SHOPPING
FOR CHANGE

Shopping
FOR
CHANGE

Consumer Activism and the Possibilities of Purchasing Power

Edited by
Louis Hyman & Joseph Tohill

ILR Press
an imprint of
Cornell University Press
Ithaca and London

First published in Canada in 2017 by Between the Lines, Toronto, Canada www.btlbooks.com

First published in the United States of America in 2017 by Cornell University Press

First printing, Cornell Paperbacks, 2017

Printed in the United States of America

Cover and text design by Gordon Robertson
Cover photo by Denis Mikheev

Library of Congress Cataloging-in-Publication Data

Names: Hyman, Louis, 1977– editor. | Tohill, Joseph, editor.
Title: Shopping for change : consumer activism and the possibilities of
   purchasing power / edited by Louis Hyman and Joseph Tohill.
Description: Ithaca : ILR Press, an imprint of Cornell University Press,
   2017. | Includes bibliographical references and index.
Identifiers: LCCN 2016049424 (print) | LCCN 2016057112 (ebook) | ISBN
   9781501709258 (pbk. : alk. paper) | ISBN 9781501712623 (epub/mobi) | ISBN
   9781501712630 (pdf)
Subjects: LCSH: Consumer movements—North America. | Consumption
   (Economics)—Political aspects—North America. | Social action—North
   America.
Classification: LCC HC95.Z9 C67 2017 (print) | LCC HC95.Z9 (ebook) | DDC
   381.3/2097—dc23
LC record available at https://lccn.loc.gov/2016049424

CONTENTS

ACKNOWLEDGEMENTS

This volume would not have been possible without the vision of Amanda Crocker, Managing Editor at Between the Lines, whose confident stewardship saw it from inception to publication. We would like to thank the staff of both BTL and Cornell University Press, particularly Frances Benson.

Two anonymous peer reviewers of the volume contributed greatly to its improvement, as did our copy editor, Cameron Duder. Gordon Robertson is responsible for the excellent design.

The editors would also like to thank the contributors, whose hard work and patience finally paid off.

INTRODUCTION

Shopping for Change

LOUIS HYMAN and JOSEPH TOHILL

T HE GREAT RECESSION reminded us that while we are all part of the economy we do not share in that economy equally. If before 2008 the two numbers that represented capitalism were the GDP and the Dow, then after 2008, thanks to the Occupy Wall Street movement, those two numbers are now the 1 percent and the 99 percent. Occupy Wall Street did not stop Wall Street's excesses. Even now, years later, after the stock market has recovered and GDP growth has returned, inequality still haunts our debates—and our economy. Yet Occupy did change our views of what a successful and more equitable economy could look like. If the Occupy movement accomplished anything, it was to reawaken our sense that change was, and *is*, possible.

The language of Occupy originated with the academic work of the then-obscure economist Thomas Piketty, but it was academics and activists working together that made this key shift in our understanding of capitalism possible.[1] Tellingly, it is the numbers highlighted by Occupy— the 1 percent and the 99 percent—that have articulated our post-recession political consciousness. Income and how we spend it defines our radical imagination today. Even though the brief surge of Occupy appeared to come to an end when police forces swept the occupiers from the streets of cities across North America and around the world in the winter of 2011–12, the new attention to power and inequality remains alive in contemporary social movements and activism from Strike Debt to Black Lives Matter, from the Fight for $15 and Fairness to Idle No More.

While we could easily think of shopping as disconnected from the rest of our economic lives, the freedom of choice we experience in stores is inextricably connected to the lack of choice in the workplace and, increasingly, in politics. Our contemporary understanding of economic inequality—also known as class difference (something most North Americans like to pretend does not apply to them)—is articulated less by our work than by our consumption. Class, in this post-recession world, is defined more by the power to consume than by the power to produce. Whether "false consciousness" or not, this experience of class as consumption fundamentally drives our politics today.

Every day we make decisions about how to spend our money, and, for the socially conscious, we want these decisions to matter. Consuming with a conscience—using individual and collective purchasing power for political ends—is among the fastest growing forms of political participation worldwide. The most common form of consumer activism, the boycott, involves collectively shunning goods and services produced or sold by particular firms, industries, nation-states, or (on occasion) ethnic groups. Another common activity is the buycott, through which activists encourage the consumption of particular goods or brands for moral, ethical, or political reasons. Such "political consumerism" (as political scientists label it) or "consumer activism" (historians' preferred term) is premised on a belief that consumption is an inherently political act embedded in a complex web of economic and social relations. This belief establishes both a framework and a prescription for grassroots collective action that makes use of the buying power of consumers to change market, business, or government practices or policies that activists find politically, ethically, or environmentally unacceptable. Recognizing the connections between our consumer choices and other issues—labour rights, civil rights, corporate behaviour, the environment, and human rights—consumer activists practise a form of long-distance solidarity that links them not only to like-minded consumers but also to distant workers, employers, environments, and nations.[2] And so, political consumers, as contributors to this collection tell us, "buy green" for the environment or "buy pink" to combat breast cancer. They boycott Taco Bell to support migrant workers or Burger King to save the rainforest.

It is easy to imagine that such politicized consumption is new, that in the past social justice movements, especially those concerned with economic

Black Lives Matter activists protest in front of Macy's flagship department store in New York City in November 2015, encouraging a boycott of Black Friday consumerism in solidarity with Ferguson, MO, where a police officer shot and killed an unarmed black teenager, Michael Brown. Photo by The All-Nite Images licensed under CC BY 2.0, www.flickr.com.

inequality, rested solely on workplace or racial and ethnic solidarities. After all, in our history classes we learn, for example, (sometimes a little, sometimes a lot) about the unions and strikes that empowered workers in an industrializing economy or the civil rights movements that empowered peoples of African, Latino, or Native descent. In activist circles, we valorize labour's radical past and the mid-twentieth century labour victories that helped usher in an unprecedented and prolonged period of decreased inequality following the Second World War. But this is a past that seems to have little to do with shopping, a past that regards purchasing power as the reward of all that labour struggle. (Hoorah postwar appliances!)

In the last few decades, inequality has resurged in both countries as unfettered global capitalism has driven capital—and with it well-paid, stable jobs—offshore, into free trade zones in the Global South. Inequality has risen faster in the United States, where the rise of neoliberalism and the decline of private sector unions has been more pronounced, and the effects of deindustrialization have been less cushioned by a widespread social safety net, including a universal, single-payer health care system.[3] At the same time, the increasing globalization of supply chains has distanced consumers even further from the production of goods they continue to consume in (over)abundance. Understandably, then, today's activists are looking for new ways to promote economic and social justice, both at home and abroad. Politicizing consumption can seem like a completely new way to accomplish old goals, with untapped possibilities.

Historians, as this volume shows, can offer some guidance, since this "consumer history" is far older than most of us realize. While the histories of other twentieth-century social movements are celebrated in activist circles, where they provide a basis for future strategy, a comparable consumer history is not. Among professional historians, consumer history is a growing but niche field, but for activists, it may as well not exist. Quite simply, they don't know their history. Instead of seeing themselves as the inheritors of a continuous political tradition stretching back to at least the eighteenth century, historian Lawrence Glickman insightfully notes, members of each new generation of consumer activists think of themselves as "political pioneers." The consumer movement is notable for "the relative absence of memory and myth that usually characterize social movements."[4]

Without knowing our history, it is difficult, if not impossible, to acquire the depth of experiences necessary to think through what is truly new (and what is not) about today's challenges. In thinking about what will work and what won't, reason alone can never be enough. We can easily convince ourselves of scenarios. Only through experience can we separate the useful strategies from the failures. Reinventing past failed strategies is a waste of time. History can help us. We hope, in this volume, to bring together these two worlds—history and activism—so that today's consumer activists may draw on the lessons of a useable past.

The broad-based transnational consumer movement that arose in the early to mid-twentieth century, leading scholars in the field persuasively argue, constitutes a social movement that deserves a place alongside the stories of modern social movements. If a social movement can be defined as a loose coalition of groups and organizations with common goals that are oriented toward mass action and popular participation and that share the intention of influencing major societal institutions or groups, then the consumer movement certainly counts as one. Generally reformist rather than revolutionary, modern consumer movements have mobilized millions of North Americans, captured (at times) the attention and imagination of the broader consuming public, greatly influenced government policies and business practices, and consistently put forward a vision of our societies and economies based on participation, access, and fairness.[5]

Moreover, forms of consumer activism—from boycotts to buycotts—have often been central to the most important struggles for social justice, like abolitionism, anti–child labour activism, civil rights, trade unionism, and anti-globalization. The Occupy movement was, after all, ignited by Adbusters, the Canadian-based radical anti-consumerist, culture-jamming organization that brought us "Buy Nothing Day," which has since 1992 encouraged consumers around the world to reconsider the devastating impact of rampant consumerism on the planet. Acts of consumer resistance in North America have a long and storied history, which stretches back to the earliest days of consumer society (tea, anyone?). Some of the most successful political struggles in history, from the American Revolution to Abolitionism, to the civil rights movement, have articulated their politics by a refusal to shop, even though their successful boycotts "have not always been understood as victories for consumer activism."[6]

Whatever their cause, consumer activists see themselves as agents of reform. Waves of consumer activism most often arise to address perceived failures in the market—or governance over the market. Political consumerism inherently involves attempts to restructure the political community, expand venues of citizens' engagement and participation in political life, and explicitly turn ordinarily private, seemingly apolitical, even conservative actions like shopping into forms of political engagement that combine self-interest and the general welfare.[7]

As so many of our contributors illustrate, consumer activism, as a form of political participation outside of the realm of traditional or formal politics, has opened up new arenas for citizen participation in public life. In fact, it calls into question the public/private divide that ordinarily defines what constitutes political participation because it recognizes seemingly nonpolitical or private arenas (such as the home or the store) as venues for political action. The traditional gender division of labour in capitalist societies has made consumer activism an important form of political participation for women, in particular, in North America and elsewhere. As a relatively low-risk political activity with a low threshold for participation (sometimes literally buying nothing), it has also appealed to oppressed groups and those marginalized by traditional political systems and voting, such as

African Americans denied the vote in the Southern United States under Jim Crow.[8] For those at the margins, shopping can be a radical activity.

All of these examples would appear to make consumer activism an ideal way to conduct activist politics. Organized and politicized consumption can exert real pressure on the powerful. In theory, this all makes sense. But, despite these advantages, movements of consumers have some serious drawbacks and pitfalls that other forms of organizing do not necessarily share. In recent years, some forms of political consumerism, such as fair trade, have faced criticism as projects of Northern consumer societies that undermine Southern economies and cultures as much as they do market-driven globalization, and that ignore voices from the Global South. Other critics argue that shopping for change is too neoliberal-friendly and cannot fundamentally change corporate practices. They argue that it directs attention away from the necessary role of the state in regulating capitalism and instead encourages corporate co-optation of consumerist goals, leading to such ethically dubious practices as "pinkwashing" and "astroturfing."[9] As "commodity activism" has come under fire in recent years for such practices as "celebrity humanitarianism" and, more generally, for grafting "philanthropy and social action onto merchandising practices, market incentives, and corporate profits," the effectiveness of consumer activism has been an important topic of debate among social movement activists and academics.[10] Many remain sceptical. As we discovered when putting together this collection, some consumer activists view the idea of "shopping for change" as thoroughly co-opted by corporations and corporate philanthropies. One activist author who we emailed about writing a chapter for this volume returned a terse rejection of the idea based on the misperception that our proposed title, *Shopping for Change*, represented everything she was fighting against!

Moreover, consuming (or not) tends to reaffirm the moral foundations of consumer capitalism as a whole. Consumer choice, a seemingly apolitical and inherently positive concept, is in fact a conservative value deeply embedded in the heart of capitalism. The right to buy or not to buy reaffirms the central tenet of the market—money speaks loudest. Choice is also one of the fundamental differences between consumer politics and, for example, worker politics. At the end of the day, consumers always have a choice to buy (or not), while workers always need a paycheque, and consumption is much more diffuse (all those shops) than production (just one workplace). Going on strike, for a worker, is always harder and involves more sacrifice than a buyer giving up a particular good. Although civil rights movements and other social justice causes have harnessed this conservative idea (choice) for progressive ends, its use nonetheless risks re-legitimizing economic inequality. Those with the means to consume, with the ability to buy, inherently have more power than those who don't. Boycotts and buycotts only work if consumers have sufficient purchasing power to withhold or to wield. Consumer power, while often a powerful tool for redressing social inequality, does not naturally lend itself to redressing economic inequality.

Furthermore, consumer activism can as easily be harnessed by reactionary movements seeking to reinforce inequality as it can by movements of the left that use it to fight inequality and injustice. In the North American context, for instance, some labour organizations in the late nineteenth century organized boycotts of Asian businesses. The 1920s and 1930s witnessed boycotts of Jewish businesses, driven by anti-Semitic and fascist-sympathizing organizations. In Canada, the "achat chez nous" movement, organized by French-Canadian nationalists, urged French-speaking Quebecers to boycott Jewish businesses. Americans were urged to do the same in the "Buy Christian" campaign promoted by the Christian Front and Father Charles Coughlin, the right-wing populist radio sensation whose infamous anti-Semitic rants reached a weekly audience of millions. These examples of "conservative consumerism" (though they are not ones we are concerned with in this work) caution against overstating the affinity between consumer activism and social justice.[11]

Fostering the consumer consciousness necessary for sustained social activism is another key challenge. While other movements have had relatively stable, definable identities and constituencies at their core, the consumer movement rarely has. When you ask someone who they are, rarely do they volunteer, "I am a Consumer!" At the workplace, you think of yourself as a worker and have friends who are the same. As someone from a marginalized group, you experience that identity every day, especially if you leave your community. This experience of identity—both as an individual and as part of a collective—has been foundational for all social movements and is often missing in consumer politics. Moreover, the "consumer interest" risks being so diffuse as to lose all value. If everyone is a consumer, then for whom does the movement speak? Being a consumer is more often a social practice than a social identity. So while African American rights' activists boycotted buses and occupied Woolworth's lunch counters to ignite the civil rights movement of the 1950s and 1960s, their struggle was (understandably) cast as civil rights rather than consumer rights.

Given the conservative nature of consumer choice and the relatively weak pull of consumer identity, turning good intentions into effective action is another challenge. An intention-action gap exists between what consumers say they believe and how they shop. While about 30 percent of people claim to care about how goods are made, for instance, ethically produced goods rarely capture more than a 3 percent market share.[12]

And yet, North American consumer activists, as several of the contributors to this volume demonstrate, have "made a difference" and continue to do so—in spite of the inherent weakness of consumer activism and frequent failures. In recent years, consumer historians have challenged the old socialist critique of the rise of consumer capitalism as an inherently conservative force and demonstrated in historical terms what political scientists, sociologists, and others (including the contributors to this collection) have shown of contemporary political consumerism: consumption can empower. Figuring out how and in what circumstances consumer activism has succeeded, what has worked and what has not, what should be emulated and what should be avoided—these are among the goals of *Shopping for Change*.[13]

Re-establishing a useable history is essential to the success of today's consumer activism. By building on a burgeoning international literature that documents the breadth and importance of consumer activism in both past and present, *Shopping for Change* seeks, by highlighting the possibilities and pitfalls of political consumerism, to contribute to efforts to address inequality and promote social justice. The American contributions to this literature are now considerable. The most important single work is Lawrence Glickman's *Buying Power: A History of Consumer Activism in America*, which spans the late eighteenth through to the twenty-first century. A similar overview of political consumerism in Canadian history has yet to be written, and there are comparatively fewer published studies of the extent and impact of Canadian consumer activism. Although most of the contributions to this volume, with one or two notable exceptions, remain rooted in national historiographies, we believe bringing them together in one volume emphasizes consumer activism as a phenomenon that transcends international boundaries.[14]

In making a contribution to reclaiming the history of consumer activism, *Shopping for Change* also seeks to overcome the almost engrained hesitancy of historians to bring their stories right up to the present. Glickman's otherwise comprehensive opus, for example, devotes less than 8 of its 310 pages to the period after 1980, despite suggesting (rightly, we think) that this was a period during which "consumer activism has flourished as never before."[15] Thus, our book contains almost as many chapters on what historians might call the "contemporary history" of political consumerism, including twenty-first-century campaigns.

This volume came from a desire to think about how shopping for change helped to remake a more just society in the past and how it can continue to do so today. Can we overcome the limitations of consumer identity, the conservative pull of consumer choice, and other pitfalls of consumer activism to marshal the possibilities of consumer power? Can we, quite literally, shop for change? This is the question that *Shopping for Change* attempts to answer. Taken together, our contributors answer with a qualified "yes." The authors of the volume share a broad commitment to thinking critically about the limits and possibilities of consumer activism, in both its past and present manifestations. *Shopping for Change*, then, brings together the historical and contemporary perspectives of both academics and activists to provide a rapid introduction into what has been possible before and what we think is possible now so that we can, together, make a more just tomorrow.

*   *   *

Economic practices and transnational capitalism can seem too large to be affected by consumers and shopping. Consumer activism, while potentially powerful, cannot alone solve the problems of inequality. Yet in the past, consumer activism has undermined the most powerful forces in our society, like imperialism and slavery. Even before the tactic got a name in the 1880s, the "boycott" was central to consumer activism. "Non-importation" and "non-consumption" movements played a key role in the American Revolution. A similar *Patriote* boycott during the unsuccessful Rebellions of 1837 and 1838 in Lower Canada (modern-day Quebec) drew inspiration from the American boycotts seven decades earlier.[16]

As our first two contributors demonstrate, consumer boycotts were key tactics of nineteenth-century American social movements. In "Consuming with a Conscience," Michelle Craig McDonald looks at how abolitionists in the mid-nineteenth century marshalled purchasing power to undermine American slavery by boycotting southern cotton and selling only "free produce." By the end of the century, the American labour movement and its allies in the National Consumers League, an organization of primarily middle-class women, had made boycotts and what would later be called "buycotts" key strategies in the fight to curb the abuses of industrial capitalism. Wendy Wiedenhoft Murphy, in "Boycotts, Buycotts, and Legislation," reminds us of the difficulties, and possibilities, of cross-class consumer legislation through her study of Progressive Era reform.

Mounting alarm over the rising cost of living in early twentieth-century North America, particularly during and immediately following the First World War, was central to the emergence of a self-conscious, politically oriented consumer movement in both the United States and Canada. The rise of the consumer movement was characterized by widespread consumer consciousness, the increasing view of the consumer as citizen, and the identification of a distinct "consumer interest." What distinguished the consumer politics of the twentieth century from that of earlier eras, not only in the United States but in Canada, Britain, and other countries that were transitioning into modern consumer societies, was the "emphasis on consumers themselves as the beneficiaries of political activism" and the emergence of groups dedicated to representing, defending, and lobbying the state to protect "the consumer." Concern over prices and purchasing power were central to the emergence of consumer consciousness and the development of the idea that there was an identifiable "consumer interest" that was in need of protection. This idea, in turn, became a foundational premise of the consumer movements that emerged in numerous countries around the world throughout the twentieth century.[17] Whether this newly identified consumer interest was allied to or in competition with the interests of labour, whose unceasing and understandable demands for higher wages tended to contribute to rising prices, remained an open question. Inflation galvanized political activism on behalf of the consumer, leading the press, social reformers, labour leaders, and women's and newly created consumer groups to advocate for government action.

Grassroots campaigns against rising prices added weight to demands for action. Dispersed and usually short-lived groups of primarily working- and middle-class women formed in response to what they considered particularly egregious cases of price gouging in meat, milk, and other staples and launched localized food and "cost-of-living" protests and boycotts. Bettina Liverant's contribution to this book, "Making a Market for Consumers," examines one such local effort in Western Canada following the First World War, that of the Calgary Consumers League to create a public market with affordable food to help working people make the most of limited budgets. As Mark Robbins explains in his chapter, municipal market campaigns were also among the tactics pursued south of the border by new white-collar consumer activists, who blamed both wealthy "profiteers" and striking workers for inflating prices at the expense of the "the public," boldly redefined as middle-class. Robbins's "Making a Middle-Class 'Public'" explains how we all began to think of ourselves as middle-class consumers and what this has meant for progressive politics.

During the Great Depression, municipalities all over North America experimented with ways to both stimulate consumer spending and keep the few spending dollars local. But, as Allison Ward shows us in her study of one Canadian city, "You Are Purchasing Prosperity!," solving local economic problems was not as simple as raising consumer awareness of the need to buy local, especially when those economic problems were part of a much larger international downturn. Nor did alternative currencies prove a cure-all for local economic woes, as Sarah Elvins shows in "Making Money in Hard Times," which examines efforts of American cities to stimulate consumer demand by injecting new currencies into struggling local economics. As it turns out, creating your own cash is not as easy as just printing it.

Hard times also fostered an explosion of consumer activism, which had begun before the onset of the Great Depression with the publication of explosive, best-selling exposés of corporate capitalism and advertising, such as *100,000,000 Guinea Pigs* and *Your Money's Worth*. The burgeoning consumer movement of the 1930s responded to the efforts of increasingly sophisticated corporate advertisers to target new markets by making protecting consumers from unscrupulous advertising and other corporate practices a key focus of its activism. In "Protecting the 'Guinea Pig Children,'" Kyle Asquith reminds us that advertising to children—the youngest and most vulnerable consumers—has long been a profitable market, but we have been able to control what advertisers can and can't do.

The economic and political ferment caused by the Great Depression and the Second World War spurred many creative efforts to channel consumer purchasing power for a variety of explicitly political ends to promote social justice at home and abroad. Josh Carreiro's "Our Economic Way Out" traces the history of "buy black" co-operative stores that flourished during the 1930s across America, illustrating the successes and failures of trying to create a truly alternative black capitalism. American Jewish-led boycotts of Nazi German products, Jeffrey Scott Demsky and Randall Kaufman argue in "Not Buying It," helped undermine Hitler's regime and bring the United States into the Second World War.

As a number of the contributors to this book show, women were both vital organizers and the shock troops of the militant consumers' organizations that proliferated in the 1930s and 1940s. The explicit "social movement consumerism" of this era was embodied in the slogan of the League of Women Shoppers, one of the most prominent American organizations of the late 1930s: "Use your buying power for justice!" Julie Guard argues in "Canada's Citizen Housewives" that politicians of this era underestimated at their own peril organized housewives who drew on their authority as mothers to demand a stronger welfare state.

Perhaps even more than the Great Depression, the Second World War fostered a consumerist vision of a more just economy because of the extent to which interventionist government came to permeate the day-to-day lives of North Americans in unprecedented and transformative ways. Through rationing, price control, and other controls on consumption, the power of the wartime state firmly backed an economy of access to "fair shares" and a decent standard of living. Joseph Tohill's "The Consumer Goes to War" compares the efforts of politically well-placed consumer activists on both sides of the border to use the war effort to mobilize consumers, particularly women, and incorporate them into the state in order to give them a key say in running the economy. However, by the end of the 1940s, both Guard and Tohill suggest, the most militant consumer groups and their radical consumerist visions were laid low by the anticommunist backlash of the early Cold War.

Red-baiting of activist consumers and organizations by powerful business lobbies and their allies in government was an important reason for the seeming quiescence of the consumer front during the 1950s. The lack of consumer activism during this decade, however, can easily be overstated, as these trough years of the consumer movement were also years that laid the groundwork for an explosion of activism in North America and elsewhere in the following decade. The cultural and political ferment of the 1960s contributed to a marked upsurge of activism and a revival of the consumer movement as a popular social movement. President John F. Kennedy's 1962 declaration of a "Consumers' Bill of Rights" helped catalyze the upsurge in both countries, as did the writing of Vance Packard and Ralph Nader.[18]

Important continuities existed in terms of personnel and organizations between the 1960s revival and the earlier era of consumer activism. In the United States, some of the presidential consumer advisers appointed by Kennedy and his successor, Lyndon Johnson, had been active in the consumer movement's earlier heyday during the Depression and war. In "From the Great Society to Giant," Lawrence Black explores the complicated political life of one of these presidential advisors, consumer advocate Esther Peterson, as she balanced government policy roles with private work for corporations.

The flourishing of consumer activism in the 1960s and 1970s also led to the creation of important consumer regulatory agencies and considerable representation of consumers in government. On both sides of the border, consumer activists revived the demands of progressives from the interwar and war years for a cabinet-level department of the consumer. In Canada, consumer activists, led by the Consumers' Association of Canada, won a partial victory in the creation of the federal Department of Consumer and Corporate Affairs, though ultimately the awkward pairing of consumer and corporate interests within a single department led (as consumer activists feared it would) to the subordination of the former to the latter. In the United States, influential muckraking consumerist Ralph Nader spearheaded a decade-long campaign for the creation of a federal Consumer Protection Agency (CPA) from the late 1960s to the late 1970s. But a rising conservative backlash against political consumerism and the liberalism associated with it, closely tied to a well-funded and skilful anti-CPA lobbying campaign by business organizations, gradually undermined congressional and public support. By 1978, supporters of the CPA abandoned their campaign as unwinnable, a failure that sped the decline (again) of the consumer movement.[19]

The neoliberal agenda adopted in North America as well as internationally by the 1980s led to political defeats and a general decline in and fracturing of consumer movements not only in North America but also across the globe.[20] Yet somewhat paradoxically despite the consumer movement's decline at the end of the twentieth century, consumer activism continued to grow, taking on new tactics and goals, as well as revisiting the tried and true. The rise of green consumerism is among the prominent developments over the past few decades. Philip A. Wight's "The Countercultural Roots of Green Consumerism" helps us see that today's eco-friendly consumerism is more than a fad, but has resulted rather from decades of activism aimed at bringing about a synthesis of shopping and environmentalism. The difficulty of actually shopping for a better world is highlighted by H. Louise Davis's "Purchasing Change," which explores the unintended consequences of the enthusiasm for "green" alternatives like biofuels. The first-world use of biofuel, Davis suggests, doesn't particularly help the environment, but it *does* drive up the price of food in the developing world.

The shortcomings of buying our way to a greener world provide but one example of the pitfalls of shopping for change. Our writers also unmask the ways that corporations have turned our willingness to shop for a cause to their advantage. Cause-related marketing, Mara Einstein tells us in "Buying a Better World," has certainly helped sell high-end goods to women but has had a more uncertain benefit for charities. Drawing on a wealth of evidence, including both American and Canadian health studies, "What about the Cause?," Daniel Faber, Amy Lubitow, and Madeline Brambilla's exploration of "pinkwashing," reveals the even more unprincipled use of cancer-related marketing to sell cosmetics, some of which are actually carcinogenic! Another ethically dubious corporate practice— "astroturfing" or corporate seeding of faux-grassroots lobbying groups— is the subject of Bart Elmore's "The Making of a Coke CAN." Elmore explains how Coca-Cola created its own "civic action network" to compensate for the loss of political support it had formerly received from Main Street America before aggressive consolidation of its supply chain put most small-town bottling operations out of business.

Efforts to organize consumers and workers along the increasingly convoluted supply chains that have driven the globalization of capitalism and rising corporate profit margins for the last forty years are the subject of many of the essays in this book. Modern supply chain capitalism, in which the world of production is hidden from consumers, obscures local, national, and global inequalities. Yet several of our authors show how real world campaigns have succeeded. In "Boot the Bell," Dawson Barrett explains how farm workers connected with student activists to successfully pressure Taco Bell for better wages for its suppliers. Katrina Lacher's "Where's the Beef . . . From?" shows how activists educated Americans that their delicious Burger King Whoppers were destroying the rainforest—and what could be done to stop it. In "The Sweatshop Effect," Meredith Katz examines one of the most successful examples of consumer activism in recent decades. Drawing on her own experience as co-founder and former president of United Students Against Sweatshops (USAS) at Virginia Tech, Katz relates how student activists pressured Nike to improve its sweatshop conditions overseas, if it wanted to sell on campus. (Now on the faculty of Virginia Commonwealth University, Katz serves as faculty advisor for the university's recently formed USAS chapter. In that capacity, she recently contributed her knowledge to the chapter's successful campaign modelled on previous USAS wins.)

Nevertheless, Jessica Stewart, in "Hating Wal-Mart, Loving Target," highlights the continued difficulty would-be consumer activists face in sorting out the good from the bad in supply chain capitalism and that they don't always get it right. She explains why American liberals who would never shop at Wal-Mart fawn over Target—even though the suppliers are the same and, in most cases, the labour conditions are worse at Target. (The recent untimely demise of Target's foray into Canada has left Canadian consumer activists with only a single target (pun intended) for their fear and loathing.) Louis Hyman suggests that attempting to boycott juggernauts like Wal-Mart is missing the mark anyway. He argues for a radical rethinking of how activists concerned about supply chain capitalism can maximize their impact. His "Ports are the New Factories" instead lays out a strategy to disable the container ports that make supply chain capitalism possible

Robert Mayer and Larry Kirsch return to the theme of the importance of coalition building highlighted early in this volume by Wendy Murphy. In "To Speak in One Voice," a thorough examination of the two-year campaign for the passage of the Dodd–Frank Wall Street Reform and Consumer Protection Act, we learn how difficult it continues to be to make meaningful political and economic reforms and regulate business in the consumer interest in the United States, even in the wake of the Great Recession. Yet Mayer and Kirsch demonstrate that, while forming political coalitions for change is difficult, it can be done, even in our neoliberal age.

Our final contributor, Tracey Deutsch, reflects on the history of shopping for change by tracing the history of the idea of demand, revealing that its assumptions are both historical and political. In "On Demand," she shows us how neoliberal thinkers contributed to the depoliticization of consumption through their efforts to reshape our ideas about consumer demand. Deutsch highlights the meaning of these intellectual trends for contemporary politics of consumption, pointing to the need to recapture an older vision of consumption and retail spaces (as she puts it "as sites of everyday struggle—places full of politics, resistance, and possibility").

In *Shopping for Change*, we hope you will see that consumers have power, though they often lack awareness of how to exercise it and do so imperfectly or incompletely. Political consumerism—such a powerful tool for reform—is alive with potential, but also vexed by snares. We think it needs to be better understood, by both academics and activists. Creating a history of consumer activism and thinking through the strategic possibilities for today are necessary to create effective movements for social justice.

1

CONSUMING
WITH A CONSCIENCE

The Free Produce Movement
in Early America

MICHELLE CRAIG McDONALD

N 1838, the Anti-Slavery Society of Newcastle, England, issued a
clarion call to United States cotton growers. In a pamphlet tellingly
entitled *Conscience versus Cotton*, it argued that the surest route to abolition was "a wide-spreading and thoughtful conviction, that the unnecessary purchase of one iota of slave labour produce, involved the purchaser
in the guilt of the Slaveholder." This was not to suggest that slaveholders escaped accountability. Indeed, Newcastle's authors reserved "well-
merited scorn and indignant execration" for enslavers' actions. But it does
imply that abolitionists recognized such castigations fell largely on deaf
ears. While a few planters saw the error of their ways and recanted—some
even becoming powerful symbols for antislavery activism—the majority
remained committed to their chosen form of labour. As debates over abolition intensified, proponents changed direction, shifting from production to consumption and asking "every righteous man and every modest
woman" to consider, "what can I do to put down slavery?"[1]

Most scholars, except the few who highlight Revolutionary-era
boycotts like those on tea, consider consumer politics to be a modern
phenomenon, but such activism was the principal tactic of the free produce movement that emerged on both sides of the Atlantic during the

early nineteenth century.[2] An effort initially dominated by Quaker and free black abolitionists, the free produce movement encouraged consumers to avoid slave-made goods—like Caribbean tropical commodities and American cotton—in favour of those harvested or manufactured by free workers. Historians have considered both the moral and economic motivations for abolition, but less often how they were intertwined. Such issues were inseparable for the free produce advocates who emerged in the United States in the 1820s and consciously modelled themselves after British antislavery sugar boycotters of the 1790s. These men and women believed that foregoing slave-made goods was only the first step in combating the institution of chattel bondage; offering a free labour alternative was essential to ensuring slavery's downfall. Fortunately, for those British buyers who wished to buy according to their conscience, help was readily at hand. "Already under the guarantee of the Philadelphia Free Produce Association," *Conscience versus Cotton* concluded, "some of this free cotton has been shipped directly to Liverpool."[3]

Historians have been less impressed with the ease of ethical buying. While the free produce movement blossomed for a short time, it did not become a viable alternative to slave-produced goods in most communities. Some historians have suggested that it failed because finding free labour cotton and sugar substitutes proved too challenging. Production levels for such goods were low compared to slave-grown commodities, and so purveyors had difficulty building a solid market despite rising disposable income in the lower and middle classes that resulted in what consumer scholars now see as a boom in spending. Buyers wanted more goods, these scholars conclude, but not pricier ones—and the market trumped morality.[4]

But profitability is only one measure of success, even in histories of the economy. The number of stores that specialized in goods produced by free labour and of free produce associations are others, as is the prominence of free labour ideology in both local and national advocacy movements. Free produce wares flourished in some abolitionist communities—particularly Philadelphia, New York, and Wilmington. Association minutes and correspondence, as well as advertising language, help illuminate how free produce vendors reached these markets while promoting a particular set of social ideals. For while American revolutionary tea party rhetoric encouraged colonists to think about their rights, free produce supporters asked consumers to consider the well-being of others, at the same time that it reinforced the value of a dollar. Free produce sought, in other words, not to distance ethics from economic concerns, but to create both profits for purveyors and consumers with a conscience.

In 1826, Quaker Friends in Wilmington, Delaware, drew up the first charter for a formal free-produce organization, and that same year Baltimore Quaker Benjamin Lundy opened a store that sold only goods obtained by labour from free people. In 1827, the movement expanded with the formation of the Pennsylvania Free Produce Society in Philadelphia. Pennsylvania quickly dominated free produce agitation, but over time more than fifty stores opened in eight other states, including Ohio, Indiana, and New York. Meanwhile, parallel movements operated in Britain and were even attempted by abolitionist advocates in the Caribbean. Such efforts not only linked buying behaviour to notions of morality but also helped promote "free" commodity industries in the East Indies and Africa. "We are too dependent upon American slavery for the supply of this important article," those targeting U.S. southern cotton argued. "The remedy for this dependence is commercial encouragement" of "the free cotton growers of British India, the West Indies, Africa," or, much closer to home, the newly independent nation of Haiti, as well as "the free cotton growers of the United States themselves."[5]

Although the free produce movement was not strictly a sectarian response to slavery, most association members were Quakers. The idea of a boycott of slave produce dated from at least the mid-eighteenth century when it was advocated by John Woolman, Joshua Evans, and others. Not all Quakers, however, cleaved to these ideals. Some, such as Anthony Benezet, tried to ensure that their marketplace matched their moral code, but others, including Thomas Willing and John Reynell, invested a significant proportion of their mercantile efforts in the slave-based economies of the Caribbean.[6]

What set the consumer activism of the early nineteenth century apart from these earlier individual efforts, however, was its shift from producers or importers, and their ability to personally decide a course of action, to the far broader base, and larger numbers, of consumers. It also emphasized the power of peer pressure over individual choice. The movement quickly became popular among many abolitionist leaders, including Frederick Douglass, Harriet Beecher Stowe, Gerrit Smith, and the Grimke sisters, who were all early supporters, consumers, and even investors in free labour enterprises, particularly during the peak of abolitionist unity in the late 1830s and early 1840s. Smith, for example, served as vice president of the American Free Produce Association for several years, and Angelina Grimke ensured that her 1838 wedding to Theodore Weld featured only free-sugar desserts made by an African American confectioner. Others promoted the project through publications, including the poet John Greenleaf Whittier who edited the *Non-Slaveholder*, the most important free produce journal of the early nineteenth century, and, for a time, William Lloyd Garrison, editor of the *Liberator*. Indeed, in the movement's early years, Garrison provided extensive coverage of, and editorial support for, the free produce movement. Still others took a more material stance. The husband of feminist Quaker Lucretia Mott ran a free produce store in Philadelphia, and David Lee Child, the husband of the famous writer Lydia Marie Child, traveled to France in 1837 to study sugar beet production in the hopes of finding an alternative to Louisiana's and Cuba's cane fields. Elias Hicks and Charles Collins, two of New York's leading Quakers, used free produce profits to finance emigration efforts to Haiti. Emigration proponents hoped that business-minded free blacks resettled in Haiti might, along with newly manumitted slaves, create a free labour alternative that challenged slavery in both the U.S. and the Caribbean. Toward that end, Collins operated a free produce store on New York's Cherry Street between 1817 and 1843, selling over fifty thousand pounds of coffee provided by Haitian President Jean-Pierre Boyer to help finance emigrants' transportation costs.[7]

Many well-known black abolitionists, including Henry Highland Garnet, William Wells Brown, and Frances Harper, also supported free produce in their writings and on trans-Atlantic lecture tours, and some, including Lydia White and William Whipper, operated free produce establishments as well. Richard Allen, leader of the African American Methodist Episcopal Church in the United States, joined the Free Produce Society in the 1820s, urging other African Americans to do so as well. He also personally contributed to the manufacture of free labour fashion by recruiting free black seamstresses to design dresses and hats to be worn as material manifestations of abolitionist sentiment.[8]

In 1838, these efforts coalesced in the Requited Labor Convention held in Philadelphia, which Garrison, Mott, and other abolitionist leaders attended and which led to the establishment of a national American Free Produce Association. In their founding charter, the association declared that "as slaves are robbed of the fruits of their toil, all who partake of those fruits are participants in the robbery." If these words implied that consumers merely enabled a crime whose main perpetrators lay elsewhere, this was not the position of the free produce activists who understood consumers to be, as one activist put it, "the ultimatum of the whole sys-

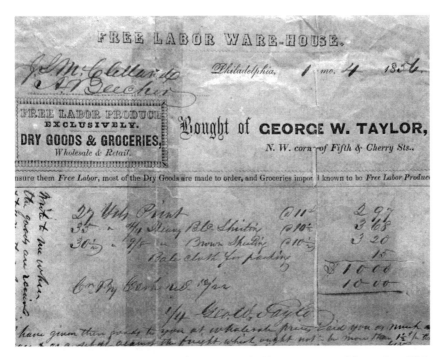

George W. Taylor warehouse receipt, January 4, 1856, property of the author. This invoice from George W. Taylor's store promoted "FREE LABOR PRODUCE EXCLUSIVELY. Dry Goods and Groceries, Wholesale and Retail." Made out to J. M. Clelland and A. Beecher, it listed twenty-seven yards print (printed cloth), thirty-five yards heavy black sheeting, thirty yards brown sheeting, and one bale "cloth for packing" for a total of $10.00.

tem" of slavery. "It is clear to those who will take the trouble to examine the subject," according to another proponent,

> that the northern merchant who purchases the cotton, sugar and rice of the southern planter . . . the auctioneer who cries his human wares in the market, and sells those helpless victims of cupidity . . . yea, even the heartless, murderous slave-trader, are each and all of them, only so many AGENTS, employed by and for the CONSUMER.[9]

Moreover the growing number of free produce stores, such advocates contended, made this kind of theft all the more gratuitous.[10]

Recognizing the necessary pragmatism of their endeavour and actually building an industry, however, were often two different enterprises. Collin's New York store, which operated for twenty-six years, was a success by most measures, but other free produce stores operated only briefly, and many were economically unstable. Perkins & Towne, for example, ran a free produce store at 141 Bowery Street in New York City from 1839 to 1841, but Hoag & Wood's store proved more tenuous. It opened in February 1848 but by October of that year had been taken over by Robert Lindley Murray, who, "having purchased the stock of Hoag & Wood, purposes carrying on the business, dealing exclusively in produce which is the result of Free Labor," at the same location, 377 Pearl Street, New York.[11] Murray himself, however, was foundering less than a year later.

Philadelphia's free produce vendors maintained viable businesses over longer periods of time. James Miller McKim, for instance, began advertising "goods manufactured by the American Free Produce Association," specifically ginghams, checks, flannels, and muslins for clothing and bed linens, as well as cotton ticking for mattresses, in July of 1848 from his store at 31 North Fifth Street; he continued to regularly run an almost identical notice through 1852. McKim's mercantile efforts formed only a portion of his abolitionist activities; he lectured extensively, worked with the Underground Railroad, co-founded the American Anti-Slavery Society, and in 1849 was the recipient when slave Henry "Box" Brown was mailed to freedom. He also frequently testified in court on behalf of freed slaves captured under the auspices of the Fugitive Slave Law, which was passed by Congress in 1850 and allowed slave-catchers to seize alleged slaves without due process of law and prohibited anyone from aiding escaped slaves or obstructing their recovery. After the Emancipation Proclamation, he organized efforts to welcome and assist the thousands of newly freed slaves who emigrated north, and in 1865 he co-ordinated the financial backing to establish the progressive magazine the *Nation*.[12]

George Washington Taylor had one of the most successful free produce business ventures of all. Taylor had been born in Radnor, Pennsylvania, and attended Quaker schools for most of his education. He was an agent of the Friends Bible Association and publisher of the periodical the *Non-Slaveholder* and a peace paper written by Elihu Burritt entitled the *Citizen of the World*. He opened his free produce store on March 4, 1847, at the northwest corner of Fifth and Cherry Streets in Philadelphia, a location which had formerly housed a free produce store operated by Joel Fisher, and he was still advertising from the same location a decade later. Taylor's advertisements emphasized both the provenance of his producers and the moral culpability of consumers. He specialized in "cotton goods

> **Groceries, the produce of Free Labor.**
> The subscribers having used some exertion to procure a supply of the above description of articles, now offer for sale the following,
> Superior New York steamed Molasses; lump and loaf Sugar; white and brown Sugar from Jamaica, Java, Canton, and Siam.—Maple Sugar in cases; double boiled Calcutta Sugar; St. Domingo, Manilla, and Java Coffee; St. Domingo honey, Chocolate, Indigo; Jamaica Ginger; Lampwick, &c. Also a small lot of superior Rice;—together with a general assortment of Teas, Lamp Oil, Spices, Fruit, Hams, dried Beef, Flour, &c.
> **C. & E. ADAMS, Temperance Grocers,**
> N. E. corner Fifth and Race Sts.
> *Philadelphia,* Fourth mo. 1 2, 1838.

C. & E. Adams advertisement, "Groceries, the produce of Free Labor," *Pennsylvania Freeman*, May 3, 1838, Early American Newspapers Series 1 and 2, 1660–1900.

manufactured by the Free Produce Association" and "provided for those who really wish to be non-slaveholders."[13]

Some free produce stores, to expand markets further still, not only serviced local needs but also operated mail order catalogues, thus expanding the potential reach of their activist impact beyond their neighbourhoods and even cities. Ezra Towne, another New York shopkeeper, assured both "dealers and families" that goods "free from the stain of slavery" were "carefully packed for the country." McKim advertised his store in both local Philadelphia newspapers as well as *Frederick Douglass' Papers* in Rochester, New York, where he noted that "Orders for Goods, or letters describing information may be addressed to J. Miller McKim, 31 North Fifth street; Daniel L. Miller, Tenth street; or to James Mott, No. 35 Church Alley."[14] Taylor likewise began his free produce store with cotton cloth and bedding, although by 1855 had expanded to include "an assortment of groceries," and two years later offered "prices, lists, and samples sent by mail."[15]

Storekeepers who opted to limit supply sources to those using free labour in commodity markets still dominated by production through enslaved workers necessarily faced price competition. Delegates of the Requited Labor Convention recognized the problem and even proposed sending a petition to Congress to repeal duties on "all goods which come in competition with slave labour produce, at least as far to place them on an equal footing."[16] Storekeepers, meanwhile, described their inventory in ways that coupled material goods with less tangible benefits to justify any extra cost. In 1848, for example, Robert Lindley Murray "opened with prices which he believes will be found (with the exception of dry goods, some kinds of which must for the present be somewhat higher) to be uniformly the market rates." But, he continued, he relied on consumers to ensure his financial success, "trusting the increased business which this fact, as it becomes known, may secure, will enable him to maintain this desirable position, notwithstanding the disadvantages which a store of this kind is under, when compared with those which make no distinction between the products of Slave and of Free Labor."

Murray's onus on the buyer—cast as a moral and economic partner rather than simply a patron—was not unusual. Value, such advertisements implied, had several constituent factors. The inherent cost of an object was important but needed to be calculated along with the social and economic conditions surrounding its production, distribution, and consumption. And while Murray focused on coffees and teas rather than clothing and bedding like McKim and Taylor, he too offered "orders by mail carefully attended to."[17]

Most free produce stores stocked similar inventories, especially cotton cloth, sugar, and coffee. But a smaller subset of enterprising vendors offered less common commodities such as free labour molasses, rice, and chocolate. Some offered alternatives, such as Eli Adams' sale of "maple sugar . . . a fair sample of free labor sugar, having been manufactured in our own state by labor-paying farmers."[18] Others included the provenance of their wares to reassure buyers of the free labour origins. Charles Wise's coffee came from the East Indies and St. Domingo, or the newly freed nation of Haiti, and his sugar from Canton. Robert McClure's sugar and candy arrived from Calcutta and his coffee from Africa, while C. & E. Adams, who advertised themselves as "Temperance Grocers," sold goods from Siam, Calcutta, Manila, and Java.[19] Place, in other words, served as a kind of geographic branding, a short-hand to buyers about the provenance of their provisions that simultaneously educated them about the relative status of free versus enslaved labour around the globe.

Other goods, however, less often associated with free labour activism also appeared in the same newspaper pages. Mark Brook's notice for "ice cream made of free labor sugar" seems a natural extension of boycotts on slave-produced cane, but it is unclear whether C. & E. Adams' "oil, spices, fruit, hams, and dried beef" were part of their antislavery inventory or were non-free labour goods included to provide prospective customers with more reasons to visit their store.[20] James Willis, who operated a shoe store at 241 Arch Street, also in Philadelphia, provided one of the only non-agricultural free labour commodity markets. His advertisement, which changed little over the eight years of his business, promoted a "FREE LABOR BOOT AND SHOE STORE—Women's and Children's Boots and Shoes, of every description, and best materials, and entirely free from the contamination of slave labor."[21]

Several historians have noted women's active role in the abolition movement, so it is unsurprising that they also appear as free produce purveyors. They made up almost half of the delegates at the 1838 Requited Labor Convention and formed an important if smaller fraction of the retail market. Lydia White, for example, operated a "requited labor and temperance grocery store" at 219 North Second Street in Philadelphia, where she sold sugar, coffee, coffee, cotton, spices, and teas.[22] By 1845, White had moved her operation to the northwest corner of 5th and Cherry Streets, where she operated the only "store in the city where free goods are sold exclusively"; two years later, however, this address had come under the ownership of George W. Taylor. Laetitia Bullock, just one block west, offered more specialized goods, including ice cream, water ices, jellies, cakes, and candies, "all the produce of Free Labor, and warranted to give every satisfaction."[23]

Interestingly, free produce and free labour initiatives emerged on both local and national agendas almost simultaneously. The American Convention for Promoting the Abolition of Slavery initially focused on ending the slave trade, but by 1827 it had appointed a committee to review the viability of "experiments [that] have been heretofore made, and are now making, on the American Continent and Islands, in relation to the cultivation of the products of Cotton, Rice, Sugar, Tobacco, &c. by free labor." The committee, chaired by the same Benjamin Lundy who operated Baltimore's first free produce store, outlined several promising possibilities, ranging from free produce sugar initiatives in parts of the British Caribbean, Haiti, and even Mexico, to experiments in growing free cotton in North Carolina and Alabama, as well as the manufacture of this cotton into coarse muslins by "a gentleman in Rhode Island." One report suggested that tobacco been "successfully cultivated in the State of Ohio, where it is known that slavery does not exist," as well as piloted by some free black migrants who moved from Kentucky to Canada.[24] While some of these schemes undoubtedly remained imagined rather than realized, they demonstrate the movement's desire to make antislavery efforts tangible rather than remaining within the realm of reified rhetoric.

By the mid-1840s, American abolitionists' focus had shifted. Garrison spoke for many when he acknowledged that the free produce "question has lost its importance with us." The World Anti-Slavery Convention held in London rejected a call to endorse the movement, and other antislavery bodies followed suit. Ironically, their decisions were in part driven by money. Despite his early support, Garrison came to believe that slaveholders were principally driven by a desire to dominate those they enslaved, regardless of whether it was lucrative to do so. Consequently, even if free produce gained widespread consumer support, he concluded, slavery would remain because its proponents valued power more than profits. By 1847, in response to a free produce motion at an antislavery convention, Wendell Phillips, once heralded as "abolition's Golden Trumpet," declared that he would happily face the "Great Judgement" attired in slave-made cotton of South Carolina. Garrison denied that "it is morally wrong to wear slave grown cotton, or eat slave grown sugar or rice," and renounced the fundamental premise of free produce even more succinctly. "The wrong concentrates," he concluded, "not on the head of the consumer."[25]

For other would-be free produce supporters, however, the decision not to buy had less to do with efficacy than with cost. Francis Ellen Watkins Harper, a popular black lecturer on the abolitionist circuit, admitted that the money she earned on stage made her decision to buy free produce goods easier than it was for many other free African Americans. Even a small price difference might be too much for those with limited or no disposable income. She agreed with free produce storekeepers like New York's Robert Lindley Murray that activist consumers gained more than the goods they brought home. But the intangible moral benefits of such purchases were only an option to those who could afford to buy.[26]

Today, labels such as "green," "organic," "fair trade," and "cruelty free" are as morally and politically loaded as "free produce" or "free labor" hoped to be, and buyers must weigh the pros and cons of a host of causes when making their consumer choices. How will what they eat, wear, or live with impact the environment, animal testing, fair labour practices, and even national boundaries? The goods that front such movements range from dolphin-free tuna and hybrid cars to cosmetics, free-trade coffee, and SodaStream, an Israeli company whose manufacturing plant is located in occupied Palestinian territory. The free produce movement was not the only effort to align moral suasion with commerce. Such considerations drove nineteenth-century reform efforts to regulate the use of child labour as well as early twentieth-century wartime government bond campaigns. Nor was free produce the only movement to link food to social good. Victory gardens claimed to "sow the seeds of victory," and vegetarian advocates, a nascent movement begun in the 1810s, declared that a meat-free diet was "the catalyst for total reform ideology."[27] But free produce did help set a precedent which regularly reappears in subsequent U.S. movements to purposefully and systemically consider morality and economy. Moreover, it required that such considerations take social context into account. It was not the welfare of the individual that rang most strongly in free produce appeals, but the obligation of the one to the many.

2

BOYCOTTS, BUYCOTTS, AND LEGISLATION

Tactical Lessons from Workers and Consumers during the Progressive Era

WENDY WIEDENHOFT MURPHY

S CONSUMPTION more than a private, economic activity that maximizes the happiness of individual purchasers? Can consumers help workers earn a living wage or eliminate sweatshops? If the answer to these questions is yes, what kinds of tactics can be used to mobilize consumers and their collective purchasing power effectively? The various ways that two organizations, the National Consumers League (NCL) and the American Federation of Labor (AFL), politicized consumption during the Progressive Era provides insight into such questions.[1] This chapter emphasizes the challenges that both organizations encountered in framing and implementing their respective tactics. It examines differences between boycotts and buycotts and why it is important to have reliable organizations endorse and monitor them. It explores the difficulties of developing cross-class and gender alliances in relation to the male-dominated, working-class AFL and the female-dominated, middle- and upper-class NCL. Finally, it asks whether legislation is a potentially more successful way to achieve structural change than consumer activism at the point of purchase. The results of these explorations are framed as four lessons that might prove useful for contemporary consumer organizations.

Organizational Tactics and the Politicization of Consumption

The AFL created two consumer tactics in its attempt to mobilize the purchasing power of its members and their households: the "We Don't Patronize" list and the union label. First published in 1894, the "We Don't Patronize" list was a blacklist of manufacturers that the AFL asked its members to discriminate against in their purchasing conduct. The "We Don't Patronize" list was published and updated every month in the back pages of the *American Federationist*, the AFL's official journal. The first union label was created in 1875 by cigar makers in San Francisco, which certified that cigars were made with union labour and not by inexpensive, unskilled Chinese workers, who union workers blamed for driving down wages. A variety of trade unions affiliated with the AFL soon adopted this tactic, placing their own labels on items such as hats, beer bottles, overalls, stoves, and paper.

For the AFL, politicizing consumption was a clever way to support its vision of "pure and simple" business unionism, which was strongly pursued under the leadership of its founder Samuel Gompers. Instead of fighting its grievances primarily in the arena of the state through trying to enact legislation or creating a political party, like most European labour federations did, the AFL decided that the struggles of organized labour in the United States would be fought on the shop floor through collective bargaining and the strike or at the store counter with its consumer tactics. The AFL claimed that this decision was made because skilled workers did not need the state to fight its battles; however, its actions were severely constrained by the state, especially the judiciary, and the influence of big business in the political realm. During the Progressive Era, the AFL faced numerous injunctions from the judiciary for striking because employers often chose to take trade unions to court rather than enter into arbitration. These strikes and court battles were costly for the AFL. Employers replaced striking union members with "scab" labour and often blacklisted strikers, making it difficult for them to find employment at all. The low job security associated with the strike made this tactic a sacrifice many AFL members did not eagerly embrace. Its consumer tactics, on the other hand, were not immediately vulnerable to the injunction. Furthermore, the AFL did not have to collect funds to support its consumer tactics as it did with strikes. Scabs could be used as replacement workers at the point of production, but not as substitutes for the loss of union patronage at the point of consumption.[2]

The NCL also created tactics to mobilize consumers at the point of purchase: a white list and a white label. However, unlike the AFL, it included legislation as a key piece of its tactical repertoire. The white list was established when the first Consumer League was organized in New York City in 1891 by Maud Frederick Nathan and Josephine Shaw Lowell. It listed merchants who treated their female sales clerks fairly and was published in widely circulated newspapers. The white label was created in 1899 when several state and city level consumer leagues consolidated into the NCL. The NCL's white label was placed on undergarments that were produced in clean and healthy work environments. Besides its consumer tactics, the NCL pursued legislation to secure and enforce labour laws, which initially bolstered but eventually made obsolete its white list and label.

The NCL politicized consumption through the lens of citizenship with a maternalist gaze. It reasoned that by voting with their purses women could reform unfair business practices, shape public policy, and in the processes become "better consumers and better citizens." Feeling that it had the duty to educate the public and organize consumers to make ethical decisions in the marketplace, the NCL especially worked on behalf of working women and children who it felt could not protect themselves. Since women did not have the right to vote yet, turning to the marketplace to enact social change was an accessible and acceptable avenue for women at the time, particularly as they did most of the shopping for their families. The NCL stressed that voting at the ballot box occurred only occasionally, while "all of us, all the time, are deciding by our expenditures what industries shall survive at all, and under what conditions." The NCL's tactics enlisted the support of wealthy women consumers, who could influence how department stores treated their female sales clerks and could afford to purchase relatively expensive consumer goods.[3]

The lessons that follow provide a more detailed description of the tactics that the AFL and NCL used to politicize consumption, including how these tactics developed over time in relation to each other. These lessons highlight how manufacturers and merchants responded and also reveal how the AFL and NCL felt about each other's implementation of them. In the process of expounding these lessons, a limited historical narrative of each organization is offered that emphasizes class and gender relations.

Lesson #1: Buycotts are Less Controversial than Boycotts

Boycotts are attempts "by one or more parties to achieve certain objectives by urging individual consumers to refrain from making selected purchases in the marketplace," while buycotts encourage "people to purchase goods following an established set of criteria." Buycotts, which are also referred to as positive boycotts, recommend instead of prohibit consumer purchases and are less controversial than traditional boycotts because they are not viewed as coercive or interfering with individual rights to produce, sell, and purchase goods. The AFL learned this lesson when its boycott, the "We Don't Patronize" list, was declared unconstitutional by the US Supreme Court in 1908 because it violated the Sherman Anti-Trust Act (1890) as a consequence of interfering with interstate trade. The AFL placed manufacturers on its blacklist for a variety of reasons, such as refusing to recognize individual AFL trade unions or neglecting to meet union standards regarding working hours and wages. Often these grievances resulted in a strike, in which case the manufacturer was also blacklisted. Because the "We Don't Patronize" list was printed in the *American Federationist* that was distributed nationwide, all local boycotts in essence became national ones. This is how the "We Don't Patronize" list could be understood as obstructing interstate trade. Ironically, a law passed to prevent the concentration of corporate power was interpreted to regulate the action of a trade union that was struggling against just such power.[4]

However, the AFL's union label remained a viable tactic to mobilize consumers without violating the Sherman Anti-Trust Act. The union label, unlike a traditional boycott, was a non-prohibitive tactic or a buycott and was therefore viewed as a "weapon" that could not be "touched by lawyers or the courts." As one commentator at the time wrote in the *North American Review*, "The label builds up the fair employer's trade instead of tearing down the unfair man's business, as did the boycott. The union label is constructive, not destructive." According to the AFL, the union label was a way for employers and employees to enter into a relationship based on co-operation rather than competition, especially because the AFL split the cost of the union label with businesses that were approved to use it. Following the court-imposed ban on its "We Don't Patronize" list in 1908, the AFL established a Union Label Department and by the end of the year 68 out of the 117 national trade unions affiliated with the AFL were using a union label, a proportion that covered the goods made by about 47 percent of the AFL's aggregate membership.[5]

Unlike the AFL, the NCL did not use any boycott tactics but did use the buycott tactics of white lists and labels to try to help female workers during the Progressive Era. The white list was intended to "keep shoppers informed of such shops that deal justly and fairly with the employees and so bring public opinion and public action to bear in favor of just employers." Thus, their "white" list differed from the typical blacklist because it recommended fair merchants for consumers to support rather than prohibiting consumers from purchasing goods from unfair firms. This meant that it could not be ruled an illegal tactic. While some department stores were dismissive of the white list at first, others came to welcome its seal of approval in order to attract a relatively wealthy customer base. Founder Maud Nathan reported that a "competitive jealously" was aroused every time the league added a new name to its white list and stores began contacting league members to find out how they too could be included on the list. Being added to the white list cost the stores no money and could be used as a form of free advertisement, providing another incentive for stores to support the tactic.

Likewise, manufacturers did not have many complaints about being approved to use the NCL's white label, even though they did have to pay a nominal amount for the labels.[6] Like the union label, the white label was not very controversial because it encouraged instead of prohibited consumers to spend their money. The white label focused exclusively on women's and children's undergarments, which limited its scope. However, manufacturers of other clothing products were eager to use the white label, asking the NCL to expand the campaign. But the NCL decided to maintain its exclusive focus on one product line because it was overwhelmingly made by the labour of non-unionized women, often in sweat shops. By 1904, sixty-four manufacturers had been approved to use the NCL's white label.[7]

Lesson #2: Boycotts and Buycotts Need to be Coordinated and Monitored by Reliable Organizations

In order for boycotts and buycotts to be viewed by consumers as legitimate they had to be certified and regulated by reliable organizations. Both the AFL and NCL struggled to keep their respective consumer tactics valid and trustworthy. The AFL tried to achieve this through its centralized authority over its affiliated trade unions, while the NCL relied on scientific investigation and inspection to ensure the integrity of its white list and label.

The initial popularity of the "We Don't Patronize" list led to it being restructured to make it more legitimate. So many firms were being blacklisted that it was becoming difficult for the AFL to monitor if manufacturers were being added to the "We Don't Patronize" list fairly. The list was also growing so long that the AFL felt it was losing its power to mobilize consumers effectively. As a result, in 1900 the AFL made the executive decision to drop all firms on the list. Affiliated trade unions were allowed to request the reinstatement of firms that they were boycotting, but the AFL now more strictly regulated the list. Before listing a firm, the AFL required that a trade union provide the Executive Council with a full statement of its grievances against the firm and an explanation of what efforts had been made to resolve them. The Executive Council then decided if the trade union had acted in good faith and made "every effort to amicably adjust the matter" with the firm in question. If this was found to be the case, then the Executive Council approved placing the firm on the "We Don't Patronize" list. Trade unions with firms on the list were required to report on the efforts being made to resolve their grievances every three months; failure to do so would result in the firm being dropped from the list. Along with these stricter criteria, the AFL also decided to limit the number of firms that individual trade unions could place on the list at a given time. Even after these rules were instated the AFL still encountered problems with regulating the number of boycotts in communities throughout the country. According to contemporary labour economist Leo Wolman, the majority of the AFL Executive Council's legislative acts between 1893 and 1908 were attempts "to control the too frequent use of the boycott."[8]

The AFL faced different problems with its union label. Rather than complain about the labels, manufacturers tried to imitate them. Counterfeit labels were partially a consequence of the AFL allowing each of its affiliated trade unions to design their own unique labels, which consequently differed greatly in shape, size, colour, and texture. Some of these union labels were stamped, others engraved, and others sewn onto products. In 1895, the AFL prepared a bill for a uniform label law and, at its 1889 convention, resolved to investigate the matter of creating a universal union label, but the Executive Council eventually decided against enforcing a universal label on its affiliates. Thus, at any given moment there existed a large variety of union labels being used across the country. This made it difficult to obtain trademarks to protect each union label from counterfeit labels, especially after some trade unions decided to change the colour or size of their labels every three to six months to avoid imitations.

Besides the problem of counterfeiting, the lack of a universal union label also complicated the AFL's goal of fostering working-class fraternity beyond each member's individual trade. For example, cigar makers might only purchase union-made cigars but would fail to purchase other union-labelled goods. A further problem associated with the lack of a universal label was that there were no clear standards of what each union label represented, apart from the fact that the products it was placed on were made with union labour.

In contrast to the inconsistent standards of the AFL, the NCL conducted social scientific research to legitimize the validity of its claims about the working conditions of female and child labourers. Before implementing its white list, the Consumers League decided on the specific standards merchants had to meet in order to be designated a "fair house." These included requiring employers to pay male and female employees equal wages of at least six dollars per week, compensate all overtime work, not employ children under the age of fourteen, keep their stores open only between the hours of eight o'clock in the morning and six in the evening, and allow employees at least forty-five minutes for a lunch break. Additionally, fair houses had to obey existing sanitary and labour laws, provide seats for female sales clerks, and establish a place where clerks could eat lunch and rest. To appear on the League's white list, merchants had to sign a letter of agreement certifying that they met these requirements and would allow a member of the League to visit their establishments and question their employees to obtain confirmation of their compliance.[9]

Like its white list, the NCL also established clear standards for manufacturers to adhere to in order to use its white label. The League demanded that goods bearing its label be made entirely within factories, not with piecework arrangements in tenements or sweatshops, and that employers obey state factory laws, require no employees to work overtime, and employ no child under the age of seventeen. Furthermore, before the NCL allowed a manufacturer to use its label a member of the league had to inspect the factory and obtain a report from the local or state Board of Health to certify that the working conditions of the establishment met health and safety laws. The NCL label stated that the product to which it was attached was "made under clean and healthful conditions" and that "use of the label" was "authorized after investigation." Unlike the union label, which appeared on a variety of products, the white label was only placed on one product line, undergarments. This choice of product was intentional, as the garment industry was notorious for employing unskilled, young women and was the main industry responsible for sweatshop production. The high standards of the NCL's white label tactic made it difficult to implement since so few manufacturers met all of the NCL requirements. For example, the stipulation that manufacturers obey state health and factory laws resulted in an uneven use of the label through-out the country. Twenty-seven of the sixty-eight manufacturers using the label were located in Massachusetts because it was a state that had not only passed regulatory labour laws but also enforced them. Furthermore, many manufacturers were reluctant to allow NCL members access to their fac-tory floors for inspections.[10]

Lesson #3: Building Class and Gender Alliances is Complicated

Political consumerism provides the potential for cross-class and gender alliances, but it may also be constrained by these social categories, par-ticularly if there are strong stereotypes attached to them. During the Progressive Era, these stereotypes situated women as the primary con-sumers in their households and men as the primary producers. On the one hand, these gender beliefs encouraged the AFL to mobilize the pur-chasing power of women to help support organized labour. The success of the "We Don't Patronize" list and union label relied on the consumer activism of the wives, daughters, sisters, and mothers of union men. On the other hand, viewing women through the lens of consumption ignored female workers and any efforts to try to unionize them. Furthermore, the AFL expressed little interest in enlisting the support of middle- or upper-class consumers, who it felt would not purchase working-class products that displayed the union label.

The NCL intentionally tried not to interfere with the AFL's consumer tactics. John Graham Brooks, the first president of the NCL, claimed that he had initially envisioned the League simply adopting the union label, but early investigations found its members were not likely to consume union-made products and that allying itself too closely with the AFL "would have killed the movement from the start." Neither the white list nor the white label demanded the use of union labour, which appealed to some middle- and upper-class consumers who viewed any talk of wages or unionization as un-American. The NCL focused its efforts on helping female garment workers who were not unionized by the AFL; therefore, the NCL label did not compete directly with the union label. However, similar to the AFL, the NCL did not view working women as active participants in its move-ment, but as victims that it could protect. Thus, the NCL both embraced and tried to challenge gender stereotypes, claiming that consumption could empower middle- and upper-class women, yet did not fully identify working-class women or men of any class as consumer activists.[11]

It proved difficult for the AFL and the NCL to form a cross-class and gender alliance. The AFL criticized the NCL's white label because it did not stipulate wage standards. Since the union label already guaranteed sanitary working conditions, the AFL felt the white label served little purpose. The AFL worried that the NCL's white label would cause "unintentional injury" to the union label. For example, the NCL did not know if a manufacturer was requesting to use its white label because the AFL failed to approve it to use the union label. When an AFL union engaged in a strike against a manufacturer that was using the NCL's white label, the AFL began aggressively attacking the League's label, accusing the NCL of awarding it to employers who were hostile to organized labour. The NCL conceded that the AFL's allegations were accurate and decided to discontinue the use of its white label in 1918. "Our position is obviously untenable as friends of labor" claimed the NCL "if we persist in pushing our label as a rival to the label of the American Federation of Labor against the protests of union officials." But, the decision to end its white label campaign was also because the NCL began concentrating on helping women workers more through legislation than consumer tactics.[12]

Lesson #4: Legislation is More Effective

Even during the NCL's list and label campaigns, the tactic of legislation occupied a pivotal position in the work of many League participants. League members had worked on securing and enforcing labour laws from the creation of the very first Consumers League. Investigative testimony from members of the New York City Consumers' League, for example, was fundamental in securing the passage of the 1896 Mercantile Inspection Act. In 1902, League president Maud Nathan was appointed as a special investigator for the New York Department of Health, which was responsible for the enforcement of the act. Nathan's experience was not unique. Many NCL members worked for state regulatory agencies. Before accepting the position of General Secretary of the NCL, Florence Kelley was appointed the first State Factory Inspector in Illinois in 1895. Achieving these positions was critical to ensuring that the new labour laws were enforced. In addition, NCL members were very active in helping to secure the passage of the Pure Food and Drug Act in 1906.

A further move toward legislation occurred at the NCL's tenth annual meeting when Kelley reported that the label tactic was not sufficiently solving the problem of sweatshop production and suggested that the League work to secure legislation to prohibit sweatshops. This suggestion came after the NCL's most remarkable victory: its instrumental work to establish a maximum workday of ten hours for women in the Supreme Court case *Muller v. the State of Oregon* (1908). League member Josephine Goldmark helped her brother-in-law, lawyer Louis Brandeis, compile a brief consisting of labour laws and medical reports demonstrating that the health and well-being of women and their families suffered if they worked long hours daily.[13] This logic fit not only the League's maternalist philosophy and its belief in scientific expertise but also the stereotypes of women at the time. Positioning women as physically weaker than men proved persuasive in convincing the Supreme Court that women needed legal protection in the workplace. When the NCL succeeded in passing labour legislation to prohibit child labour and protect female workers, it no longer needed its list or label tactics. The NCL grew into a lobbying association and made consumers not only a third party in economic transactions between employers and employees, but also a third party in government labour regulations—and its lobbying and legislative successes achieved more long-lasting, structural change compared to its white list and label.[14]

Conclusion

In conclusion, the consumer tactics of the AFL and NCL can inform the practices of current social movements that turn to the realm of consumption to effect social change. First, consumer sovereignty is important and attempts to restrict the freedom of consumer choice may limit the number of potential participants or be deemed coercive or even illegal if they obstruct so-called free trade. This is why buycotts will almost always be more successful than boycotts. It may also explain why current consumer campaigns that use label buycotts, including the fair trade and organic movements, are experiencing success. This is not to claim that boycotts never work; indeed, boycotts may gain more initial attention and reaction because they go against consumerism, like Adbusters' "Buy Nothing Day" campaign. But anti-consumer sentiments are not likely to attract many mainstream participants. Second, too many simultaneous consumer boycotts or buycotts may backfire if participants find them redundant, confusing, or illegitimate, which is why reliable organizations are necessary to co-ordinate and monitor consumer tactics.[15] When one particular product contains a variety of labels consumers may be confused as to the authenticity of the claims these labels represent and question what organizations exist to justify these claims. Third, consumers have diverse interests, and consumer movements may have difficulty bridging class and gender divides, especially if the products they are endorsing are expensive, unusual, class specific, like working uniforms, or difficult to find outside of exclusive specialty stores. Finally, consumer activism may not engender long-term structural change. Indeed, movements may find that consumer power might be best organized and most influential not in the market-place, but in the realm of the state through lobbying and working to enact legislation. However, in today's global marketplace where manufacturers and consumer goods easily cross national borders, consumer tactics at the point of purchase may prove more powerful than laws that are not privi-leged to such mobility. In addition, consumer organizations may find that they need to incorporate a more global approach to their consumer activ-ism, especially because international nongovernmental organizations have become key actors in certifying and monitoring key global buycotts, like fair trade.

3

MAKING A MARKET FOR CONSUMERS

The Calgary Consumers League and the High Cost of Living

BETTINA LIVERANT

I N 1913, the Calgary public market was a forlorn and drowsy place: a few stalls offering overpriced mouldy cabbages and limp carrots; flies circling exposed blocks of butter; and the smell of incontinent dray horses in the air. The market, owned and paid for by the city since 1885, had occupied a succession of sites chosen by way of real estate deals rather than for public convenience. Now it stood virtually abandoned by housewives and farmers alike. A year later, regenerated by efforts of the new Calgary Consumers League, the same building presented a very different picture. The aisles were crowded with shoppers and the stalls filled with fresh produce offered at good prices; vendors were wait-listed for space. Taxpayers voted funds for an expansion that would double the size and modernize facilities.[1] The league's success captured the imaginations of Calgarians and inspired group action across Canada. In a time of rising prices and uncertainty, the women of Calgary had done something effective to lower the high cost of living. Although they adopted a broad program of action in the period 1913 to 1917, it was this rapid and highly visible triumph that won the league local and national attention. And, while the league benefited from the publicity, the effort drained energy and focus away from their broader platform. Five years later, the market was under threat of closing. Key leaders had moved on to other issues. Calgary grocers had become more competitive, and the city council was no longer interested in supporting a public utility supplying staple foods at lower prices.

How do we understand the story of the Calgary Consumers League, hailed in its day for improving the lives of Calgarians but subsequently reduced to a footnote or passing reference? In the years immediately before the First World War, rising food prices, exacerbated by a global recession, were a concern throughout the developed world. While experts debated the causes and statisticians sought to measure the precise degree of inflation, ordinary people took to the streets in Europe and America.[2] In Calgary, Alberta—a small city in Western Canada—women confronted the same "arch enemy" of high living costs. Their protest, however, was not in the streets but in public meeting rooms and the city council chambers. The efforts of many consumer activists are organized to effect change in other areas: improved working conditions, for example, or desegregation. The Calgary Consumers League sought to lower costs and raise the quality of everyday foodstuffs for working- and middle-class families, leveraging their energy and their gender to prove that bringing the consumer and the producer closer could benefit all parties: lowering prices and improving quality for consumers, raising returns for farmers, and, ultimately, benefiting retailers as consumers and farmers spent their savings on dry goods, groceries, and machinery. The public market, they insisted, was not an attack on existing retailers but reform within capitalism.

The Calgary league rose to prominence during the same period as the better known National Consumers League in America, and indeed the two organizations were aware of each other. Although the American organization urged Calgary to adopt the NCL constitution with its focus on social reform, local leaders believed that the conditions each community had to overcome differed too greatly for a uniform line of action. Perhaps, the Calgary league acknowledged, it had "set sail under the wrong flag," but its leaders believed that they were "laying the foundation here for a new order of things wherever trade conditions touch the household."[3]

The Calgary Consumers League

At the beginning of the twentieth century, Calgary was a rapidly growing city in Canada's booming west. The population, just 4,091 in 1901, officially reached 43,704 by 1911 and 56,514 by 1916. Unofficial estimates for 1913–14 ran as high as 70,000 to 90,000. The dramatic scale and speed of urbanization, typical throughout Canada's midwest, created housing shortages and high prices. In Canada, the cost of food rose by one-third between 1900 and 1910. At the end of 1912, the economy slipped suddenly into recession. Unemployment and wage cuts further strained the resources of working class and low salaried families. When the Local Council of Women reorganized in 1912, one of its first actions was to appoint a Home Economics Committee to investigate what might be done about the high cost of living. The leaders of this committee called a series of mass meetings the next spring, requesting that "Everyone interested in the reduction of the high cost of living" gather in the public library to discuss possible solutions.[4] Attendance was high and the consensus, particularly among the "experienced housewives" in the audience, was that a public market could be a great aid in reducing household expenses. As Mrs. Georgina Newhall, soon to be the league president, explained, a "market built by the people for the people, with its expenses and profits open to investigation, enables the consumer to properly estimate the cost of production and distribution, and allow a reasonable margin of profit."[5] Interest in the problem of the high cost of living was widely shared, requiring an organizational commitment well beyond the scope of the Local Council. United by their commitment to fight high prices, those present voted to form a Calgary Consumers League, the first of its kind in Canada, with a membership fee of 25 cents for one year to cover the costs of postage and stationary needed to communicate the league's objectives to a broad audience. A constitution was devised, with three objectives:

1. To investigate the increasing cost of living and to counteract the same by any legitimate means within their power.
2. To study and teach the principles of co-operation in connection with home economics.
3. To watch, influence and promote civic legislation in connection with either of the foregoing clauses.[6]

A week later, at a third public meeting, this draft constitution was approved and the Calgary Consumers League formally launched. Calgary's mayor was in attendance, and he challenged the women to demonstrate they truly wanted a market by "patronizing the one which had been built for them."[7] With sufficient evidence of support, he implied, the city would be willing to consider improvements, including a new building in a better location.

The methodologies of investigation, education, and improved legislation were consistent with moderate Canadian progressivism. Although it had been developed as a clearing-house rather than a centre of retail trade, a public market had existed in Calgary since 1885. Advocacy for the market was often seen as an attack on local retailers, but league leaders insisted that reducing high food costs would benefit consumers, producers, and retailers when money saved on food was spent on other goods and services. The league frequently received—and always rejected—offers proposing preferred pricing for members. The market was open to all. The league would not abandon those "who cannot afford to put up the money for crates of fruit or vegetables or twenty pound lots of sugar," but proposed to "show the way towards cheaper and better living to all the people of the city, whether members or not."[8]

If the agenda was not especially radical, neither were those most directly involved. Although there were businessmen in the league, the executive positions were held by middle-class women. Most had come to Calgary from the United States or Britain as the wives of middle-class professionals. Although not particularly wealthy, they benefited from access to higher education and were notably articulate, confident, and energetic. Politically, league leaders held a range of commitments, spanning from the radical socialist Annie Gale (the league's corresponding secretary) to the home-centred feminism of Elizabeth Deachman, who led the league during the war years. Claiming authority as experts in the workings of the economy as it affected the household, they represented a rising generation of women organizing to reform public life. In the case of the Calgary Consumers League, the driving concern was not social or moral reform, but what historian Meg Jacobs has named "pocketbook politics." With incomes squeezed by inflation, middle-class housewives discovered a bond with the working poor. Charitable and patriotic organizations would help the unemployed, Newhall observed, but there was no one "taking care of the man who is holding onto his position by the skin of this teeth. . . . The Consumers' League is going to benefit the people who are straining every nerve to make a cent do the work of a dollar."[9]

Not inherently radical, they found themselves at odds with local merchants (who regarded a public market as a threat to their trade) and a business-oriented city council (who regarded intervention into food prices and the retailing of foodstuffs as well beyond the role and responsibility of municipal government).[10] Challenged by the mayor to show that the market was viable, and determined to make a difference, the leaders spoke with conviction and promised to back up their rhetoric with action, threatening to import a train car of fruit and vegetables from the neighbouring province of British Columbia and to sell this produce in a tent beside the market building. By early June, the war of words between the Consumers League and city council began to yield results. An experimental one-day market was held on June 21, with a large central stall in the market hall staffed by league members, offering plentiful produce at lower prices. Before the opening day, league representatives had promoted the market with women's groups and contacted almost five hundred local and regional producers to convince them that interested buyers would come. That morning an estimated five thousand shoppers representing all classes, ages, and genders arrived, some lining up even before the doors opened. Shoppers were reported to be pleased with the bargains, and farmers were well satisfied with the prices received.[11]

Opening day was a media sensation. One of the local papers took up the cause; others covered the story. The market, once a deserted wilderness, was now filled to overflowing. The league continued with its own stall through the summer, adding local produce as it became available. By August, the remaining stalls were fully leased. By the following spring, crowds were so large "as to interfere with business and the comfort of customers."[12] Taxpayers supported a bylaw that would almost double the space and modernize the facilities.

The league's success in restoring the market to profitability and reducing prices received widespread and very positive attention. Consumer and gender themes were co-mingled in the reportage which credited women with putting the market (previously described as a "white elephant" in the hands of the city) on a working basis and effecting real reductions in the cost of living by bringing the bringing the producer closer to the consumer. The league was besieged by requests from across the country for advice, written materials, and speakers. New consumer leagues agitating for public markets appeared in Brandon, Red Deer, Edmonton, and Saskatoon. Articles appeared in daily newspapers from Victoria to Toronto and Quebec City. In Calgary, the league moved to broaden its lobbying power by rejoining the Local Council of Women. A larger membership, it was understood, would help persuade the city to carry out promised improvements and give the league added weight in achieving municipal, provincial, and federal legislation.

Descriptions of the league's triumph, whether in the daily press or accounts shared among women, were told in much the same way, celebrating "the success of the ladies" where the men had failed and describing the persuasive power of women. There was clearly a performative aspect to their efforts, with women asserting their power as shoppers (no longer victims taking what retailers gave), as voters (lobbying for changes to the bylaws that regulated business), and as individuals willing to work in the market to prove their point. Even while styling themselves as advocates for the "defenseless housewife, the weakest member of society," they employed gender tactics to advance their objectives. The *Morning Albertan's* account of Mrs. Newhall's address to City Council, for example, noted that her purse full of housekeeping money was displayed "just conspicuously enough to impress married aldermen."[13] A letter written by a suffragist who had immigrated to Calgary to her friends living in the United Kingdom explained that the women

> frequently had to haunt the City Hall to get various grievances redressed, but it was a brave man who dared say them nay. One who was rash enough to say, "Let the women go home and clean their kitchens before they worry about cleaning up the market," found out on election day that his services were no longer required; he also had his telephone kept busy for days by women inviting him to visit their kitchens.[14]

A campaign to reduce the cost of butcher licences brought a delegation to Calgary City Council the day before the municipal election. The motion passed under the "glittering eyes" of the "ladies." The presence of women in the audience was also a factor in the motion that followed. After a brief discussion, the word "male" was removed from the bylaw providing for the election of hospital trustees. A reporter remarked "the fair sex scored again," adding that the mayor "shot a beaming smile in the direction of the feminine contingent, with the remark that he hoped the ladies would take notice that all the aldermen were in favour of the motion."[15]

The league leveraged its success in the market to secure other reforms, some related to the market, others involving broader concerns; some more progressive and some, perhaps, more reactionary in nature. Although it was unable to have the market moved to a better location, the league campaigned successfully for reduced street car fares on trips to and from the market and for the free delivery of goods bought at the market (apparently the only market in the whole of the Dominion to do so). Further lobbying resulted in the purchase of new scales, the hiring of an inspector of weights and measures, and the appointment of a meat inspector (enabling small farmers to retail meat in the building). In October 1914, the league gained public attention again when it brought in a train carload of flour and sold it at cost in an effort to "break" the flour monopolies.[16]

The success of the market was also instrumental in campaigns for other reforms, including the introduction of copper coinage and cash sales. In their campaign for copper coinage, league representatives visited each trader in the market hall, explaining the advantages of a few pennies saved. Those who "refused to see the point" found themselves targets of "a gentle boycott" that "leavened the whole in a few weeks."[17] The league also used the market to promote cash sales and, in a related effort, to campaign for the payment of regular weekly wages. The use of cash rather than store credit, it asserted, would eliminate both favouritism and the risk of unpaid bills. Complaints that the market was taking away business from other grocers were dismissed outright. Money saved on foodstuffs could be spent elsewhere, as Newhall explained: "cash set free in one direction sweeps round in a circle . . . the cash taken in at the market is dispensed at dry goods stores . . . a system of cash payment is being established, the ripples of which are bound to be far-reaching."[18] Other aspects of the agenda sounded a reactionary note. The league objected to the added expense of telephone delivery and encouraged housewives to "Carry the Basket," to do without frills, to use their labour and time to reduce costs.[19] Provisioning would take longer, but time, Newhall eloquently argued,

> is the one available right of every woman. It is her own unalienable possession to throw into the breach whenever financial stringency assails and compels a reduction of the food supplies. When women are paid by the hour for their household duties, it will be time to consider the economic loss of going to the market. Until then she will do as she has always done, cut out all that is eliminable in her housework or work longer in the evenings to complete her duties—but food for her beloved—she must have the best foods—the most food—and at the least possible real cash price.[20]

By late summer of 1913, the *Morning Albertan* reported that the market was essentially paying for itself. With the exceptions of flour, sugar, and imported groceries, the prices of foodstuffs in Calgary had stabilized. Fruit from the neighbouring province of British Columbia was arriving, plentiful and cheap. Vegetables were better and somewhat cheaper than usual. The league now resolved to reach even further in its "war on the high cost of living" by campaigning for a wholesale market and working for a bylaw (on the "New York model") that would require all Calgary merchants to list the ingredients on packaged goods. Announcing its fall meeting, the league executive aimed to reset the broader agenda, asking "Will you help to form an intelligent public opinion as to the responsibilities of consumers?" Attendance was high and enthusiastic. Mrs. Singley, the league secretary, reported on the challenges of the past four months, highlighting work done to recruit regional producers to assure an ample supply of fresh produce. The future of Calgary, she asserted, depended not on real estate speculation but factories offering steady employment backed by affordable food and shelter. The Consumers League would help by identifying "a saner solution" to these challenges. Newhall then expounded on the unexpected success of the public market:

> The fact of the matter is that the establishment of a market . . . was a side issue not contemplated in the programme of the league. It was a dramatic coup scarcely contemplated before it was achieved.
>
> If you were to ask me the reason for its sudden success I should tell you that some of us say: it was the psychological moment for the establishment of anything that seemed to point toward a reduction of the cost of living; some of us say it was pure luck; some say hard work. While none of us will deny the strenuosity of our endeavors, none of us will willfully deceive you by saying that it was the result of organization. We are willing to confess looking back over the summer that this dramatic stroke did more for us, perhaps, than months of cold-blooded organization might have done.[21]

Although bringing in a carload of vegetable and fruit had "caught the popular fancy," Newhall promised there would be nothing as "dramatic or spectacular" going forward. The purpose of the Calgary league was not civic boosterism, nor were the members of the league responsible for maintaining the market. The market was owned and paid for by the city, and it was the city's responsibility to put the market on a business basis. The league kept "its part of the compact," proving that shoppers would come and that produce was available. It was "now up to city to put that public utility, in which the people's money was invested, on a proper business basis." Turning to broader concerns, Newhall explained that national consumers' leagues already existed in Germany, France, and the United States. In these older countries, she proposed, the principal duty of consumers was to find out under which conditions the articles they purchased were produced and distributed, and to insist that these conditions be wholesome and consistent with respectable existence on the part of workers. The league's job in a new country, however, was to "regulate profit to a fair percentage" by bringing the consumer and producer closer together in an open marketplace. "Our position is this: Consumers are the object of production. They possess, as buyers, an incomparable economic power, and should organize to make themselves a beneficent influence in society."[22]

The league's goals for the coming year included the establishment of a wholesale market, a commitment to affordable housing for workers, passage of bylaws to compel the publication of ingredients and package weights, and a program of public education to encourage more cost-effective ways of buying, cooking, and storing foods. By September of 1914, however, many of the initial leaders had reached their physical limits. The most committed had been running the league's market stall as volunteers for over a year, receiving produce, moving crates, keeping books, and personally staffing the stall for several days each week. Their goal was to prove that it could be done, and they believed they had succeeded.[23] The league now called for the operation to be handed completely over to the city and monitored by a Market Advisory Board, to consist of three women and two men. Newhall resigned as president. Handing over responsibilities for the market would also free the league to take on new roles, particularly in relation to the war effort. Indeed, the membership embarked on a number of new initiatives, including the creation of the Vacant Lots Garden Club (organized to grow vegetables on vacant civic property), canning projects in the market hall, and educational lectures that encouraged thrift on the home front as part of the war effort.

The withdrawal of the league meant that the city, as well as operating the market, would be selling produce in the market in direct competition with local retailers, often at lower prices. A provincial bylaw, supported by the league, was required and obtained for this purpose. By summer 1915, however, city council, never wholly supportive, began to undercut the viability of the market. New regulations were introduced: first ending the sale of groceries in the building (adding inconvenience for the shoppers); and then declaring that any remaining perishable produce would be auctioned off at 4:30 every afternoon (reducing returns to the farmers). Although representatives of the league were in attendance at the April 1915 city council meeting, they were unable to alter the outcome.

The market continued to generate income from stall rentals and consumers continued to benefit from lower prices on staple foods such as eggs, butter, and potatoes, but market attendance began to decline. Newspaper reports in the spring of 1916 mention unspecified dissension within the executive of the league. A petition circulated, calling for Mrs. Newhall to return as president. She declined, and, while the election proceeded peacefully, membership numbers began to fall. Accusations that some city officials received goods better in quality and cheaper in price than the general public—although investigated and dismissed—further undermined goodwill. In June 1916, the sale of produce was reduced from three to two days each week. Fewer consumers led to fewer farmers, and fewer farmers led to fewer consumers. For many years the public market continued to be publicized by city council, used in booster propaganda to portray Calgary as a progressive community even as it began to undercut the success of the enterprise as a business venture. However, the market increasingly suffered from poor management and little advertising. The streetcar subsidy was ended. Local merchants combined to sponsor a rival market in a better location. Although the city continued to support the development of other public utilities, including gas and transportation, the market was delisted as a public utility by 1925. The building was sold and burned down in an accidental fire in 1954.

Key actors moved on to new initiatives, bringing their energy and skills to other causes. Newhall worked to establish a nation-wide association that would allow local organizations to share their successful experiences and work together to secure legislation and educate the public. Unfortunately, her campaign of letters, press articles, and addresses met with limited success. Newhall believed that war effort, the franchise, and modern expectations displaced concerns about the cost of living.[24] Gale moved directly into civic politics, organizing Canada's first Women's Ratepayers Association in 1916 and winning elected office as a Calgary alderman in 1917. She was a fierce advocate for a range of radical causes; however, by 1919 she was forced to acknowledge that little business was being done in the market. Gale responded with comprehensive recommendations, calling for the municipalization of basic food commodities, a network of branch markets, and a municipal Jersey herd to supply milk for babies. Her proposals seem to have met with little response. After an unsuccessful run for a seat in the provincial legislature, Gale retired with her family to Vancouver in 1925. The work of Mrs. Deachman, the president of the league through the war years, was less radical in approach. Deachman organized an extensive canning program in collaboration with the Red Cross Society, using part of the market as a depot to supply military hospitals with canned goods prepared under the auspices of the Consumers League.[25] Deachman continued to advocate for lower prices in the marketplace, but her primary focus was on economies that could be achieved in the home. In a familiar pattern, the Deachmans left Calgary, in their case moving to Ottawa in 1926.

Is Politics Local?

The history of the Calgary Consumers League suggests a dynamic to consumer activism: energy is mobilized by a problem and coalesces around a visible project, but is not sustainable. The heyday of the Calgary public market was brief. The causes of its decline were multiple and common to such projects: fatigue, internal dissension, and the redirection of energies to other concerns. The league naively believed that if they proved the market was viable, city council would continue to support it. This was not the case. Although council (predominantly male) continued to support utilities seen as beneficial to business development (including electricity, water, and streetcars), there was no commitment to support food distribution as a not-for-profit public utility. It is also the case that markets were becoming less relevant to daily provisioning as shopping patterns changed. Cold storage, railways, streetcar lines, and suburban development supplied dispersed populations with foodstuffs; consumer tastes shifted to branded, packaged goods and imported produce sold in self-serve grocery stores. Low prices became associated with advertised sales rather than local produce and public markets. Women joined the workforce, and time could no longer be thrown into the breach. The legislative legacy of the league's efforts was more long-lasting. Changes in coinage and campaigns for high standards in processing and packaging helped pave the way for federal legislation.

The success of the Calgary Consumers League mobilized women in ways that had other impacts. When women self-consciously identified themselves as consumers, their consumer identities became the basis for collective action.[26] Campaigns for reform in the marketplace drew some women from private life into public politics. Gender played a role in the league's success, not only as an effective vehicle for grassroots organizing but also because the novel presence of women in the city council chambers and their success, particularly as women, in reinvigorating the market and lowering food costs garnered them considerable attention and publicity. The triumphs of the Calgary Consumers League correlated with the early high point of women's influence in civic affairs, and it both benefited from and contributed to the expanding influence of women in public life.[27]

Local Calgary leaders, just like those in America's better known National Consumers League, understood the problems they saw as the result of the increasing distance between consumer and producer. The focus of concern in Calgary, however, was not horrific conditions of production in the needle trades but problems of distribution that were seen to threaten every household. In both situations, individuals identifying a consumer interest stepped forward to engage in political action as a counterweight to perceived inefficiencies and unfairness in the structures of capitalism. In Calgary, the logistics of daily provisioning were shifting from small proprietorships to national chains and globalized networks of food distribution, but the transition was incomplete. The idea of the public market held considerable appeal in part because it drew on recent memories of simpler, less expensive times. The market also spoke to the ideal of transparency. It would be a place where consumers and producers could come together without the intervention of the middleman, using cash rather than store credit, and the most accurate weights and measures available. Transparency would result in fair exchange, and fair exchange would lead to lower prices. Transparency was the consumers' defence against "the rapacity of private interests."[28] The Calgary league, which focused on the household, insisted that consumer activism had to be situated in time and place. The impetus for reform was not social change but the provision of affordable, reasonable quality staple foods. It was as spenders in the local economy that league leaders claimed a role in civic affairs. In the home, the housewife was alone; as a consumer, she was a force to be reckoned with.

The league's call to reduce the distance between producer and consumer was not unique, nor was its conviction that running the market as a public utility would eliminate the profit component and reduce costs. Today, however, the provision of public services continues to move away from government and toward privatization. The development of covered, conveniently located spaces for shopping is almost entirely the domain of private enterprise and organized for profit. Perhaps the Calgary public market was only a manifestation of local concerns, outmoded by the efficiencies of scale introduced by private capital. In its day, however, it was also the manifestation of a larger vision of a common consumer interest in which household provisioning was a civic responsibility rather than a private act. It was this vision that energized the Calgary Consumers League. By withdrawing support for the public market, Calgary ended an experiment that sought to model an alternative within capitalism.

4

MAKING A
MIDDLE-CLASS "PUBLIC"

Middle-Class Consumer Activism
in Post–First World War America

MARK ROBBINS

N THE MIDST of an upsurge in labour unrest and soaring prices for the
necessities of life immediately after the First World War (1919–22),
Vice President Thomas R. Marshall observed that the "middle class"
was "rapidly coming together" to protect themselves from the selfish
actions of capital and labour.[1] Marshall was among the many politicians,
commentators, and activists to take notice of a rise in "middle-class" consumer activism by white-collar workers and their families in one of the
most significant attempts in U.S. history to organize the middle class.
As part of newly formed consumer groups, ranging from new clothing
boycott clubs to tenants' leagues, these activists blamed striking workers and wealthy "profiteers" for driving up prices for innocent consumers
and boldly defined the middle class as "the public," "the people," and the
"backbone" of American society.

Through an examination of postwar middle-class consumer activism,
this chapter considers the political implications of what scholars such as
Marina Moskowitz and Jennifer Scanlon have elucidated as middle-class
Americans' growing consumer identity in the early twentieth century.[2] It
discusses how white-collar activists mobilized to protest the high cost of
living in the postwar period, forming consumer organizations, including
tenants' societies, new clothing boycott clubs, home garden committees,

and municipal market campaigns. By drawing on the actions and statements of members of these organizations and their contemporaries, this chapter illustrates how white-collar activists used their consumer identity to define themselves as both the middle class and as the "public," against the supposed selfishness of organized labour and elite "profiteers."[3] Much like the Calgary Consumers League, discussed by Bettina Liverant in the previous chapter, these activists did not seek change through radicalism, instead pursuing goals and strategies within the framework of capitalism. Despite the short timeframe of their activism, popular portrayals of the middle class as the public interest continued to have a presence in American political discourse throughout the remainder of the twentieth century and beyond.[4]

The Emergence of Middle-Class Consumer Identity

The early twentieth century brought significant changes to the composition of the U.S. middle class. During the nineteenth century, most Americans defined the middle class as consisting of owner-operators, skilled artisans, or small merchants. Termed by scholars the "old middle class," they often worked with their hands in small environments and, in many cases, produced a product or crop. Popular writers celebrated the producer values that shaped the identity of this middle class. As the *San Francisco Bulletin* declared in 1878, "Quiet, deliberate, persistent hard work, and honest workers—these are what California needs. The middle class of the State."[5] When the United States experienced rapid industrialization and urbanization during the late nineteenth and early twentieth centuries, a "new middle class" of white-collar workers grew in size and prominence, expanding by 200 percent from 1880 to 1920, relative to the rest of the population.[6] This "new middle class" worked in stores, offices, and classrooms, largely did not physically produce a product, and often did not own their businesses. Artisans, small shopkeepers, and other members of the "old middle class" remained a prominent part of American society but were increasingly displaced by economic change.

Unlike the producer-centred "old middle class," consumption increasingly shaped white-collar workers' "middle-class" identity. By the early 1900s, the United States had become a consumer society, which featured a proliferation of mass-produced goods, advertisements, and popular print media. A number of scholars have noted how this growing consumer society offered Americans a plethora of new products that acted as visual markers of class distinction.[7] Many white-collar workers and their families took cues from department store displays, trade cards, and national popular magazines like *Ladies' Home Journal*, which standardized the types and styles of consumer goods and shopping experiences that signified a middle-class lifestyle. They sought to live in middle-class neighbourhoods, comprised of similar homes, filled with the same kinds of consumer products.

During the Progressive Era, a number of middle-class Americans drew on their consumer identity to politically mobilize in support of the working class. Like the consumer activists of the previous two centuries, who, as Lawrence Glickman notes, had organized boycott or buycott movements in support of causes ranging from the American Revolution to abolitionism, they reconciled the seeming private and passive nature of individual consumption with active citizenship.[8] As part of the National Consumers League or local women's clubs, these progressives encouraged middle-class shoppers to avoid buying items that had been produced under unjust labour conditions, but they often neglected to advocate in concert with the goals, strategies, and organizations developed by working class groups themselves.[9]

Rising prices during the 1910s led many white-collar Americans to lobby overtly for their *own* interests as consumers. From 1913 to 1920, the consumer price index increased by 97 percent, mostly due to wartime inflation.[10] A wide range of Americans lamented "the high cost of living," but white-collar workers felt especially impacted. Whereas the wages of a sample of blue-collar professions increased by 55 percent between 1913 and 1919, white-collar salaries purportedly remained the same.[11] As one of many white-collar consumer organizations reacting to these changes, a newly-formed Tampa anti–high cost of living organization characterized "salaried men" as the greatest sufferers of price increases and sent a petition to elected officials promising that they would make no new clothing purchases "until the different branches of government show an honest effort" to reduce the cost of living.[12] In testimony before a U.S. Senate committee, the leader of a like-minded organization in Chicago complained of the hardships high prices had caused for "the so-called middle class, the so-called white collar class . . . the class that is suffering." In most cases, such individuals and organizations saw virtually only white-collar workers as within the boundaries of the middle class.[13]

Middle-Class Activism

By the end of the war, white-collar workers and sympathetic commentators often identified elite profiteers and organized labour as the two primary culprits of the high cost of living. Newspaper articles, letters to the editor, correspondence to government officials, political speeches, and congressional testimony commonly noted how middle-class consumers suffered from the greed of both organized labour and wealthy profiteers. Writing in 1919, a year in which 22.5 percent of all workers went on strike, one Montgomery, Alabama man was among those to express this common sentiment. He complained, "Labor is already more highly paid than any other class of our citizenship" and "Capital, of course, get 'his'n.'" It was "the great 'middle class'" that suffered, he concluded.[14] The anti-labour sentiment in these types of critiques often took on the antiradical language of the first red scare, which posited the American public and its traditional institutions against labour, immigration, and political radicalism. As John Corbin wrote in *The Return of the Middle Class* (1923), the American Federation of Labor was "selfish," "reckless," and "honeycombed" "with Bolshevism," while "the salaried folk were submerged" by the high prices resulting from battles between labour and capital.[15]

Many middle-class Americans labelled themselves the public as they expressed their grievances. C. L. Elliott, a white-collar worker in Portland, Oregon wrote, "We, the middle-class, are the chief consumers," "the majority and the backbone and the gray matter of the country." According to Elliott, they were the victims of economic greed, as "labor and capital are fighting . . . to be the devourer of—us." Elliott's characterization was not unique. Helen Fletcher, a former teacher, likewise defined the "middle class" as "the public" and "the backbone of business," "who calmly sits by and foots the bills, not striking [or] grafting." Similarly, Charles Nesom, a salesman, argued that the white-collar "middle class," "said to be the backbone of a nation," needed protection from "being ground to pieces between the upper and lower mill stone." In the context of the postwar strikes, middle-class consumers were particularly hostile to the organized working class, a sentiment which largely persisted even after the general failure of the 1919 strikes, due to the rhetoric that accompanied the open shop politics of the 1920s and the lingering power of the anti-union discourse established during these strikes.[16]

During this postwar labour unrest, newspaper editorials and politicians reinforced the characterization of white-collar, middle-class citizens as the public based on their seemingly neutral consumer identity, which they contrasted with the self-interest of profiteering elites and striking labourers. The *Rocky Mountain News* wrote of the "awakening of the middle class to the realization of its own peril as the battle ground over which labor and capital fight. . . . For when we talk of the 'public' . . . it is really this middle class we mean." Vice President Thomas Marshall called the middle class "the backbone of the Republic" while lamenting the impact of the "never-ending quarrels between capital and labor." More optimistically, Governor of Illinois and presidential candidate Frank Lowden, in a 1921 speech, emphasized how buying power gave "the public" the tools to defend itself against the greed of labour unions and elites.[17]

Drawing on this national discourse, which defined the middle-class public as victimized consumers, many white-collar citizens formed consumer organizations. They created a variety of local organizations to conduct consumer boycotts. In mostly urban localities spanning from Los Angeles to Washington DC, white-collar consumers formed clubs or committees to co-ordinate the planting of home gardens in backyards and vacant lots to circumvent food "profiteers." Building on their patriotic efforts as part of wartime liberty garden campaigns, which promoted both supporting the war effort and counteracting the high cost of living, these white-collar gardeners celebrated the producer values of hard work and thrift, even as they condemned actual producers, such as striking railroad workers, for purportedly not living up to these values. While proclaiming that hard work and thrift were the neutral values of the public, they symbolically and literally performed the hands-on labour of agricultural production that did not typify white-collar professional work. They also lobbied for municipal markets to obtain fair prices for consumers by bringing them in direct contact with farmers, who they largely defined as "honest" producers but not middle-class.

In actuality, this activism was far from neutral. Even though the white-collar "middle class" accused the working class of greed and extravagance, they aimed to uphold their own ability to consume according to a middle-class lifestyle. With less purchasing power and the potential of more spending ability on the part of blue-collar workers, they were increasingly less able to differentiate themselves through consumption. As author John Corbin queried of the impact of declining middle-class purchasing power, "what distinction have the Forgotten Folk with which to feed their inward pride?"[18] Their activism, which blended a self-righteous promulgation of producer values with consumer protest, thus sought to safeguard both their pocketbooks and their sense of social superiority.

In the spring of 1920, scores of middle-class Americans also took part in the "wear overalls movement." "Striking" against profiteering in the clothing industry and the supposed greed of striking textile workers, white-collar participants formed "overall clubs" and agreed to wear nothing but overalls until prices returned to acceptable levels. They performed producerism by ironically wearing working-class clothing to show that the working class was not living up to the values of diligent production and thrift. As part of the movement, judges heard cases in overalls, club members held dances in them, Hollywood and Broadway actors and actresses wore them on set and stage, couples were married in them, national politicians donned them in the U.S. Capitol, and overall-clad residents staged parades down the streets of cities across the nation.[19] Like home garden and municipal market activists, the overall movement celebrated the producer values of hard work and thrift as the neutral and universal values of the nation and the middle class. One supporter stated, "the vast army of 'white collar' salaried men, such as clerks, teachers, etc. whose salaries have not begun to increase in proportion to the cost of living . . . [now] must practice the most rigid economy to combat the H.C.L. [high cost of living]," while blue-collar workers are "demanding and receiving the elusive dollar in ever increasing amounts."[20]

Even though women were frequently represented in popular culture as the nation's chief consumers, many people defined the overall movement as a masculine protest. As one newspaper put it, overalls conveyed "the grass roots of Americanism . . . the bed rock of honest and honorable, stout and clean manhood."[21] When white-collar men put on overalls, they projected a masculine sense of righteousness that both relegated the difficulties of female shoppers in navigating high prices and acted as a cultural weapon against the supposed greed or underproduction of the working and elite classes. The words and actions of overall movement supporters often implied that a blend of masculinity, honesty, and production reflected the nation's values and that people who did not adequately produce or who charged dishonest prices lacked Americanism. Although some women joined overall protests, many ultimately formed clothing boycott clubs around the use of other kinds of inexpensive clothing. While not all activists or commentators used gendered cultural symbolism or language, it had a meaningful presence across postwar middle-class anti–high cost of living movements, with the overall movement serving as a prominent example.

White-collar Americans also formed "middle-class" tenants' unions during the immediate postwar period in protest of both profiteering landlords and graft among contractors and labour unions in the building industry. On popular moving days, white-collar tenants in middle-class neighbourhoods coordinated rent strikes, in which they collectively refused to move out in order to pressure landlords to withdraw rent increases and to influence city and state governments to pass legislation to empower tenants in rent disputes with landlords. White-collar tenants' unions, appropriating from the working class the "rent strike" tactic (previously used in only blue-collar neighbourhoods), sought to safeguard their middle-class lifestyle. Escalating rents made it more difficult for them to live in homes that were located in middle-class neighbourhoods and to fill them with the proper consumer goods. As John Patterson, a librarian, participant in the overall movement, and president of the Rogers Park (Chicago) Tenants' Protective Association (RPTPA), stated, "They feel that they are fighting for the preservation of the home, for a wholesome community, in which to bring up their children," and proclaimed, "the public has a right to protect itself."[22]

In defending their consumer identity, middle-class tenant activists like Patterson also saw themselves as acting as the public and in the name of American values. Speaking for the newly created Denver Renters and Consumers League, Leslie Hubbard asserted that the organization defended the middle class as the public interest. According to Hubbard, "It is time that the majority of people—the great middle class . . . should have a voice as to the conditions under which we are forced to live." Reflecting the popular xenophobic language of the first red scare, Hubbard elaborated,

> We are preaching Americanism and yet no day passes that the financial back of Americans is not broken under the burden of increased prices. The time has come for the owners of apartments and houses as well as those who deal in other necessities of life to realize that they are striking against the public interest and are therefore subject to condemnation equally with labor organizations that strike against the public interest.[23]

In conjunction with forming groups aimed primarily at reducing the cost of clothing, rent, and housing, a number of white-collar Americans organized broader "middle-class unions," which focused on using boycotts to defend consumers from unjust price increases for all commodities. These middle-class unions, which sprung up in cities such as Chicago and New York City, ironically used the name "union" while organizing at the point of consumption rather than at the workplace. They developed an anti-labour agenda, drawing inspiration from the British Middle Class Union, which had been formed in 1919 to oppose profiteering and organized labour. Similar to the other forms of self-interested white-collar consumer activism in the postwar period, middle-class unions depicted the middle class as the public, taking on official names such as the "People's League" and the "Public's Union."[24] They viewed their consumer identity as a major source of cohesion, power, and righteousness.

Although relying on the "buyers' strike" instead of the labour strike, middle-class unions once again turned to the imagery of organized labour while condemning them for exploiting the consuming public.[25] Public statements by middle-class union proponents indicated that they stood for "true democracy," "the public interest," "justice," and "fair play for all," whereas labour unions, middlemen, and elite profiteers promoted "tyranny and greed."[26] The Secretary of the New York Middle Class Union bluntly declared, "We are the public and we do not intend to be sent to hell to oblige millionaires or laborers."[27] During a New York/New Jersey railroad strike, some white-collar middle-class union proponents made headlines for serving as temporary replacement workers.[28] More commonly, middle-class unionists threatened to boycott pertinent consumer goods if labour unions went on strike for exorbitant wages, or if merchants charged too much. Their anti-union behaviour also evinced features of the red scare, in which organized labour was commonly branded as radical, with newspapers referring to them as "anarchists," "socialists" and "Bolsheviks."[29]

By 1922, white-collar Americans, politicians, the press, and other commentators had established in American society a popular characterization of the middle class as the public based on their neutral and defensible consumer identity. Leaders in the labour movement denied accusations of their greed and indolence and took offence to white-collar men mocking them by wearing overalls.[30] Nevertheless, they found themselves up against unpopular public opinion and repression from capital as they entered the "lean years" for labour activism during the 1920s.

Legacies of a Middle-Class Public

The economic crisis that had spurred the eruption of middle-class consumer activism against the high cost of living dissipated just four years after the end of the war. As prices stabilized, white-collar citizens took off their overalls, ceased to participate actively in middle-class tenant associations, reduced their commitment to growing gardens or supporting municipal markets as methods to fight high food prices, and no longer joined middle-class unions. While middle-class organizing in the name of the consuming public subsided in conjunction with economic change, the

An example of the popular belief that a middle-class union would serve as a bulwark against the selfish actions of labour unions and elites. "The Revolt Between the Upper and Nether Millstones," *New York Tribune*, January 11, 1920.

discourse that was firmly established during these campaigns continued to reoccur throughout the twentieth century and beyond.

During the 1930s, when the nation felt the effects of the Great Depression, popular writers continued to depict the middle class as the public, or, at least, as representative of the public interest. Kansas newspaper editor William Allen White, for instance, declared in 1938 that "this is a middle class country" and that "the middle class thinks and feels chiefly as the consumer."[31] Similar to the white-collar consumer activists of the postwar period, some activists and commentators continued to condemn the labour movement under the logic that higher blue-collar wages threatened their ability to consume. However, many other middle-class activists during the Depression lobbied on behalf of the working class as part of pro-labour segments of the burgeoning "consumer movement."[32]

After the Second World War, popular writers celebrated how mass consumption offered freedom and fulfilment to the nation and its middle class.[33] During subsequent years, the middle class continued to engage in consumer organizing, especially during periods of inflation when their ability to comfortably consume seemed to be under threat.[34] Significant moments in middle-class consumer activism persisted in featuring an interchangeable popular usage of the terms "middle class" and "the public," or "the people." Amid a spike in meat prices in 1973, for instance, middle-class consumers organized boycotts as part of groups such as "Citizens' Action Program," and participants like Ellie Bassett, a forty-year-old Massachusetts woman, lamented how politicians had failed to look out for them as "the middle class" and the "common man."[35]

This discourse, which equated the middle class and the public based on their consumer identity, continues to have implications. At times, middle-class Americans, armed with the label of being "the public" or the "backbone" of society, have acted with a sense of righteousness for justice for working people. However, as Dana Frank has noted, middle-class consumer campaigns, ranging from early twentieth-century National Consumers League efforts to label garments made under safe working conditions to recent anti-globalization boycotts, have often failed to work within the organizations developed by the very people they claim to help. The category "middle class," after all, implies exclusive boundaries. By playing to its boundaries, "middle-class" Americans and sympathetic commentators have seamlessly and powerfully defined the middle class as victims of the selfishness of those who reside outside of its limits. Their simultaneous characterizations of the middle class as the centrepiece of society have only increased their self-righteousness by positing it not as an interest group but as a neutral representation of America. Epitomizing the continued expression of middle-class victimhood, Lou Dobbs' *War on the Middle Class* (2006) positions the middle class as "the bedrock of American society" and "the core of [the nation's] work ethic," and he includes many sectors of the American public in the category as he complains of how corporate greed has squeezed the producer and consumer. Yet he also draws clear boundaries of exclusion as he scapegoats undocumented immigrants. His words are a reminder of the multifaceted possibilities of equating the categories middle class and public.[36] Under the right circumstances, this potent combination can be a political force for social justice. On other occasions, such as in many of the consumer activist movements discussed in this chapter, it can and has offered a supposedly neutral basis to define American values and the public interest in narrow and self-aggrandizing terms. Whether deployed on behalf of or against the needs of others in society, a middle-class consumer politics continues to be a powerful force in American life.

5

YOU ARE PURCHASING PROSPERITY!

Local Buying Initiatives and Women as Conscious Consumers in the Great Depression

ALLISON WARD

N JUNE 1, 1929, a crowd of over 100,000 flooded Hamilton, Ontario's armouries. There were no "huge spectacles of circus methods used to attract people."[1] Visitors came purely to see what the city manufactured and to give their support to the Hamilton branch of the Canadian Manufacturers' Association's extremely popular "Produced-in-Canada" exhibition, which filled two huge halls. Hamilton itself embodied the "Produced-in-Canada" movement. With close proximity to natural resources, masses of skilled craft workers, and a well-developed industrial core, it was the city that made everything. The city boasted over 500 unique manufacturers in 225 different industries, despite having a population of only 155,547.[2] These enterprises ranged from small businesses, such as Hamilton Soaps, to multi-national corporations, like Canadian Westinghouse.[3] This profusion of manufactories put the "Made-in-Hamilton" stamp on nearly everything a person or business could want and served as a point of pride in the 1920s. Depression-era efforts in Hamilton increased this focus on manufactured goods and exclusionary image of the Canadian economy. The local branch of the

Canadian Manufacturers' Association (CMA), the city's government, and its boosters repurposed this national campaign to suit their own purposes and ensure that Hamilton products were front and centre. For them, local business interests superseded national protectionist rhetoric.

Hamilton's good economic times ended with the stock market crash of October 1929, but encouraging local pride through buying goods marked with the "Made-in-Hamilton" stamp became an important strategy to escape the effects of the Depression. John Maynard Keynes's theory that consumption could chart North America's way out of Depression has been much debated by both his contemporaries and later scholars.[4] However, for the politicians, retailers, consumers, and businessmen in the city that made everything, this approach seemed to suit both their resources and the previous protectionist rhetoric in which they were well versed.[5] It fit well into the industrial boosterism that the locally successful Conservative Party of Canada had been promoting for the last half century. The urgent need for this program to succeed repositioned the boosterism of the 1920s as the solution to the depression of the 1930s.

Breaking with the previous nationalist focus, "Buying Hamilton" became a consciously executed plan to save the city from the Great Depression. During the lean years of the 1930s, the city's municipal government, business organizations, retailers, labour organizations, and women's groups all discouraged Hamilton's women from supporting their families by working. Rather, they encouraged women to prop up the city's economy and preserve local jobs by shopping for locally produced goods. These women responded by forming local consumer organizations that sought to benefit their community through informed purchasing practices. Hamilton's consumers may not have identified themselves as activists, but their actions powerfully demonstrated that conscious consumption, used as what Lawrence Glickman calls "an instrument of solidarity," could be an expression of citizenship, one that, all Hamiltonians hoped, might carry the city through tough times.[6]

From Produced-in-Canada to Made-in-Hamilton: Buying for Community Prosperity

When the Depression hit Hamilton, its civic leaders and citizens were hopeful it would be short-lived, but this initial optimism had dissipated by the spring of 1930. Faced with the need to provide long-term aid to the city's unemployed, municipal leaders instituted extensive relief programs beginning in October 1930. These programs overtaxed the city's resources. Meanwhile, local industries carefully calculated rotating shifts to spread around what little work there was and thereby keep families afloat.[7] As the crisis deepened, Hamiltonians fought against unemployment and municipal bankruptcy using the only resource their city had—its massive manufacturing strength and relatively large consumer base.

The first step to selling Hamiltonians on buying locally involved hosting exhibitions—an approach that had worked well for the city in the past. In 1925, the CMA had revived the pre–First World War practice of holding Made-in-Canada exhibits to celebrate the growing strength of Canadian industry and encourage consumption of Canadian goods.[8] Though the "Produced-in-Canada" campaign was presented as a national effort, the displays primarily featured the central Canadian goods that had thrived thanks to protective tariffs, especially on American trade. Western and Atlantic Canadian provinces felt increasingly alienated by this focus on and protection of centralized manufacturing efforts, which closed down manufacturers in their regions, raised shipping costs, and led to inflated prices for consumer goods.[9] This exclusionary approach to Canadian industrial development benefited Hamilton's manufacturers. As the city's industries grew, its city council worked with the local branches of the Imperial Order Daughters of the Empire, the Canadian Club, the Chamber of Commerce, and the CMA itself to adapt the trade show model to its own purposes. These groups launched their own locally organized "Produced-in-Canada" exhibition in 1926. Though the event attracted producers from around the country, it featured Hamilton products especially heavily. By 1928 it was drawing ninety-three thousand people to the city. Becoming "the foremost affair of its kind," the event highlighted Hamilton's diverse industries and products for a wider audience, attracting investment and consumers to the city's industrial wares.[10] This strong support from the public invested justifiable pride in the "Made-in-Hamilton" label most ads in the city's newspapers seemed to bear.

Funded solely by the local association, Hamilton's Produced-in-Canada exhibitions continued during the Depression with renewed purpose and drive. Hamilton's CMA branch chairman advised the mayor, city council, and its board of control that "during times of stress such as at present, every effort should be made to insure as far as possible the purchase of Canadian made goods."[11] It was generally understood by CMA members that supporting national production also meant supporting Hamilton products and producers, especially when such a show was held in Hamilton. Holding the show locally allowed manufacturers to participate without investing in travel or the transportation of their goods. The CMA, retailers, and civic leaders wanted to make sure this manufacturing reputation continued to serve as an effective tool to draw tourists, retailers, and consumers to the city and its wares. So the vast Produced-in-Canada exhibitions continued, and there remained a special focus on what Hamilton contributed to the country's industrial landscape. The exhibition's attendance continued to rise in these years of hardship, and in 1934, 133,000 people attended, many of them visitors to the city. The Hamilton branch of the CMA hoped that the Depression-era exhibitions would reinforce to those present "in a very real and practical way . . . its underlying principle of providing more employment to Canadian workmen."[12]

The plea to buy national goods was reinforced by the federal government. As Christmas approached in 1930, H. H. Stevens, Minister of Trade and Commerce to the Conservative government of Prime Minister R. B. Bennett, wrote numerous open letters, which ran in city newspapers, on consumer spending. These national efforts overlapped with local campaigns and continued discussions about Hamilton's strength as a manufacturer. Acknowledging the hardships faced by Canadians, Stevens suggested that "with unemployment so prevalent in all parts of the country, with so many fellow Canadians dependent upon charity even for the bare necessities of life . . . the moral obligation rests heavily on all of us to govern our Christmas gift buying by the 'Produced-in-Canada' policy."[13] Editorials in the *Spectator*, Hamilton's most important newspaper, drove home Stevens's message for readers who questioned their role in the cycle of prosperity: "The extent to which Canadian prosperity depends upon the response to the sort of advice being tendered by the minister of trade and commerce is little realized by the average person. . . . But individual action does make a tremendous difference."[14] The Hamilton Chamber of Commerce's annual report made it clear that manufacturers and businesses understood that these efforts to buy Canadian products would directly improve their own fortunes, due to the breadth of products the city produced.[15] The Produced-in-Canada exhibits and the local newspaper editorials left little doubt in the minds of Hamiltonians of the need to buy Canadian, but optimally one should buy Hamilton products first of all. The direct and visible impacts of civic unemployment caused Hamiltonians to prioritize their own jobs first, over those of both the country and the empire.

"That Factory Chimneys [Would] Once More Smoke:" Shopping for Jobs in Hamilton

Prior to the Depression, there had not been any real distinction between local products and national or imperial ones. Shopping to support either the country or the empire was broadly promoted and bolstered through the government's implementation of protective tariffs. Hamilton products were only singled out in year-end reports on city progress published in its newspapers. During the Depression, local boosters and politicians felt the need to break this implicit connection between national and local goods and hold Hamilton's wares up for distinction. Buy Hamilton efforts aimed at manufacturers, tourists, and corporate investors extended to a number of special "Hamilton Day" sales focused on city retailers. In 1931, the Chamber of Commerce, with support from the Advertising Club of Hamilton, restaurants, manufacturers, the press, city council and many of its committees, theatres, and as many retailers as possible, introduced this new sales day. This development followed similar efforts in Buffalo and Rochester, New York, which shared cross-border trade ties and business links with Hamilton. "One Great All-Buffalo Bargain Day" was held for the first time on September 4, 1931, and though it was not a resounding financial success it boosted the image and morale of its business community.[16] The Hamilton Day sale similarly served as an opportunity to promote city-wide shopping for locally produced products and was planned to coincide with the start of Christmas shopping.[17] In the words of an editorial in the *Hamilton Herald*, this shopping was about more than sales:

> A lot of money is lying idle, and if put to work it begins to travel rapidly from pocket to pocket. It goes to the retail store, from that to the jobber, and from him to the manufacturer, from him to the raw material man in farm or lumberyard or mine or furnace or spinning mill or weaving factory. It starts with the wheels moving and once they start the workers get paid and there is more money to send to the store so that the whole machinery of society gets going. . . . It will be worth anybody's while to take out all his loose cash and turn it into household and personal necessaries.[18]

The idea that success would be immediate and visible in the community was one of the important factors behind the inception of Hamilton Day. Descriptions of Hamilton Day emphasized the visual ties that the city had with manufacturing. Unlike in many other Canadian cities, Hamiltonians would actually be able to see "that factory chimneys [would] once more smoke" if spending increased.[19] These ties to the visual landscape of the city firmly connected Hamiltonians to the success of their campaign. They provided tangible signs of success and decline that could not be seen consistently in numbers such as profits and tax revenues. With many of their houses within mere blocks and none out of sight of the city's factories, the skyline served as an inescapable sign of the source of the city's prosperity. It provided a constant reminder of where it had come from and what, it was believed, would bring it back to its former glory. The city's physical landscape and its connections to employment provided a connection people living near them could recognize as beneficial to themselves, as workers and citizens of the city, rather than just to its big businesses and manufacturers.

The first Hamilton Day, October 27, 1931, was perceived to be a smashing success by manufacturers, retailers, and shoppers alike. Shop windows and storefronts shone with the local football team's black and gold colour scheme. Shops sacrificed their window space to displays advertising manufacturers Hamiltonians may not have known had local ties, like Firestone and Tuckett Tobacco. The Independent Labour Party gave over a page of its paper, the *Labor News*, to the "Anti-Chain Store News," where they advised their readers: "For your own self protection—it will pay you to buy from the independent home-owned stores and keep your money here."[20] It advised its readers that Hamilton's retailers served as more than just stores, they were a part of the community, and "the community owes some of these independent merchants a debt that it will never pay—a debt that at least is worth the patronage of the citizens."[21] Hamilton pride was front and centre. The great prices were intended to lure rural shoppers who may otherwise turn to closer but smaller towns in the area. In spite of otherwise declining sales that year, most participating businesses reported that purchases just about doubled during the promotion and retailers were optimistic that these shopping habits would remain ingrained after the sale and Christmas were over. The Chamber of Commerce declared it "one of the most outstanding and successful events of the nature ever attempted in this City."[22] The event was so successful at increasing business that it remained a staple throughout the 1930s, reminding citizens of their ability to contribute to success in the city. The event became part of "Made in Hamilton Week" in 1933, also held during the first week of November, "designed to impress upon the people of Hamilton and this district the numerous products made in Hamilton which can be purchased by them to advantage over the counter in Hamilton stores."[23]

"You are Purchasing Prosperity":
Hamilton's Women Confront the Depression

Shopping the city out of Depression relied on the co-operation of the city's women for its success. Businesses recognized that women wielded household purchasing power. In Depression-era advertising campaigns, this was presented as a crucial contribution that women could make to recovery. These campaigns reinforced the move to send women back into the home after the economic crash. During the Depression, especially its early years, women, especially married women, in Hamilton and throughout Canada were actively dissuaded from working. Even when their husbands were unwilling or incapable of finding work to support their families, women were fiercely discriminated against in the job market. While employers and labour organizations had never fully supported women's employment prior to the Depression, it was explicitly discouraged once it began.[24] Unemployed women were truly without options. They were encouraged to keep themselves afloat through the informal labour market of housekeeping, cooking, and child-minding. These attitudes relied on the expectation that ultimately a woman would get married, and her support would become her husband's responsibility, not the city's.

With little opportunity for work, women were stripped of their earning power but retained their economic influence as the household spender. As early as the turn of the century, advertisers and women themselves began to recognize that that meant they had some potential to exert force on the markets.[25] During the Depression, local organizations such as the Women's Fair Price Commission and the Housewives' Association were formed to give an organized voice to women's concerns as shoppers, which were very different from those expressed in the producer-focused, male-dominated forums of the city's branches of the Chamber of Commerce and CMA. Despite their different perspectives on the Depression, both price-conscious consumer activists and the protectionist nationalist campaigners came up with similar solutions. Women's consumer groups advocated shopping locally and the formation of local co-operatives as solutions to both the crisis of unemployment and the potential that rising prices could come about as companies struggled to stay open during the Depression.[26] Hamilton's Depression-era advertisements demonstrated that women were beginning to be recognized for their power over the household spending and how this power became pivotal to their role in economic recovery.

The housewife of the Depression did not have time to waste wandering the aisles; her time and money were valuable resources. She shopped with a clear sense of direction and purpose: "She shops at *home* before she buys. . . . She prefers to ponder, consider, compare, and she is confident she will save as she opens her purse to buy."[27] As the *Spectator* advised its prospective advertisers: "Shopping is a serious business." "ACT!," the smiling housewife was advised in one advertisement, "Confidence and normal buying will bring prosperity."[28] This advertisement, sponsored by some forty local businesses, implored women to consider the political, social, and economic importance of their consumption. They were not just buying for frivolity's sake; they bought to sustain their community. These ads frequently invoked maternal feelings by suggesting to women that their families, neighbours, and even children were depending on them to reinvigorate Hamilton's industry with their purchasing power. These campaigns and organizations recognized that while a man's domain may be making the money, a woman's was in spending it, but with moderation, careful thought, and consideration. In Depression-era Hamilton, these decisions took on a more militant tone of industrial protectionism. It was not enough to shop and spend money; one had to shop Hamilton, since the whole city depended on it.[29]

Newspaper columnists proffered similar advice in the women's pages of both of the city's major newspapers. The *Herald's* Nora-Frances Henderson was a strong proponent of women remaining in their home, especially if working outside it might mean taking jobs from men. Yet she was very clear that this did not mean that women had no role in solving the current economic crisis. She encouraged all of the city's women to open their household budgets by just a little bit, even a single dollar. She posited that, by doing so, just ten thousand women could put men to work. By putting in just a little extra work and buying Hamilton, women could work together to improve the community. Henderson proclaimed: "Our houses thrive by it and our hearts are warmed by it. . . . Homemakers and housekeepers know better and understand from their own experience how [purchasing and job creation] are inseparably mingled."[30] This advice carried through most of her Depression-era columns on shopping and was echoed by women's organizations across the city. The National Council of Women went so far as to suggest relief should be distributed to women, by women, because it was women who understood how household money worked.[31]

During the Depression, job losses, relief limits for single women, and hiring freezes for married women cut women's earning power significantly and their ability to contribute to the household economy as wage-earners. However, women's growing role as shoppers and "Buy Hamilton" initiatives during the Depression politicized their decisions about where to shop and what to buy in order to best serve their communities. Buying cheap, mass-produced American imported goods or European glassware may have seemed friendly on the pocket book, but Hamilton's women were encouraged to look past price and toward the benefits that their spending could bring to their husbands, fathers, and brothers. They were repeatedly told that, through these efforts, they could do what the government could not, and bring Hamilton out of the Depression. As activities like Hamilton Day, local Produced-in-Canada initiatives, and the formation of organizations such as the local Housewives' Association and Women's Fair Price Commission indicated, women listened to and engaged with these messages.

Conclusion

It is difficult to assess the full success of these buy local initiatives, especially since Hamilton was hit so hard by the Depression. As Canada's third largest manufacturing centre, after Toronto and Montreal, its producers paid wages and salaries worth over $26 million to the over 25,000 individuals directly employed in manufacturing in the city, and so it had a lot to lose.[32] By 1933, the peak of the Depression in the city, there were 8,149 families receiving some form of direct relief from the municipal government, whether this meant work, housing, medical care, or one of the other supplementary supports offered.[33] However, that number began to decrease rapidly as the city's economy strengthened and industry again expanded, with 6,476 families on the relief roll by 1934.[34] To say the situation was challenging for the city's workers who had moved there with the promise of prosperity, dependent on production, would be an understatement. However, the records of the city's manufacturers and businessmen at the very least demonstrated that buying locally had kept businesses open and pay cheques coming. Many businesspeople pointed to changes in favour of local purchasing and protective tariffs as among the most important reasons they were able to continue operating and, in slowly growing numbers, expanding and hiring.[35] In spite of grim unemployment numbers, Hamilton's manufacturers and retailers perceived the "Buy Hamilton" campaigns to be essential to keeping employment levels from dropping ever further, and "Buy Home Products" became a slogan for all.[36]

Before online shopping, the explosion of foreign manufacturing, and the North American Free Trade Agreement, buying locally had a meaning that extended beyond contemporary campaigns' pleas for consumers to shop at brick-and-mortar stores or eat local foods. In the case of Depression-era Hamilton, Ontario, it literally meant buying everything you needed for your household, from radios to radiators, from city merchants and sourced from the city's factories, often themselves within blocks of the consumers' homes. Doing so was alleged to be the best way to support the city's economy and keep Hamiltonians working. Fed by federal initiatives, local advertising, and a fierce campaign by local boosters, Hamiltonians were implored with greater urgency than ever before to think about what their city's factories meant to household and local economies and how they could be sustained, for the good of the whole city. The movement politicized a decision Hamiltonians had previously made without even thinking about it. Women had no place in Hamilton's workplaces but were expected to contribute to the city's prosperity through thrift, good household management, and, above all, supporting the city's industries through consumption. Their role in the cycle of consumption and the conscious decisions they were expected to make regarding their purchases integrated them into the city's recovery in an integral way, politicizing their decision to "Buy Hamilton" to preserve prosperity. Their example continues to offer an alternative way of thinking about how communities envision their role in the cycle of consumption and what impact buying local can have.

6

MAKING MONEY
IN HARD TIMES

Scrip and Grassroots Efforts
to Solve the Great Depression

SARAH ELVINS

N FEBRUARY OF 1933, Karl Starkweather of the small community of Plymouth, Michigan, wrote to Professor Irving Fisher of Yale University for advice about ways to "climb out of the doldrums" of the Depression. Describing himself as a "down-and-outer," Starkweather outlined a plan to print special certificates to be used in exchange for services or goods in his town. Although his family's savings were depleted, Starkweather noted that his wife regularly went to the Red Cross room to make dresses for the "poor people," adding sarcastically "which is not supposed to include us." Tired of waiting for the economic situation in his community to get better, Starkweather wrote, "Even though I have nothing else, I still have the optimistic attitude, time and energy." He sought advice to put a scrip, or alternative currency, plan into operation. He offered to give Fisher credit for any guidance, noting, "I should be sending you some real money as compensation, but I have none." [1] Starkweather was not alone in his search for a grassroots solution to the hard times of the 1930s. In the years after the stock market crash, Americans across the nation struggled with the inability to make purchases. Crippling levels of unemployment and depleted savings accounts quickly ended the consumer spending spree that had characterized the culture of the 1920s.

In the early years of the crisis, many argued that the key to recovery was in the hands of the private consumer: in order to restart the wheels of business, individuals needed to stop "hoarding" money and put it back into circulation. This focus on currency and individual spending suggested a new form of consumer activism during the Depression. According to this view, consumers needed to make a commitment to spend, to overcome their fears and hesitation and resume their role as the engine moving the economy forward.[2] But just how to convince people to put money into circulation remained unclear. Even prior to the March 1933 Bank Holidays declared by Franklin Delano Roosevelt, which prevented individuals and businesses from withdrawing funds, a shortage of money made everyday purchases challenging. "Delayed spending—hand-to-mouth purchasing—both on the part of the storekeeper and of the consumer, is steadily holding production and employment at low levels," proclaimed an editorial in the *Syracuse Herald*.[3]

Under such conditions, barter organically reappeared. In Nyack, New York, an informal barter system allowed residents to swap everything from "Dogs, furniture, vegetables, phonographs, Christmas trees and vinegar." A local dentist even offered dental work in exchange for a meal in a restaurant. "It was an easy matter," claimed Mrs. Wharton Clay, the coordinator of the local trade group, "to find a restauranteur who needed bridgework."[4] Across the South, country merchants accepted oil and cotton in exchange for goods, and communities organized barter exchanges to facilitate trades of farm produce and other items.[5] Co-ordinating barter exchanges beyond standard commodities or necessary medical transactions, however, proved frustrating. For barter exchanges in hundreds of communities, the use of scrip seemed to provide the answer. Printing their own coupons allowed people to swap goods and services for scrip, which facilitated more precise transactions.

In the early 1930s, as newspapers trumpeted scrip as a panacea, city councils, politicians, retailers, economists, and groups of the unemployed eagerly sought information about this route to recovery, and observers flocked to towns where scrip had been put into action. Towns, cities, and even entire states experimented with scrip, in schemes ranging from simple barter coupons to elaborate plans to increase the speed of consumer spending.[6] The Natural Development Association, an exchange in Salt Lake City, Utah, did estimated sales of $20,000 per month in early 1933 by allowing participants to set a price in scrip for items they brought in instead of having to negotiate a direct exchange of one item for another.[7]

At Antioch College in Yellow Springs, Ohio, a clearinghouse was set up to enable students, local farmers, and other businesses to exchange labour, produce, and materials. Some transactions were quite complicated, involving multiple parties. Antioch students were employed in a local foundry, which paid the exchange in a shipment of excess rubber tires. These tires were exchanged to some local businesses for other items to stock the clearinghouse store. The students worked part time, earning enough to "pay their way through" at college.[8] A reporter from the *Literary Digest* noted approvingly the multiplying transactions that were sweeping through the community, all made possible by the use of scrip: "Each transaction immediately spreads out in many directions. Shipments split up and chase each other around the circuit of wholesaler, retailer and consumer; but it can be taken for granted that every swap has pleased both parties."[9]

In cities facing a lack of tax revenue, scrip seemed a means to both pay municipal employees and enable citizens to meet their outstanding tax bills. Other communities experimented with printing coupons to offer relief for the unemployed. In most cases, scrip schemes were designed to circulate within a particular local area. This added to their grassroots appeal: advocates emphasized that this would be a way to concentrate recovery, allowing individuals to help their neighbours and friends. While not always organized by consumers, scrip plans relied on the good faith and participation of consumers to succeed. In Salt Lake City, men were employed on local farms and in trades and were paid in scrip, which could be exchanged for groceries, furniture, or other items in the organization's warehouse. In Boston, the unemployed were organized into labour pools to be paid in scrip. Local companies donated space and equipment in order to put some sort of currency in the hands of workers, who then could go out and consume. One day, organizers promised, "Machinery restarts, goods of all descriptions come to the warehouses and retail store of the corporation and the man again carrying his dinner pail comes with his token of service and buys a hat, a toy for his children or a pair of shoes."[10]

The Organized Unemployed of Minneapolis drew national attention for the success of their warehouse and work relief program. Reverend George Mecklenberg of the Wesley Methodist Episcopal Church spearheaded the initiative, which put crews of the unemployed to work chopping wood or on local potato farms, and in its own sauerkraut factory, restaurant, bakery, shoe repair shop, and clothing factory.[11] Workers were paid a dollar a day in scrip which could be redeemed in the Commissary, "which is like a small-town department store," stocked with new, used, and reconditioned consumer goods. Furniture, cooking utensils, clothing, and books flew off the shelves, with a complete turnover of goods occurring every four days as thousands visited the exchange.[12] An account in a local magazine described how local housewife Mary would be able to exchange a few phonograph records for some shoes for her child, while Joan had some baby shoes but hoped to get a bottle of milk and two loaves of bread from the bakery. Joan and Mary did not know each other, and so would not be likely to trade directly, but they could turn in their excess goods for scrip and get exactly the items they desired.[13] Others who had nothing to trade could turn their labour into scrip and purchase meals at the restaurant or a bed in the organization's dormitory. The Organized Unemployed became a model for roughly two hundred similar associations across the country.[14] By 1933 the Department of Commerce reported over three hundred barter organizations and one hundred unemployed groups and municipalities using scrip in some form.[15]

Barter exchanges could allow individuals to turn their excess labour or goods into coupons that could then be spent on items they needed. But a more ambitious variant of alternative currency aimed to increase the number of transactions within a community. In Hawarden, Iowa, local businessman Charles Zylstra proposed a stamp scrip plan, which was reported in newspapers and magazines from coast to coast. A Dutch immigrant who had experience working at a credit union in Europe, Zylstra was likely influenced by the monetary theories of Silvio Gesell, an early advocate of depreciating currency (which would penalize those who held onto wealth without spending or investing it).[16] Key to Zylstra's scheme was the sale of stamps, which would have to be purchased by users of the scrip. On the back of each scrip certificate was a grid of thirty-six squares. Each time a certificate changed hands, a stamp worth 3 cents would be attached to one square. This was self-liquidating currency—as it moved from hand to hand, it accumulated value until it would finally be worth $1.08 (the extra 8 cents charged was to cover printing and administrative costs of the program).[17] At this point, it could be redeemed for one dollar of "real" currency. Zylstra proposed that unemployed men be paid a "living wage" in scrip for working on municipal improvement projects. This would provide a boost to the community, without requiring a costly liquidation fund to be set up in advance. To critics who complained about having to purchase stamps in order to use the scrip, Zylstra argued that a few cents was a small price to pay for the creation of new business. In October of 1932, Hawarden's City Council agreed to issue $300 in scrip.

Unemployed workers were paid a rate of $1.00 in scrip and sixty cents in cash for one day's work. Most area merchants and utilities accepted the certificates, which they could use to pay wages and utility bills.[18]

Yale economist Irving Fisher was among the hundreds of observers who visited Hawarden to learn more about stamp scrip. Fisher was not only prominent in academic circles but also the author of a nationally syndicated newspaper column.[19] In a letter to Fisher, Zylstra explained that he had started the plan "to increase buying power, relieve suffering and provide a credit to the community without having them pay interest."[20] Fisher was intrigued by the possibilities of stamp scrip but felt that its main flaw was the requirement of a stamp for every transaction. This, he argued, was a disincentive for people to spend and a penalty imposed on the very people helping to get the economy moving again. Instead, Fisher proposed that stamp scrip be given a series of "expiry dates," so that it could circulate freely up until a stated date, at which point a stamp would have to be purchased. For example, the scrip might require a new stamp every Wednesday, and so consumers would try to pass it on as quickly as possible, so as to avoid having to buy a stamp. Fisher wrote a manual about dated stamp scrip, offering advice to communities hoping to implement a similar program.[21] He saw these plans as a means to "prime the pump" so that eventually real currency would return to flow in full force through the economy.[22]

While Irving Fisher developed technical instructions about the circulation of alternative currency, other proponents repeated folksy stories about money being "nothing but a piece of paper." *Time* printed a likely apocryphal story about a stranger who came into town and left a $100 bill in his hotel bank vault, for which he was issued a receipt. When the local butcher came to collect money on an overdue account, the hotel owner borrowed the bill and erased the debt. The butcher took the money and paid his rent, his landlord paid his lawyer, and eventually the money circulated back to the hotel and was put back in the vault. Eventually, the salesman returned and announced that the bill was fake, a prop for the stage. To the shock of observers, he used it to light his cigar.[23] But although the bill was not actually U.S. currency, it had the real effect of circulating and wiping out debt. In Enid, Oklahoma, promoters of scrip wrote a poem describing a similar trip of a single piece of scrip through a town, which concluded,

> The check had made the full round trip
> And everyone who handled it

Feels times are better—so, they are!
Soon stocks and bonds head back to par
And so, by simply keeping moving
It made folks feel times are improving.[24]

Beyond the economic function of scrip, it had a psychological benefit. By making "folks feel times are improving," alternative currency could help consumers move past their fear of spending and help put more hoarded dollars into circulation. Stuart Chase, the nationally recognized economist, consumer advocate and advisor to FDR who coined the term "New Deal," argued that scrip could help to coax more "real" money out of hiding. He argued that for consumers facing the "intolerable ravages of the depression," scrip could help restore self-respect and tangible comfort.[25]

In late 1932 and early 1933, alternative currency seemed to capture the imaginations of disparate groups across the U.S. Indeed, as Loren Gatch has noted, scrip spread "because it meant different things to different people."[26] To independent merchants in Evanston, Illinois, it seemed a means to discourage patronage of out-of-town mail-order and chain stores.[27] To city bureaucrats in Detroit, Michigan, it was a means to pay municipal employees who had been without salaries for months.[28] To unemployed residents of Harlem, it could form the basis of a new exchange.[29] To the city council of Atlanta, Georgia, it was the only form of currency available to pay local teachers.[30] In Anderson, Oklahoma, it promised to provide "honorable work" to unemployed men without the stigma of direct relief payments.[31]

In most cases, supporters of scrip were not interested in overthrowing the capitalist system, but in finding a way to help the economy back to its feet. Zylstra saw scrip as a way to avoid more radical upheaval. Writing to Irving Fisher, he argued, "Somehow people will have to be able to buy the things that they need to live, or the pressure can not be retained and revolution will result."[32] Instead of destroying people's morale by collecting donations and handing out charity, Zylstra claimed, scrip could provide a credit extension and create new work within the community. Scrip seemed a common-sense, practical solution to communities facing unemployment and a lack of buyers for surplus goods. An account of the National Development Association in Salt Lake City noted,

While the parlor pinks have been chinning about the philosophies of Communism and Karl Marx over bath-tub gin in New York hideaways ... the N.D.A actually got to work on a simple program. Here were men without work, here were farms with surplus produce, here were idle factories and shops. Here were families that needed the necessities of life.[33]

Although some celebrated the new sense of common cause they enjoyed as part of a barter group, few advocated a complete overhaul of the monetary system.

Traditional American notions of self-help also bolstered support for scrip. Instead of waiting for the government to take action, one account of the scrip movement noted, "Vast numbers of people ... have decided quite shrewdly that if anything is to be done about getting food and clothes and housing, to say nothing of the amenities of life, they themselves will have to do it."[34] The grassroots nature of scrip was also reflected in promoters' emphasis on helping friends and neighbours in the community. The notion that currency could be circulated "at home" was not new—throughout the 1920s, independent retailers facing new competition from chain stores argued that consumers should make an effort to spend their dollars "at home" rather than patronize businesses based outside of the area. When the Depression hit, exhortations to spend money locally became common tropes in advertising and newspaper editorials.[35] Merchants in Key West, Florida emphasized how patronizing local grocers, garages, department stores and other businesses helped to increase tax revenues in the municipality, to the benefit of all. "Remember," they argued, "your neighbor will take better care of you than a stranger. It is in his interest to do so. His future depends on his winning and holding your confidence and friendship."[36] In reality, it was very difficult for businesses to limit the scope of their transactions to a prescribed area. Merchants protested that while they were interested in local improvement, they owed debts to suppliers across the country. Nevertheless, promoters of scrip routinely appealed to local loyalty to encourage participation by consumers. Given this emphasis on local community activism, there was less appeal for national scrip plans. Irving Fisher testified before Congress and helped to promote a bill to administer scrip though branches of the Post Office, but the bill did not come into effect.[37]

Eventually, after the arrival of Franklin Delano Roosevelt into the White House in March of 1933, the momentum behind the scrip movement began to slow. Programs that had been adopted with enthusiasm in the fall of 1932 began to face challenges and were not renewed. Some issuances of scrip faltered when merchants or employees refused to accept scrip. Detroit used scrip to pay teachers in April 1933, and retail stores discounted it so that it was quickly worth only 75 cents on the dollar. Wholesalers were even more reluctant to accept it, *Business Week* reported, because "they buy 85% of their merchandise outside Michigan, where the scrip is worthless."[38] Larger communities that had considered putting scrip into circulation abandoned their plans after witnessing the limitations of existing experiments.[39] The announcement of federal relief plans under the New Deal also diverted attention and initiative away from scrip. In some cases, the federal government took over the administration of barter groups, as was the case with the Organized Unemployed of Minneapolis, which came under the control of the Federal Emergency Relief Administration and eventually was disbanded as the unemployed were put on federal relief lists.[40] Arthur E. Morgan, the founder and president of the Yellow Springs, Ohio, Midwest Exchange (and also the president of Antioch College), announced the liquidation of all merchandise in the organization's warehouse and retiring of scrip in August 1933. Morgan himself went from scrip activist to New Dealer, becoming chairman of the Tennessee Valley Authority.[41] The eventual waning of scrip does not, however, erase its significance as an indicator of the faith of Americans in private consumption. Particularly between 1929 and 1933, the widespread appeal of scrip rested on the notion that individual consumers could use their own buying power to help speed recovery. In hundreds of communities, people like Karl Starkweather educated consumers, persuaded businesses to participate, printed scrip and put it into circulation in the hopes of turning the tide of the Depression.

For those without work, alternative currency seemed a route to acquiring not only the necessities of life but also the types of consumer goods that had become a defining part of individual identity and self-expression in modern American society.[42] Scrip was not a form of charity, organizers emphasized, but a way of turning the unemployed into consumers themselves. As late as 1939, the Washington Self-Help Exchange boasted that its members rejected handouts, but were given self-respect along with their scrip:

> Many young people come in, shabby and disheartened. They go to work in the sewing room, in the laundry or in the kitchen. Before long they can exchange their hours of work for beauty parlor treatments, for a complete new outfit of clothes, shoes, etc. In no time

they are looking for a job with an entirely different approach for they
have an improved appearance and can face the world with courage.[43]

In the depth of hard times, allowing the unemployed to find a new outfit
or hairstyle was thought to make all of the difference. A nineteen-year-
old girl who earned scrip for doing clerical work boasted that her home
was furnished and her brother was able to have proper haircuts and shoe
repairs, which allowed him to remain in school. Scrip became a way for
thousands of Americans to continue to consume despite job losses and
depleted savings. Its supporters presented scrip as a common-sense solution to the Depression, a way to act without waiting for Washington or
Wall Street to "show the way out."[44]

Given the benefit of hindsight, it is easy to dismiss the scrip phenomenon as a futile exercise in wishful thinking. We now know that it would
take far more than a community printing its own money to end the Great
Depression. Yet scrip had widespread appeal to a range of thinkers, academics, politicians, business leaders and average citizens. The language of
self-help and community activism mobilized by advocates of scrip encouraged individuals to believe that they could personally play a role in helping
recovery. The hundreds of communities that considered or implemented
scrip were motivated by sheer desperation as the economic crisis stretched
out longer than any had imagined it would. Scrip did not end the Depression, as many of its supports had promised. But it signalled a role for ordinary consumers and communities to take charge of the economy, to take
action rather than passively submitting to the larger forces of the business
cycle.

Today the rhetoric and promise of scrip is very much alive. Since the
1980s, local exchange trading systems (LETS) have developed in North
America, South America, Africa and Europe, which enable members to
barter goods and services and encourage spending in the local community.[45] In the age of globalization, local money advocates promote alternative exchange systems as a way to empower citizens and undercut the
power of multinational corporations.[46] Critics of the conventional banking system and the control of currency by governments on both the right
and the left have been attracted by the "virtual currency" of the software-
based digital payment system Bitcoin, which allows peer-to-peer transactions without using a traditional bank. The grassroots nature of scrip has
proven a key part of its appeal.[47] Looking back at the history of scrip in
the 1930s, we should remember that the focus on the local which seemed

to make so much sense to supporters also posed real challenges to the circulation of alternative currency. Any future efforts to mobilize consumers using scrip will need to build on the imaginative appeal of "local money" while acknowledging that successful trading systems are necessarily larger than a single community. The irony of scrip is that the larger it became, the less likely it was to succeed. Small farming communities like Hawarden were able to keep alternative currency in circulation much longer than larger centres like Chicago or Detroit, where businesses resisted taking on currency they could not use for outside suppliers. National scrip plans like those envisioned by Irving Fisher never got off the ground. Individual consumers responded to appeals to help their neighbours through the use of scrip. Currency advocates will have to find ways to empower consumers to trace the path of their spending through the local community and beyond.

7

PROTECTING THE "GUINEA PIG CHILDREN"

Resisting Children's Food Advertising in the 1930s

KYLE ASQUITH

OVER THE LAST DECADE, advertising food to children has become a prominent consumer issue, public health crisis, and policy concern. In the wake of a childhood obesity epidemic, some critics have called for complete advertising bans. In response to threats of regulatory intervention, including outright prohibitions, food brands ranging from McDonald's to General Mills have altered products, revised marketing practices, and launched major public relations campaigns to convince parents and policymakers that they are part of the solution.

Although frequently framed as a public health issue, this controversy runs deeper than accusations—or public relations defences—related to Happy Meals. While we are very conscious of child-only goods, such as toys, the more important commodities for children, in the long run, are food. We may think that child-focused advertising began with toys, but in the 1930s—long before direct-to-child toy advertisements of the television era—food manufacturers targeted children. Attention given to toys, moreover, renders child-focused advertising as more innocuous because toys are temporary. Food preferences, however, can be life-long. Through the small everyday food staples and indulgences, advertisers invite children to be demanding participants in a brand-laden marketplace. Advertising food to children is controversial because food is the quintessential product category linking children to the branded marketplace of monopoly capitalism. Food can be relatively inexpensive, and of course, necessary, but through these routine purchases children become part of a system of capitalist consumption.

Despite being significant and worthy of analysis in light of contemporary debates, efforts to limit advertising to children receive comparatively little attention in American histories of Depression-era anti-advertising activism.[1] In the 1930s, as national food brands began marketing directly to children, mothers, medical officials, and numerous organizations condemned food advertisers for utilizing unfair sales pitches, harming the health of children, and socializing young people to want only branded goods. Notably, critics in the 1930s touched on both the public health and consumer socialization consequences of advertising food to children. Activists also posited arguments that resonated with a broader consumer movement that expressed concerns over food and drug regulations, advertising claims, and the oligopolistic power of large corporations. This chapter, focusing on the American context, examines the tactics and arguments of 1930s authors and activists who took aim at children's food advertisers. More specifically, my objective is to make visible how the controversy of advertising food to children at the present juncture is remarkably similar to one faced by citizens in the 1930s. Important lessons can be drawn, such as the role of commercial media and how self-regulation cannot be trusted to significantly alter the commercialization of childhood. Drawing on articles from newspapers and the advertising trade press, newsletters of parent groups, and consumer movement publications, this chapter provides an overview of advertising food to children in the 1930s, spotlights key texts and groups resisting these practices, and offers socio-historic reflections on the long history of challenging children's food advertising.

The Early History of Advertising Food to Children

Long before the 1930s, food advertisers had children on their radar. As early as the nineteenth century, advertising agencies strategized that mothers were the prime targets of food advertisements and advised their clients to make their promotional materials mini-lectures on child feeding. Such advertisements commonly included a list of healthy ingredients, some information on how the product was made, and images or other signifiers of innocent, healthy, and happy children. Mothers, according to the business community, viewed advertisements and made purchases with their young ones in mind. Here, advertisers considered children as a kind of "bait" to secure the purchases and brand loyalty of mothers, who marketers believed put the needs of their children first. By the late 1920s, advertisers of national food brands started to consider children themselves as a key target audience, and this marked a critical juncture in the history of children's advertising. Advertisers increasingly communicated directly with children and sought to turn young people into demanding, brand-loyal purchase influencers.[2] New advertising platforms aided this new strategy.

The remarkable growth of network radio explains why advertising food to children took off in this era rather than earlier. Radio allowed advertisers to communicate their message directly to children from a variety of age groups, geographical regions, class positions, and reading abilities. In a time of economic downturn, children, a group of consumers who had little direct purchasing power, became important to the medium's commercial development. In 1928, listeners in New York City could tune in to thirty-four hours of total children's programming per year; by 1933, this number had risen to over one thousand, and food advertisers backed the majority of these hours.[3] According to one agency account manager in April 1930, radio allowed advertisers to speak directly with "the primary customers" instead of selling "indirectly, through the mothers to the children."[4]

Food-sponsored children's radio programs shared common formats and sales strategies. Most programs aired for fifteen minutes during the afterschool hours and used gimmicks such as "listener clubs," contests, and "premium" or free prize offers to foster brand loyalty. For example, on September 25, 1933, Ralston-Purina debuted the *Tom Mix Straight Shooters* program to promote Ralston-Purina's Hot Wheat Cereal. Children who submitted a proof of purchase, a box top, joined the "Straight Shooters" club, received the club manual, and signed a pledge to "shoot straight with their parents, friends, and Tom Mix by regularly eating Ralston, Official Straight Shooters Cereal." In exchange for mailing additional box tops, Straight Shooter members received badges, comic books, toy guns, flashlights, and even a toy telegraph set. Ralston-Purina considered these offers powerful mechanisms to promote brand loyalty in a cereal market in which dozens of corporations sold nearly identical products. Members of the club may have considered themselves loyal "Straight Shooters," but Ralston-Purina saw the membership as brand-loyal purchase influencers. Dozens of other food advertisers followed this same strategy of programming combined with other offers made in exchange for proofs of purchase. Notable examples included *Little Orphan Annie* (1930, sponsored by Ovaltine); *Singing Lady* (1932, sponsored by Kellogg); *Skippy* (1932, sponsored by Wheaties); *Bobby Benson* (1932, sponsored by Hecker H-O Oats); *Buck Rogers in the Twenty-fifth Century* (1932, sponsored by Cocomalt, Cream of Wheat, Kellogg, and eventually Popsicle); and *Lone Wolf Tribe* (1933, sponsored by Wrigley).

Food advertisers, innovators in children's radio, also invested in sponsored comic strips, which became another way for advertisers to communicate directly with children starting in the 1930s. Full-page comics—produced by advertising agencies and inserted into the Sunday comics section of newspapers—featured sidebars and other promotional features that accompanied the actual comic storyline. Post cereals, for example, launched the "Melvin Purvis America's No. 1 G-Man" comic strip in early 1936. Post described the comic serial as an opportunity to reveal "the methods used in capturing desperate criminals" and promoted Purvis's adventures as being "inside stories" that proved "crime does not pay." The instalments invited children to join the "Junior G-Men" club in exchange for box tops. Members received manuals and badges and had the opportunity to exchange additional Post box tops for premiums, such as magnifying glasses and toy guns. Long before the television age, then, advertisers enjoyed strong partnerships with children's media, and food sponsors wove their products, brands, and special offers into children's entertainment.

Consumer Resistance and Industry Responses

The rapid discovery and growth of advertising to children coincided with a wave of consumer activism. During the Depression, a rising "consumer consciousness" motivated individuals, academics, women's groups, and consumer groups to confront corporate power.[5] Activists questioned an American society dominated by oligopolistic corporations that manufactured similar products and competed solely through advertising and branding. Several books laid the foundation for consumer activism. In 1927, Stuart Chase, a liberal economist, and Frederick Schlink, who at the time worked for the Bureau of Standards, published *Your Money's Worth*. Chase and Schlink argued that manufacturers failed to provide consumers with sufficient and accurate information; consumers, in turn, wasted money on useless products that they would have otherwise not purchased if fully informed. As a follow-up, in 1933 Schlink and Arthur Kallet published *100,000,000 Guinea Pigs* with Vanguard Press—a publisher that federal politicians accused of being a "communist enterprise" by the 1940s—an exposé on the dangers of mass marketed foods and drugs. Schlink and Kallet highlighted both the fraudulent claims of food and drug advertisers and the lack of sufficient regulation or product testing in the United States. The hardships of the Depression made citizens aware of both the greed of corporations and the structural biases of capitalism, such as price fixing, a lack of competition, and the inefficient allocation of resources. Despite offering at times radical criticisms of the way in which capitalism cannot take care of basic human health and safety, these books resonated with American citizens, and many libraries held multiple copies of each.[6]

Criticisms of advertising directed at children appeared in several books associated with the Depression-era consumer movement. Peter Morrell devoted an entire chapter to food advertising on children's radio in his 1937 polemic, *Poisons, Potions and Profits*, which criticized the consumer socialization of children. Morrell compared sales pitches on radio to the "medicine tent-wagon that was so common on the American scene before the days of radio."[7] He condemned radio advertisers for "bullying" parents into purchasing "worthless and sometimes dangerous" foods because of pressure from children. Recognizing that "it takes a thrilling juvenile adventure story to get the average juvenile interested in anything as unadventurous as cereal," Morrell affirmed that food advertisers manipulated children through program narratives. Morrell also criticized the club and premium offers that resulted in children developing a habitual preference for branded, packaged, advertised foods.

Rachel Palmer and Isidore Alpher wrote the most direct, substantial, and well-researched attack on children's food advertising, *40,000,000 Guinea Pig Children* (1937), the title of which played on Schlink and Kallet's *100,000,000 Guinea Pigs*, also published by Vanguard Press. Like Schlink and Kallet's earlier work, *40,000,000 Guinea Pig Children* offered an institutional critique of advertising, its biases, and its long-term impact, and the text focused on food, beverage, and drug advertising. The book's opening declared, "health rightly comes first among the things parents desire for their children."[8] The authors argued that poor diets represented the "greatest hazard to children" and attributed this hazard to the quantity of advertisements to which children were subjected. Advertisers offered an abundance of biased "free" nutritional information, while children and parents could not easily access "unbiased" nutritional recommendations. Sponsored radio programs caused children to be "subjected to the influence of advertising" during most of their leisure hours at home. These arguments are remarkably similar to ones launched at children's food advertisers in the twenty-first century.

The co-authors also took issue with the content of sponsored programs and the way advertisers exploited children's enthusiasm and insecurities. Palmer and Alpher found fault with radio shows such as *Little Orphan Annie* that threatened, implicitly or explicitly, to go off the air if children did not get their parents to purchase the product. Purchasing tins of Ovaltine, the show's sponsor promised, represented a way for children to demonstrate their friendship with the fictional Annie, and purchasing additional tins allowed children membership in Annie's circle of special friends. The authors further lambasted food advertisers for exploiting children's love of mystery, sleuthing, adventure, aviation, sports, and cowboys. Attacking advertiser comic strips such as Post's G-Man series, Palmer and Alpher wrote that a child who became "all wrapped up in the detection of crime" would need to consume "enormous quantities of cereal just to acquire the necessary equipment."

The overarching thrust of *40,000,000 Guinea Pig Children* exposed the ways in which food advertising negatively influenced the finances of parents and the health of children. Because commercial media only promoted more expensive branded, packaged foods, selling to children meant that parents paid more than necessary to feed their families. The book advised parents that manufacturers hid the costs of "free" premiums in the higher prices of branded products. Advertising also placed too much emphasis on breakfast cereals, often enjoyed with a heavy helping of sugar, and candy. "Buck Rogers [1930s radio action hero] may successfully dazzle youngsters into eating Cream of Wheat," Palmer and Alpher noted, but there was "no hero who roams the stellar regions to convince children that an egg is as important as cereal at breakfast time." Advertising to children, the authors claimed, contributed to the rising consumption of sugar, one of the most damaging recent changes in the American diet, and rising rates of both tooth decay and diabetes followed.

This bias toward processed, branded foods also had long-term consequences. "A child trained via radio to look to Ovaltine for 'Orphan Annie pep and energy,'" Palmer and Alpher forewarned, "will grow into an adult who will try first one patented product after another to banish constipation, get rid of that tired feeling, and cure all his other ills, fancied or real." The authors were cognizant of what was arguably the most significant consequence of advertising to children: the long-term socialization of children to habitually turn to branded, packaged, and advertised products. The authors concluded that food manufacturers did not just promote goods. Rather, advertisers attempted to train consumers—a sophisticated critique that went beyond early twentieth century debates over fraudulent advertising "puffery."

The advertising industry trade press took notice of these books. The October 7, 1937, issue of *Printer's Ink* reviewed *Poisons, Potions and Profits* and *40,000,000 Guinea Pig Children*. The joint review dismissed *Poisons, Potions and Profits* as sensationalist and "by far the poorest of the consumer books." On the other hand, the reviewer declared that *40,000,000 Guinea Pig Children* warranted "serious consideration" by advertisers because it avoided "the meretricious sensationalism that mars so many consumer books." The review noted, "thousands of children are being deprived of their full share of certain elements of nutrition because of selfish advertisers." Warren Dygert's 1939 *Radio as an Advertising Medium*, a text aimed at a business audience, acknowledged the work of Palmer and Alpher. He agreed "exploiting Young America via radio" was a "great American pastime," but stopped short of recommending changes.[9]

An attack on children's food advertising was even written for children. In 1938 Ruth Brindze published *Johnny Get Your Money's Worth (and Jane Too!)*, a book for children.[10] While Palmer and Alpher placed responsibility on the shoulders of parents to help protect their children, Brindze's story recognized that children could be educated as critical consumers. An early example of teaching media literacy, *Johnny Get Your Money's Worth* addressed children as critical consumer-citizens rather than mere dupes of food marketers. A section of the book advised young readers about "how to choose candy." The book cautioned children that although "manufacturers may say that if you send a certain number of wrappers from their candy by a certain date they will give you a prize," to get this number of wrappers "you would have to eat far more candy than your regular share." Warning that contests functioned solely to sell more candy, Brindze concluded, "a prize is a first-rate advertisement." Finally, addressing the issue of long-term consumer socialization, Brindze instructed: "When you are collecting coupons or wrappers, you form a habit of buying a certain kind of candy. And long after the prize contest is over, you may continue to buy the same kind of bar. You have developed a taste for it. This is good business for the manufacturer. It helps him to sell more of his candy."

Resistance went beyond consumer movement books. Throughout the 1930s, grassroots movements of parents and teachers worked to improve the state of children's commercial radio. Concerns over food advertising combined with fears over the poor quality of children's radio programming. Ridding radio of sensational, non-educational programs became a top priority for parents and parent-teacher associations. A campaign started in 1933 by New York parents' groups to improve children's radio programming garnered considerable media attention. In January, mothers in Scarsdale met to discuss how their children suffered from emotional and anxiety problems because of radio. The mothers constructed a survey and distributed it through their local parent-teacher association. The survey results revealed that the majority of parents in the neighbourhood agreed that popular children's programs were of "poor" or "very poor" quality. A month later, the parent-teacher association and the Scarsdale Women's Club began a letter-writing campaign, aimed at the radio networks, to protest sponsored radio programs. In a February 28, 1933, *New York Times* piece covering the campaign, NBC's president gave a vague answer to these complaints, stating that broadcasters and sponsors always attempt "to make their form of entertainment as acceptable as possible to the greatest number of people."[11] As the *Nation* reported two months later, the broadcasters' lukewarm response made clear that poor programs "will continue to blight the homes of Scarsdale and all of America."[12]

Unsatisfied, the Scarsdale group continued their letter-writing campaign. In May, *Parents' Magazine* ran an editorial instructing parents to "write to the sponsor of the [offending] program and tell them why you object to it."[13] This editorial recognized the sponsors, not network, as the key party to influence and urged parents to simply "say so" if "critical of the type of program which the radio is supplying for children." Given the prominent role in shaping radio, threatening sponsors appeared promising. In 1934, the Michigan Child Study Association sent a petition to Ovaltine, protesting that *Little Orphan Annie* was "unwholesome entertainment for children."[14] As complaints continued to mount, the National Congress of Parents and Teachers discussed boycotting national sponsors at its 1935 convention in Washington.[15] However, this period saw more threats of sponsor boycotts than actual boycotts. Despite receiving press attention, the Scarsdale Women's Club did not have the resources to mobilize a national boycott and largely dropped the issue after 1933. Likewise, discussions at the National Congress of Parents and Teachers remained discussions. Nevertheless, radio networks, sponsors, and industry associations worked to subdue this resistance.

To appease their critics and proactively protect their sponsors, broadcasters frequently introduced self-regulatory measures. The National Association of Broadcasters (NAB) introduced its first advertising code of ethics in 1929, prior to the issue taking hold, which it touted as an attempt to "raise the bar" against false advertising. A revised NAB code, adopted in 1935 at the height of children's radio controversy, included a section dealing exclusively with children's programming. This code can be read as a largely a token effort, as it only limited the most malicious practices. For example, the code prohibited sponsors from requiring children to partake in dangerous activities in order to enter contests. CBS introduced an internal "statement of policies" on children's programming in 1935 and 1939, the NAB and NBC jointly created the Radio Council on Children's Programs, intended to be a "watchdog" for children's programming.[16] This council invited participation from women who led groups such as the United Parents Association and the Progressive Education Association. The Radio Council on Children's Programs' code included standards for "reasonable suspense" and "correct English and diction," yet said nothing about advertising practices and offers. Furthermore, the council did not actually review shows before they aired and had no regulatory authority to discipline offending networks. The council, demonstrating commercial radio's ability to co-opt resistance, functioned as a gesture of goodwill to these formerly critical groups rather than a publicly accountable regulator.

Writing about this era of radio, Joel Spring argues that the 1935 CBS self-censorship code "was part of a well-orchestrated public relations campaign."[17] Such self-regulatory efforts to convince citizens that sponsors acted responsibly may have also been effective in avoiding regulatory action. Despite powerful critiques from Palmer and Alpher, as well as organized campaigns from a variety of groups, regulators took a limited interest in children's food advertising practices during the 1930s.

The 1934 Communications Act charged the Federal Communication Commission (FCC) with ensuring that the "public interest, convenience, and necessity" would be paramount when granting and overseeing broadcast licences. The FCC paid attention to broadcast advertisements, but only intervened in the most egregious cases of advertising to children. In one instance in 1935, the FCC held hearings over the national *Jack Armstrong* radio program, sponsored by Wheaties.[18] A 1935 episode told listeners that Jack's mother was hospitalized and waiting for an expensive operation. Jack took to stamp collecting, in search of rare stamps to pay for his mother's operation. The episode ended with an invitation for children to get their own *Jack Armstrong* stamp by sending in a nickel and a Wheaties box top. With the pitch, "you'll be doing Jack a mighty big favor if you join his stamp club right away," children may have thought their nickel and box top were helping Jack's mother get her operation.

The FCC investigated the program after parents complained that their children believed Jack's mother would die if they did not participate in the promotion. Wheaties immediately cancelled the offer, but it continued to promote many other premiums directly related to the show—such as Egyptian Whistle Rings or Hike-o-meters—without raising the eyebrows of broadcast regulators.

Although the federal government signed several new advertising and product regulations into law during the 1930s, none dealt exclusively with advertising to children. The multitude of parties involved in the policymaking process left the issue of children's advertising off the table as the Tugwell Bill evolved into the Wheeler-Lea Amendment of 1938, which gave the Federal Trade Commission (FTC) the power to prosecute false or misleading advertisers.[19] The Wheeler-Lea Amendment left the FTC with no special standards or procedures for dealing with children's advertising. Policymakers did not consider how advertising to children required different ways of defining "false" or "unfair" practices.

On the other hand, the new Food, Drug, and Cosmetics Act, implemented in 1938, gave the FTC power over certain manufacturing and retail-level practices that appealed to children. This Act prohibited manufacturers from adding "inedible substances" to candy. Confectioners had been embedding small premiums, often metallic toys, within candy. *Consumers Guide* wrote about the risk of children "unsuspectingly swallowing" prizes along with the candy.[20] *Consumers' Research Bulletin* advised mothers to make candy at home so as to save money and eliminate the potential for such danger.[21] The FTC also objected to retail "lotteries" used to sell candy. Stores lured children with games. Children could buy a single piece of penny candy and with that purchase have the opportunity to punch a slip of paper on a large board. If the child punched a lucky name or winning number, she or he received bonus candy. If a child did not win on the first try, alleged *Consumers Guide*, "the gambler's fever gets a hold of him, and in the heat of it away goes his pocket money, not to mention his appetite."[22] Other retailers offered "break-and-take" lotteries where children broke off a piece of chocolate from a wrapped bar and if under the wrapper the piece was coloured, the winner received an additional chocolate. The FTC, in keeping with the Food, Drug, and Cosmetics Act, determined such lotteries as unfair methods of competition.

In summary, federal regulators only cracked down on some of the most extreme sales techniques (e.g., candy lotteries or *Jack Armstrong's* stamp premium) while leaving untouched the vast majority of national advertising practices and the powerful ways in which sponsors shaped children's media for commercial goals. Despite powerful critiques from authors and grassroots parent organizations, policymakers and regulators took a limited interest in children's food advertising practices during the 1930s. Unlike twenty-first century debates concerning the marketing of food to children, no 1930s policymaker proposed a total prohibition of advertising food to children.

The 1930s furnished an opportunity to limit or possibly prohibit children's food advertising. A window of opportunity existed because these years saw an active consumer movement, as well as political debates over advertising and broadcasting. Additionally, funding children's media via advertising was still relatively new and restricted to several product categories, such as cereal and candy. However, owing to a lack of interest from regulators and proactive attempts to self-regulate, children's food advertisers and media traversed a decade of resistance relatively unscathed. The positioning of children as brand-loyal consumers would prove significant during the postwar decades when thrift became un-American, credit became plentiful, the ownership of suburban houses filled with appliances defined "freedom," and the consumer movement retreated.

Lessons for Today

Children, open to new ideas and able to bring them into the household, motivate social change, which is precisely why both advertisers and activists have paid close attention to them for nearly a century. Although attempts to stop children's advertising in the 1930s were at best mixed, we can consider several important lessons from this early history.

First, the availability of commercial mass media represented an important pre-condition. Because food advertisers and children's media have enjoyed such a close relationship for almost a century, to discuss the problems of advertising to children often means discussing the commercial nature of children's media. We cannot deal with advertising controversies without considering the commercial contexts in which advertisements are distributed. If sponsorship did not become the "default" business model for funding American radio in the 1920s, or if newspapers were not so desperate for ad sales in the early 1930s, advertising to children would not have taken off in the way that it did. It is interesting to note that although activists often took aim at sponsors, the radio networks themselves reacted; commercial media acted to protect their revenue streams. Consequently, activists should focus on the conditions that allow for advertising as much as the regulation of the advertisements themselves. We should push for vibrant public media that can produce quality children's content (print, broadcast, online, and mobile) without the need for advertising funding. Likewise, we should push for sufficient public school funding. Admittedly, in a neoliberal political economic context, these are no small feats.

Second, despite claims by advertisers and commercial media, self-regulation cannot be relied on to substantially alter the children's food advertising landscape. The broadcast industry utilized self-regulation in the 1930s to combat rising anti-advertising opponents and parents concerned about program quality. Food advertisers in the twentieth-first century continue to implement self-regulatory codes to stave off criticism and regulation.[23] Bill Jeffery, from the Centre for Science in the Public Interest, argues that advertisers "have both a vested financial interest in weak standards and a professionally honed skill for 'selling' such weak standards as tough regulatory oversight."[24] Self-regulation appears to be merely a public relations tactic to quell criticisms.

As Lawrence Glickman's history of consumer activism traces, new forms of consumer resistance follow the new practices of corporations.[25] Even more interesting, this dialectic of power and resistance can unfold during tough economic times. The Depression represented a critical juncture that produced new advertising methods but also a powerful consumer movement. The new millennium marks another critical juncture, as it has witnessed economic crisis, new forms of advertising (especially online, interactive, social, and mobile), and another wave of resistance. For activists seeking to resist corporate power and capitalism's tendency to commodify, this economic context is both a threat and opportunity. The context is a threat because economic recessions or depressions make advertising and media issues seem small by comparison to job numbers. The context of economic collapse can also be an opportunity. According to media historian and political economist Robert McChesney, the Depression marked one of the few moments in American history when institutional and, in a few instances, "radical" criticisms of the role of advertising and branding in capitalist consumer culture were permissible in mainstream political discourse.[26] Books such as *40,000,000 Guinea Pig Children* are, indeed, remarkable. Considering the present context, perhaps there has never been a better time to challenge advertising and the consumer socialization of young people.

8

OUR ECONOMIC WAY OUT

Black American Consumers' Co-operation in the First Half of the Twentieth Century

JOSHUA L. CARREIRO

ONTEMPORARY CONSUMERS' co-operatives tend to be associated with the middle and upper classes, "foodies," ex-hippies, and health foods. However, modern consumers' co-operatives originated in nineteenth-century working-class England. Although consumers' co-operatives existed before, the Rochdale Pioneers established what would become *the* model of consumers' co-operation still in practice today. In 1844, in the midst of England's "hungry forties," twenty-seven men and one woman came together to form the Rochdale Society of Equitable Pioneers, a co-operative store in Rochdale, England. Faced with reduced wages and a higher cost of living, the workers of the Rochdale mills went out on strike. Their strike unsuccessful, the workers turned to consumer activism and established one of the first successful consumers' co-operatives. Consumers' co-operatives, stores democratically controlled and owned by their members, are a working model of an alternative to capitalist organization of consumption. They are not profit-driven; any surplus capital is reinvested as collectively decided by the member-owners or returned to member-owners in proportion to their purchases. Consumers' co-operation is based on a set of principles, commonly referred to as the Rochdale principles, which include: open membership; democratic control; a return of surplus to members based on each member's purchases; a no-credit policy; an educational component; political neutrality; and co-operation among co-operatives.[1]

Scholarship on consumers' co-operatives in general is limited, and there is a dearth of material on nineteenth- and early twentieth-century consumers' co-operatives specifically. Lost in the historical accounts of consumers' co-operatives are the stories of the black American consumers' co-operatives that blossomed in the early to mid-twentieth-century United States.[2] This chapter provides a brief history of that movement, its key figures and organizations, and its successes and failures. Despite the movement's lack of grand success, it played an important role in the development of twentieth-century black American consumer activism and provides us with valuable lessons going forward.

The Origins of Black Consumers' Co-operation

Despite some ties, black Americans were largely excluded from the broad, predominantly white consumers' co-operative movement of the late nineteenth and early twentieth centuries. Therefore, black consumers' co-operatives developed within the context of increased black American consumers' activism in general. During the Great Migration between 1910 and 1930, close to two million southern black Americans moved to northern and midwestern cities. Due to migration and increased urbanization, black Americans' influence as consumers increased in relation to their buying power. Although organized black consumer activism existed before the late 1920s, continued discriminatory practices against black American workers and consumers and the disproportionate economic effect of the Great Depression on black Americans led to a flourish of activism in the 1930s.

When white employers in segregated black neighbourhoods refused to hire black workers, black consumers used their buying power to demand more employment opportunities. The "Don't Buy Where You Can't Work" campaign was perhaps the most well-known example of black consumer activism of the 1930s. Led by Joseph Bibb, the editor of the influential black-owned newspaper the *Chicago Whip*, the first "Don't Buy" campaign was launched in Chicago in 1930. Due to the success of that campaign, black community organizations in other parts of the United States adopted Bibb's tactics. The "Don't Buy" campaign organized boycotts and pickets of white retailers in predominantly black neighbour-hoods who did not employ black workers at all or only employed them in menial positions. In addition to Chicago, the campaign resulted in gains in Harlem, Cleveland, Baltimore, Newark, and Washington, D.C., as well as other primarily black cities and neighbourhoods, and served as a nucleus of other consumer activism.[3]

Despite the fact that black-owned businesses were most likely to be successful in areas characterized by residential segregation and large black populations of disadvantaged workers, white-owned businesses contin-ued to dominate the consumer landscape in segregated black neighbour-hoods. In response, community leaders initiated "buy black" campaigns. For example, the "Double-Duty Dollar" campaign encouraged black consumers to shop at black-owned businesses to fulfil their own needs as consumers and simultaneously help develop the black business commu-nity.[4] Despite the relative success of these campaigns, several prominent black Americans were concerned that "buy black" campaigns would grow a black bourgeoisie at the expense of the black worker-consumer.[5] St. Clair Drake, a black American anthropologist, criticized the "Don't Buy" and "Double-Duty Dollar" campaigns as self-serving and short-term solutions. The campaigns increased black employment in white-owned businesses and the success of black-owned businesses in black communi-ties, but the consumer received little in return. Even if both the business owner and consumer were black, their interests under capitalism were not necessarily the same. The dollar could serve triple duty, Drake argued, if it was used to start black consumers' co-operatives, which would support black-owned businesses, increase black employment, and return profits to black consumers in the form of dividends.[6]

The encouragement of black consumers' co-operation began in the early 1900s, but the idea gained traction in the 1930s. Like the "Don't Buy" and "buy black" campaigns, co-operators agreed that black economic empowerment and advancement could only be achieved through buy-ing power. However, whereas the "Don't Buy" campaign supported and sought to develop a black bourgeoisie, the consumers' co-operative move-ment advocated collective control of business. And while other forms of black consumer activism encouraged support of white-owned businesses that employed black workers, the black consumers' co-operative move-ment supported varying forms of self-segregation. These differences were significant enough to define the black consumers' co-operative movement as a distinct form of consumer activism.

The actual establishment of black consumers' co-operatives began on a large scale in the late 1920s and early 1930s, but a history of black American consumers' co-operation should begin with an analysis of the early foundation laid by W. E. B. Du Bois. Du Bois, an influential American sociologist, co-founder of the National Association for the Advancement of Colored People (NAACP), and civil rights activist, began exploring the possibility of a black consumers' co-operative economy in the early twentieth century and committed himself to developing and promoting the idea soon after he assumed editorship of the *Crisis*, the official publication of the NAACP, in 1910 (a position he held until 1934). Du Bois was faithful to the idea that black Americans required an economic foundation before substantial advances in racial equality could be made. His search for an economic foundation and burgeoning advocacy of black self-segregation led him to consumers' co-operation.

Du Bois based his advocacy of black consumers' co-operation on two central premises. First, he held that modern capitalism was an inherently oppressive economic system. Black workers were uniquely exploited by white employers who used them as strike breakers and a means to drive down wages. Additionally, black workers were largely excluded from the American labour movement due to white racism and segregationist practices and policies.[7] Unlike other black leaders who encouraged the development of a black capitalist class, Du Bois cautioned that black Americans "must avoid, in the advancement of the Negro race, the mistakes of ruthless exploitation which have marked modern economic history" and sought to "spread the idea among colored people that the accumulation of wealth is for social rather than individual ends."[8] Thus, he concluded, consumers' co-operation was black Americans' "economic way out, our industrial emancipation."[9]

Second, because of the reality of both de jure and de facto racial segregation, Du Bois argued that black Americans should define segregation on their own terms rather than seek integration into the larger economy as second-class citizens, workers, and consumers.[10] As an alternative, Du Bois advocated the creation of a parallel, quasi-socialist black economy. As early as 1906 Du Bois argued that the efficacy of a black co-operative economy had already been established in post-slavery southern states that had been characterized by "group economies"—"cooperative arrangements of industries and services within the Negro group that tends to become a closed economic circle largely independent of the surrounding white world."[11] Almost three decades later, in one of his last articles written for the *Crisis*, Du Bois stated confidently that "the great step ahead today is for the American Negro to accomplish his economic emancipation through voluntary determined cooperative effort."[12]

Following a 1918 conference of individuals interested in black consumers' co-operation, Du Bois and other conference attendees founded the Negro Cooperative Guild (NCG). The Guild was established to develop propaganda materials, create educational programs for the study of consumers' co-operation, and encourage and support black Americans interested in starting consumers' co-operatives.[13] Despite the intentions and efforts of Du Bois and his colleagues, the Guild lasted less than two years. Its efforts, however, did result in two successful co-operative stores—one at the Bluefield Institute in West Virginia and another in Memphis, Tennessee.[14] Undaunted, Du Bois continued to use his position as editor of the *Crisis*, which at its peak reached more than one hundred thousand readers, to advocate for black consumers' co-operation. His editorials and reports on the subject helped maintain a national network of practitioners and advocates of co-operation.

Ten years after the dissolution of the NCG, journalist, novelist, and civil rights activist George Schuyler founded the Young Negroes Cooperative League (YNCL) determined to build a black consumers' co-operative economy led by young black Americans (those thirty-five and younger). In "An Appeal to Young Negroes," Schuyler urged young black Americans to reject the "old Negroes" and their leadership. The elders, claimed Schuyler, had failed because their plan for racial uplift emphasized conciliation, a bourgeois ideology of individualism, employment through appeals to "good white folk," and an over-reliance on the church. The YNCL and the establishment of consumers' co-operatives, Schuyler argued, provided an opportunity for immediate and proactive solutions to the problems faced by black Americans.[15] Schuyler maintained that the movement needed to be self-segregated because white Americans were not sufficiently aware of the plight of black Americans and therefore "Negroes [could not] trust their destinies to mixed organizations" and that "the leadership and control of these enterprises must be . . . by those within the group rather than those outside it."[16] He argued that poverty, unemployment, and growing residential and industrial segregation uniquely positioned black Americans to benefit from segregated consumers' co-operation. Schuyler, himself thirty-four at the time of the founding of the YNCL, believed that only the young could embrace a new way forward. The "old" had grown jaded or lulled into believing capitalism and individual economic achievement were the way out and up for black Americans.

Schuyler quickly recruited Ella Baker to head the YNCL. As director, Baker—who went on to leadership positions in the NAACP, the Southern Christian Leadership Conference, and the Student Nonviolent Coordinating Committee—stressed the importance of establishing functioning co-operatives to illustrate the change the movement sought. In a short time, the YNCL had organizers in twenty-eight cities and, with more than six hundred attendees at its first annual meeting, appeared to be off to a strong start.[17] But organizing the YNCL at the start of the Great Depression promised financial difficulties that the League was unable to overcome and by 1934 it had disbanded. However, the YNCL did help grow the black consumers' co-operative movement. By the end of 1931, members of the YNCL had established consumers' co-operative councils in Pennsylvania, Ohio, South Carolina, Washington D.C., Arizona, Louisiana, Virginia, and New York.[18] By 1934, several of these councils had established successful consumers' co-operatives.[19]

Neither the NCG nor the YNCL succeeded in developing an umbrella organization to co-ordinate a national system of black consumers' co-operatives. However, a loose network of co-operatives did develop between 1930 and 1950. These co-operatives illustrate the promise and struggles of black consumers' co-operatives as a form of black economic development. Their success was due to a combination of factors that allowed them to overcome economic obstacles, racism, and a general lack of formal education among the membership. In some cases, successful consumers' co-operatives grew out of educational programs. In others, churches provided the organization and foundation for their establishment. Housing developments, segregated by race, proved to be a fertile ground for the growth of black consumers' co-operation as well. Despite differences, what most successful co-operatives shared was a social context that provided resources not readily available to a disparate group of potential black co-operators.

The Consumers' Cooperative Trading Company of Gary, Indiana was one of the most successful examples of black consumers' co-operation during the Depression. Black residents made up about 20 percent of Gary's population of one hundred thousand, which made Gary a disproportionately black northern city. Of the twenty thousand black residents, most had migrated north between 1910 and 1930 looking for work in the city's steel mills. A full half of Gary's black population was dependent on relief programs.[20] Recognizing the dire circumstances of the city's black population, J. L. Reddix, a black high school teacher, began a study group with the intent to publish a newspaper reporting on the conditions of the black population of Gary. The discussion quickly turned to the possibility of starting a consumers' co-operative. Building on the momentum of the study group, Reddix offered a night course to educate community members on the benefits of consumers' co-operation.[21] The class provided the foundation on which the Consumers' Cooperative Trading Company was built. By 1935, just three years after the formation of Reddix night course, the store was doing $35,000 in monthly business—$10,000 more than any other black-owned retailer in the country.[22] Despite limited financial resources, the educational program provided training and a foundation that proved essential to the success of the co-operative.

Students' Cooperative Store, another successful black consumers' co-operative established within the context of an educational institution, began in 1924 under the guidance of Professor W. C. Matney and the Department of Business Administration at the Bluefield Institute, a historically black college located in Bluefield, West Virginia. The co-operative, established and run by students of the college, lasted until 1934 when the state of West Virginia disallowed the presence of independent businesses on state school property.[23] The co-operative served as a business "laboratory"—a functioning store, owned and managed by the students, prepared students to manage co-operative enterprises on graduation. Matney, a founding member of the Negro Cooperative Guild and the first black American to attend the National Cooperative Congress in 1928, was a leading figure in the black consumers' co-operative movement and advised other schools on the establishment of their own co-operatives.[24]

Other successful black consumers' co-operatives developed educational components despite not growing out of formal educational institutions. Two examples from Harlem, the Pure Food Cooperative Grocery established in 1935, and the Modern Co-op started in 1940, both illustrated the importance of member education.[25] Large-scale co-operatives with hundreds of members each, the Pure Food Cooperative Grocery and the Modern Co-op instituted well-organized educational systems intended to teach the tenets and benefits of black consumers' co-operation and buying black. In addition, both emphasized the ideological basis of co-operatives, encouraging members to view consumers' co-operation as a transformative social and economic form of organization, not just a business style. The members viewed consumers' co-operation, which was less "glamorous" than other movements such as socialism or communism, as a more effective, practical response to the economic and social conditions of black Americans.[26] In addition to meeting the immediate needs of black Americans, consumers' co-operation, argued many of its advocates, provided a means by which capitalism could slowly be dismantled and replaced by an economy based on collective control of the means of consumption and, ultimately, the means of production.

Despite Schuyler's reluctance to collaborate with black churches, several successful black consumers' co-operatives grew out of faith communities. Opposition to the involvement of the black church in economic and racial uplift was based on the suspicion that black churches only promoted a small number of elite black capitalists, doing little or nothing to benefit the masses of poor, black consumers.[27] Du Bois, however, correctly predicted that black churches could be useful to the co-operative movement if they utilized their presence and influence in black communities to organize and educate the black working class on consumers' co-operation.[28] Partnership with churches also encouraged greater participation by women, those most likely to be responsible for a household's consumption.

In 1936, encouraged by their reverend, the all-black congregation of St. Simeon Church just outside of Cincinnati, Ohio started a small buying club to reduce their food costs. With over 90 percent of the congregation on public relief, the reverend viewed black consumers' co-operation as a form of self-help. The congregation bought into the co-operative model and by 1943, despite minimal financial resources, established the Valley Consumers Cooperative. With over two hundred members, the co-operative became the largest black-owned grocery store—and one of the largest black-owned businesses—in the Cincinnati area.[29] Other black churches, such as Harlem's Church of the Master and Abyssinian Baptist Church, encouraged their congregations to use their church buildings as "incubators" for consumers' co-operatives until the members were able to move to storefront locations.[30] The success of the movement's close work with churches foreshadowed the important role that religious organizations would play in the civil rights movement.

In addition to religious and educational institutions, segregated black housing developments often provided the spatial intimacy and social cohesion necessary for the establishment of successful consumers' co-operatives. Black housing developments were commonly located in "food deserts"—residential areas characterized by a lack of access to affordable and healthy food. Without a grocery store in a two-mile radius, the residents of the Frederick Douglass housing development in Washington, D.C., formed a group to study the possibility of establishing a consumers' co-operative to fill the void. The residents organized a buying club in 1941 and by 1944 established a successful consumers' co-operative adjacent to the housing project that met the needs of residents.[31]

Where residents of black housing developments did have access to grocery stores, the businesses were most often white-owned and charged higher prices for inferior goods, which was a common problem faced by black Americans nationally. In response to these exploitative conditions, the residents of the Rosenwald Apartments, a black housing development in Chicago, organized a boycott of the white-owned neighbourhood stores. Simultaneously, the residents formed a consumers' co-operative that by 1939, just two years after opening, claimed a membership of 450 members—a membership equal to the number of apartments in the development.[32] Black co-operators responded to residential segregation by creating separate black institutions under democratic control, a tactic advocated by Du Bois years earlier.

Finally, black consumers' co-operatives occasionally formed and succeeded as a collective response to the development of chain stores in predominantly black neighbourhoods. Although chain stores were likely to offer competitive prices, they were unlikely to hire local black residents. The presence of chain stores often meant disaster for black consumers' co-operatives, but in some cases, their presence encouraged a collective response from local black residents. One example, the Red Circle Stores of Richmond, Virginia, which opened in 1938, faced early competition from the grocery chain A&P but eventually claimed a membership of over one thousand.[33] Unable to attract customers from the Red Circle Stores, the A&P began to hire black workers in an attempt to curry favour with black residents. When the residents stuck with the co-operative store, the A&P cut prices to a level that Red Circle could not match. Despite the price cuts, black consumers remained loyal to Red Circle. Eventually, the Richmond A&P closed, illustrating that black consumers' co-operatives could compete with the chain stores that were beginning to take over the American consumer landscape.[34]

Discussion

To be sure, there were many unsuccessful attempts to establish black consumers' co-operatives in the first half of the twentieth century. Those that failed shared several deficiencies. First, although consumers' co-operation is a means by which those with small amounts of capital can collectively start a business by combining their resources, in some communities individual financial resources were too paltry to provide the needed capital to sustain the co-operative even when pooled. The participation of the black middle class was one possible solution to the problem of insignificant capital, but inter-class co-operation was less common than intra-class co-operation. In addition, as mentioned above, competition from chain stores posed a serious challenge to the development and success of black consumers' co-operatives. Even though some co-operatives were able to overcome this competition, many were unable. Withstanding the often lower prices offered by chain stores required a co-operative membership committed to the ideals of consumers' co-operation and an understanding of its long-term benefits (for example, the return of profits to the membership, which could lead to greater savings in the long run). Finally, community members often lacked proper education of the consumers' co-operative model and doubted their ability to successfully and co-operatively operate a business. In these cases, the consumers' co-operative often reverted to a traditional business model or folded.

However, despite examples of failure, there were enough successful black consumers' co-operatives to prove that co-operation was a viable response to the economic and social conditions faced by black Americans. Historical analysis of the black consumers' co-operative movement reveals several key factors responsible for the success. The incubation of consumers' co-operatives within an existing organization contributed significantly to success, as did formal educational programs. The established networks of socially and economically similar individuals in churches and segregated housing developments, for example, provided the social cohesion and spatial proximity necessary for success. An examination of black consumers' co-operation reveals that success was unlikely to be achieved via race loyalty alone. Success appears to have been built on a solid social foundation in addition to a commitment to "buy black."

While churches and segregated housing developments provided social cohesion and infrastructure for burgeoning consumers' co-operatives, educational institutes and programs provided necessary training in addition to a social foundation. Because few black Americans (or Americans in general) were accustomed to consumers' co-operation as an alternative to a capitalist organization of consumption, successful stores relied on a membership familiar with the basic principles of co-operation. Du Bois cautioned that no group should attempt to start a consumers' co-operative without careful study of the philosophy, business model, and history of co-operatives. Numerous successful black consumers' co-operatives adhered to this advice. The Bluefield Institute's co-operative "laboratory" not only operated a successful consumers' co-operative but also trained students to establish and manage co-operatives after graduation. The Consumers' Cooperative Trading Company of Gary, Indiana, perhaps the most well-regarded black consumers' co-operative of its time, owed much of its success to the educational program developed by J. L. Reddix.

Conversion to the co-operative model required more than technical education; it also required a change in consciousness and an ideological shift. Consumers' co-operation is a business model based on shared wealth. Profits are divided among members according to their purchases and the remainder reinvested in the co-operative. Du Bois insisted on the need for black Americans to renounce a belief in bourgeois individualism and the idea that business exists solely for profit and accept that wealth should exist for social, not individual ends. The failure of the Young Negroes Cooperative League, and the Negro Cooperative Guild before it, impeded the development of a large-scale propaganda and education program to promote consumers' co-operation. Du Bois's work as editor of the *Crisis* and the support of the major black newspapers fostered a network of black consumers' co-operatives, but a disorganized network was no replacement for nationwide organizations.

The many successful black consumers' co-operatives of the first half of the twentieth century illustrate the promise of co-operation as an economic way out for black Americans. Because of the similarity between the contemporary economic and social conditions of black Americans and conditions in the early to mid-twentieth century, consumers' co-operatives should be considered a viable tactic for black economic development today. Just as the Great Depression disproportionately affected black Americans, the 2007 Great Recession hit black Americans harder than any other racial or ethnic category. Looking at 2010 data (the first year of recovery following the recession) black households experienced a negative 10 percent change in income since the start of the recession while white households experienced a negative 5 percent change. That same year, the median white household income was $65,135 compared to $39,715 for black households. The black unemployment rate at the end of 2010 levelled at 15.5 percent compared to 8.5 percent for white Americans. And coming out of the Great Recession, black Americans faced a

27.4 percent poverty rate compared to a 9.9 percent rate for white Americans.[35] Black Americans continue to be concentrated in central-city locations and segregated from white Americans. Due to this concentration, black Americans are disproportionately located in "food deserts" without access to affordable and nutritious food.[36]

The civil rights movement proved that consumer activism, such as the boycott, is an effective instrument for social change. However, the success of black consumers' co-operation illustrates that other forms of consumer activism can also force change. Consumers' co-operation serves a practical purpose—providing decent products at fair prices—but it also holds transformative promise. Consumers' co-operation allowed racially marginalized groups to achieve self-reliance, to challenge and even remove themselves from exploitative economic relationships, and to disrupt racialized power structures. At the beginning of the twentieth century, black academics and activists recognized the importance of buying power for racial uplift and looked back to the Rochdale Pioneers for guidance. In the twenty-first century, many acknowledge the primacy of consumption in the economy and society and should therefore study the successes and failures of the first black consumers' co-operative movement and apply those lessons to the organization of consumption in a way that empowers marginalized populations as consumers and citizens.

9

NOT
BUYING IT

Reconsidering American Consumer
Opposition to Nazi Anti-Semitism

JEFFREY SCOTT DEMSKY
and RANDALL KAUFMAN

S HORTLY AFTER Adolf Hitler became German chancellor, pockets of Jewish and Christian American opposition formed. Some people denounced the Nazi hostility to democratic values, while others condemned their anti-Semitism. At times, these strains overlapped. Such opposition, however, shared one recurring theme: Americans must combat—not placate—instances of intolerance both overseas and at home. Condemnation took many forms, from lawmakers' speeches[1] to journalists' articles[2] and even actors' films.[3] Opposition also took a lesser-known economic form—a boycott and non-consumption campaign.[4] Among experts that specialize in American resistance to Nazism, most agree that this boycott campaign was a well-intentioned failure, indicative of a larger set of deficiencies. Military action, not consumers, ultimately stopped Nazi Germany, ending the war and the Holocaust.

During the last four decades, a powerful set of remembrances has formed around this finding. What has come to be known as the "abandonment" of the Jews holds that a legacy of Christian antipathy, prevalent during the 1930s, helped scuttle relief efforts.[5] In this sequence of "angry days," one would not expect much support for such things as

an anti-Nazi boycott.[6] While reasonable, this context ingrains a meth-
odological tendency—diminishing opposition tales—that can result in
scholars beginning their investigations with conclusions already in sight.
While acknowledging the damaging effects of domestic anti-Semitism,
we want to push past this familiar terrain. Our boycott study does not ask
how many additional Jews might have been helped had the U.S. been
more welcoming. Rather, we are focused on intention, trying to learn why
the movement formed, how it operated, and what its legacy teaches about
prejudice and pluralism in the U.S.

Well before Hitler's regime appeared, the members of such Progressive organizations as the Anti-Defamation League (1913), American
Civil Liberties Union (1920), and National Conference of Christians
and Jews (1927) forecast their social preferences through consumerism.
In one instance, boycotters targeted advertisers that supported Henry
Ford's anti-Semitic newspaper, *Dearborn Independent*.[7] In another case,
they helped convince Congress to abrogate a long-standing trade treaty
in protest of Russian pogroms.[8] Such episodes appear relatable to subsequent anti-Nazi activities. They point the way to an alternative narrative, or at least a side conversation that does not cast Americans as having
turned completely away. This innovation offers fresh glimpses of the boycott movement, reframing it both as a foreign policy effort and a domestic
movement to marginalize social bias.

It is true that the boycott's leaders never fashioned a cohesive strategy,
such as the non-importation effort that eighteenth-century colonists used
against the British.[9] The campaign also competed with other non-consumption movements during the period, arguably with less success. For
example, by 1937, the American silk boycott against Japan prospered.
Evidence indicates that the movement achieved its economic end, damaging foreign silk producers.[10] It also took hold as a wider social movement.
Americans across the nation, inspired to protest Japanese fascism, invented
unique ways to publicize their non-consumption. College students in the
Northeast held "bonfire boycotts" featuring participants communally dis-
robing and setting their silk apparel aflame. Hollywood luminaries staged
a vampy "strip tease" performance in which the actresses' silk undergarments came to rest in a red-white-and-blue garbage pail.[11] Unlike the
more ambitious anti-Nazi effort that endeavoured to restrict all German
wares, the decision to target one decisive product resulted in what one
observer called "a nation-wide movement of unprecedented propor-
tions."[12] This process naturally references an interesting question, one

that rests a bit outside our focus, whether consumers' ire was more effect-ively directed against Japanese or German products.[13]

We argue that American consumers, repelled by accounts of Nazi racism, attempted to use their purchasing power to sculpt a new epoch in which prejudice was taboo. These efforts were national in the sense that the campaign was visible in such urban centres as New York, Los Angeles, Philadelphia, and Cleveland. But the campaign was also localized, con-ducted on a day-to-day basis, between consumers and the entrepreneurs whose businesses they patronized. This dichotomy, between a national and localized movement, is something not frequently discussed in stan-dard interpretations of the boycott campaign. In order to bring this more nuanced story into focus, we perceive a need to reconsider the protean nature of the 1930s.[14] Searching for residues of earlier Progressive mind-sets, instead of re-treading over instances of the era's well-documented nativism, will pump fresh air into what has become a flattened portrait of the decade. Sceptics may characterize examples of this bustle as boosterism or rhetoric. Admittedly, when cast against the later memories of the mil-lions of victims, consumer opposition arguments face a rather high thresh-old. However, if enough activity existed, and the rationales informing the activity persisted, later generations might wish to take notice.

The boycotters' actions were not significant because they helped save lives or changed the course of history. Rather, they are important because they contradict the canon of well-known academic debates that set the contours of public memory. We have already learned a great deal from studying those figures that displayed personal prejudices and pro-fessional shortcomings with regard to European Jewish suffering. The opportunity now exists to learn from those who tried to ensure that bigots everywhere learned that their unwelcoming opinions carried with them potential costs.

Part One: Efforts to Change Nazis' Behaviours

In January 1933, most Americans probably had little knowledge of Weimar Germany's new chancellor. At the exact time that Adolf Hitler and his Nazi Party formed their government, the U.S. was struggling with the economic and personal costs of the Great Depression. An attempted assassination of President Roosevelt, as well as sensationalist reports that a Wall Street cabal wanted to overthrow his administration, were main topics of public conver-sation. Some people, however, had knowledge of what Nazism meant for Jews.[15] They took steps to raise domestic awareness levels. "Who Stands behind Hitler?" asked a February 1933 headline in the *Nation*. Listing several Nazi goals, such as abjuring the Versailles Treaty and reviving the German economy, the article closed with the observation that Germany's new leader "emphasized the anti-Jewish position."[16] "Leave the Jewish Problem Alone!" read the headline of another piece in *Christian Century*, the period's most influential Protestant journal. "Since Locke," the reader learned, "religion, opinions, and philosophies are personal matters." "If we are to carry on Western civilization . . . neither the state nor society has the right to deny the Jews."[17]

It was people possessed of this ecumenical mindset who devised the American anti-Nazi boycott movement. Such activities represented an increase in the scope and intensity of domestic opposition directed against German militarism. During the First World War, for example, no American boycott of German goods took shape, although "hate-the-Hun" sentiments resulted in sporadic outbreaks of violence against people of German heritage and the banning of German language courses taught in many states' public schools.[18] The absence of economic resistance during this period perhaps renders what later emerged as the anti-Nazi boycott movement something worthy of greater retrospective analysis. Banding people together against Hitlerism signalled citizens' learned awareness of the threats associated with German bellicosity, as well as an understanding of how they might help combat the dangers. The campaign found its initial expression in late March 1933, within weeks of Adolf Hitler's consolidation of dictatorial powers, when thirteen thousand members of the Jewish War Veterans laced up their boots for a public march in New York City. These men had fought Germans in battle two decades earlier. This time, however, their mission was consumer-based. If Americans could not directly blunt the Nazis' intolerance, these former soldiers reasoned, perhaps organizing a boycott would lend indirect pressure.[19]

Media reports celebrated the rally's success. A *New York Times* story, entitled "Protest on Hitler Growing In Nation," stated that one million people lined Manhattan's streets in a show of solidarity.[20] Alongside a bevy of dignitaries, the city's mayor issued a supportive proclamation. Such activities spurred additional efforts. A few days later, more boycotters, including American Federation of Labor president William Green, Senator Robert Wagner (D-NY), and Rabbi Stephen S. Wise from the American Jewish Congress, convened a gathering in Madison Square Garden. More than fifty thousand people came out in support. Countless more listened to the proceedings on a national radio program.[21]

Jewish war veterans marching in Manhattan, March 23, 1933. National Museum of American Jewish Military History.

Events that soon followed demonstrate both the power of the emerging boycott movement and the complicated nature of taking such steps. Nazi propaganda minister Joseph Goebbels monitored American media. He knew the clamour. Within days of the American rallies, Goebbels planned a German pushback. Several *New York Times* articles make clear the reciprocity. In one story, readers learned of plans for a "sweeping

National Socialist boycott that is to be Germany's answer to demonstrations in the US."[22] Discussions about this action occurred at the regime's highest levels. A second piece informed American readers that Minister Goebbels and Chancellor Hitler had a "long conversation" in which they settled on "sharp, though perfectly legal, measures to reach those that are benefiting from this agitation."[23] On April 1, 1933, the Nazis attacked. They painted the Star of David across thousands of Jewish-owned stores. Notices exclaiming "Don't Buy from Jews" and "The Jews Are Our Misfortune" appeared in German cities and towns. Hermann Goering, who held various Nazi leadership posts, including Director of the Four Year Plan in the German economy, also stirred. He summoned several prominent German Jews to his office and demanded they try to block the proposed American embargo.[24]

Hitler's government was not the first to enact anti-Jewish boycotts.[25] Nevertheless, these steps indicate that Nazis leaders viewed the North American campaign with concern. They went so far as to direct their consul in the U.S. to speak with Rabbi Wise about ending the demonstrations.[26] Such anxieties, however, may also have increased the potential danger for German Jewry. As some witnesses observed at the time, American calls for social justice had only hurt those whom the boycotters were trying to help.[27] Calls for a consumer campaign, specifically, bolstered Nazi charges that Jews used economic levers to control global events.[28] As additional boycott activities took shape in other nations, this mentality only served to heighten the Nazis' anxieties, making them more bellicose toward Jewish interests.

American plans for a consumer opposition against Hitlerism resonated globally. Shortly after the American boycott rally, British advocates plastered signs proclaiming "Boycott German Goods" around shops and restaurants.[29] Newspapers touted the Nazis' belief that the American and British efforts were interrelated.[30] In summer 1933, over thirty thousand East End labourers marched noisily to the Hyde Park business district.[31] Along the route, protesters distributed thousands of so-called closing cards imploring merchants to shutter their shops in opposition to German fascism. Such activities were not symbolic. The day after the Hyde Park demonstration, a *Manchester Guardian* article reported the story of a woman who had noticed the words "Made in Germany" printed on boxes belonging to a toy importer. Within minutes, the account tells, hundreds had gathered with such a fury that neither foot nor mounted police could scatter them. "Things were looking very ugly," remarked a law enforcement official identified in the story. "Not until every case had been taken away from the warehouse," the constable recounted, "did the people fully disperse."[32] Newspaper accounts report additional examples, such as twenty-five British passengers that declined to sail aboard the German steamship *Europa*, and a manufacturer that dropped a £14,000 order for German goods.[33]

Of course, these sporadic, private efforts lacked an imprimatur. They also belied a larger reality, one that stymied the boycotters throughout. Prior to the Second World War, dozens of German-American corporations flourished. Particularly this was the case in the entertainment industry.[34] Despite its clear repugnance at what Nazism denoted, Britain nevertheless remained Germany's largest European trading partner. Both democratic governments sustained full diplomatic ties with Hitler's foreign office; both sent delegations the 1936 Berlin Olympics.[35]

This does not mean, however, that consumer opposition was insignificant. Particularly in the pre-dictatorship era, there is some evidence of contest among the parallel issues of Nazi anti-Semitism, and retaliatory boycotts. The German financial paper *Borsen Zeitung* observed, "It is useless to shut our eyes to the fact that boycott propaganda abroad is producing serious results." "Gradually," the account continued, "German products are being replaced by British, Swiss, or Italian goods."[36] This line of reasoning hinted at a subtle prospect. Just as the March 1933 American rally may have had the unintended result of damaging Jews, this article suggests the potential for German misfortune resulting from continued expressions of anti-Semitism. Before 1935, the Nazis regime had not codified its anti-Jewish policies. In this atmosphere, North American activists may have concluded that their pressures were having an effect.

In May 1933, Nazi Economics Minister Alfred Hugenberg decreed certain Jewish retailers exempt from a wave of new anti-Semitic regulations.[37] This moderation also influenced hiring practices, as a few German exporters replaced Christian employees with Jews.[38] However, any moderation of Nazi anti-Jewish policies was fleeting. While some may conclude the Nazis wanted to avoid further provocation, others might observe that such vacillations provoked calls for stricter adherence to Nazi racial mandates. This appears to have been the case. One month after his gesture of philo-Semitism, Minister Hugenberg resigned his post. His successor, Hjalmar Schacht, proved less charitable toward Jewish interests. Speaking in August 1935, Schacht warned, "The Jew must realize that their influence is gone for all times. We desire to keep our people and our culture pure and distinctive."[39] The subsequent institutionalization of these mindsets was not open for public debate. The Nuremberg Laws (1935) were the culmination of proscriptions that appeared soon after Hitler gained power. It is unclear, and scholars must continue to research the issue, whether American pressures softened, exacerbated, or had no meaningful impact on expressions of Nazi anti-Semitism.

The philosophical basis of German fascism was the destruction of European Jewry. North American consumer resistance was not going to alter that ambition. During the 1930s and 1940s, an unlikely relationship emerged in which the non-importation campaign grew in size and scope but was less capable of influencing outcomes. A more pressing question then becomes why the boycotters continued with their work. Short of regime change, what were some of their additional objectives? Moving beyond the received narrative, one that narrowly depicts the boycotts' failures,[40] we hope to reconsider the movement's domestic significance as a device for promoting pluralism. Although American consumerism did not blunt Nazi bigotry, it may have had some impact in helping to confront domestic intolerance, intensifying the drive to transform the national identity, making it more secular.

Part Two: Efforts to Change Americans' Behaviours

On November 21, 1933, Joseph Broadman, a Manhattan doctor, typed a message to the New York offices of the R. H. Macy Company. "You may have noticed," he mentioned, "Mrs. Broadman's account has been quite dormant as of late." The reason for the drop off, he explained, was "we do not wish to purchase anything in your store because of your position on the question of boycotting German merchandise."[41] Indeed, Macy's was one of several New York retailers that rebuffed the non-importation calls, citing a view that consumer institutions should be "kept free from racial, religious, or political considerations."[42] Set against the grittiness of Hitler's regime, however, some people demanded greater vigilance. In Dr. Broadman's case, not only did he shut his family's account, but he also shared his intention to "voice his sentiments with nearly all our friends."[43]

Such letters speak to the domestic side of the anti-Nazi boycott movement. It represents an effort to change American behaviours—both corporate and private—through non-consumption. These sorts of localized tales are not very well remembered. While there is some work that explores the campaign's domestic activities,[44] the dominant boycott discourse remained fixed in global foreign policy questions.[45] Researching the papers of such opposition groups as the "Joint Boycott Committee" and "Non-Sectarian Anti-Nazi League," however, it appears that monitoring local businesses for compliance was a recurring concern. During the 1930s, so-called vigilance committees lodged thousands of reports against non-compliant merchants. These allegations, in turn, unloosed strident letters, such as Dr. Broadman's, leafleting, and also picketing.[46]

These episodes were irregular and did not always produce a tangible gain. But they are not ephemera. Instead, the documents illustrate boycotters contributing to one of the period's social debates, focused on re-sculpting civic attitudes. Americans, too, maintained a heritage of ethno-racial hostilities. While Jim Crowism and Nazism were not the same things, going public in support of persecuted Germans allowed pluralist-minded boycotters to signal their wider preferences.[47] This activity is significant precisely because it was not oriented to harm Nazis. Instead, it was intended to advise Americans that Nazism was dangerous; anti-Jewish bigotry was abhorrent; and consumers should join in efforts to marginalize both phenomena.

Through its radio, print, and press releases, the anti-Nazi campaign led this charge. A primary argument advocates used to convey the rationale was that Nazism threatened more than just German Jews. For example, in April 1934, "Joint Boycott Committee" member Moses Schenkman delivered a radio speech. His remarks opened by noting the specific dangers that Nazism posed to Jews. By his closing, however, he had reframed the risk more broadly. Schenkman told listeners that German anti-Semitism threatened "human justice." "We must stand first as human beings," he declared, "to see that the rights of all human beings are preserved."[48] Sceptics might characterize such language as hyperbolic. Such judgment, we contend, misses a subtler point. During the early 1930s, people in the U.S. were only first envisioning Adolf Hitler.[49] They did not know what, if anything, his worldview had to do with their lives. Radio addresses such as Schenkman's, steeped in universal claims of human security, represented a method by which boycotters attempted to sculpt public knowledge.

Such arguments also permeated the halls of Congress. During the so-called hundred days Congress of 1933, dozens of lawmakers spoke out about the dangers Nazism posed to the U.S. One figure was Loring Black (D-NY). In May 1933, he proclaimed, "I stand before you on the theory this country . . . must not in any way allow our economic resources to continue in power the present government in Germany." Commenting directly on the boycott movement, he continued, "We call upon our people to do something in an economic way to help."[50] Emanuel Celler (D-NY) reinforced these sentiments. "Recent events," he announced to the chamber in mid-April, "seem to indicate that Chancellor Hitler has not moderated his zeal against the Jews and things Jewish." "Hitler," Celler exclaimed, "may not be murdering Jews, but he is undoubtedly killing them economically."[51] Samuel Dickstein (D-NY) was another member sympathetic to boycott plans. In 1934, he had a series of correspondences with Samuel Untermyer, president of the "Non-Sectarian Anti-Nazi League," centred on the conclusion that non-consumption was the "only effective weapon in defense of the basic human rights so ruthlessly destroyed by the Hitler government."[52]

Such legislative pronouncements may have had the effect of rendering boycotters' claims more credible. Themes embedded in congressional discourse influenced public conversations. These connections indicate that, far from "abandoning" imperilled Jews, American boycotters, and some elected officials, sounded an alarm. In October 1937, a boycott group called the Federation of Women's Clubs passed a resolution asking Congressman Dickstein to renew his domestic investigations of German subterfuge. Their message trumpeted familiar creedal ideas. "The ideology and philosophy of Nazism," members asserted, "is calculated to undermine our American institutions of democracy and freedom."[53] This theme also found common cause in a public essay contest, sponsored by officials at the "Non-Sectarian Anti-Nazi League," which focused on the topic of "The Nazi Menace in the US."[54]

However, as was the case with efforts to mould Nazi attitudes overseas, the campaign to prod Americans' behaviours at home was uneven. Evidence of the movement's successes dots the landscape of the period's consumer culture. More than one thousand retailers signed a boycott pledge to avoid German wares;[55] pamphlets and bulletins stoked interest globally;[56] there were high-profile conventions.[57]

Some non-compliant retailers, notably the F. W. Woolworth Company, acquiesced to the pressures and stopped selling German products."[58] But this was not the case for all American concerns. Continuing to tender German merchandise may have reflected practical considerations, such as the New York florist that had accumulated a large inventory of German products prior to Hitler's government.[59] Likewise, a theatre manager at New York's Fifty-Fifth Street Playhouse declared himself "much in sympathy" with the boycotters aims, but was contractually obligated to screen certain German films, as discontinuing the run would

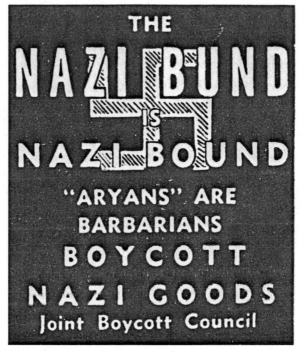

Joint Boycott Committee envelope stamp (1936). Author's personal collection.

produce "unemployment and suffering to our employees, many of whom are Jewish."[60]

In other cases, however, such as with the General Motors Corporation, boycotters' rationales proved ineffective. General Motors' president, Alfred Sloan, despised Nazism. He recognized that Hitlerism posed hazards to world peace. However, he also concluded that corporations must conduct their foreign business irrespective of a government's political orientation.[61] Sloan saw in the German market a potential for great profit. Under his leadership, General Motors had acquired Opel, the most venerable German automobile manufacturer. Defending this investment was an obvious reason for Sloan to eschew American boycott calls. However, there is also evidence that prominent executives, those who worked with Sloan, supported various Nazi goals.[62] Reviewing snippets of communications between American boycotters and General Motors executives does not reveal anything unexpected. What the back-and-forth illustrates, primarily, is the ways that non-consumption calls continued to crop up in domestic debates.[63]

On March 11, 1936, "Joint Boycott Council" Chairman Joseph Tenenbaum sent a letter to Sloan. The purpose of his message was to learn if the carmaker was shipping merchandise aboard a Nazi-owned vessel. In addition, Tenenbaum asked Sloan why he conducted business with a nation that had a "policy of persecution toward Catholics, Protestants, Jews, and Labor."[64] In some ways, the letter seems cursory. A familiar template, unpacked in secular, creedal language presses the idea that Americans of all stripes had cause to fear from Nazism. But Tenenbaum certainly knew that Sloan would not abandon his controlling interest of Opel. It was a significant asset on his balance sheet. When viewed in this light, Tenenbaum's letter appears less intended to persuade than to put General Motors on notice.

Predictably, the boycotters' pleas did not convince the carmaker to alter their practices. Sloan's reply message acknowledged that General Motors contracted with German ships. "As a matter of fact," he told Tenenbaum, "our policy in such matters is to use all the transportation companies that we can." Sloan only indirectly addressed the issue of German persecution of its citizens. "General Motors," he explained, "deals with problems without respect to politics, religion, or any other consideration . . . without discrimination and without prejudice."[65] Later messages to Tenenbaum, authored by additional company executives, also noted this policy of "dealing equally with all parties . . . in perfect fairness and without discrimination or prejudice."[66]

Such communications did more than rebuff boycotters' calls. They contested the boycotters' self-appointed positions. During challenging economic times, General Motors' managers may well have resented the efforts to infuse social and ethical questions into their affairs. To spend time answering harrying letters, rather than running their operations, could bolster perceptions that the boycotters—not Nazis—posed the truest danger to General Motors' bottom line. The residue of this frustration is visible in an exchange of letters between Tenenbaum and the corporate general manager, E. C. Riley. "I am very glad that you have brought to our attention your understanding that we were showing favoritism toward German shippers," he wrote to Tenenbaum. "Particularly as this understanding is incorrect," he continued, "perhaps you in turn will want to correct your source."[67] Riley's message then proceeded to list various minutiae related to General Motors' shipping. Not to be outdone, Tenenbaum shortly replied, including in his missive brochures for non-German steamships that he averred the company might wish to patronize.

These letters teach us about the intersection of consumerism and politics in 1930s America. On the one hand, there were people that concluded that Hitlerism represented a grave threat to collective liberty. They wanted to use their purchasing power to isolate Hitler and the ideas he spewed. On the other hand, however, there were citizens willing to accommodate the new German regime. They didn't mind Nazism and wanted to conduct business as usual. Such divergences produced a great deal of acrimony at the time. It remains a source of disagreement in public memory. Studying the boycotts as part of this domestic debate teaches us more about the overall movement. It also shines a light on the period's larger conversations about the future world that Americans hoped to fashion.

Conclusion

When asked about the efficacy of the non-consumption campaign, Rabbi Stephen Wise explained, "We must speak out. If that is unavailing, at least we shall have spoken."[68] In voicing this sentiment, Wise betrayed his belief that words matter. Language cannot be undone. Sceptics, however, might recall the adage "talk is cheap." They would contend the support shown to the anti-Nazi campaign is unworthy of greater retrospective analysis. In this essay, however, we have argued that this view misses the wider mark. What makes the boycotters' activities pertinent to later generations is their relevance to an interpretation of U.S. responses to Nazi anti-Semitism that does not restate the claim that Americans turned away.[69]

Shortly after Adolf Hitler's rise to power in Germany, some in the U.S. initiated arguments that held that Nazi anti-Semitism did violence to democratic freedoms. Repudiating Nazism—and, specifically, its negative portrayal of Jews—contributed to a much larger campaign to reconfigure mainstream American attitudes. Evidence that citizens, both private and public, opposed Nazi bigotry appeared in periodicals, political statements, and cultural products. It also coalesced around a non-consumption effort. During the 1930s, this movement attained global recognition. In the U.S., specifically, it became part of a larger effort in which citizens promoted a more pluralist worldview. This existing drive received additional momentum with the nation's entry into the Second World War, and the movement that emerged ultimately outstripped all efforts that preceded it.

10

CANADA'S CITIZEN HOUSEWIVES

Cold War Anti-Communism and the Limits of Maternalism

JULIE GUARD

ROM THE LATE 1930s until the early 1950s, the Housewives Consumers Association (HCA) mobilized thousands of women and men across Canada in campaigns for fair prices, a managed economy, and state ownership of essential foods such as milk, meat, and bread. The HCA accused elected officials of pandering to business and demanded public policies that advanced the interests of ordinary people rather than those of capital. It pushed for the appointment of genuine consumer and labour representatives to government policy-making bodies (such as the Milk Control Board) and the investigation of illegal price-setting in major food industries. To press its demands, the HCA organized boycotts, rallies, pickets, parades, conferences, and petition campaigns. It mounted a series of delegations to Ottawa, where the Housewives and their allies buttonholed MPs to lobby support for their demands and came face-to-face with Cabinet ministers, whom they boldly accused of ineptitude, duplicity, and deceit. In short, they caused a ruckus.

Some Housewives were not only mothers and homemakers but also communists and left-leaning social democrats, and they demanded many of the same reforms as the rest of the left. But the organization's apparent conformity to prevailing gender norms effectively obscured their radicalism. At a time when women were barely-tolerated interlopers in politics, the Housewives' gender was critical to their ability to initiate and sustain this broadly based social movement. Indeed, far from presenting a problem for the HCA, their domestic identities shielded them from criticism by providing what the historian Temma Kaplan has called "maternalist cover."[1] Like generations of politically active women, they used the pervasive notion that motherhood was inherently apolitical to advocate radical social and economic change without appearing to challenge the social order.[2] In contrast to the labour, party, and ethnic left, the Housewives spoke as consumers, a categorization that identified them as safely apolitical. The Housewives thus achieved that to which the male left could only aspire: they united middle- and working-class women and men of all political stripes in a grassroots social movement while advancing a left-wing agenda and engaging citizens in a wide-ranging debate about the proper role of the state. Tapping Canadians' widespread outrage, they raised popular expectations about the responsibilities of government and enlarged popular notions about the rights of citizens, helping to shift mainstream public views to the left.

Women in mid-twentieth century Canada were, and arguably continue to be, political anomalies—out of place, susceptible to ridicule, and tolerated so long as they appeared to conform in all other ways to unthreatening femininity. The Housewives, like other politically active women in many times and places, overturned the obstacles they encountered by virtue of their gender by using motherhood as a justification for political action. Their ability to present themselves as innocuous homemakers motivated solely by their concern for their own families and those of others legitimated their incursions into male-defined public space as a form of activist motherhood. Arrayed in matronly frocks and picture hats, the Housewives embodied conservative maternalism even as they marched down the streets of cities and towns across the country bearing picket signs denouncing high corporate profits and urging others to "buy no butter"—or meat, milk, or other essential items—until the state intervened in the market to "roll back prices."

The HCA was originally established as the Toronto Housewives Association in 1937 by a small group of neighbours, all of them political neophytes, who were outraged that the province was allowing milk prices to rise while Depression-era wages stagnated or fell. These apolitical women were soon joined by communist women who had been organizing for some time against rising prices and who, along with eight hundred others, founded the Toronto Housewives Association at a noisy meeting in

Toronto's Labour Temple in November 1937.[3] Communist Housewives distinguished between their party work, which they perceived as political, and their participation in the HCA, which they regarded as an expression of their concerns as mothers and homemakers. Even so, as left activists, they embodied a form of radical motherhood that impelled them to take action against injustice. In a 1938 article in the communist *Clarion*, Housewives member and communist Alice Cooke reminded women that the Depression "very seriously threatened" their homes, but there were "things we can do as good housewives" to defend "that which women cherish, the welfare of their homes and families." She urged them to join the Housewives, an organization committed to a "program of work and wages, and to fight the monopolies which are responsible for the high cost of living."[4] Communist labour activist Pat Chytyk, a Housewife from Sudbury, interviewed many years later, explained that, unlike her other activities, which included organizing for the left-led Mine, Mill and Smelter Workers union and involvement in the Mine-Mill women's auxiliary and the left-identified Association of United Ukrainian Canadians, her work in the Housewives was "not political." On the contrary, she explained, organizing against high prices was "just the [natural concern] of women."[5]

From 1937 to 1939, the last years of the Depression, the Housewives mobilized women and men in at least three provinces to protest the government's failure, despite stagnant wages, widespread poverty, and most outrageous of all, rising corporate profits, to ameliorate the rising cost of essentials, such as milk, bread, and fuel, or to provide relief for single men or unemployment insurance. When Canada entered the Second World War in September 1939, Housewives organizations were well established in three major cities, Toronto, Montreal, and Vancouver, as well as in small and medium-sized cities across Ontario and British Columbia, with a total membership of about fifteen thousand women who mobilized against rising prices, high rents, and low relief rates.[6] Through the war years, they played an important and highly visible public role as volunteer price-checkers for the federal government's very popular program of wartime price control, which, as Joseph Tohill observes in this volume, was both more successful and less ambitious than its U.S. counterpart, the Office of Price Administration. But despite their commitment to the Wartime Prices and Trade Board's Consumer Branch, whose program, as Tohill points out, presented no threat to either Liberal policies or business interests, they also remained vigilant in their defence of consumers.

When federal officials blamed shortages of essential items on hoarding by consumers, the Housewives pointed instead to profiteering and the state's failure to control it.

At war's end, they galvanized thousands in a campaign supported by a majority of Canadians that called on the state to maintain into the peace the price control legislation that had kept prices low, halted inflation, and ensured equal access to essential items during the war. They launched their new round of protests in spring 1946, less than a year after war's end, when the Liberals' attempt to wind down the price control program led to sudden and drastic price increases. Despite government assurances that the process would be well-planned and orderly,[7] a divided Cabinet, advised by inexperienced bureaucrats, bungled the economic transition from state control to the free reign of the market.[8] Prices on essential goods, especially food, rose across the country, creating significant hardships for some wage-dependent families. A study by the Toronto Welfare Council found that a family of five needed $40.11 per week, or an annual income of $2,085.72, for food and other basic needs, but 1.75 million earners had an income of under $2,000 in 1946.[9] Canadians responded with a rising tide of anger, and consumer protests, led by the Housewives, quickly became front-page news.[10]

"Buyers' Resistance" Threatens the State

The HCA grew steadily through the next two years as inflation continued to erode people's standard of living. By the end of 1947, inflation had increased by almost 15 percent over the previous year, while food costs had increased by over 22 percent.[11] Manitoba HCA president Anne Ross warned that housewives like herself were "at our wit's end trying to make ends meet" and "getting progressively more disillusioned with the Government's attitude."[12] Mrs. E. Molinski, president of the Mothers' Club of the politically progressive All People's Church and an ally of the Manitoba Housewives, accused the government of hypocrisy, noting that politicians "express concern over the nutrition and health of the citizens" but then "jeopardize the health of children" by failing to control rising food prices. Such policies were "not sensible," she lamented, "not to mention [not] being Christian."[13]

In the context of the continuing crisis, the HCA's maternal appeal, combined with their extraordinary ability to mobilize popular support for campaigns demanding more government accountability, policy in the interest of ordinary people, and state intervention in the economy, became toxic to the Liberals. HCA campaigns fuelled what the press dubbed a "rising tide" of public protest that kept price control on the agenda of the House of Commons through the latter half of the 1940s.[14] To the embarrassment of the government, the Housewives used official Dominion Bureau of Statistics data to prove their argument that the average wage earner was unable to "provide adequately for family needs," and that welfare agencies were becoming "seriously alarmed" about rising rates of malnutrition. The press confirmed the severity of inflation. Although overall weekly wages rose an average of 10.7 percent between 1947 and 1948, the official cost of living rose even more, by 16.8 percent, cutting real wages by 6.1 percent.[15] By eliminating "luxuries" such as tea and coffee, the Toronto Welfare Council calculated that a family of four could subsist on $45 a week, but even such a minimal diet would have been beyond the means of the many households that survived on the average weekly wage of $41.25. The Housewives disputed even that figure, arguing, along with organized labour, that the official cost-of-living index, developed during the war, significantly underestimated real costs.[16]

From 1946 through 1948, HCA-led boycotts of over-priced food and other essentials became front page news, not only in Canada but also abroad.[17] In January 1948, *Time* reported on Canada's "price war," in which shoppers fought meat prices that had risen as much as 25 percent in two months.[18] Even basic foods such as cabbage rose from five cents to 15 cents a pound. Lettuce, which Finance Minister Douglas Abbott had labelled a "luxury" vegetable, was selling at 59 cents a head.[19] The Housewives' national "buyers' resistance" campaign, together with many women demanding "the cheapest" items "in the store," forced Toronto retailers to drop meat prices by as much as 8 cents per pound. Yet even with lower prices, meat sales declined by as much as 50 percent, prompting the liberal-populist *Toronto Star* to encourage the Housewives to "hit 'im again, Missus," while announcing, "we are winning!"[20]

By their peak in early 1948, consumer activists in some thirty-nine Housewives associations across the country were mobilizing their friends and neighbours in protest against the government's failure to contain the rising cost of living. They tapped the collective outrage of a nation that had been promised a peace dividend of prosperity and full employment but instead faced spiralling inflation, stagnant wages, and widespread profiteering. Women across the country organized under the Housewives' banner, constituting a nation-wide network that stretched from coast to coast with thousands of members and the support of a small army of allies.[21] Their unfeminine tendency to confront prominent politicians and criticize the heads of powerful industries was not merely masked by their maternalism, but construed, instead, as the very embodiment of responsible motherhood. The Housewives were endorsed by community, service, religious, and professional organizations; labour councils, federations, unions, and auxiliaries; clerics, social workers, and public health authorities. Its leaders served on prestigious committees alongside well-known philanthropists, rabbis, pastors, social reformers, business leaders, and socialites, and they were interviewed frequently by the press.

"What a Band of Determined Women Can Do"

In reality, the Housewives were both married women who managed households *and* vociferous critics of the business-friendly policies of Prime Minister William Lyon Mackenzie King's Liberal Party. As homemakers themselves, they consistently identified women's "hot button" issues with precise accuracy; as activists, they provided opportunities for ordinary people, particularly women, to take direct action without having to join a "political" organization or embrace unfamiliar doctrines. Their linkage of maternalism and activism, long a strategy of women on the left, deployed in many times and places, including by middle-class women in the early twentieth-century women's movement, helped make the Housewives the best-known and broadly subscribed social movement of the postwar period. Its leaders were recognized as authorities on matters of specific concern to women, as well as economic issues that mattered to the nation.[22] Indeed, the reputations of several prominent women with established records of public service, such as Elizabeth Brown, Lily Phelps, Dorise Neilsen, and Rae Luckock, were enhanced by their role in the Housewives. Others, such as the Canadian novelist Margaret Laurence, who began her writing career as a fledgling journalist under the byline of Peggy Laurence writing for the Manitoba *Housewives' News*, the communist *Westerner*, and the short-lived, left-wing *Winnipeg News*, later became famous.[23]

Powerful links to their communities affirmed the Housewives' authenticity as mothers and homemakers and reinforced their claim that they were ordinary women motivated only by their concern for families, not abstract political philosophies. They were active and engaged members of their communities, applauded for their civic responsibility, and familiar to their neighbours. The Housewives transformed traditional women's social events into progressive political activism. Women across the country chatted with Housewives across the back fence and at the doorstep as the HCA canvassed for signatures. Members attended regular monthly meetings and raised funds through euchre parties, book fairs, and white elephant sales. Their friends and neighbours joined them in rambunctious "bread-and-butter" and "prices" parades and rallies in the streets of their towns and cities. Thousands attended Housewives-sponsored public meetings and conferences at local schools, churches, and community halls; attended their fund-raising social teas, dramatic evenings, and picnics; and signed their protest postcards on local street corners.

The Housewives were most passionate about and rallied the broadest support for the campaign for peacetime price control, affirmed by years of consistent lobbying, including countless delegations to city councils, many to provincial legislatures, and five to Ottawa. Countless supporters wrote letters to their local newspapers encouraging others to join the organization and support their boycotts, congratulating the housewives for forcing the government into action and for providing an inspiring example of how much "a band of determined women can do."[24]

Price Control and the CCF

The Housewives' maternal appeal created a "Housewives" problem for the Liberal government, which was exacerbated by Canadians' shift to the political left in the mid-1940s. The rising popularity of the social-democratic Co-operative Commonwealth Federation (CCF), a party to the left of the Liberals, was a result, at least in part, of its vocal support for continuing federal price controls in peacetime. The CCF's 1948 campaign, for example, called for the "re-imposition of price controls on all the necessities of life—food, clothing and fuel," a renewal of subsidies, and a new tax on excess profits. Such demands echoed those of the Housewives.[25] The connection was more than incidental, as CCF leaders openly allied themselves with the Housewives. M. J. Coldwell, the party's leader, and Stanley Knowles, its most prominent member of parliament, congratulated the Housewives on their "roll-back-prices" campaigns, assuring them that, together, the Housewives and the CCF could "influence" the government on the price issue.[26]

With elections in the offing and the CCF's popularity surpassing that of the Liberals, the latter had to take seriously the imminent threat of a CCF victory in Ontario and the possibility, albeit still remote, of an eventual CCF government in Ottawa.[27] The Housewives exacerbated that threat by contradicting government reassurances that Canadians were relatively well off and that real prosperity was imminent. Their press releases, leaflets, and briefs to Royal Commissions, the cabinet, and other government bodies regularly cited government data, including wage and profit rates and the cost-of-living index, together with evidence from health experts demonstrating that high prices pushed "protective foods" out of reach and led to malnourishment. Their demands that government take action to control rising prices were a constant reminder that the Liberals had failed to meet popular expectations of a postwar world of general prosperity, full employment, and social and economic security—expectations that had been encouraged by the government's own wartime promises.

By mobilizing women on everyday concerns, they not only reminded voters of the Liberals' failures, but they helped to normalize the previously unthinkable possibility of a CCF government. On countless occasions, the Housewives had organized dozens, hundreds, and even thousands of members and supporters, often on short notice, in response to a sudden price increase, a change in policy, or a speech by a cabinet minister or other public figure. In communities across the country, supporters— both women and men—had expressed their dissatisfaction with the government by sending hundreds of letters and postcards to Prime Minister King demanding government accountability and state control of prices. The HCA's support for state control of at least some aspects of the economy and direct democratic participation in policy-making, proposals they shared with the CCF, helped to advance such ideas as reasonable socialist alternatives to a system that was demonstrably not working.

Fostering Communism

Liberal anxieties reached a peak in April 1948, when the Housewives, their popularity undiminished despite relentless red-baiting, led some 500 delegates from across the country in a mass rally on Parliament Hill, bringing with them the biggest petition ever received by Parliament, signed by over 740,000 Canadians who called on the Liberals to "roll back prices."[28] By this time, the Housewives had become a serious irritant to the Liberal government, which had already gone so far as to fund a rival consumer organization, the Canadian Association of Consumers (CAC), led by elite women with ties to the Liberal party and the socially conservative National Council of Women of Canada. CAC President Mrs. R. J. Marshall did her best to downplay the Liberal connection, insisting that, despite receiving $15,000 in start-up funds, the organization would henceforth be "self-supporting" and "free of political, industrial, and trade control."[29]

This, their fifth delegation to Ottawa, was a turning point for the Housewives, who had so far managed to survive anticommunist attacks with minimal damage. The Cold War anticommunism that had taken hold across the continent emboldened the government that had previously met with them, however reluctantly, feeling obliged to do so by their maternalism and the breadth of their support. By redefining them publicly as radical political agitators who were not genuinely interested in prices or the well-being of ordinary people, and indeed, were neither loyal Canadians nor genuine housewives, but agents of a hostile foreign power, it could safely refuse to see them. Invoking anticommunist rhetoric, Finance Minister Abbott announced to "thunderous applause" from all but the CCF MPs in the House of Commons that the government would no longer receive Housewives' delegations. Because the delegation's "primary purpose" was to "foster communist propaganda," he argued, the government actually fulfilled its duty to citizens by refusing to "facilitate movements of this kind."[30] Not only did the government refuse to receive the delegation but it detailed Royal Canadian Mounted Police (RCMP) officers to bar them from attempting to enter the visitors' gallery of the House.

What made it possible for the Liberals, who had endured the Housewives' criticism for years, fearing the political consequences of ignoring this very popular movement, to turn against them? Escalating Cold War anxieties in general, bolstered by a media campaign that targeted the Housewives as not only a particularly dangerous threat to the state but an outrageous fraud perpetrated against naïve but well-meaning Canadians persuaded the Cabinet that they could snub the Housewives with little political risk. As the Housewives prepared for the culmination of their biggest campaign, right-wing newspapers across the county ran articles couched in hyperbolic Cold War rhetoric that purported to expose them as a secret "Communist front" organization whose real objective was not lower prices, but the "the violent seizure of Canada's material and human resources to enrich the world's most tyrannical dictatorship." Sneeringly suggesting that their very name was a fraud, and, invoking the pervasive nativism and xenophobia of the times, these "so-called" housewives, they reported, were not even real Canadians. On the contrary, they warned, the recently formed CAC advised real housewives to beware of alleged consumer organizations which did not contain "Canadian" in the name.[31]

Maternalism had not only enabled the Housewives to claim political space; it had shielded them, for almost a decade, from precisely this kind of demonization as political subversives. Inevitably, as in any post-war organization that did not exclude communists, accusations of "communist domination" erupted periodically, but the Housewives' claims to domestic femininity had inoculated them, at least temporarily, against the red-baiting that decimated the male-dominated left. But Cold War tensions were escalating just as the Housewives' popularity was at its height and they believed their goals were within reach. Internationally, the 1948 Prague coup, the Berlin Blockade, and the inauguration of the Marshall Plan evinced the hardening of East-West antagonism. Domestically, official anticommunism—including the 1946 Taschereau-Kellock Commission on the Gouzenko affair and the subsequent spy trials of twelve Canadians, security screening of public employees, and the reactivation, in February 1948, of Quebec's anticommunist Padlock law—signalled the government's turn from a policy of apparent liberal tolerance to the explicit suppression of dissent. Such measures both encouraged and reflected hardening popular attitudes toward communism. By the late 1940s, Cold War anticommunism was no longer just a weapon of political conservatives and corporations against their critics; liberals and especially noncommunist leftists, anxious to avoid accusations of "Communist control," denounced communists and purged anyone suspected of being one from their organizations.[32]

A "Communist Racket"

In anticipation of the HCA's April 1948 delegation, anticommunist attacks on the HCA erupted in the right-wing press. Encouraged by the Finance Minister's refusal to receive the Housewives, anticommunist papers launched a frenzied attack in which they claimed that the Housewives were not really housewives at all. Instead, they insisted, they masqueraded as housewives only to "dupe" innocent women into supporting their "protest-against-prices business," which, they charged, was no real social movement but a "Communist racket."[33] Seasoned Cold Warriors decried the Housewives as by far the worst kind of subversives and ranked them as "the most effective Communist front the Reds have had for a long time."[34] In the hyperbolic context of the Cold War, the Housewives were transformed in these accounts from outraged mothers and therefore merely irrelevant into a sinister and dangerous fraud.

What made these housewife-activists so dangerous? Some were, in fact, active in the broad procommunist ethnic and labour left, including some Communist Party members. Although a tiny minority of Housewives, communists were disproportionately represented among the HCA's most active members, making it an easy target for red-baiters. But the Housewives' worst offence appears to have been their shattering of traditional notions of femininity. Anticommunists drew on specifically gendered arguments to denounce communist Housewives as imposters; as exceptionally dangerous subversives who used "high-sounding names" to trap "unwary" (but real) housewives into "doing the work of Moscow."[35]

Gender, as Cold War history demonstrates, plays an important albeit largely unrecognized role in the definition of political subversion. The right's persecution of the left and liberal women who played an important role in the New Deal administration, as the historian Landon Storrs has so compellingly shown, vilified progressive women, many of whom were also feminists, by portraying them as inherently unfeminine and over-sexed. These traits, the New Deal's opponents charged, were not only unseemly but also rendered such women susceptible to radical and un-American influences.[36] Radical women have typically faced accusations that they are unnatural mothers, fraudulent housewives, and immoral women, on the assumption that their unorthodox political views are de facto proof of their failure as women. The exaggerated suspicions of Communist women were clearly at work in the 1949 McCarthy-era show trials of the House Committee on Un-American Activities (HUAC). Former U.S. Communists and HUAC star witnesses Elizabeth Bentley and Hede Massing, who testified against their former comrades, were portrayed as both dangerous subversives capable of twisting the minds of unwary women and as naïve and gullible women whose subversion was directed by men.[37] By the late 1940s, the conviction that Communist women were, by definition, women of bad character was so entrenched that the logical inconsistency of these beliefs proved no obstacle to their assertion by a wide range of commentators.

But radical women have also resisted these damning indictments of their femininity. Consider, for instance, the wives of Communist Party leaders and activists who were arrested under the U.S. Alien and Registration Act of 1940—commonly called the Smith Act—which provided the legal justification for official persecution of Communists. Like Canada's Housewives, these women deployed maternalism to legitimate their activism. Challenging the assumptions that denied maternal identities for communist women, their public appeals for aid for the families of the Smith Act victims asked potential supporters to consider whether "Family Devotion" was truly "Subversive."[38]

Like the Smith Act organizers in the U.S., members of the House-wives Association identified themselves as "ordinary women" with the same concerns as others, regardless of their political views. Their claims were supported by their noncommunist sisters. Housewives President Rae Luckock, a left-wing social democrat and long-term member of the CCF, responded to anticommunist attacks that demonized particular Housewives by instructing the press that, although she was not a Communist, it should not matter if she was. "I'm a democrat," she snapped at reporters. "Are you?"[39] Red-baiters asserted that the association was "under the direct control of Communists," although the evidence to support that claim was thin, based in part on assumptions that, as women, they were incapable of mounting such successful campaigns on their own and particularly susceptible to party guile.[40] Even the "Communist officials" who were said to "head up" Housewives groups were assumed to be "dominated" by their male comrades. Not only was their family status no longer an antidote to red-baiting, but the political affiliations of their husbands, brothers, and other relatives had become evidence against them. Ignoring the women's own activist histories, some of them extensive, attackers cited Housewives' marriages to known communists as evidence that the HCA was "contaminated" by "Reds."[41]

The Limits of Maternalism

By the 1950s, red-baiting had eroded the Housewives' credibility by undermining the maternalism that had shielded them from attack. The CCF quietly dropped its demands for postwar price control, and, at the urging of its Ontario Women's Committee, expelled Rae Luckock, a former CCF Member of the Ontario Legislature and one of its most prominent activists, from the party.[42] Thoroughly demonized, their good reputation in tatters, and their collective voice silenced, the HCA lost its broad popular appeal and thus its ability to influence state policy in the interests of consumers. The Cold War demonization of those who dared to challenge the state as dangerous subversives eventually silenced not just the HCA, but virtually all community-based protest. The socialist reforms that many people had accepted as practical solutions to the social and economic chaos of the previous decades were discredited and their proponents silenced. The Housewives were particularly vulnerable to anticommunist attack, both as women who, despite their maternalist credentials, engaged in political activism that subverted feminine norms of docile domesticity, and because of their close ties to the broad communist left. After more than a decade of struggle for the interests of consumers, by the end of the 1940s, the Housewives were marginalized and demonized as enemies of the state. Yet their decade of successful organizing testifies to the largely unrecognized power of women who have used their genuine identities as housewives and mothers strategically to demand concessions from the state. It reminds us, as well, of the historical continuum of activist citizen-consumers who have contributed significantly to the shaping of the progressive state.

11

"THE CONSUMER GOES TO WAR"

Consumer Politics in the United States and Canada during the Second World War

JOSEPH TOHILL

ORTH AMERICAN CONSUMERS experienced little deprivation as a
result of the Second World War. "Never before in the history of
human conflict," the Canadian-born, American price controller
John Kenneth Galbraith later said, "has there been so much talk of sacrifice and so little sacrifice." Recent studies of the wartime home front
have confirmed that, for consumers living the high life on full employment, higher wages, and controlled prices, the Second World War really
was "the good war." The orgy of consumer spending, which raised the
spectre of the kind of inflationary spiral and collapse that had followed
the First World War, led to a wartime politics of consumption focused on
discouraging selfish behaviours, like frivolous or black-market spending.
Yet wartime consumer politics also involved high principles: if not exactly
sacrifice, then public service, fair shares, and democracy.[1]

This side of wartime consumer politics, which was not confined by
national borders, made the war years a crucial but understudied phase
of the twentieth-century consumer movement.[2] Drawing ideas and
lessons from one another, American and Canadian consumer activists
sought to organize consumers while mobilizing for war. The creation of

agencies responsible for regulating consumption and stabilizing the cost of living provided activists with an opportunity to mobilize consumer citizens and expand consumers' rights and representation in economic policy-making. Anti-inflationary measures, particularly the price control and rationing programs implemented by the U.S. Office of Price Administration (OPA) and the Canadian Wartime Prices and Trade Board (WPTB), imposed a raft of new public obligations on consumers—to buy wisely, to never pay more than ceiling prices, to obey rationing regulations, and to actively monitor compliance with price and rationing regulations in their everyday purchases. In exchange, state policy-makers assured consumers of the benefits of "economic citizenship"—a "Wartime Consumer's Bill of Rights," in the words of the OPA—which included the right to economic stability, fair dealings in the marketplace, and equal access to essential goods in short supply.[3]

Consumer activists seized the opportunity presented by the creation of wartime controls on consumption to advance their agenda. Through a succession of consumer agencies primarily within the OPA in the United States and the WPTB in Canada, they aggressively promoted consumers' rights and representation, and they actively mustered unprecedented mass support for their social democratic vision of consumer society. Mobilized consumer-citizens were the "shock troops" in the home-front battle against inflation, but they also gave weight to the efforts of consumer activists to wrest from other economic interests—and often-reluctant politicians and policy-makers—a greater share of economic and political power for consumers.

Broad similarities as well as differences characterized the visions and agendas—and successes and failures—of activists within these government agencies, and a range of views and political orientations characterized consumer activism within and across national borders. Yet Canadian and American wartime consumer activists saw themselves as part of a transnational consumer movement, united across national borders by a belief in empowering grassroots consumers not only as savvy shoppers but also as a collective force deserving of a vital role in political and economic decision-making.[4] Wartime consumer activists on both sides of the border envisioned a more humane economic system that would uplift those with the most meagre pocketbooks, give a voice to the voiceless, democratize economic decision-making, and, thus, make the capitalist economy itself more democratic.

They believed that realizing this vision required consumer representation in government and the backing of a mass movement of consumer

citizens—particularly but not exclusively women—who identified themselves in a political sense as consumers. In essence, activists sought to make
the vast consuming public not just the beneficiaries of, but also active
participants in, the state's protection and promotion of the consumer
interest. By connecting mostly female middle- and working-class consumers to national policy-makers, consumer activists within the OPA
and the WPTB hoped to facilitate policy-making from the bottom up.
Their long-term goal was not only to help win the war, but also to "win the
peace" by making the consumer's significant role in the political economy
of the war a permanent fixture of postwar society.[5]

During the war, political consumerists successfully mobilized consumer citizens and enjoyed some limited success in shaping wartime economic policies and controls. However, their attempts to extend wartime
achievements into peacetime largely failed, as would-be national consumer organizations faltered and the influence of consumerist policy-
makers sharply declined.[6]

*   *   *

No one articulated the consumerist vision of the era more strongly than
prominent and politically well-connected American consumer activist
Caroline Farrar Ware. "We consumers have a big job to do in this war,"
she declared in the opening salvo of her wartime manifesto, *The Consumer
Goes to War: A Guide to Victory on the Home Front.* "No one of us consumers
can escape his wartime duty. We must be at our battle stations twenty-four
hours a day. . . . We must learn to be good consumers [and] understand the
strategy and tactics of the consumer front." A strong "consumer front,"
asserted Ware, meant "wise buying by consumers and careful conservation" in order to "release all possible resources to work for our fighting
men." It meant consumers playing an active part in protecting the American standard of living through "an all-out attack on inflation, with war
bonds, taxes, and effective price control." And it meant "responsible consumer citizens" playing "an intelligent part in shaping national policies"
and ensuring that the new national agencies created for war and the peace
to follow would be "conceived in the spirit of democracy and develop
democratic procedures."[7]

Ware's book, published in late 1942, was in part a practical guide to
wartime living, in part a political and economic polemic. It encapsulated
many of the ideas and goals that had, during the 1930s, motivated Ware's

public life as one of the central figures in the consumer movement and would, during the war, shape her actions as the driving force behind every permutation of consumer representation within the Office of Price Administration. Along with wise buying and conservation advice, Ware's wartime treatise advanced the movement's two interrelated political objectives: first, a permanent, national department of the consumer, which would give consumers a "seat at the table" and protect and promote consumers' interests in the way that the commerce and labour departments did for business and labour, respectively; and, second, mobilizing consumers as a powerful countervailing force to the business and corporate interests that dominated the American political economy. At her most radical, Ware (a social and economic historian by training) envisioned the achievement of these goals as the basis for a dramatic reordering of political and economic relations that would give consumers a central role in the political economy of consumer capitalism. Such an outcome, Ware suggested, would constitute a "revolution" that would "reshape our way of life."[8]

Even before the United States had entered the war, American consumer activists such as Ware had drawn on a well-developed consumer movement and precedents set by New Deal consumer agencies to establish the first war-related consumer agency in North America. Ware was the motive force behind the Consumer Division of President Franklin D. Roosevelt's National Defense Advisory Commission (NDAC), insisting that her boss, Harriet Elliott, assert her equality of status with fellow commissioners who represented industry and labour.

Yet even before Pearl Harbor brought America into the war, some of the Consumer Division's erstwhile New Deal allies and the ascendant anti–New Deal coalition of industry lobby groups, the right-wing press, and conservatives in Congress had already both done much to check the ambitions of Ware and the Consumer Division. Within the OPA, into which the Price Stabilization and Consumer Divisions of the NDAC were merged in mid-1941, the technocratic vision of Leon Henderson's price controllers clashed with the participatory policy-making vision of the Consumer Division. The Price Division's male economists and lawyers, who dominated the OPA, regularly dismissed the Consumer Division's would-be policy-makers—most of them women—as wide-eyed idealists and cast themselves in the role of "hard-headed" realists and experts. At the same time, the mounting political attacks on the OPA in the fall of 1941 often focused on the Consumer Division and its appointees. It was largely to blunt such attacks that the circle of New Deal policy-makers

Caroline Farrar Ware, seated at her desk in the Consumer Division of the OPA in October 1941. Ware (right) was the key person in the Division and the lobbying effort for the creation of a consumer department. Here she converses with an assistant. Although Ware was adamant that the Consumer Division was not a woman's division, women made up most of its staff at all levels. Library of Congress LC-USE6-D-000393.

around OPA Administrator Leon Henderson sacrificed the controversial division, downgrading it to the point of irrelevance in late 1941 and 1942.[9]

Only in late 1943 did consumerists succeed in re-establishing a role in OPA policy-making. By then the anti–New Deal coalition had succeeded in purging the OPA of Henderson's "clique" of "arrogant left-winger bureaucrats" and "Communistic" New Deal professors (notably John Kenneth Galbraith) who sought "to strangle the normal and healthy activities of business."[10] Henderson's replacement in summer 1943, New York advertising executive Chester Bowles, initially placated the OPA's conservative detractors. As a successful businessman, he "passed [their] acid test." Bowles, who brought the salesmanship and finesse of an advertising man to a job that required both, reorganized the OPA, opening the door for the first time to input from business into the agency's policy-making.[11]

But Bowles was also an ardent New Dealer who possessed sufficient liberal credentials that his appointment counteracted the negative effect on labour, consumer, and other liberal groups of the forced resignation

of Henderson's circle.[12] Bowles's conception of the OPA also created
space for the revival of consumerist hopes. He envisioned the OPA as an
exemplar of what he termed "Big Democracy in Action"—vigorous public
administration backed by widespread input from all stakeholders, including consumers. Among the host of new policy advisers he appointed were
a consumer relations adviser and a consumer advisory committee, a veri-
table who's who of the most prominent American consumer activists of
the era, including Ware.

Yet despite Bowles's New Deal proclivities and his support for political consumerist goals of representation and mass organization, the OPA's
consumer advisers struggled to make their voices heard in the wake of
the OPA's political struggles in 1943, which left the OPA chastened and
enhanced the influence of business throughout the organization. Unlike
its now-defunct Consumer Division, the new OPA Consumer Advisory
Committee possessed only consultative powers and was excluded from
most of the OPA's policy-making councils. Under pressure from business
lobby groups, the OPA abandoned key consumer initiatives that would
have strengthened price control and empowered consumers, most notably the plan to put pocketbook-sized price ceiling lists in the hands of
individual consumers (rather than relying on stores to post their ceilings
behind store counters).

The travails of American consumerists within the OPA contrasted
with the experience of their Canadian counterparts within the WPTB.
The U.S. Consumer Division's slide into irrelevance in late 1941 and
1942 coincided with the surfacing in Canada of the WPTB's Consumer
Branch, an agency largely fashioned in the image of the American division. When the WPTB announced plans in December 1941 to use volunteer housewives to police its newly imposed blanket retail price ceiling,
leading Canadian women's organizations leveraged their co-operation
into the creation of a "consumer representation branch" within the board.
The branch quickly mobilized thousands of women to check prices and
ultimately contributed greatly to the success of price control in Canada.
Its nationwide network of Women's Regional Advisory Committees, with
liaison officers in virtually every women's and consumer group and (eventually) many labour organizations, made the branch a two-way conduit
between national policy-makers and grassroots consumers.

The relatively uncontroversial mobilization of Canadian women to
police retail prices contrasted with the hotly contested efforts of the
OPA's Consumer Division to do the same. Five months after Canada's

price freeze, the OPA put its own price freeze into effect, very publicly crediting Canada's example as its model. The attempt by the OPA's then-faltering Consumer Division to consciously emulate the volunteer price checking aspect of Canada's plan, however, was met with vehement opposition. Retail spokespeople and their congressional allies, in particular, condemned the idea, and the OPA's top policy-makers rejected it both to appease these critics and because they favoured plans (ultimately no more palatable to their foes) to have trained "professionals" rather than "amateur" housewives do the job. While women's groups expressed their eagerness to help, as their sister organizations were doing in Canada, price officials instructed them not to act as "snoopers," "price-policemen," or, as OPA price deputy Galbraith infamously termed them, a "Gestapo of volunteer housewives."[13]

The OPA's initial rejection of consumer participation struck a blow not only against the Consumer Division's hopes to revive its fortunes by mobilizing consumers en masse but also against the overall effectiveness of American price control efforts. Not until a year later did the OPA under Chester Bowles, struggling to get inflation under control, finally call on women to volunteer for price checking. Yet after a year of stigmatizing such activity, the number of volunteers continually fell far short of expectations, despite the OPA's attempts to recast price checking as "American as baseball" and consistent with good citizenship and "the American way."[14] Comparing the much better job Canada had done in keeping a lid on inflation during the first years of the war, one senior Office of War Information official concluded wistfully that "enlistment of women's organizations was an important advantage enjoyed by Canadian price controllers that was not present in this country at the beginning of price control."[15]

The relative lack of controversy surrounding the creation of Canada's Consumer Branch, in general, and its mobilization of volunteer price checkers, in particular, points to a major irony: Canada's WPTB, an organization seemingly dominated by industry administrators and headed by Donald Gordon, a banker who recruited businessmen into his board's key positions, proved a more welcoming home for political consumerism than the OPA, an agency headed from conception to closure by New Deal liberals. The reasons for this, as well as for the different outcomes of Canadian and American wartime consumerism more generally, were more political than cultural or economic. Activists in both countries envisioned their political consumerism and their challenge to the political economy of consumer capitalism in terms that transcended national boundaries,

An early experiment with using trained women volunteers to check OPA price ceilings, September 1942. It would be almost another year before the OPA began making systematic use of volunteers in price checking, and recruitment efforts were seriously undermined by the earlier characterization of price checkers as a housewives' Gestapo. Edward Gruber/Library of Congress LC-USW3- 055125-C.

and debates and events on either side of the border were influenced by and intruded on those on the other side. However, the actions of activists and policy-makers were shaped and constrained by different national political-institutional contexts.

Different American and Canadian political institutions and processes, the dissimilar political contexts in which the war efforts began and were waged, and the different political orientations of key policy-makers and consumerists in each country contributed to a more auspicious outcome for Canadian consumer activists. Canada's centralized parliamentary system facilitated more decisive, co-ordinated action than the decentralized U.S. political system allowed. Canada's cabinet government shielded Ottawa policy-makers and consumerists-in-government from the legislative interference and withering political attacks that bedeviled their American counterparts and often thwarted decisive (and especially progressive) action in wartime Washington. The constancy and efficacy of the WPTB and its Consumer Branch relative to their American counterparts owed a great deal to these facts.

In addition, organizing for war in Canada was not fraught with the polarizing legacy of the New Deal, and so Canadian political consumerists did not have to contend with an already-mobilized opposition. Although the political consumerism that animated wartime activism had its origins in the cost of living protests of the 1910s and 1920s, it had taken more concrete form in the 1930s when consumer activism exploded in response to the crisis of capitalism that was the Great Depression. By the late 1930s, in the United States especially, widespread consumer activism had coalesced into a formidable "consumer movement." More than at any other time in the twentieth century, the consumer movement was then truly a social movement—a sustained, organized, and collective effort to produce social change. The movement's adherents, conscious of the political impact of consumption and public-oriented in their activism, sought to use the market as an arena for influencing policy. By the Second World War, both the movement's supporters and critics in the United States viewed it as a significant and more or less permanent force in politics and the economy.

As was the case for the labour movement in both countries, the role of the state was an important reason for national differences in the consumer movement's development during the Depression, as well as its growth during the war. The rise of the American New Deal state in the 1930s had helped transform the American consumer movement into an influential political force. Although the New Deal introduced no consumer equivalent of the Wagner Act, which legitimized unionization and catalyzed the phenomenal growth of the American labour movement in the late 1930s, it nonetheless left a legacy of consumer representation in government, institutional links between activists and agencies, and considerable public support for the idea of a permanent federal consumer department. The OPA was the last of the great New Deal programs, and both it and its various consumer sections drew broad support from the same left-liberal coalition of progressives, African Americans, labour organizations, and consumer groups that backed the New Deal. But as noted above, they also provoked a vicious backlash from an increasingly powerful anti-New Deal coalition of industry groups, the right-wing press, and a congressional alliance of conservative Republicans and southern Democrats.

In Canada, however, the absence of New-Deal-style state-building meant that Canada had neither a well-connected consumerist lobby in federal politics nor a legacy of consumer representation in government; in other words, Canada's "No Deal" response to the Depression contributed both to the more nascent state of the Canadian consumer movement at the outset of the war *and* to its greater success during the war. The differing institutional and political contexts outlined above meant that it was in Canada, the prewar consumer movement laggard, rather than in the United States, the consumer movement leader, that political consumerists experienced the most success.

Also key to the Consumer Branch's success was the better fit between its goals and political orientation and the political and institutional context of the nation's war effort. The radical social democratic vision of Ware and the US Consumer Division's leadership contrasted with the more moderate views of the leaders of the Canadian Consumer Branch. The branch was led not by the militants of groups like the Consumers' League of Edmonton or the Housewives Consumers Association (the subject of Julie Guard's chapter in this collection) but rather by moderates closely associated with the governing Liberal Party. Under the guiding hand of journalist and magazine editor Byrne Hope Sanders, the Consumer Branch pursued a less openly articulated—though clearly less radical—agenda.

To a great extent, Sanders and the branch achieved more than their American counterparts did because they sought less. The branch's vision of the citizen consumer was "Mrs. Consumer," whose activities as an efficient household manager using her skills for the benefit of the war effort certainly blurred the boundaries between public and private, between production and consumption. But Mrs. Consumer—at least in the Consumer Branch's hands—lacked much of the transformative potential of Ware's vision of the citizen consumer demanding an equal seat at the policy-making table with producers. The political consumerist vision pursued by Sanders and the Branch did not hold the interests of business and consumers to be as inherently in conflict, nor the interests of labour as inherently aligned, with those of consumers.

Sanders shied away from the class-conscious consumer radicalism of Ware and militant Canadian groups and instead couched the branch's work almost solely in a maternalist tradition of middle-class women's activism. Like their more militant counterparts, Consumer Branch leaders advocated key consumer protection issues, such as mandatory grade labelling, quality standards, and food subsidies. But securing a "seat at the table" was less central to their demands. "Too many people are apt to think of the Branch as in there fighting against vague foes for the consumer," Sanders stated at the branch's national conference in January 1944, when in fact "the whole Board works for consumer protection."[16] Such a characteriza-

"Thank You Mrs. Consumer," Wartime Information Board poster for Mrs. Consumer Week, May 1944. Mrs. Consumer Week encapsulated the distinctly gendered vision of the citizen-consumer in wartime Canada. As in this illustration, the housewife-consumer played a supporting role to male producers and warriors. G. Fairbairn/Library and Archives Canada E010857472.

tion of the role of consumer representatives would have struck militant political consumerists, like those who peopled the OPA's Consumer Division and radical Canadian groups, as odd. Caroline Ware and her activist colleagues viewed fighting for the consumer against competing interests as precisely the role of government consumer representatives.

The more moderate views and ambitions of Sanders and other branch leaders, their close ties to the governing Liberal Party, their portrayal of themselves as part of a tradition of maternal activism rather than consumer radicalism, and their less confrontational attitudes toward business and more reserved attitude toward organized labour made them less of a threat to WPTB policy-makers and business interests. Certainly, neither Sanders nor anyone else in the Consumer Branch's leadership ever spoke openly, as did Ware and Canada's more militant groups, of a desire to subordinate corporate power to the state or the consuming public. New Deal consumer activists saw themselves as closely allied with labour in the fight to curb corporate power and create prosperity through a high-wage, low-price economy. Consumer Branch leaders were more apt to see the interests of organized labour, especially its demands for ever-higher wages, as inherently in conflict with the interests of the consumer.

Despite its more moderate political stance, the branch nevertheless sought to give consumers a voice in economic decision-making. During the war, the branch did, in fact, constitute a popular movement, a broad coalition of women crossing class and party lines. Both French- and English-speaking women, moderates and radicals, Liberals and Conservatives, social democrats and communists co-operated in a somewhat uneasy alliance under its umbrella. The Canadian branch quickly forged an effective link between grassroots consumers and policy-makers and exercised an influence in the WPTB that (limited though it was) made it the envy of the faltering Consumer Division and its successors in the American OPA. The branch played a limited though important role in policy-making, but its most significant achievement was the creation of a vast grassroots network of consumers that was linked into the policy-making process and became the base of Canada's postwar consumer movement. Thus, it still represented a considerable challenge to the economic status quo.

*   *   *

Yet even in Canada, the wartime accomplishments of political consumerists were limited and, for the most part, temporary. Consumer activists contributed meaningfully to the success of wartime programs such as price control and rationing, often helping to shape and refine these programs in ways that were beneficial to consumers. But their attempts to implement key consumer movement priorities, such as grade labelling, were rebuffed by industry, and they exercised little influence over the larger direction of wartime economic policy-making. Moreover, during the period of decontrol that followed the end of the war in both countries, the influence of consumerists steadily declined.

Amid the decontrol process, political consumerists refocused their efforts on creating mass-membership consumer organizations to build on their wartime work of representing the consumer interest in the market-place and governing policy councils. The leaders of the OPA's Consumer Advisory Committee and the WPTB's Consumer Branch were pivotal figures in the newly formed National Association of Consumers in the United States and the Canadian Association of Consumers. On both sides of the border, postwar activists envisioned these mass organizations as powerful and democratizing forces in politics and the economy.

But the political ambitions of both national organizations quickly faltered. Both recruited only a small fraction of their membership goals. The reasons for this were many. The end of the war sapped the consumer movement of the sense of crisis and urgency that had animated wartime political consumerism. The winding down of the operations of the OPA and the WPTB—and the inability of consumer activists to find new homes within the postwar state—deprived the movement of its institutional base. Support for the organizations was also certainly undermined by the general stability of the postwar period in both countries after 1947, which confounded wartime fears of a postwar economic disaster. In Canada, former Consumer Branch leaders faced a challenge from the left, as the militant Housewives Consumers Association vied with the Canadian Association of Consumers to be the voice of the consumer interest. By the end of 1948, the perceived failure of postwar consumer organizations to influence economic decision-making in the face of government policies that led to higher consumer prices led to a precipitous drop in support for the already struggling associations.

The failure of would-be national consumer organizations in either country to organize consumers on a mass scale also resulted from the reactionary political climate of the emerging Cold War. The Second Red Scare arose amid the divisive politics of decontrol between 1945 and 1947, and the profound political and economic reforms sought by militant consumer activists—and their limited yet real wartime successes—made political consumerists in both countries the targets of anticommunist attacks and scrutiny by the burgeoning national security state. Anticommunists targeted the most militant and populist consumer groups, driving them from the political mainstream to the margins. In this political and economic climate, the moderate Canadian Association of Consumers survived (in part because of its close ties to the still-governing Liberals), but more militant groups, such as the Housewives Consumers Association in Canada and the National Association of Consumers in the United States, did not. The Red Scare thus greatly contributed to the directing of postwar consumer activism into more moderate channels. More importantly, the very concept of the consumer as an economic citizen with a vital contribution to make to economic decision-making withered.[17] By the end of the 1940s in both Canada and the United States, the idea of mobilizing grassroots consumers as a countervailing power had failed.

Yet in both Canada and the United States, despite the waning of the militant consumerist vision that had emerged out of the Great Depression and Second World War, the destruction of the most radical consumer groups, and a general decline in organized political consumerism, the consumer movement did not die. However, what remained of the consumer movement in the 1950s and what has been grafted onto it since has, with perhaps the exception of the movement's resurgence in the 1960s and 1970s, lacked the transformative social movement potential of the wartime political consumerist vision. The wartime generation of prominent consumer activists such as Ware had sought to use their nations' mobilization for war to advance an agenda of consumers' rights and representation, and they believed that organized consumer-citizens could use their purchasing power to shape public policy and influence corporate behaviour in both wartime and peacetime.

The hopeful foundations on which such lofty dreams were built had been laid down during the Depression and war years, a period of unprecedented consumer activism. Animated by an expansive vision that emphasized collective action and the potential for grassroots consumers' democracy, consumer activists in both countries during the Second World War had sought to mobilize consumer citizens around the politics of purchasing power into a countervailing economic power, giving a voice to the voiceless and empowering women, in particular. They hoped to build a mass movement that possessed the political influence to reshape and reform politics and the capitalist economy in the consumer interest and to ensure that consumers were strongly represented in government. It was a tall order and still is, but it is one that may offer some hope to consumer activists committed, at the very least, to curbing the abuses of consumer capitalism and empowering ordinary citizens.

12

FROM THE GREAT SOCIETY TO GIANT

Esther Peterson and the Politics of Shopping

LAWRENCE BLACK

"After Ralph Nader," Lawrence Glickman's history of consumer activism notes, Esther Peterson "was the leading consumer advocate of the postwar era . . . although she spent a good part . . . in the employ of the federal government and the Giant supermarket chain." It is precisely this mix of government, voluntary, and private sectors that makes her compelling. Peterson's career as President Johnson's Special Assistant on Consumer Affairs (1964–67), a post she resumed under President Carter, is well documented. But her time as Giant's Consumer Advisor (1970–76) was no less significant. Giant's consumer-centred program was part of a broader experimentation in consumerism in the 1970s and ranks alongside radical retail models like consumer co-operatives, worker-owned partnerships, ethical stores, and, in the 1910s, the National Consumers League's (NCL) own store in New York. Since Giant "adopted many of the changes opposed by industry when Esther Peterson was the White House consumer adviser," her time at Giant can be interpreted as an application of Johnson's "Great Society."[1] It allows us to ask: was this more a case of corporate culture and the state assimilating the consumer movement's aims, or of the consumer movement infiltrating the retail and political mainstream?

Most consistently framed and mobilized by the NCL belief in "using our purchasing power to guide social policy," Peterson's vision was of a consumer movement that benefited and engaged the whole of society. Peterson's labour, consumer, and women's movement credentials linked the Great Society and New Deal. Raised a Mormon, she was radicalized by women's garment workers strikes and summer schools in 1930s' New England, meeting Colston Warne, later the leading figure in the Consumers' Union, and joining the NCL. By 1938 she was an organizer for the Amalgamated Clothing Workers' Union. Esther and her husband Oliver, a State Department labour attaché in Europe (where the couple upset diplomatic protocol by shopping at co-ops), were targets of McCarthyism and federal loyalty boards. Having campaigned for John F. Kennedy, Peterson headed the Women's Bureau in the Labor Department. She promoted the Equal Pay Amendment to the Fair Labor Standards Act, which saw the 1964 Civil Rights Act prohibit sex discrimination in employment. Making good Kennedy's 1962 Consumer Message—which Peterson regarded as "the Magna Carta for the consumer movement worldwide"—Johnson made her his Special Assistant in 1964.[2]

By the 1960s Peterson was an important voice in a movement that produced abundant critiques of consumer culture and made Ralph Nader, Rachel Carson, Vance Packard, Paul Ehrlich, David Caplowitz, Betty Friedan, and herself public figures.[3] Consumerism fed the Great Society in the Fair Packaging and Labeling (1966) and Truth-in-Lending (1968) Acts, a product safety commission, and a proliferation of federal, state, city, and voluntary education initiatives. What had been a single 1962 federal program, the Consumers' Advisory Council, numbered twenty-six when Peterson re-entered the White House in 1977. In 1966, the NAACP's eighteen hundred units developed consumer protection programs and in retail itself "consumer advisors" flourished.[4] Women were prominent consumer voices: Peterson, Betty Furness (the actress with whom Johnson replaced Peterson), Virginia Knauer (Nixon and Reagan's Special Assistant), economist Persia Campbell, and ex-model Bess Myerson Grant in New York. Moving between the worlds of government, the consumer movement, and the private retail sector, Peterson developed a unique practice of engagement.

When Peterson became Johnson's Special Assistant in 1964, she envisaged her office re-balancing the market in consumers' favour. That supermarkets had quintupled their product range in the preceding decade meant consumers had to make "more decisions in a more impersonal marketplace." Countering Republican charges of a federal "power grab," Peterson forwarded a moral and economic agenda that echoed both Johnson's Great Society and the NCL's belief in the power of consumer choice for shaping society.[5] She often cited the President's 1964 Special Message to the Congress on Consumer Interests to explain how her program would "pursue the excellent and reject the tawdry . . . in every aspect of American life."[6] Her 1967 Presidential Committee on Consumer Interests (PCCI) report to Johnson argued:

> What American families do with their money . . . determines the material shape of American Society. . . . The excellent and the tawdry are on sale today. . . . If, over the next decades, the American society becomes the great society, their choices will have done much to make it so. . . . Expressions of taste have to be based on knowledge of quality, quantity, durability, performance, cost, and charges of the items chosen. With this knowledge, the American consumer can choose well.[7]

Johnson seemed to have made an adroit move when on Peterson's appointment correspondence flooded into the White House for her. But she soon felt "duped in a major consumer fraud." Johnson's advisors, Jack Valenti and Joe Califano, were better at relaying business discontent to Peterson than her concerns to the President. Peterson complained of limited access, that Johnson did not attend the PCCI, and that she was not consulted on the Packaging Bill. With just one assistant and expected to continue as Secretary of Labor, she was a "political instrument," a front to give the pretense of interest, "rather than a real instrument for consumer action."[8]

A flashpoint between Peterson and Johnson came during supermarket boycotts in 1966 against price rises and sales gimmicks like stamps and bingo. Republicans blamed inflation on federal spending; Democrats countered it was an industry issue; housewives blamed supermarkets; supermarkets blamed producers; and the Super Market Institute (SMI) alleged housewives who "were not ready to listen" bore some responsibility.[9] Peterson's office took no official position but was in the forefront of media coverage, especially when she was pictured embracing the leaders of the highest-profile protest in Denver. But she was also critical of shoppers. She advised buying chicken instead of pricier beef and suggested the problem was that "many women don't know how to shop." Peterson claimed the protests forced "the large, impersonal chain store operations to improve their public relations" and to explain their pricing regimes, but she was perceived by the press and the Administration as supporting consumers against business.[10]

Advertising also brought Peterson and the Administration into conflict. Valenti was an ex-advertising executive, whereas Peterson thought advertising "respectable humbug." With the Fair Packaging and Labelling legislation before Congress, advertising journal *Printer's Ink* asked, "does the President know what she is doing?" When the Advertising Federation of America—who, quoting *Printer's Ink*, described Peterson as "the most pernicious threat to advertising today"—invited Johnson to their convention, she felt accepting "would pull the rug from under your consumer program."[11]

Peterson's eventual political demise in 1967, *Advertising Age* reckoned, was because her "instructions were to project a pro-consumer image for the administration," but "she had yet to find a way to accomplish this without setting off alarms on the business front." Indeed Administration reports were wary of consumerism's "inability to reach and affect the general public," and thus the "political strategists decided that there is little . . . consumer vote."[12] Peterson refuted this. The advertising fracas and boycotts demonstrated the "new awareness of . . . Americans that they have rights and responsibilities as consumers, just as they do as voters or wage earners or producers." Noting how some "economists have argued the consumer 'votes' each time he makes a purchase," Peterson welcomed the housewives' protests as evidence of the consumer's "more direct participation in the economy." The protests, moreover, heightened business "awareness of consumer dissatisfaction and led to stronger efforts to explain the industry's problems." The 1967 PCCI report duly noted business efforts on this front.[13]

Peterson's fraught tenure in office evinces Storrs' argument that 1930s New Deal radicalism became moderated in the face of attacks on the postwar consumer movement. Historians have noted an additional fracturing of the consumer and labour movements in this period. Nader's more legal strategy marked a shift away from any remnants of New Deal–style fusion of radical labour and consumer politics.[14] Evidence of this was to be found when Peterson left the White House and became the Amalgamated Clothing Workers' legislative representative. The union was not interested in her consumer strategies. She regarded this as a missed opportunity, and it was a reason why she accepted the offer in 1970 from the Giant supermarket chain to become their Consumer Advisor.[15]

The move to Giant was not incongruous for Peterson because Giant wore its liberal politics openly. Peterson saw an opportunity to apply her progressive philosophy and its essence—building dialogue and trust between retailer and shopper—promised competitive benefits to Giant as well as appealing to its politics. Giant opened Washington's first supermarket in 1936 and ran stores in Virginia and Maryland. Paul Forbes (head of Public Affairs) met Peterson at a Johnson inaugural ball, for which Giant supplied a cake. Forbes confessed, "I envy you the opportunity you had to serve the new frontier and now the great society." After the 1968 riots (which spared Giant's 14th Street store), Giant President Joseph Danzansky chaired the Urban Coalition's Emergency Food Committee.[16]

But retailers and activists speculated that Peterson might revise her opinions now she had swapped sides. As Danzansky put it, the "consumer thought she had sold out, whilst the executives thought she would keep them from selling out." Jac Lehrman (Giant's co-founder) told her, "the sooner you get out of here, the better." But in Peterson's vision, there were no sides to swap: her reform agenda, consumer and business interests were compatible; retail could be a neutral meeting place of producer and consumer. She kept an arms-length relationship to management, determined to be an "ambassador to the company *for* the consumer, not the ambassador of the company *to* the consumer." She did not join the Society of Consumer Professionals ("people who knew their bread was buttered by the big corporations"), took no Giant stock, and remained active in the consumer movement. In 1973, while working for Giant, she was elected NCL President.[17]

For Peterson, this was all part of a continuing political project. As the NCL explained, "Watergate and inflated supermarket prices have the same root: a few people or organizations . . . have bought a corner of the marketplace." She participated in Democrat study groups, convinced the consumer agenda was "closer to the public interest than any other category of political issues."[18] Criticizing Republicans as unpatriotic, she warned that if government only supported business "free market balance is destroyed, quality is lowered, prices run wild. . . . Only a free market economy—involving consumer/buyers and producer/sellers of equal political and economic strength—can turn this tide." This meant support for a Federal Consumer Protection Agency (CPA) and recognition that "a growing proportion of business is creating a new climate of social accountability." The latter, Carter insiders Stuart Eizenstat and Mike Pertschuk noted, distinguished Peterson since most consumer activists and Democrats mistrusted business.[19]

Driving Peterson's Giant agenda was a Consumer Advisory Committee (CAC) of teachers, home economists, and nutritionists. The CAC piloted initiatives on unit pricing (to show cost per weight or size as well as of an item or package, to allow comparison with other brands and stores), bar-coding, open dating of products, nutritional labelling, and education. They employed Howard University laboratories and interns; touted bussing from poorer communities to big suburban stores; introduced recyclable products, a Senior Citizen Committee, in-store "Pester Esther" forms, radio shows, and newsletters; and abolished trading stamps. A longstanding bugbear of Peterson's, trading stamps were to her a gimmick, inducing shopper loyalty by collecting stamps which could later be cashed in for certain gifts rather than winning loyalty through value, quality, and service.[20]

Giant adapted from Kennedy a "Consumer Bill of Rights" promising the right to safety, to be informed, to choose and be heard, and adding redress and service. Unit pricing, bar-coding, and computer checkouts fulfilled the consumer's right to be informed by providing detailed till receipts, enabling comparative shopping. They reduced human pricing errors. Open dating informed shoppers when products had been packed or displayed. These initiatives included a deal to avoid job losses—indeed, they promised, if adopted industry-wide, to create employment.[21] Peterson exploited the expertise of her many networks, such as Dr. Arnold Elkin, Chair of the Consumer Product Safety Commission. On nutritional labelling, she consulted Dr. Jean Mayer (Chair of the White House Conference on food, nutrition, and health); Jim Turner, one of Nader's Raiders and author of *The Chemical Feast*, an exposé of food safety and the Food and Drug Administration (FDA); and the FDA. Danzansky sold this nutritional initiative to an industry wary of Peterson and unconfident it had the requisite data, on the grounds that Giant could "be the guinea pig for the industry."[22]

The 1970s were testing times for innovation. Inflation posed problems for unit pricing. Giant's competitor, Safeway, announced when prices changed, but lower price stock remained on shelves. Giant resisted following suit, concerned that smaller stores would have to put prices up first and explained why transport and labour inflation meant mark-ups on existing stock. But in 1974 it backed down, even reintroducing discount trading stamps. "We aren't taking this step because we think it is right," the company conceded, but because "we must bow to realities of marketplace," at least (in a telling phrase) "until consumers become sufficiently knowledge-able to separate real from counterfeit consumerism."[23] Equally, inflation was a stimulus to bar-coding. Inflation negated the value of printing prices on goods (though many shoppers favoured this) and was labour-saving. Giant insisted to Virginia's General Law Committee this was a market not legislative issue: "Consumers will cast their $ votes . . . but before legislation is considered, let's give computer-assisted checkouts a chance to develop."[24]

Such developments have become norms but were achieved despite industry scepticism, shoppers' indifference, and resistance within Giant itself. The "roof fell in" when Gerson Barnett, head of grocery, discovered all policy changes were subject to Peterson's approval. Open dating, he feared, would see shoppers messing up displays looking for newer pro-duce. Unit pricing required shelving redesign. Giant's schemes gener-ated FDA interest, allowing Giant to allay fears over bar code scanners by assuring shoppers of their safety and that the FDA was checking their accuracy. The FDA also monitored nutritional labelling, in 1972 finding 62.4% of shoppers aware and 85% of those wanting it extended.[25]

But there were problems with unit pricing. Peterson asked the CAC for ideas to convey their uses "to a low-income, non-reading, non-mathe-matical group."[26] A 1975 survey found 92.5% could identify prices, 48% kept their sales receipt and of these, 30% compared prices. This picture of a minority using this information and comparatively shopping emerged in other surveys. Shoppers, it was concluded, needed time "to learn the new method."[27] Even if only 20% looked at labels (a figure Peterson doubted), that did not undermine their value—many didn't vote, but that was no reason to end elections.[28]

When unit pricing replaced individual pricing (directly on each item), it was assumed this was a tribute to the trust Giant had earned with its shoppers, but disquiet was persistent.[29] A grandmother in 1975 declared herself "against any form of pricing that takes the price directly off the merchandise." She disliked Peterson's "shop elsewhere if-you-want" phi-losophy, which she felt was "thumbing a nose at shoppers." Detailed labels showed that shops want us kept "in a maze."[30] Peterson's aim was the oppo-site—a risk-reducing guide to shopping that, for instance, decoded adver-tising language. But its demands on shoppers' knowledge led to Peterson's schemes being accused of "taking the romance out of shopping."[31]

Peterson was not a born shopper. "My forays into supermarkets have always been as short as I could make them" she admitted, nostalgically longing for "the butchers, bakers . . . who wouldn't dream of . . . wrapping cellophane around a loaf of bread." But at Giant, people followed her trolley around. Peterson had fostered scepticism of shopping as a risky business (as had books like *The Supermarket Trap*) that she now looked to overturn in asking shoppers to trust her schemes.[32]

Giant marketed their program aggressively—part of consumers' right to be informed—often featuring Peterson, which was ironic, given her run-in with the ad industry. During 1972's inflation, a Giant ad showed Peterson suggesting a solution for high beef prices was for shoppers to "buy something else" (lentils and dried beans were protein-rich alternatives). This won a *Family Circle*–SMI award and annoyed the beef industry. In 1975, the Advertising Club of Metropolitan Washington made Peterson their "Advertising Woman of the Year."[33]

Peterson resisted any implication she was compromising with commercial practices and values, but either way, the company sought commercial and competitive advantage. Giant saw these schemes as competitive tools. Even when they came to little, ads made a merit of the effort; Peterson was their unique selling point. Many initiatives more than broke even and won management around. Unit pricing paid for itself (productivity gains offset start-up costs); open dating aided stock rotation and Giant's own brand sales (since some brands would not comply); and nutritional information increased sales, for example of broccoli.[34]

In Washington, where supermarkets were engaged in "the country's most gruelling struggle for market domination," this added up to a vital advantage over Safeway.[35] Peterson justified it as setting standards competitors would have to follow, but she often sprang to a partisan defence of Giant. As Safeway had consulted Nader on nutritional labelling, Peterson felt it "important that we move expeditiously," to secure Giant the credit.[36] She defended Giant in 1971 when the Price Commission of Economic Stabilization found it had exceeded a price cap. Peterson alleged the violation was technical and nothing to besmirch shoppers' trust. In 1972, she told a disgruntled shopper she was right to be "upset with the big increases in food prices . . . but we have very little control over them" and had not passed them on for longer than competitors.[37]

Peterson's first full year, 1972, as she explained in the *Harvard Business Review*, saw record Giant sales. Peterson-style consumerism was of value to the shared interests of shoppers and retailers. Danzansky told the 1972 SMI Conference, "everything she's touched has turned to gold" and proposed, "let's call in the Ralph Naders and Esther Petersons." This was met with boos, but Danzansky felt it held out the "real promise of voluntary consumer reform" which was "preferable to the . . . deadening effect of regulatory legislation."[38]

Peterson saw herself as "the guardian of the gullible" since, as Giant's *Consumer Guide to . . .* leaflets put it, "shopping in today's abundant and complicated marketplace is not easy."[39] This was why consumer programs flourished. Business had a responsibility not to violate its power. Underpinning this was a belief in market democracy—"consumers are to economics what voters are to politics"—so long as it could contain corporate power. To this end, retailers should be "as much buying agents for the consumer, as selling agents for the producer," and this was Peterson's mantra.[40]

Peterson found "many businessmen" gave her "the impression that if only I would only go away, the consumer movement would disappear." But she and Giant knew "that the best way to keep the government out of the marketplace is to meet the legitimate needs of consumers." Peterson supported the push for a federal CPA later in the 1970s but was mostly loyal to the ideals of the market, wary of postwar attacks on consumerism's regulatory propensities. In this Cold War context, the consumer movement posed as a loyal opposition, simultaneously critical of business and pro-free market. Danzansky reiterated how they had brought retailers, government, manufacturers, experts, and consumers into "dialogue . . . in these times of polarization" and showed it was "possible to work within the system." Giant's program could "serve as a model for the nation."[41]

Peterson's farewell gift from Giant was a "cake of equal parts of politics, business sense, street savvy" and garnished with "chopped Chambers of Commerce." But was this sufficient? Under Carter the battle for a CPA was lost by a combination of weak executive lobbying, Nader's strong-arm tactics, and the unprecedented scale and militancy of the business lobby and a major advance for the New Right. Peterson had realized "how powerful the big corporations were at . . . shaping the marketplace" when she could make no headway at Giant rearranging shelving for consumer use rather than to ensure big brands were at eye level. It was a tribute to the growth in consumer awareness that "our opposition has organised more strongly," but the anti-CPA lobby left Peterson "terrified of . . . the growth of corporate power on the Hill."[42]

Peterson was formidable and after Carter turned to lobbying for the International Organisation of Consumer Unions at the UN. The sexism she experienced in Johnson's White House ensured she stood up to Giant executives. Still, Giant presented her as "a matriarch . . . honest and reassuring." What Glickman terms "the feminizing of the consumer movement" saw the New Right in the 1970s target figures like Peterson, mothering the gullible shopper, as part of an overweening, overreaching government bureaucracy.[43]

Peterson's experimentation and experience suggested that change was possible and that retail was a plural, flexible system. Peterson's Giant successor noted in her obituary: "Her friends in consumer activism asked, 'How can you work for a business and represent the consumer?' She showed it could be done." But Peterson had recurring doubts that these efforts could reign in corporate power. A persistent beef in this regard was the relative weakness of the consumer movement or that shoppers were not up to its ideal practices, not "sufficiently knowledgeable." This was a pervasive view. Interviewed by David Frost in 1969, Nader reckoned the consumer movement's power "doesn't amount to a whit" because everyday consumers "don't do much about it. They're pretty complacent. They just sit and watch television."[44] Both factors—shopper apathy and the consumer movement's reservations about consumers—explain much about what limited more extensive reform.

13

THE COUNTERCULTURAL ROOTS OF GREEN CONSUMERISM

PHILIP A. WIGHT

WHAT DOES IT MEAN to be an environmentalist in contemporary America? According to one popular theory, modern greens can awake and slip comfortably into $245 "eco-501" Levi's jeans and $200 organic cotton Patagonia pullovers. After consuming a guilt-free breakfast of organic tropical fruit (regardless of season) and Fair Trade coffee, they might commute to work in a Lexus hybrid. Environmentalists have so emphasized the importance of lifestyle choices and shopping that "consumer agency" is now the most pervasive form of eco-activism.

By purchasing volumes of eco-friendly products, Americans have invested great faith in green consumerism. Advocates of green consumer agency contend that individuals are both the cause of and the solution to environmental ills. When enough consumers purchase "eco-friendly" products, they contend, the market will offer more sustainable alternatives. By this logic, consumers hold all the power, as each time they swipe their credit card they are "voting" for a more sustainable way of life. Since proponents believe consumer choices lead to ecologically sounder modes of production, green consumption constitutes a dominant element of *demand-side environmentalism*. Pollution stems primarily from consumers' lifestyles in a free market, the argument goes, rather than the underlying structures of the nation's political economy.

The strange reality of contemporary American environmentalism—namely the ideals of green consumption that encourage individuals to purchase their way to sustainability—begs for historical context: When and how did *personal* consumer decisions come to be seen as the answer to a problem of *collective* global sustainability?

While green consumerism's origins are often traced to the 1987 Brundtland Report on "sustainable development," civic and labour advocates have long emphasized consumer decisions as a tool for social change. Consumer and labour activists in the early twentieth century made political consumerism an indispensable tenet of responsible citizenship. Yet as Tracey Deutsch highlights, following the Second World War neoclassical economists reframed consumer market "demand" as the ultimate signifier of public will, "neglecting the structures that shape[d] that demand."[1] As environmental concerns reached crisis levels in the 1960s, economists and activists imbued personal consumer decisions with an even more powerful valence.

The American counterculture of the 1960s and 1970s was the first social movement to advance green consumption as a theory of environmental change. Coined by historian Theodore Roszak, the "Counter Culture" envisioned changing society through lifestyle politics and a cultural rebellion. The counterculture's ideas of social change proved resonant with American culture and greatly affected the environmental movement. Indeed, the modern usage of the term "green" stems from Charles Reich's countercultural classic, *The Greening of America* (1970). By the early 1970s, millions sought lifestyles of simplicity and "right livelihood" to transform the nation. Paradoxically, in the late 1970s and early 1980s, entrepreneurs, marketers, and status-seeking individuals supercharged this focus on responsible consumption into an affluent green *consumerism*. While the counterculture was far from monolithic, four intellectual currents connect it to America's contemporary paradigm of green consumerism: personal responsibility, the rejection of social-democratic governance, "appropriate technologies" (human-scale tools like solar panels) and faith in consumer activism.

The era's single most important publication to advance shopping for change was the *Whole Earth Catalog* (1968). As the founder and editor of this classic text, entrepreneur Stewart Brand established himself as the progenitor of green consumption. While health enthusiasts had sold "organic" and "natural" products for decades before, Brand's *Catalog* disseminated an entire worldview of green lifestyles and demand-side solutions that forever changed American environmentalism. It was perhaps the first popular publication that advanced the "heroic" consumer life-style—social change through everyday consumption.[2]

As countercultural environmental ideas gained traction, critics warned of the limits of individual lifestyles and argued for controlling pollution through collective political action. Leftists like the nation's foremost ecologist, Dr. Barry Commoner, dismissed Brand and his fellow counter-culturalists as reactionaries—the unwitting rearguard of corporate capitalism. Commoner refused to criticize consumers for the ecological crisis and instead faulted America's capitalist system of production. He argued that individuals must engage politically as citizens—not merely consumers—to create a more sustainable society. Commoner's *supply-side environmentalism* held that since producers were most responsible for pollution, environmental public policies—not ethical consumption—could provide the only enduring remedy. Brand and Commoner's theories offer a useful foil to understand the evolution of environmental politics and the rise of contemporary demand-side environmentalism.

Despite their divergent theories of social change, the ideas of Brand and Commoner emerged within the same postwar milieu of rising environmental concern. The conclusion of the Second World War ushered in an era of widespread prosperity, rampant suburban development, and unprecedented mass consumption. The ecological consequences of these developments, in conjunction with the pervasive presence of new chemicals like DDT and radioactive fallout from atomic testing, alarmed both professionals and lay citizens alike. Rachel Carson's *Silent Spring* (1962) arose as the most eloquent and persuasive rebuke of these new developments and consequently galvanized an emerging environmental movement. In the early 1960s, Carson and other critics of unbridled capitalism succeeded in ushering in a "liberal hour" of environmental public policies. Yet others, like Brand, rejected government intervention and sought their own anti-statist solutions—what would become demand-side environmentalism.

Brand was born in Rockford, Illinois in 1938 and enjoyed the prerogatives of a privileged middle-class upbringing, including enrolment at New Hampshire's prestigious Phillips Exeter Academy. While attending Stanford University under the direction of soon-to-be-famous professor Paul Ehrlich (author of 1968's best-selling *The Population Bomb*), Brand studied ecology and humanity's perilous relationship with the biosphere. After graduating and serving in the army, he grew restless with America's prepackaged mass culture. In the early 1960s, Brand travelled across the United States and explored bohemian lifestyles, Native American traditions, psychotropic drugs, and communal living.

Brand soon found himself, in the words of historian Andrew Kirk, "in the center of the San Francisco counterculture at its apex."[3] After reading Ken Kesey's best-selling *One Flew Over the Cuckoo's Nest* (1962), Brand introduced himself to the author—a fellow Stanford graduate—and they became good friends.[4] Through Kesey and his "Merry Pranksters," Brand participated in the era's famous "Acid Tests" and befriended several of the counterculture's most iconic figures: Jerry Rubin, Richard Alpert, Jerry Garcia, and Timothy Leary. Most memorably, the Pranksters organized an electronic art "happening" known as the Trips Festival. The festival marked Brand's emergence as a countercultural innovator for his multi-sensory art exhibit, "America Needs Indians." The psychedelic exhibit proved to be the first manifestation of his environmental model—rebellious, entrepreneurial, libertarian—that would imbue the *Whole Earth Catalog*.

In March of 1968, a family tragedy—the death of his father in Illinois—precipitated Brand to materialize his worldview into what would soon become a countercultural classic. The event proved cathartic for the young innovator, and on his return flight to California following the funeral, he conceived a provocative idea. "I was reading *Spaceship Earth* by Barbara Ward," Brand recalled. "Between chapters I gazed out the window into dark nothing and slid into a reverie about my friends starting their own civilizations hither and yon in the sticks and how I could help." He envisioned a parallel to the L. L. Bean catalog that would provide "an exchange for interesting ideas and heresies" for a new generation seeking cultural rebirth.[5]

By the fall of 1968 Brand transformed his romantic vision into the sixty-four-page *Whole Earth Catalog*. Between the oddly shaped covers of the *Catalog*, readers could find product reviews and learn where to buy geodesic domes, solar hot water heaters, and 135 tools for rural self-sufficiency. Emphasizing a holistic worldview, self-education, and home provisioning, Brand designed the publication to empower pragmatic individuals. *Time* described the *Catalog* as the "Boy Scout Handbook of the counterculture."[6] Following favourable reviews in *Esquire*, *Time*, and *Vogue*, the homespun catalog became a commercial phenomenon, selling 60,000 copies within the first year. "Success is going through here like a thunderstorm that won't quit," Brand wrote a friend in 1968.[7] The *Catalog* went on to win the U.S. National Book Award in 1971 and the public purchased over 2.5 million copies by the mid-1970s.

The *Catalog's* initial success reflected the counterculture's enthusiasm for communalism, appropriate technologies, and living "off the grid." Brand told *Rolling Stone* that the *Catalog* was "strictly an outgrowth of the commune movement."[8] Between 1965 and 1972, as many as 750,000 lived in more than 10,000 communes nationwide.[9] Ironically for a movement that praised Native Americans, nearly all of the back-to-the-landers were white, young, and financially privileged—an ideal combination to embrace Brand's libertarian model of "dropping out" and building communities in their own image.[10] For many in the counterculture, Brand included, traditional institutions and politics offered little hope for meaningful social change. "You don't change a game by winning it or losing it," he explained. "You change it by leaving it and going somewhere else and starting a new game from scratch."[11] The counterculture envisioned starting anew with human-scale communities, decentralized production, and eco-conscious lifestyles freed from the pressures of big government and big business.

In his "purpose statement" of the 1972 *Catalog*, Brand rejected the ability of "government, big business, formal education, [and the] church" to advance meaningful social change. He argued against the perception that environmental issues were "vast . . . and unapproachable by an individual," and instead advocated "intimate, personal power."[12] To this end, he promoted the *Catalog* as "a book of tools for saving the world at the only scale it could be done, one hand at a time."[13] Chief among these personal choices was rejecting procreation, as Brand and most environmentalists of the era feared overpopulation. He believed all individual actions had profound cultural implications. "Individual lifestyle choices became political acts," historian Fred Turner writes of Brand's thinking, as "both consumption and lifestyle" took on "a new political valence." The *Catalog*, therefore, was profoundly consumer-centric.[14] "Individual buyers have far more control over economic behavior than voters," Brand summarized in 1971.[15] Ironically, the countercultural rejection of big business and mass culture lent itself surprisingly well to a new rebellious consumerism.

Rather than rejecting capitalism, Brand embraced it. From the inception of the *Catalog*, he aimed to create his own countercultural business model and a more eco-conscious capitalism. He explained that the *Catalog* emerged in response to those in the counterculture who "dropped out of the economic system in despair that there's nothing worth buying."

Rejecting such anticonsumer sentiments, Brand embraced both appropriate modern technologies and traditional instruments and asserted, "There
are a lot of tools that are worth sustaining."[16] To critics who chided his
commercialism, he replied, "You may not think capitalism is nice. . . . But
we should both know that the *Whole Earth Catalog* is made of it."[17]

Despite Brand's assertions that the *Catalog* was an apolitical publication, in rejecting government intervention, Brand advocated a libertarian worldview. Objectivist philosopher Ayn Rand especially influenced
his thinking. Brand found her "intuition amazingly reliable" and credited
her novel *Atlas Shrugged* (1957) with inspiring "a lot of our operational
stuff."[18] His aversion to government interference became apparent during the world's first major global environmental governance event, the
United Nations' "Conference on the Human Environment," which he
attended in Stockholm, Sweden in 1972. "*My* people," Brand wrote
to his wife, "turn out to be a few poets, diggers, malcontents who also
feel that 'one planet' is what's real and 'one world' is what's happening in
Stockholm—transnational unrooted bullshit." The fact that the conference took place in socialistic Sweden did not help: "Sweden gives me the
creeps," he confided, "Too goddamned rational, controlled."[19]

While Brand maintained his distaste for traditional political activism
and government intervention, with time he fell out with elements of the
counterculture and renounced his former faith in off-the-grid communes.
As early as 1971, Brand confided his "increasing disaffection with long
hairs," hippie "superstition," and the excesses of the drug culture.[20] Four
years later, he repudiated a central pillar of the *Catalog's* original purpose.
"'Self-sufficiency' is an idea which has done more harm than good . . . it
is flawed at the root," he admonished. It "is not to be had on any terms,
ever. It is a charming woodsy extension of the fatal American mania for
privacy. . . . It is a damned life."[21] Ultimately, he rejected the counterculture's back-to-the-land survivalism and instead embraced cybernetics,
"co-evolution," and systems theory—which fortified his faith in technology and commerce stronger than ever.

As the 1970s progressed, Brand's green consumption shifted from its
countercultural roots to mainstream America's corporations and suburban
neighbourhoods. He increasingly called for more institutional solutions
to the ecological crisis, such as investing in ethical companies, innovative
foundations, and providing grants to entrepreneurial environmentalists.
His emphasis on "access to tools" in the *Catalog* evolved into advocating
liberating computer technology—the early Internet. Brand co-founded

the first online community, coined the term "personal computer," and reflected that the computer revolution represented the greatest legacy of the counterculture. His individual-centred demand-side environmentalism evolved in time to be the guiding light of Silicon Valley and all those who strove for a greener capitalism. Yet leftists like Commoner remained wary of Brand's model of consumer agency and instead implored citizens to change the political economy of capitalism.

On February 2, 1970, *Time* hit the newsstands across the United States with an unlikely figure hailed as the "Paul Revere of Ecology" adorning its cover—Dr. Barry Commoner. *Time* lauded the microbiologist as a "professor with a class of millions" who "has become the uncommon spokesman for the common man." He was "endowed with a rare combination of political savvy, scientific soundness and the ability to excite people with his ideas," the article concluded.[22] Connecting the ecological crisis to the logic of America's consumer capitalist economic system, Commoner emerged as a pioneer of supply-side environmentalism during the 1960s and 1970s and a stark foil to Brand's green consumption.

Born in 1917 in Brooklyn, New York, Commoner rose to prominence for his intellectual prowess. The son of Jewish-Russian immigrant parents, he supported prominent leftist causes of his day and grew to maturity under the austerity of the Great Depression. Commoner graduated Phi Beta Kappa with a degree in zoology from Columbia University and then matriculated to Harvard as a prestigious University Fellow, where he earned a PhD in cellular physiology. After joining the faculty at Washington University in St. Louis, he tackled controversial issues like nuclear fallout and DDT and became famous in the 1950s as a tireless advocate for environmental public health. Emmy Award-winning newsman Jim Clarke hailed Commoner as the "nation's foremost ecologist" and even conservative critic William F. Buckley lauded the leftist as the "father of ecology."[23]

Commoner argued that pollution did not originate from wasteful consumers, but rather "the very structure of our modern productive system."[24] "The only explanation which can be offered for the irrational, counter-ecological" direction of the U.S. economy was "the drive—natural in our economic system—to increase the rate of economic return," he asserted.[25] The single-minded pursuit of profit, in short, fuelled the environmental crisis. Commoner often cited Henry Ford II's remark that "mini-cars produce mini-profits." Detroit manufactured massive automobiles with powerful but inefficient engines that emitted more pollutants because large cars were more profitable than smaller ones. "I don't think that you and I are to blame for the fact that if you want to buy a car," Commoner reasoned, "the chances are you have to buy one that pollutes the environment." He asserted the "fault is not the consumer. The fault lies with the producer."[26]

Commoner marshalled evidence to reframe environmental pollution as a social crisis of private enterprise rather than a problem of ignorant individuals. Unaccounted costs of private enterprise, he explained, like noxious overflow into waterways, smog, and toxic wastes were costs "borne not by the *producer*, but by society as a whole." Thus, businesses were "not wholly private," as the consequences were "paid by the lives of the present population and the safety of future generations." Since "unmet environmental costs benefit the producer," Commoner argued the public unfairly subsidized billions of dollars in private profits.[27] Corporations privatized profits while socializing the costs of pollution.

Yet as ecological awareness grew in the late 1960s, activists like Brand increasingly blamed individuals' lifestyle choices—especially mass consumption and procreation. The most popular representation of this idea was cartoonist Walt Kelly's "Pogo" cartoon. Kelly depicted his main character "Pogo" stumbling on a dump of disposable consumer goods in the woods and lamenting, "We have met the enemy, and he is us."

Commoner wasted no time in rebuffing the cartoon's argument, especially the contention that overpopulation and personal consumption caused pollution. During a speech in Toronto, he asked his audience to

Walt Kelly, "We Have Met the Enemy and He Is Us," Earth Day Poster, 1971. Image used with permission from Okefenokee Glee & Perloo, Inc.

choose between the burden of "not having so many children" or to "change those social relationships" responsible for polluting the environment and the health of its inhabitants. "The problem is fundamentally economic," he continued, "and it's not going to get cured simply by calling for recycling and cleaning up."[28] Commoner dismissed "Pogo" as a "kind of propaganda" and claimed Kelly "misled a lot of people with his famous slogan."[29] Systemic problems, he stressed, simply could not be overcome solely through lifestyle politics.

Rejecting the assumption that "if we all did our part it would be solved," Commoner explained that individuals were not equally complicit.[30] "Some people cause more pollution than others," he reasoned, and "some people are responsible for the decisions that cause pollution." An early advocate of the Environmental Justice movement, Commoner blamed the rich for "polluting the environment in which the poor live." While he recognized people could "vote with their pocketbook," he dismissed green consumerism as inherently undemocratic. An affluent environmentalism that neglected the ghetto and the grape fields, he suggested, would not provide sufficient justice. "The best way to reduce pollution," he argued, was direct political action regulating pollution at its source.[31]

Commoner's political philosophy would in time be called eco-socialism. He contended the environment could not be commodified as private property, and therefore the production system should be treated as social property. Rejecting Brand's vision of a cultural rebellion, Commoner emphasized, "The thing to do is not to develop a counter-culture but to take over the establishment-culture and make it run right." As a self-proclaimed "democratic socialist," he prescribed massive public investments based on the science of thermodynamics and "social need": electrified railroads, sewage pipelines, and renewable power generation. To achieve these objectives he advocated uniting "the economic democracy of socialism with the political freedom that is such an important part of the American heritage."[32] The economic and political crises of the 1970s, he hoped, presented the opportune moment for the emergence of this supply-side environmentalism. Unfortunately for Commoner and his fellow leftists, the 1970s witnessed not the dawn but the decline of the "liberal hour."

By the 1980s Americans looked increasingly to the counterculture's ideal of green consumption rather than government regulation to protect their environment. The political and economic consequences of the Vietnam War, Watergate, and the Oil Crises precipitated the marginalization of social-democratic environmental solutions.[33] The Reagan administration reduced the EPA's budget by a third, removed the solar panels President Carter installed on the White House, imposed a cost-benefit standard to ensure that environmental regulations would not burden corporations, and enshrined consumer spending as the leading indicator of economic progress. While the counterculture's communes collapsed in the 1970s, paradoxically, a decade later its commercialized legacy endured stronger than ever. Buying green became a status symbol and a lucrative marketing mechanism to distinguish a new class of upwardly mobile connoisseurs. Green consumption perversely encouraged ever-more consumerism. By April 1990, *Time* could bemoan the twentieth anniversary of Earth Day as a "commercial mugging."[34]

Despite the marginalization of Commoner's prescriptions, the intensifying climate crisis validates the indispensability of supply-side environmentalism. In his phenomenally popular 2012 essay "Global Warming's Terrifying New Math," journalist-turned-activist Bill McKibben argued that the proven oil and gas reserves of fossil fuel companies reveal that humanity is poised to burn five times more carbon than the amount scientists warn can be safely combusted. Without a supply-side limit on carbon pollution, in short, these fossil fuels will be consumed and ensure runaway climatic warming. "People perceive—correctly," McKibben concludes, "that their individual [consumer] actions will not make a decisive difference in the atmospheric concentration of CO_2."[35] A recent MIT study came to a similar conclusion: no matter how simple one's lifestyle, each American's carbon footprint is nearly double the global average. Carbon-intensive societal services like infrastructure and defence are carried out on individuals' behalf, regardless of one's personal consumption.[36] Even Brand now stresses the importance of government solutions as a strong proponent of nuclear energy—despite its historical reliance on big government for research, subsidies, and security.

All of this evidence suggests, as Commoner argued, that demand-side solutions remain insufficient. Because carbon pollution remains external to the costs of production and exchange, climate change represents the single greatest market failure in history.[37] Consumers cannot achieve social change solely through their wallets since the requisite reforms are not available within the sphere of the market.

Yet if Commoner's supply-side environmentalism remains most relevant, Brand's insights on the cultural dimensions of demand-side activism should not be neglected. Cultivating a green culture and a sustainable political economy does require personal change. Demand-side actions are essential, though ironically they should not be viewed solely through the lens of "demand" in a market system. Individual actions often make the most difference for the cultural signals they send rather than their effect on aggregate demand. Take the example of the "contagion effect" for residential solar power. When a household instals solar panels, that action greatly increases the chances their neighbours will too. Individual actions communicate what is permissible and ethical. These "neighbour effects" suggest that personal responsibility is essential in advancing the cultural change required for a sustainable society.[38]

While environmentalists have exaggerated the importance of consumer demand, individuals can influence markets. The specific variants of personal power that most influence harmful modes of production are tactics that directly disrupt supply, increase capital costs, pressure investors, alarm insurers, create new infrastructures of provision, introduce sociopolitical risks for polluters, and innovate new forms of production and ownership. Since recalcitrant governments often fail to protect the commons and markets only offer limited reform, citizens must cultivate forms of voluntary association and power beyond the market and state alike. As climate justice advocate Tim DeChristopher urges, "We must be the carbon tax."[39]

Brand and the counterculture were not misguided in cultivating a social politics of right livelihood. Social change requires the personal to be political—so long as cultural rebellion does not marginalize collective political action. The recent acceleration of renewable energies, the dramatic decline in U.S. meat consumption, the emergence of a widespread fossil fuel divestment movement, expanding community-supported agriculture programs, and popularity of sharing economies offer a tantalizing—if limited—glimmer of a cultural shift that could stimulate the collective political action needed to forge a more sustainable economy. Cultural reformation prefigured collective political action in nearly all twentieth-century social movements—although it furnished no substitute for it. Innovating new strategies that unite right livelihood, collective action, and supply-side environmentalism remains an imperative for all those who call Earth home.

14

PURCHASING CHANGE

The (Un)Intended Consequences of Biofuel Consumption on the World's Poor

H. LOUISE DAVIS

N APRIL 2008, political cartoonist Patrick Chappette produced a cartoon that humorously exposed the unintended consequences of the Global North's new reliance on biofuels. The image depicts an obese white man feeding the fuel tank of his car with bio-ethanol fuel while two emaciated people of colour, presumably from industrializing nations, stand in the background with empty bowls in hand. The man seems unconcerned by the unspoken needs of his fellow global citizens and responds to their silent presence with a simple yet dismissive statement: "Sorry, I'm busy saving the planet." The image reflects what many U.S. citizens have slowly started to realize—that biofuels are not as unproblematic a solution to our addiction to oil as they may seem. Chappette's cartoon illustrates the ridiculousness and naiveté of those of us in the Global North trying to "save the planet" without fully understanding the consequences of our choices. A growing body of evidence indicates that, while biofuels might reduce dependency on foreign oil, their production potentially reinforces existing global economic inequities separating the Global North and Global South.

The production of biofuels has proven extremely detrimental to poor people around the globe. The impact is particularly severe for the impoverished in industrializing nations who are most adversely affected, not only by food price hikes, but also land use change necessitated by the consistent increase in demand for first generation biofuels. Since the mid-2000s, food prices have spiked to such an extent that over 3.5 billion people currently spend 50 percent or more of their income on food.[1] While the causes of food shortages and price increases are multiple, there is a definite correlation between recent food crises and the production of first generation biofuels made from food crops. Converting food into fuel has exacerbated shortages and price increases in a global food market already volatile due to climate change, unexpected reductions in crop yields worldwide, the use of edible crops for animal feed, and the production of non-edible commodities such as bio-plastics.

To make matters worse, scientific evidence now indicates that the production and use of first generation biofuels has had a detrimental impact on the environment. Current studies illustrate that "renewable" fuel sources potentially exacerbate climate change through increasing emissions of greenhouse gases (GHG).[2] The increase of emissions indirectly impacts food production, particularly for farmers in parts of the world most susceptible to climate change, and potentially damages ecosystems on which many poor in the Global South rely to sustain life.

Integrating research provided by scholars in a diverse range of disciplines, as well as writings by entrepreneurs in the biofuel field and non-profit organizations focusing on poverty, this chapter identifies several of the social, economic, and environmental concerns surrounding the production and use of first, second, and third generation biofuels. Paying attention to the nature of global grain and fuel markets, the economic and environmental theories that underpin U.S. government policies on biofuels and U.S. sustainability criteria, and biofuel related land use change (LUC) in the Global South, I unpack the complexities of biofuel production and consumption.

Global Food Prices

Two-thirds of the world's caloric intake is through grains such as rice, corn, and wheat.[3] The development of biofuels made from food grains has led to what many analysts have described as the "food vs. fuel" dilemma, where grains originally consumed as food are now being processed into biofuels. The result of the increased demand for grains produced by biofuel mandates throughout the U.S. and EU has led to a worldwide spike in food prices. While there are a number of other causes to which such spikes can be attributed—climate change, conflict, population increase, grain market fluctuations—many economists and scientists argue that, even if the price jumps are not directly attributable to the production of first generation biofuels, biofuel demand has adversely affected the grain market. Biotechnologist and biofuel entrepreneur Steven Mayfield challenges the common food vs. fuel view that the production of biofuels led specifically to a food shortage worldwide but notes that while "fuel was not the dominant economic force driving the cost of food" over the past seven years, "as the price of energy goes up, it becomes more significant a component of cost."[4]

Paradoxically, as the price of both food and energy increases, so too does the production of food and fuel crops and the amount of land devoted to their production. Despite the increase in yield, however, the amount of food consumed per capita in developing nations has declined. This is unfortunately because, in many food insecure locations, land previously used to grow food crops has been reallocated to fuel crop production. This is especially the case in Latin America and the former Soviet Union, where LUC from food crop production to fuel crop production is increasing rapidly.[5] Throughout the industrializing world, global corporations are taking possession of local farmland through illegal land grabs and expanding agricultural operations into fragile ecosystems, such as virgin rainforests in Indonesia and South America. Such illegal and ecologically damaging practices are no doubt stimulated by the need to meet government mandates and, of course, increase profit.

The impact of grain price increases has proven most devastating for small-scale farmers and low-income peoples in the Global South. Recent shifts in the market price of grains have had a direct and lasting impact on those most impoverished, whose main source of calories come from the very same grains used to produce biofuels. LUC has exacerbated the problem for rural farmers, often making not only access to food but also to farmable land more difficult.

According to Mayfield, part of the reason for food insecurity is a lack of agricultural innovation. He argues that there has been little incentive to increase efficiency in the agricultural system over the past fifty years because the system has seemed to produce enough for the world's growing population and has continued to prove profitable. In his analysis of energy inputs and outputs, Mayfield illustrates how agricultural practices are inefficient. He notes that, when energy was cheap, so too was the price of agricultural production; but as fuel costs become more expensive, so do all aspects of agricultural production. This is because all agricultural processes currently rely on the expenditure of energy (fuel) to produce energy (in the form of calories or renewable fuels). Agricultural economists and social scientists support Mayfield's assumption that our agricultural system is in part to blame for current food shortages, noting that current land management policies worldwide result in gross agricultural inefficiencies.[6]

Agricultural economists have also illustrated how the food price increases of the past ten years have been exacerbated as much by the inefficient functioning of the grain markets as by agricultural production inefficiencies. Before 2007, price hikes were often buffered by the market as commodities traders assumed that any shortfall in supply, and corresponding reductions in consumption due to price increases, could be absorbed until the next period. While this system can work even when mandates exist, such buffering only works if mandates are temporary and when, as Brian Wright explains, in "the next period, the market demand curve reverts to its original kinked form, and part of the reduction in supply will in turn be shared with future markets if the harvest is large enough to allow carry-out storage."[7] Since 2007, however, demand for grains has done nothing but increase, and as a result, no future market has been able to absorb the shock of increased demand caused by the limited supply of grains in future markets.

Global Fuel Usage

During 2014, 2.1 trillion gallons of oil were consumed globally.[8] This number, excessive as it may seem, is only set to increase as energy requirements are constantly on the rise. Energy demand increased 2.4-fold between 1971 (the year in which the United States reached peak oil production) and 2010, and 70 percent of that increase in demand came from developing nations in Asia.[9] The increased demand in Asia is not surprising, especially given that millions in India and China desire the same energy exhaustive lifestyle they see enjoyed by citizens in the Global North. It is estimated that energy demands will continue to rise in the future, increasing by 1.5 times again by 2035. If this current rate continues, global oil reserves will be most likely be exhausted by 2050.[10]

Each year the United States uses an excessive amount of fuel. In 2014 alone, over 374 million gallons of fuel were consumed per day, totalling

136.78 billion gallons (3.26 billion barrels) over the course of the year.[11] The U.S. government has developed initiatives and incentives to produce and use renewable fuel sources to reduce reliance on foreign oil and meet increased demand for fuel. Biofuel development started in the U.S. in the mid- to late 1970s. The 1978 Energy Tax Act was the first political move to provide energy companies with large-scale financial incentives to produce and use renewable energy sources. From 1978 until 2004, biofuel companies received federal excise tax exemptions of 40 cents per gallon of pure ethanol.[12] In 2005 the EPA instituted a Renewable Fuels Standards (RFS) program. RFS established biofuel mandates and changed tax exemptions to tax refunds.[13] The RFS program "initially mandated that 4.0 billion gallons of renewable fuel be blended into gasoline in 2006 and increased to 7.5 billion gallons by 2012." In 2007 it implemented more complex rules and placed more emphasis on GHG emissions.[14] RFS2, as the program is now called, requires a consistent increase of biofuel usage every year and mandates that, by 2022, 36 billion gallons of fuel be acquired from "renewable sources."[15] To encourage the use of next generation biofuels, RFS2 mandates that 16 billion gallons be advanced cellulosic biofuels. However, given the inadequate supply of cellulosic ethanol, such targets seem unrealistic.[16]

Types of Biofuels

Biofuel can be defined generically as "any *biogenic* form of liquid or gaseous fuel used predominantly in the transport sector, but may include fuels used for the production of electricity or heat."[17] Distinctions between generations are based on crop type, location grown, production method, and level of efficiency.

First generation biofuels (1G) are produced from a range of food crops, including corn, soy, wheat, sugar cane, rapeseed, and palm seed oils. These food crops are used to produce the two most common biofuels: bioethanol, which is used as a blend; and biodiesel, which can be blended with fossil fuel diesel or used by itself. Bioethanol is produced by the digestion or extraction of sugars from crops. Biodiesel is produced by the esterification of seed oil.[18]

Second generation renewable fuel sources (2G) are produced from non-edible biomass, also known as cellulosic products, such as straw, woody biomass, and organic waste produced from the non-edible parts of food crops.[19] Processes to break down sugars from such biomass are somewhat more complicated than with 1G, and a number of distinct processes are used to convert raw products into liquid biofuels: thermochemical processing can be used to convert any organic material into liquid biofuel; mechanical extraction is used to expel crude oils from oil seeds; briquetting of biomass crushes and macerates woody biomass and organic waste; and distillation—the most common method employed—evaporates essential oils and condenses them back into liquid form. Direct combustion and gasification of biomass (which produces synthesis gas or syngas) are also employed by the 2G industry.[20]

Third generation biofuels (3G) are produced from non-edible biomass that is grown on sites unsuitable for crop production, such as saline land or in water. 3G consists of organic materials from which scientists have produced biomethanol, syngas, biochar (charcoal stored in the soil as a carbon sink), and biohydrogen. 3G includes: halophytes (plants that thrive in saline environments, such as mangroves and salt marsh grasses), from which oils can be derived from fatty acids or ash;[21] algae, which can be grown quickly and creates a concentrate almost identical to crude oil;[22] and photosynthetic bacteria, which needs neither land nor supplementation to grow, grows quickly, and is used to produce biohydrogen and biomethane.[23]

Despite the potential sustainability of 3G and the fact that the production of 3G does not compete with food production, 1G biofuels are still by far the most common. This is not only because 1G are the easiest to produce, but also because the infrastructure to manufacture and distribute them already exists. In attempts to address the food vs. fuel debates, governmental agencies around the globe, including the EPA, are currently touting 2G fuels as viable alternatives because they are not produced from food sources. However, to assume that the mandated use of 2G will counteract the negative impact of 1G is naïve for a number of reasons.

First, the raw materials used to produce 2G are also used in animal feed. Thus, the increasing demand for woody biomass and organic waste has led to an increase in animal feedstock prices and meat. While the majority of the world's poor do not derive a significant portion of their calories from meat, the demand for meat around the globe is on the rise, and the use of 2G could send meat prices soaring because 2G and animal feed are derived from the same sources. Second, despite 2G being touted by the EPA as a better alternative fuel source compared to 1G, the sustainability of 2G is questionable. Energy conversion for 2G fuels is inefficient, requires significant water and energy input for conversion, and produces pollutants in its waste streams.[24] Furthermore, it is still unclear whether

2G will reduce or increase GHG emissions.[25] Third, the removal of raw materials for 2G fuels has a negative impact on soil nutrients and soil structure.[26]

The 3G renewable fuel sources are of course more sustainable because they can be grown on barren saline lands using saltwater irrigation. As Abideen et al. note: "Biomass produced using saline land and saline water may supplement biofuel production without compromising food security."[27] However, despite their promise, 3G are significantly underfunded and technologically immature.[28] More infrastructure is needed in order to render them viable alternatives to 1G and 2G biofuels.

Sustainability of U.S. Biofuel Mandates

Despite government subsidies being provided at various points in the supply chain,[29] the oil and gas industry has continued to protest against mandates that require them to purchase and blend a certain amount of bioethanol and biodiesel with transportation fuels.[30] Such resistance to RFS2 results, in part, from the fact that producers of 2G renewable fuels cannot presently fulfil demand.

Food animal farmers, disturbed by increased costs of animal feed, have also voiced concern at U.S. biofuel mandates.[31] Scientists and economists have raised concerns regarding the adequacy of economic theories on which biofuel mandate policies are based.[32] Environmentalists have criticized the use of 1G and 2G because both generations lead to soil erosion, air and water pollution, and an increase in GHG emissions.[33] NGOs have exposed how biofuel production in the Global South has violated human rights and irreparably damaged fragile ecosystems.

While acknowledging some of these concerns, the EPA has refused to alter mandates to help alleviate cost for food animal producers. They have also proven incapable of addressing many of the concerns raised by academics, environmentalists, and human rights activists. This is in large part because of the inadequacy of the sustainability criteria used by the U.S. government to determine the economic, environmental, and social viability of biofuel production and usage. Current criteria focus only on lifecycle stages of biofuels: raw material acquisition; raw material preprocessing and transport; liquid fuels production; product transport and refuelling; and use.[34] In focusing their sustainability assessments solely on the supply chain of renewable fuel sources, the EPA fails to take into consideration any indirect social and environmental consequences of biofuel production. To fully assess the sustainability of the U.S. renewable fuels policies and systems, the EPA needs to consider the social and environmental consequences of LUC beyond the supply chain in both the United States and other biofuel producing nations. This will entail a significant overhaul of sustainability criteria and an opening up of debates about LUC, debates that are currently lacking throughout the energy community.[35]

While a significant amount of bioethanol is produced within the U.S. (in 2014, 40 percent of all corn grown in the U.S. was converted into biofuel),[36] U.S. manufacturers cannot fully meet demand for renewable fuel sources, particularly biodiesel and 2G fuels. A significant portion of renewable fuel sources used in the U.S. is imported from countries in the Global South such as Argentina, Brazil, and China.[37] Throughout the Global South, LUC and illegal corporate land grabs have led to the displacement of subsistence farmers, loss of livelihood, destruction of rural communities, and forced migration. None of these social impacts are currently considered in the EPA's sustainability criteria. As a result, the production of renewable fuel sources for U.S. markets and by U.S. corporations replicates and reinforces the same global social inequities that existed before their development and mandated use.

The displacement of local populations also has a detrimental impact on the environment. When displaced subsistence farmers clear forests and grasslands to plant food, they destroy the carbon sinks that "keep greenhouse gases out of the atmosphere until they are ploughed up." In doing so, they inadvertently exacerbate climate change.[38] Like the negative impacts of biofuel production, the impacts of climate change are also unevenly distributed: the most vulnerable and food insecure populations of global southerners tend to be the most immediately and severely affected.[39] Despite such environmental damage being a direct result of biofuel production and use, the EPA does not take it into account when assessing the ecological impact of biofuels. This is because, in these particular cases, damage results not from biofuel lifecycle processes but from the actions of local populations. According to their own criteria, neither the U.S. government nor the corporations from which they purchase renewable fuels can be held responsible for this environmental damage. Instead, the blame for GHG emissions increases is placed firmly at the feet of displaced populations that suffer most from, but are least prepared to deal with, the impacts of climate change.

Unregulated LUC leads to human rights abuses and environmental injustice, the consequences of which will impact generations to come. The irony is that, if energy and food producers were to establish better land management policies, such extensive LUC might not even be necessary.[40] However, there are few incentives for energy producers to develop more efficient use of current land resources and, at this present time, there is "no sustainability scheme [that] can counterbalance the powerful incentive to produce ever more biofuels at the expense of people's rights and the environment."[41] Without a form of global governance, such illegal and exploitative practices will continue. Such global governance, however, must be created collaboratively by all impacted nations. It must be designed to protect the rights of all citizens and provide nation-states the power to govern biofuel production within their borders.

Conclusion

Biofuel disrupts social, economic, and environmental systems all over the world, as corporations search for the easiest and most profitable way to meet government mandates. Energy corporations, particularly those trading in the U.S., reap the benefits of biofuel production in both government subsidies and sales. In contrast, impoverished populations around the world assume all of the economic risks. Some of the world's poorest people are paying the price of the world's addiction to oil. The answer to global warming should not be starving the poor.

As the largest consumer of fuel and a nation with strict government mandates regarding biofuel, the U.S. needs to take responsibility for the direct and indirect consequences of renewable fuel source production and use. Farmers, scientists, agricultural economists, environmentalists, and human rights activists have all clearly illustrated the flaws in systems of biofuel production and U.S. government policies. Given the evidence we currently have regarding the unsustainability of 1G and 2G, the EPA needs to acknowledge the inadequacy of the economic theories and sustainability criteria they use to determine policy and the plausibility of current biofuel mandates. They, along with other governments, need to incentivize the production and use of 3G, support the development of 3G infrastructures, and subsidize 3G industry initiatives.

Like the EPA, citizens and consumers need to be educated about the broad global impacts of biofuel production and use. Citizens in the Global North have the power to pressure their governments to take account of the multiple consequences of biofuel production and to develop, along with other nations, certification systems that force corporations to develop sustainable practices. While debates abound regarding the potential of consumers to fight against human rights abuses and environmental injustice, one can only hope that through consumer pressure and ethical consumer practices, it becomes possible to pressure energy corporations to assume the risk of renewable fuel source production and use.

In order to remedy some of the negative and unintended consequences of renewable fuel source production and use, systems of production and assessment must be revised considerably. At present, however, only impoverished rural populations and underfunded governments in the Global South bear the burden of requesting and enforcing such revisions. To develop a fair system in which the most vulnerable populations do not assume most of the immediate risk—a system in which *all* global citizens are both afforded their rights as humans and required to take the responsibility to protect their collective environment—citizens and consumers in wealthy nations like the U.S. need to share the burden, even if that means taking big corporations to task or paying a little bit more for fuel.

15

BUYING A BETTER WORLD

From Cause Marketing to Social Innovation, Can Consumption Create Positive Social Change?

MARA EINSTEIN

JUST READING THROUGH a single magazine in October 2013, I was asked—in a deluge of pleas—to support breast cancer charities. The publication began with a letter from the editor, flanked by an advertisement for a pink Ralph Lauren leather bag, of which half the $2500 purchase price would go to the company's Pink Pony Fund should I choose to purchase it. Saks Fifth Avenue offered a "Key to the Cure" t-shirt hawked by Jennifer Aniston. Ford Motor Company was selling its "Warriors in Pink" gear promising, "100% of the net proceeds from each sale supports one of four breast cancer charities." I could buy shoes for half price on QVC and "net proceeds benefit breast cancer research and education." More engaging for consumers was a two-page spread that provided a wealth of consumer products to choose from, including a pink ukulele, a $649 pink bicycle, or a $1,365 diamond and gold bracelet, from which 20 percent of the "proceeds will aid Susan G. Komen Foundation."

Why are so many companies jumping on the cancer charity bandwagon? Breast cancer charities are especially appealing to marketers. This is because they target women—the purchasers of more than 80 percent of consumer goods. Also, the pink ribbon is a readily recognizable symbol, so simply putting it on a product package is an easy promotion to implement and there is no consumer learning curve. Finally, helping breast cancer patients tends not to be controversial—who doesn't want to help women overcome a terrible disease?

But breast cancer is not the only issue that ties companies to female-friendly charities and causes, from health to childhood education to the environment. Rather, this is just one example of the thousands of cause-related marketing (CRM) campaigns that companies use to promote a growing number of products and services, from makeup to power tools, from Nike to the NFL. A recent public relations industry survey states that 75 percent of brands used cause marketing in 2010, up from 58 percent the previous year. Moreover, 97 percent of "marketing executives believe it is a valid business strategy."[1] Spending on CRM campaigns doubled between 2001 and 2009, reaching $1.5 billion a year.[2]

Cause-related marketing has become so pervasive because tying products to charities helps sell more products. Period. According to the *Cone 2010 Cause Evolution Study*, "85% of consumers have a more positive image of a product or company when it supports a cause they care about" and "forty-one percent of Americans say they have bought a product because it was associated with a cause or issue in the last year." Those are compelling statistics. Yet supporting charities through product sales is not new. Procter & Gamble, for example, has been subsidizing the Special Olympics for more than thirty years. Rather, what is novel is that CRM has moved out of the purview of the public relations department and into the marketing silo, where it is expected not only to improve corporate reputations but also to contribute to the bottom line. Profits improve for two reasons: cause campaigns are specifically tied to sales, that is, charities are promoted as product benefits in order to sell more goods and, as just noted, this is a successful strategy. In addition, companies benefit from a lower tax burden: because these campaigns are part of marketing, they are a deductible business expense. As an added benefit, most of these campaigns include a social media element, so they provide important consumer data. A win-win-win for the corporations.

However, the same is not true for charities. What does "net proceeds" mean, and how much money, if any, is really going to charity? Of concern is whether the charity is truly being provided support or, more important, whether that support is having any significant and substantive positive change on the underlying issue that makes the charity necessary.

Marketers have increased their use of cause marketing, as consumer response has been overwhelmingly positive. Consumers like these campaigns because they provide justification for spending money on (mostly high-end) consumer goods. Second, brands have become tools in identity creation. As consumers use brands to define who they are, they expect corporations to create brands that reflect their personal belief systems. And, buying a product attached to a cause allows consumers to cross charity off their to-do list.[3] These elements, in part, explain why consumers demand that corporations have a social mission even if they do not hold them accountable for their efficacy. Companies continue to use cause marketing campaigns, even while Carol Cone—the so-called mother of cause marketing—has proclaimed the practice dead, and *Advertising Age* recently trumpeted the death knell for purpose driven marketing.[4]

Some companies, however, are transforming their strategy in light of growing criticism and because of the proliferation of social media, which requires corporations to have increased transparency. Specifically, more companies are implementing what has become known as social innovation, a strategy whereby companies embed social justice and sustainability into the work that they do. This practice has also been called the triple bottom line (TBL), whereby a company ensures that the work it does is in alignment with people, profits, and the planet. In this chapter, I will argue that social innovation strategies can make improvements in the areas of social justice and sustainability. However, true and substantive social change cannot be achieved through the consumer marketplace.

The Growth of Cause-Related Marketing

Marketing research firm Mintel defines cause marketing as "when companies partner with charitable organizations to help non-profits better achieve their goals. CRM is attached to a media campaign, with money generated for the cause through the sale of products."[5]

The first cause-related marketing campaign in the United States was the American Express/Statue of Liberty initiative in 1983. For this campaign, American Express donated money to the Statue of Liberty Restoration Project for each new card that was issued during the fourth quarter of that year as well as giving a percentage of all charges made on Amex cards. This campaign raised $1.7 million and garnered considerable positive press for the corporation.

It is important to note the timing. During the 1980s, the Reagan administration significantly cut corporate taxes while simultaneously gutting the

social safety net. In an attempt to fill the void, charities turned to corporations for financial support. Corporations increased their philanthropic
giving, though it did not come near to making up the monies the government no longer supplied.[6] By the 1990s, however, corporations were looking for ways to improve profits, particularly through cost cutting. In this
economic landscape, cause initiatives had to be not only about good corporate reputations but also about creating a good corporate bottom line.
Thus, a campaign like the Statue of Liberty no longer made sense unless it
could be aligned with the strategic marketing objectives of the company.
To that end, companies developed campaigns that opened markets, gener-
ated sales prospects, or created partnerships with nonprofits.[7] In so doing,
cause marketing moved out of public relations groups and into the marketing departments of most corporations.

Changes in technology, particularly social media, created another
shift in the 2000s. The holy grail of marketing is word-of-mouth, when
one person recommends a product to their friends and acquaintances.
Social media, such as blogs, Facebook, Twitter, YouTube, and Pinter-
est, have enabled the trust that word-of-mouth traditionally garnered in
the real world to be transferred to the online space. Research has shown
that consumers are more likely to purchase and have more positive brand
attitudes when they learn about products from blogs as opposed to traditional media.[8] According to Nielsen, people trust acquaintances and even
unknown consumers who post online more than they trust advertising.[9] It
shouldn't be surprising, then, that within this environment, in which one
person can recommend a charity to another with a simple mouse-click,
cause marketing flourished. People readily share information about causes
they care about, because it is easy and because it shows the world they are
a good person. Thus, while people may hesitate to spread the word about
a product or service because it might make them look shallow or materialistic, not so when "liking" a page raises money to feed the homeless or
sending a tweet buys a book for a library overseas. That the link might
also promote a product is often forgotten or overlooked in this exchange.
As consumers share the cause, the marketer gets more positive promotion for their product and a better ability to customize consumer interactions and further develop customer relationship management through
sophisticated database marketing.[10] Every click of the mouse, every "like"
of a Facebook page provides marketers with information about a visitor's
interests; they, in turn, use this information to sell more products, and
Facebook uses it to sell more advertising.

Social factors—notably the events of September 11, 2001, the coming of age of millennials, and the rise of neoliberalism—contributed to the increase in socially responsible consumerism. September 11 spurred an increase in connecting products to causes.[11] Millennials (those born from the early 1980s to the early 2000s) use brands as building blocks for their identity, so what a product stands for has great significance for this generation. Finally, neoliberalism framed corporations over nation-states as the institutions that would solve social ills.[12] These factors combined perpetuated tying causes to the market well into the 2000s.

Responding to CRM

Early writings about CRM were decidedly pro-business. Initially, industry insiders delineated positive reasons for using these strategies.[13] Researchers in marketing and management provided tactics to make these campaigns more effective.[14] Business and academic writings alike proposed best practices for selecting a nonprofit partner, whether to do a cause campaign or to integrate a social responsibility campaign into the workings of the company and how best to promote it to consumers. In addition, an industry grew up around these initiatives, producing research supporting the expansion of cause marketing. Notable marketing firms specializing in these campaigns include Cone Communications and Edelman's goodpurpose.

Increasingly, however, critics question both the existence and execution of these campaigns.[15] They cite long-term issues such as reduced donations for charities, favouring charities based on their ability to assist corporate sales, misleading consumers in terms of the cause/corporate partnership, and changes in the cause's activities to be more in alignment with corporate needs. Neither marketers nor consumers consider these long-term issues, however, because brand managers' focus is the campaigns' short-term success and consumers focus on what they see as a positive brand benefit or simply the joy of shopping. As Eikenberry correctly notes, "The short-term benefits of cause marketing—also known as consumption philanthropy—belie its long-term costs. These hidden costs include individualizing solutions to collective problems; replacing virtuous action with mindless buying; and hiding how markets create many social problems in the first place."

Blatantly hypocritical cause marketing campaigns draw the most vitriol. In one well-known example, KFC sold pink buckets of chicken in support of breast cancer charity Susan G. Komen. Yet fried chicken contributes to an unhealthy diet leading to obesity, which is a contributing factor in breast cancer. Another example: Wal-Mart ran a Thanksgiving food drive for needy families in Canton, Ohio. However, those needy families were Wal-Mart "associates." When the public discovered that the company ran a food drive for their employees rather than pay a living wage, the campaign went viral.

Even if a cause campaign is inoffensive, the execution of the campaign is at issue, particularly when it comes to transparency. One of the biggest complaints about these campaigns is that consumers rarely know how much money is going to charity or if they are truly contributing to the cause. The vast majority of companies put a cap on how much money they will donate. In a typical example, Anne Klein promotes the sale of a bracelet and notes in their advertising that $50,000 will go to the Breast Cancer Research Foundation. However, the company does not announce when the cap has been reached. Consumers keep buying this and other cause connected products feeling good about their purchases because they believe they are donating to charity, never knowing that they are not.

Social Innovation—Good and Not So Good

Sceptical millennials and the proliferation of social media are moving companies toward a more integrated form of doing good, known as social innovation. As I have noted elsewhere, the hallmarks of social innovation include authenticity, customization, transparency, and sustainability.[16] Unlike cause marketing, which tends to be a promotional add-on, social innovation embeds social justice and sustainability into the day-to-day workings of a corporation.

Social innovation is a nascent business strategy, and companies are seeing mixed results in its implementation. What has been true thus far is that social justice initiatives are easier to embed within a new company than to integrate into an existing organization, particularly one that is publicly traded. We will see that here in looking at TOMS shoes and Warby Parker glasses versus the fast fashion retailer, H&M.

Buy One, Give One Model

Any list of socially innovative companies is likely to include TOMS shoes. Started in 2006 by Blake Mycoskie, this company created the buy one, give one model of philanthropy. Buy one pair of TOMS shoes and one pair will go to a child in the third world through what the company calls a "shoe drop." The company does not use advertising (other than having the owner appear in an American Express commercial), but rather relies on social media, which is in alignment with their millennial target audience. In addition, the company does promotions on college campuses and holds an annual event called "One Day Without Shoes," where devoted TOMS customers are asked to spend an April day barefoot to raise awareness for children's health and education.

TOMS came under fire in 2012 when fastcoexist.com, *Fast Company* magazine's blog, posted an article called "The Broken Buy One Give One Model," one of the most widely read articles the website has ever published. [17] The author noted two glaring problems with buy-one-give-one. First, it doesn't solve a social problem. What is needed in the countries receiving the shoes is "long-term, multi-faceted economic development, health, sanitation, and education solutions." Instead of improving conditions, dropping shoes into these societies undercuts local businesses and distorts the economy. Second, TOMS has built its business on a nonfunctional attribute—the buy-one-give-one model. TOMS shoes are good, but they are expensive, and it is the philanthropy that feeds that higher price point. Feeling good about one's purchase is a key benefit of TOMS and other social campaigns. But now, TOMS is not alone. Other companies have taken up the model. In response, TOMS expanded into selling eyewear and more recently, coffee. It is with this last that the company has improved on one-for-one, working directly with farmers in local communities under an economic development model in which consumers buy premium coffee while the farmers get a fair wage and the community gets clean water systems. [18]

Warby Parker, a seller of reasonably priced eyewear, is another company using the one-for-one model. However, Warby Parker has improved on it. Unlike TOMS' expensive (and to my eyes, unattractive) shoes, Warby Parker eyeglasses are affordable and far cheaper than most of its competitors' products, which are artificially overpriced because of severe consolidation in the industry. All frames sell for $95. Started as an e-commerce company, it has since expanded to include brick-and-mortar retail outlets in New York, Los Angeles, and Boston. The company embodies the "do-good" model, from selling reasonably priced products to donating eyewear to assisting employees in volunteering with charitable organizations. All these activities are not just for show; they are the essence of the company.

Philanthropically, Warby Parker works with VisionSpring to distribute eyeglasses to people around the world. Donations occur in the form of funding and/or product. Unlike TOMS, however, non-profit partners not only provide people in developing countries with eyewear but also with training so that they can become entrepreneurs with their own business, selling eyeglasses. Thus, those selling can make a living, people in the local community have access to glasses they would not have had, and the glasses are provided at a cost they can afford. According to the company, this model of philanthropy "provides community members the dignity to choose whether or not they want glasses and thereby avoids the culture of dependence that often accompanies foreign aid." To date, the company has given away one million free pairs of glasses.[19]

H&M

Social innovation is easier to integrate into new, privately owned companies like TOMS and Warby Parker than it is for existing corporations. This has not, however, stopped companies from attempting to incorporate this consumer-friendly strategy. A notable example is Swedish clothier H&M. This publicly traded company has implemented a plethora of social innovation strategies, yet it has had limited success. These failures are due in large part to sustainability being fundamentally at odds with the company's core business—fast fashion.

In 2012, H&M launched its Conscious Collection, a sustainable line of clothing made with eco-friendly materials like organic cotton and recycled polyester. Promoting social consciousness and sustainable products has been an increasingly popular strategy for marketers over the last decade as part of social innovation initiatives. However, a sustainable clothing line from H&M seemed out of place, as they are one of the world's leading "fast fashion" retailers. The store by definition is about churning out low-priced clothing and rotating the designs every few weeks to continually generate interest on the part of consumers. In line with the company's prevailing strategy, the Conscious Collection disappeared from store windows almost as soon as it got there. In truth, I thought it was a one-shot promotional opportunity.

It turns out that Conscious Collection is only one aspect of an overall sustainability strategy. According to the Global Sustainable Textiles Market Report, H&M has been the world leader in organic cotton use for the last two years, which aligns with the company's initiative to source only sustainable materials, including cotton, by 2020. Even so, sustainable cotton is used in only 11.4 percent of the company's clothes.[20]

However, sustainability goes beyond clothing materials. Initiatives include creating a more ethical supply chain by improving worker conditions (particularly in light of the 2013 tragedy in Bangladesh factory in

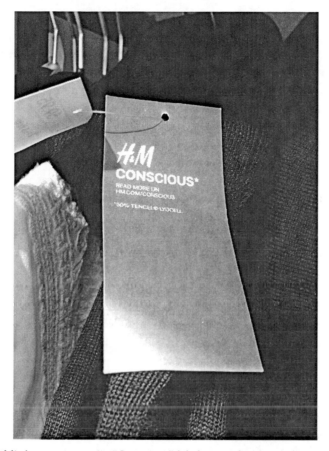

H&M did little to promote its "Conscious" label, part of its corporate sustainability strategy. (Author photo)

which more than 1100 people died), reducing water usage, and increasing recycling of clothing by allowing customers to bring clothing they no longer use back to the store in return for a 15 percent discount on the next item they buy.

H&M has clearly put a lot of effort into their sustainability initiatives as well as making them transparent. Their website bristles with pages and pages of information, including a rating system to measure the effectiveness of their initiatives and show where they still need to make improvements. One has to question their commitment, however, when assessing how the company promotes—or rather does not promote—these initiatives to consumers. H&M has long established itself as a low-cost, "throw away" consumer brand. Other than a week or two of promoting the

Conscious Collection, they have done little to make customers aware of it. I recently went into one of their stores in New York City expecting to see a big display of these clothes. I couldn't find it anywhere. When I asked a salesperson, they told me to look in "trends" on the wall. I looked where he pointed, and only after several minutes of digging did I find a shirt with a green label marked "H&M CONSCIOUS." I did find several more items mixed in with the new fall collection. While I admire that the company is attempting to do the work of social innovation and not simply put social change on the backs of consumers, one wonders why they are doing this without informing customers just a bit more. Only time will tell if fast fashion and sustainability can co-exist. I have serious doubts.

Shopping for Change?

In the end, making the world a better place is not about shopping for change. For sure, attaching a charity to a product makes consumers feel better about buying (usually high-end) goods. However, social justice and sustainability are not achieved through the consumer marketplace. At best, the money raised can offer some kind of symptom relief—providing support for breast cancer patients or food for the hungry or shoes for the poor. Underlying these causes are more substantial social issues like lack of access to health care and joblessness, which can only be affected by governments and corporations, not by individual consumer purchases.

The hope is that companies will move away from cause-related marketing and more toward social innovation. As this occurs, there will be fits and starts as companies learn what works for their product, their employees, and the environment. As we saw here, some initiatives work better than others, but in all cases openness and transparency are key. A great example of this is salesforce.com's 1/1/1 model. Quite simply, the company contributes "1 percent of profits, 1 percent of equity, and 1 percent of employee hours back to the communities it serves."[21] Admittedly, this is more difficult for existing, publicly traded companies. But it would be heartening to see more companies move in the direction of Warby Parker and think along the lines of one of its founders, Neil Blumenthal: "we started this business to radically transform the optical industry, bring down prices, and transfer billions of dollars from these multi-national companies to normal people. And, thinking more broadly, . . . we wanted to demonstrate that business can be profitable and can do good in the world, and it doesn't have to charge a premium for it."[22] That's something that's worth opening your wallet for.

16

WHAT ABOUT THE CAUSE?

The Campaign for Safe Cosmetics and the Pinkwashing of Breast Cancer Activism

DANIEL FABER, AMY LUBITOW, and MADELINE BRAMBILLA

THE LAST DECADE has witnessed the growth of a new movement devoted to the reform of chemicals policy in the United States and Canada. Grassroots organizing efforts focused on dangerous toxins in consumer products are a major component of this effort. Founded in 2004, the Campaign for Safe Cosmetics ("the Campaign" hereafter) is exemplary of a new form of consumer activism that highlights links between human health problems and hazardous chemicals in personal care products—especially cosmetics. Uniting over 170 environmental, health, worker, environmental justice, consumer, faith, and women's organizations into a broad-based national coalition, the Campaign has directly pressured leading personal care product companies to remove hazardous chemicals from their products through a variety of tactics, including public shaming. In so doing, the Campaign has drawn greater public attention to the issue of toxic chemicals, enlarged the constituency base of the movement, helped to reform industry, and encouraged the adoption of government regulations.

Drawing on social mobilization around the breast cancer epidemic, the Campaign has also used the same strategies to organize consumers against "pinkwashing." Coined by Breast Cancer Action, the term "pinkwashing" is adapted from "greenwashing," the practice whereby businesses deceptively promote themselves and their products as "eco-friendly," even though their overall practices are detrimental to the environment. "Pinkwashing" refers to marketing actions by companies and groups to position themselves as leaders in the struggle to eradicate breast cancer while engaging in practices that contribute to rising rates of the disease.[1] Since 1991, the colour pink and pink ribbons have been internationally recognized symbols of breast cancer awareness, and companies have used them in their marketing and merchandise to indicate that they have joined the philanthropic fight against breast cancer. Yet many of these same companies continue to use cancerous chemicals in their manufacturing processes or consumer products, including their "pink ribbon" product lines. By appealing to the sensibilities of health-conscious consumers, pinkwashers enlarge the market for their toxic commodities. Pinkwashing has provided a way for petrochemical dependent corporations, in particular, to focus the conversation on scientific *cures* rather than environmental causes. By distracting breast cancer and consumer activists from focusing on the environmental and corporate *causes* of breast cancer, it has contributed to framing breast cancer as a disease to be *cured* by medicine rather than *prevented* by halting corporations from using carcinogenic toxins.

The implications of pinkwashing are profound. Studies show that the mass media pays scant attention to the environmental causes of breast cancer, especially with respect to corporate and governmental responsibility for chemical exposure. Instead, the media emphasizes genetic causation or the role of improved diet and other personal behaviours, even though these factors explain only a small fraction of breast cancer incidence. Moreover, pinkwashing is deterring the scientific and advocacy solutions to the causes of breast cancer.[2] The Campaign for Safe Cosmetics challenges the practice of pinkwashing, illustrating the potential for consumer-based movements to create positive change in economic markets and policy realms. By asking "what about the cause?" the Campaign has become a vital component of a more radical environmentalism that is necessary to transform the toxic nature of contemporary consumer capitalism.

Cosmetics and Toxic Chemical Trespass

The chemical industry is among the most profitable industries in the world, generating annual revenues of $1.3 trillion. American chemical companies alone command $698.9 billion of these earnings.[3] In Canada, chemicals and plastic production was valued at more than $73 billion in 2013, with exports (primarily to the U.S.) totalling nearly $40 billion.[4] Chemicals are a ubiquitous part of the North American economy, being used in the production of everything from food and clothing to high-tech electronics and children's toys. In fact, the U.S. annually produces or imports twenty-seven trillion pounds of some 6,200 chemical substances alone—the equivalent of 925,000 tractor-trailer truckloads every day.[5] The Silent Spring Institute recently tested a variety of common cleaning, personal care, and household products, including cosmetics, sunscreens, perfumes, toothpaste, and air fresheners, for the presence of some 66 types of asthma-related and endocrine disrupting chemicals (EDC) chemicals linked to cancer. They found 55 of these harmful chemicals in these products, demonstrating widespread exposure to consumers.[6] In fact, one study found that 1 in 5 of the 29,000 personal care products surveyed by the Environmental Working Group contains chemicals linked to cancer.[7]

The toxic chemicals present in these products often pass into the human body. The Centers for Disease Control and Prevention (CDC) routinely conducts biomonitoring studies that test the blood and urine of Americans for chemical toxins. A 2009 survey found that nearly all of the 2,500 participants had detectable levels of harmful substances such as perchlorate, mercury, BPA, perfluorinated chemicals, and flame-retardants.[8] The CDC estimates that the average person living in North America carries more than 150 different chemicals in their body at any point in time. The environmental movement terms this *toxic trespass*. In Canada, preliminary testing of the umbilical cord blood of newborn babies found each child was born with 55 to 121 toxic compounds and possibly cancer-causing chemicals in their body. Of the 137 chemicals found in total, 132 are reported to cause cancer in humans or animals, 110 are considered toxic to the brain and nervous system, and 133 cause developmental and reproductive problems in mammals.[9] In effect, North American babies are born pre-polluted.

The presence of toxic chemicals in consumer products and the environment is implicated in rising incidences of asthma, cancer, and many reproductive, neurodegenerative, and learning disorders. Research suggests that as much as 70 percent of breast cancer cases may be attributable to environmental causes.[10] A 2007 statement from the International Conference on Fetal Programming and Developmental Toxicity reported that chemical prenatal and early postnatal exposures were capable of influencing health throughout a person's life and that "certain environmental chemicals can alter gene expression [and] cause lasting functional changes in specific organs and tissues and increased susceptibility to disease."[11] Furthermore, multiple chemicals that are considered relatively benign in isolation can combine inside the body to profoundly harm our health in ways that scientists are just beginning to map out.[12]

Since no amount of individual "self-vigilance" can safely quarantine consumers from chemical trespass, the failure to protect the public from toxic chemicals resides in government policy, especially the Toxic Substances Control Act (TSCA) in the U.S. The TSCA inventory now lists nearly 85,000 substances for sale. Some 62,000 of these were grandfathered in when TSCA was passed in 1976, exempting chemical producers from having to disclose information about potential hazards. In fact, the law creates powerful disincentives for manufacturers to investigate health problems related to their products. Over 1,000 new chemicals are synthesized each year. Complete toxicological screening data are available for just 7 percent of these chemicals, and more than 90 percent have never been tested for their effects on human health.[13] Instead, the Environmental Protection Agency (EPA) has partially regulated only five classes of chemicals since 1976, and fewer than 250 chemicals on the market have undergone health and safety tests.[14] Similarly, Canada's Chemicals Management Plan (CMP) has only reviewed 200 chemicals for their impact on human health and the environment, with plans to review an additional 300 by 2016.[15]

Health problems stemming from toxic trespass are fuelling the growth of a transnational movement to reform chemicals policy. In Canada, Environmental Defence has advocated for the elimination of carcinogenic and hormone-disrupting toxins in everyday products, including personal care products like shampoo and soap. Despite some progress under the country's Chemicals Management Plan, such as the banning of bisphenol A (BPA) from baby bottles and phthalates in children's toys, major gaps remain in Canada. Similarly, environmental health advocates in the U.S. and Canada have built campaigns headed by the Coming Clean collaborative and other organizations to reform chemicals policy. Since 2004, Coming Clean has provided a forum for sharing information and strategy among a diverse network of nongovernmental organizations (NGOs) working for environmental and occupational health and justice at the local, state, and national levels.

In the United States, the movement has also created the State Alliance for Federal Reform (SAFER) to advance new, far-reaching chemical policies at the state level—policies that indirectly help drive federal reform efforts. Over the last decade, grassroots mobilization around the dangers of chemical substances has resulted in the passage of over seventy chemical safety laws across eighteen states, including the adoption of comprehensive chemical policies in four states. This mobilization has contributed to numerous attempts to reform TSCA by progressive Democrats. In response, the chemical industry has fielded over five hundred lobbyists and spent over $330 million since 2005 to weaken the push for meaningful reform.[16] Repeated efforts to pass strong TSCA reform have so far failed in the face of strong opposition offered by the chemical industry and their political allies on Capitol Hill. Given this political landscape, the Campaign represents an interesting example of a consumer-based movement to enhance environmental health outcomes.

The Birth of the Safe Cosmetics Campaign

In the U.S., personal care products are part of a $50 billion industry, yet there is no meaningful regulation ensuring that these products are free of chemicals linked to cancer, reproductive harm, and other serious health problems. The health dangers posed by these products thus provide a powerful example of the need for overhauling federal chemicals policy. The U.S. Food and Drug Administration (FDA) lacks the authority to require basic health testing of personal care product ingredients before they are released into the market. Unlike food or drug manufacturers, a cosmetic maker may use almost any raw material as an ingredient in their products (with the exception of colour additives and nine specific chemicals) without approval from the FDA. In the event that a product or ingredient appears to be hazardous to health, the FDA has no authority to require a product recall. Instead, the agency can request that the company issue a voluntary recall or can take the issue to court.[17]

To fill the void left by insufficient governmental oversight, the cosmetics industry (in negotiations with the FDA) formed the Cosmetics Industry Review (CIR) panel in 1976. Funded by the Cosmetic, Toiletries, and Fragrance Association, the industry's trade association, the CIR gives the appearance of an effective regulatory body, with a panel of seven scientists and physicians. However, CIR safety suggestions are not mandatory. Furthermore, the Environmental Working Group (EWG) estimates that the CIR panel has failed to assess 90 percent of cosmetic ingredients in use today. In fact, many products violate the few suggestions that have been made.[18]

For some environmental advocates, the presence of hazardous substances in cosmetics and personal care products represents an opportunity to connect the public as consumers in a more personal manner to the larger movement to reform chemicals policy. The average American woman uses twelve personal care products per day, resulting in exposure to over 120 chemicals.[19] These dangers are not restricted to women, as the average American man uses six personal care products per day containing over eighty different chemicals. More than one in five of these are chemicals linked to cancer. In Canada alone, the men's personal care industry is worth more than $690 million, and is growing by an average of 2 percent every year. A recent Canadian study of seventeen common men's products (including aftershave, body wash, shaving cream, and deodorant) found chemicals linked to cancer, birth defects, sperm damage, obesity, asthma, and other chronic health problems. These products also commonly contain phthalates, a group of chemicals linked to testicular cancer, the most common cancer among men 15–29 years old.[20]

At the first meeting of the National Alliance for Cancer Prevention, pioneered by the Breast Cancer Fund in 2003, several organizations agreed to mobilize around the issue of toxins in personal care products. This project launched at the March for Women's Lives in 2004 under the name "Because We're Worth It: The Campaign for Safe Cosmetics" (later shortened because of copyright concerns from the L'Oréal company, whose slogan "Because You're Worth It" inspired this early language). Participating groups included the Breast Cancer Fund, Friends of the Earth, National Black Environmental Justice Coalition, National Environmental Trust, Alliance for a Healthy Tomorrow, EWG, and Women's Voices for the Earth. Building on this legacy, the Campaign continues to push for the removal of hazardous ingredients from personal care products in the U.S. By focusing on health dangers posed by products that ordinary people use daily, the Campaign enlarges the constituency base of the movement. Unions, occupational health and safety advocates, parents and religious groups, women's health organizations, networks of nurses and medical professionals, and other organizations that otherwise would not be involved are now part of a broader movement for a more precautionary approach to chemicals policy. The leveraging of several different stakeholder groups as a part of a broader consumer movement to reign in toxic chemical use in personal care products has been part of more than a decade of active strategic organizing.

People over Profits: The Strategic Vision of the Campaign

When the Campaign was established in 2004, activists faced a daunting challenge at the federal level. First, the petrochemical industry had linked with other major industrial polluters to create a vast infrastructure of think tanks, policy institutes, and research centres devoted to weakening chemical policies and environmental regulations. Second, corporate polluters had created one of the most powerful political lobbies on the planet. In the last half of 2005, over $200 million a month was spent on lobbying by what we term the "polluter-industrial complex." In addition, petrochemical companies had flooded the electoral process with campaign funds for anti-environmental Congressional candidates and contributed mightily to the election of George Bush as president in the 2000 and 2004 elections. As a result, the corporate "foxes" of the petrochemical industry were in charge of the federal government "hen house," including the EPA.[21]

Given the hostility of the G. W. Bush Administration and Congress to environmental regulation, it was clear to the Campaign (and the anti-toxics movement more broadly) that any call for meaningful reform of federal chemicals policy in general, and TSCA in particular, would not be heeded. Therefore, the Campaign sidestepped the federal government by placing direct pressure on manufacturers to move toward using safer alternatives. Retailers were targeted to stop carrying products containing harmful chemicals. Such pressure was applied through media events, consumer education, and highly public "shaming" actions, including campaigns targeting individual companies, such as OPI and Johnson & Johnson. Although consumer-oriented activism is often criticized for failing to bring about significant changes in the production processes responsible for environmental health problems, the Campaign sought to mobilize consumers as a force for cleaner production. If the Campaign could secure agreements from leading companies to eliminate toxics, then other companies would likely follow suit. In so doing, the Campaign would break down one of the most central arguments made by manufacturers and politicians against government regulations—that it is too expensive or technically unfeasible to use safer alternatives to toxic chemicals. In that respect, the Campaign would lay the groundwork for moving beyond non-binding voluntary actions to the passage of more comprehensive and mandatory federal regulations further down the road.

The Campaign's consumer-oriented strategy forces leaders in the industry to reformulate product ingredients and serves as a catalyst for shifting the market. For example, the Campaign has worked to organize consumer boycotts that target specific cosmetics companies. The Campaign provides "toolkits" that contained scientific information and talking points to help consumers pressure cosmetics companies and cosmetics retailers directly. In 2007, the Campaign targeted the nail polish company OPI to encourage them to remove a "toxic trio" of contaminants (formaldehyde, toluene, and phthalates). This effort inspired consumers to call and write to OPI, request alternatives at nail salons, and ask retailers and drug stores to stock nail polishes with fewer toxic ingredients. As customers increasingly demanded safer nail products, OPI responded, and a spillover effect occurred as well; other nail polish companies followed suit in phasing out the "toxic trio" in order to maintain their consumer base. For instance, competing brands Sally Hansen and Orly both independently committed to product reformulation without extensive additional pressure from the Campaign. The voluntary agreement to make safer products by one or two leading brands created a domino effect where product labels listing "formaldehyde, toluene, & DBP free" have become more common. The nature of capitalist competition and the increasing salience of claims to safety for consumers create important moments of opportunity for consumer activists. Similar pressure applied by the Campaign later compelled L'Oréal to phase out the toxic pesticide triclosan from their products.

The Campaign has also targeted Johnson & Johnson for manufacturing products contaminated with formaldehyde (including their iconic baby shampoo!). In May 2009, two months after the release of product-testing results in the report *No More Toxic Tub: Getting Contaminants out of Children's Bath and Personal Care Products*, the Campaign organized the first letter sent to Johnson & Johnson's Chief Executive Officer, signed by forty organizations and groups. The emphasis on children's exposure to toxins via personal care products resulted in intense media publicity and facilitated coalition building among the Campaign's member groups (particularly for groups like the American Nurses Association, Physicians for Social Responsibility, and the National Association for Pediatric Nurse Practitioners). Members of the American Nurses Association accompanied Campaign representatives to a meeting with Johnson & Johnson executives in August 2009 to negotiate the need for product reformulation. Despite this initial pressure, the company did not comply with the demands of the Campaign until an even broader consumer movement created additional pressure in 2011–12.

After a year of silence from Johnson & Johnson, the Campaign released a second product testing study in November 2011 entitled, *Baby's Tub Still Toxic*. Products were tested from thirteen countries in which Johnson & Johnson items are sold to highlight inconsistencies in product formulations. The report found that many Johnson & Johnson products sold in Europe and Japan were free of formaldehyde-releasing ingredients due to stronger cosmetics regulations in those countries.[22] In August 2012, Johnson & Johnson succumbed to the additional movement and consumer pressure and pledged to remove carcinogens and other potentially toxic chemicals from its products by 2015. The Campaign has since initiated a "Meet it or Beat it" campaign targeting other major cosmetics companies to follow suit. In this instance, the effort to challenge Johnson & Johnson to reformulate their products was bolstered by ongoing consumer-based organizing. As with the OPI effort, the Campaign again provided materials to help consumers with talking points about the harmful ingredients in Johnson & Johnson products and provided language for requesting change.

This example demonstrates the importance of the complex constellation of pressures that are required to force major companies to revise their practices; long-term pressure from established organizations and engaged consumers combined with strong scientific evidence are critical components of this success. The framing of Johnson & Johnson's actions as contradictory in the 2011 report was also arguably quite important in forcing the company to shift their practices. Important here as well were strategic uses of traditional media such as publishing the two product test reports, but then also leveraging these reports and their implications through consumer outreach via social media on Twitter and Facebook. Since its inception, the Campaign has leveraged print media and imagery to help create consumer interest and demand for safer products. It should be expected that the Campaign's utilization of various forms of social media would continue to evolve along with these technologies.

As demonstrated by the above examples, the strategies utilized by the Campaign create results. To date, more than 1,500 companies have signed on to the "Compact for Safe Cosmetics," a tool to differentiate industry leaders from the laggards and to encourage a "market shift" toward safer products. Between 2004 and 2011, the Campaign received commitments from 321 "Champion" companies to meet all of the goals of the Compact by avoiding chemicals banned by health agencies outside the U.S. and fully disclosing product ingredients. An additional 111 companies achieved "Innovator" status by making significant progress toward these goals. These voluntary pledges demonstrated to policymakers that it is "possible to make safe, effective products without using the hazardous chemicals that are all too common in conventional personal care products."[23] The Compact lays a solid foundation for ongoing pressure to establish meaningful regulatory change.

In addition to applying direct pressure to manufacturers and retailers, the Campaign also mobilized their constituencies to push for meaningful regulation of toxic chemicals at the state level. Voluntary pledges by companies to remove toxic ingredients from their products lack enforcement mechanisms, and in the end are inadequate. Just as pushing for voluntary agreements from companies to reformulate products in favour of safer substitutes can break down Congressional opposition to the reform of TSCA and other chemicals policies, the adoption of state-based reforms can break down industry opposition. In the U.S., the prospective adoption of a "patchwork" of state-level regulations (such as the California Safe Cosmetics Act of 2005) puts pressure on industry to accept federal reform as a more manageable alternative. Having fifty different sets of laws for fifty states is too unwieldy for industry to manage. In the same manner, the adoption of comprehensive chemicals policy reform in the European Union (under a program called REACH) is compelling much of the industry to alter their products. As a result of these state-level changes, opportunities to initiate serious consideration of major federal reforms are now present, especially around cosmetics and personal care products. For instance, the Safe Cosmetics Act introduced in the U.S. House of Representatives in 2010, and re-introduced in 2011, aims to restrict or phase out chemicals linked to cancer, birth defects, and developmental harm (among other things). In Canada, there is a general ban on toxic substances in cosmetics, as well as a cautious list of substances that are listed as harmful. And even though the Chemicals Management Plan has banned BPA from baby bottles and phthalates in children's toys, Canada needs to follow Europe and develop a much more comprehensive list of prohibited or restricted substances. These organizing efforts and achievements are creating much broader political opportunities to shift chemical regulatory mechanisms.

These dynamics within the realm of the personal care industry provide an important venue for exploring how consumer movements can build momentum for broader environmental changes. We next consider how similar consumer-based efforts create opportunities for important change in relation to breast cancer.

The Campaign, Breast Cancer, and Corporate Pinkwashing

Breast cancer affects over one million women every year worldwide and is the leading cause (14 percent) of cancer deaths in women.[24] Women in more industrialized nations experience the highest rates of disease. Today women in the U.S. have a one in eight lifetime chance of being diagnosed with breast cancer. Some forty thousand American women die of the disease each year. In fact, between 1973 and 2008, the incidence rate for American women rose by over 40 percent. This increase cannot be explained by improved diagnostics. Despite the widely held assumption that most breast cancer cases are caused by genetics, only 5–10 percent of diagnosed women carry a gene or have a family history of the disease. Additionally, less than 50 percent of all cases are related to individual risk factors such as diet. Instead, environmental exposures to toxic chemicals—through air, water, food, plastics, cosmetics, and other consumer products—are suspected factors in a large number of cancer cases.[25]

"Finding a cure" for breast cancer has become the rallying cry of races, walks, and fundraisers organized by the curative-oriented wing of the breast cancer movement. Mainstream breast cancer organizations such as Susan G. Komen for the Cure engage corporate sponsors that produce pink ribbon products supporters can purchase to fund research on cures. However, if women are encouraged to wear pink as a primary response, then a proper focus on "finding the *cause*" of breast cancer is absent. An exclusive focus on "the cure" displaces public dialogue related to the social and environmental implications of disease causation and suggests that consumer-oriented responses alone are adequate. The burden of action is borne by consumers rather than the corporations producing toxins that spur breast cancer. In 2010, American medical costs associated with cancer were projected by the National Institutes of Health at $124.6 billion, with the highest costs associated with breast cancer ($16.5 billion). By 2020 these costs are estimated to reach $158 to $207 billion. [26]

While funds raised from foundation-corporate breast cancer partnerships have undoubtedly served to further treatment and early detection of breast cancer (which does save women's lives), the lack of focus on identifying the causes is misguided. Moreover, the capacity of corporate entities to decide where hundreds of millions of dollars for research can be spent confers enormous power on these companies and allied foundations. According to the Federal Interagency Breast Cancer and Research Coordinating Committee, only 7 percent of nongovernmental organization funding for breast cancer research—from entities like Susan G. Komen for the Cure and Avon—goes toward projects focused on breast cancer prevention.[27] For instance, less than 2 percent of the funds raised by the Boston Avon Walk benefited environmental research regarding breast cancer prevention in Massachusetts.[28] This is proving to be a health disaster for the people of North America. As stated by Dr. Margaret Cuomo,

> More than 40 years after the war on cancer was declared, we have spent billions fighting the good fight. The National Cancer Institute has spent some $90 billion on research and treatment during that time. Some 260 nonprofit organizations in the United States have dedicated themselves to cancer—more than the number established for heart disease, AIDS, Alzheimer's disease, and stroke combined. Together, these 260 organizations have budgets that top $2.2 billion. . . . It's true there have been small declines in some common cancers since the early 1990s . . . that's hardly cause for celebration. Cancer's role in one out of every four deaths in this country remains a haunting statistic. . . . Simply put, we have not adequately channeled our scientific know-how, funding, and energy into a full exploration of the one path certain to save lives: prevention. That it should become the ultimate goal of cancer research has been recognized since the war on cancer began."[29]

The practice of pinkwashing further exacerbates this philanthropic focus on "the cure." Prominent pinkwashers include cosmetics giant Avon, which has raised over $472 million since 2003 but also initiated the "Kiss Goodbye to Breast Cancer" fundraising campaign that featured six varieties of lipstick that contained endocrine disruptors linked to breast cancer. Additionally, over 250 Avon cosmetic products are in the "highest concern" category for containing endocrine disruptors, neurotoxins, and possible carcinogens. Likewise, the Campaign has exposed Revlon for selling products containing carcinogens, although the company helps to sponsor the "Look Good Feel Better" program that gives makeovers to cancer patients, utilizing these same carcinogen-containing products.

These examples illustrate how companies benefit from pinkwashing: by creating favourable images of the company while obscuring the harmful nature of their products. Marketing around breast cancer has become a strategy for selling products, rather than an altruistic corporate behaviour. In fact, more and more corporations are turning to breast cancer campaigns as a way to differentiate their products and cut through the clutter of commercial advertising. Some have argued that pinkwashers are exploiting the breast cancer cause through their increased sales, tax deductions, and advertising advantages such that they have a stake in the continuation of the disease.[30] This exploitation becomes even more apparent as corporate profits from pink ribbon products greatly exceed the dollars actually donated.

However, public shaming tactics by activist organizations like the Campaign have begun to put a dent in this business strategy. The prevention-oriented wing of the breast cancer movement, of which the Campaign is a central component, has elected to advance a precautionary approach to the disease that targets the replacement of chemicals linked to cancer with safer substitutes. For these organizations (such as the Campaign, Breast Cancer Action, Breast Cancer Fund, and the Massachusetts Breast Cancer Coalition), this includes not only eliminating the use of carcinogens in personal care products but also phasing out chemicals linked to cancer in the economy as a whole. The capacity of the Campaign and its partners to generate long-term, consumer-driven pressure on corporate manufacturers demonstrates that such directness can be successful: ongoing shifts in production and manufacturing of these goods are notable successes of the Campaign. While building momentum for broader policy changes reflects a strategic focus for the Campaign, the consistent pressure and payoff in the marketplace cannot be underestimated; these smaller wins change "business as usual" in the short run while building consumer support and political momentum in the long run.

The comprehensive set of approaches taken by the Campaign can transform individualized consumer responses into more meaningful political change. An October 2002 National Breast Cancer Coalition poll reports, "although 50 per cent of the population believes that wearing a pink ribbon is a somewhat effective tool to fight breast cancer and 32 per cent has worn a ribbon as a symbol of support, only 6 per cent has contacted an elected official to push for Congressional action."[31] If purchasing pink ribbon products has little effect on Congressional action, then organizations such as the Campaign have a critical role in bridging the gap between consumers, policy-makers, and manufacturers who truly wish to develop safer business practices.

Conclusion

The Campaign for Safe Cosmetics emanates from the larger movement to reform chemicals policy in the U.S. and Canada. Lack of adequate governmental oversight of the chemical ingredients in personal care products is part and parcel of outdated chemical management policies and under-regulation of chemical manufacturing and use. Although consumer-oriented activism is often criticized for failing to bring about significant changes in the production processes that create environmental health problems, the Campaign has successfully mobilized consumers as a force for cleaner production. By securing agreements from leading companies to eliminate toxics, the Campaign has broken down key arguments made by manufacturers and politicians against government regulations—that it is too expensive or technically unfeasible to use safer alternatives to toxic chemicals. Furthermore, by revealing the hypocrisy of corporate pink-washers that use cancer-causing chemicals in "pink" products, the Campaign has teamed with the prevention-oriented wing of the breast cancer movement to refocus attention on exposure to toxics as a cause of breast cancer. In so doing, the Campaign is laying the groundwork for moving beyond nonbinding voluntary actions to the passage of comprehensive state and federal regulation of toxic chemicals that plague the environment and health of people across North America.

17

THE MAKING
OF A COKE CAN

Coca Cola's Civic Action Network (CAN) and the Seeding of Corporate Astroturf Campaigns, 1995–2015

BARTOW ELMORE

O N JANUARY 29, 2013, historian Grace Hale published an op-ed in the *New York Times* entitled "When Jim Crow Drank Coke." The piece detailed Coca-Cola's troubled relationship with race, including its history of discriminatory hiring practices that kept black Americans out of the firm's highest offices for years.[1]

That morning, I received some correspondence from the University of Virginia's history department announcing the publication of the op-ed, and I forwarded the news on to family and friends. At the time, I was finishing my book manuscript on the environmental history of Coca-Cola, a project I had started as a dissertation at Virginia under Grace's tutelage several years earlier. With Coke on the brain, I naturally engaged in a back-and-forth email exchange with folks, then returned to what was in all likelihood another arduous day of manuscript editing.[2]

Then, that afternoon, I received a jarring email in my inbox. It was from the Coca-Cola Company, and the subject line read: "Setting the Record Straight—Coca-Cola Responds to NY Times Op-Ed." Yes, hours after hearing news about Professor Hale's *New York Times* publication, Coca-Cola was writing to tell me that my advisor was an untrustworthy historian. The body of the message explained that Grace's op-ed was "a faulty history lesson on Coca-Cola" and directed me to a company website that would correct alleged errors.[3]

How did Coca-Cola know to contact me? Why was I hearing this news about my advisor from a corporate email account? As it turns out, there was a logical explanation for this bizarre sequence of events. In the summer of 2010, while researching the Coca-Cola Company in the basement of the American Beverage Association's (ABA) Washington, DC, lobbying headquarters, I came across a 1995 memorandum distributed by an organization called the Coca-Cola Civic Action Network (CAN). The Coca-Cola Company set up this organization to help co-ordinate grass-roots campaigns against legislation that might hurt Coke's bottom line. As any good graduate student would do, I scoured the web and realized that the organization was still in operation, so I decided to become a member. It turned out to be a smart move; primary sources concerning Coke's political lobbying campaigns came straight to my inbox.[4]

By joining Coke's Civic Action Network, I found that I was participating in a new corporate lobbying strategy developed roughly two decades earlier because of big changes in the soft drink industry. By the 1990s, Coca-Cola and other soda firms had begun aggressive efforts to consolidate their distribution networks to achieve economies of scale and thereby improve profits. But following consolidation, Coca-Cola and other soft drink businesses found that they had lost something very important: valuable political capital accrued by small town bottlers. The shift to centralized bottling operations meant that Coca-Cola no longer had as many political partners on Main Street to fight local legislation that could damage Coke on Wall Street.

Thus, Coca-Cola's CAN was a response to structural changes within the soft drink industry, but it was also a response to changing political conditions. In the 1990s, several Congressmen proposed substantial amendments to the Federal Elections Campaign Act of 1971 that would have severely limited corporations' ability to channel "soft money" toward political campaigns. Commenting in 1997 on the emergence of Coke's CAN, the *Atlanta Business Chronicle* explained the connection between changing campaign finance rules and the emergence of new lobbying techniques: "Should corporate PACs [Political Action Committees] ever be outlawed," the *Chronicle* reported, "it might be possible for the corporate grass-roots networks . . . to be far more influential than traditional PACs or lobbyists ever were."[5]

In these uncertain times for campaign finance reform, CAN's objective was to ensure that Coca-Cola could mobilize a broad network of shareholders, employees, and consumers if indeed alternate routes to political power dried up. This was to be a high-tech endeavour, one that used the emerging tools of the Internet to co-ordinate lobbying strategies across broad geographic areas in real time.

To the public, Coca-Cola pitched CAN as a tool of empowerment for ordinary citizens. "This is democracy in action," Coca-Cola spokesman Rob Baskin told reporters when speaking about CAN in 1997. Baskin made clear that Coke wanted CAN to be "strictly voluntary," adding "You don't want people to be forced into this, you want them involved because they want to be." According to Baskin, Coca-Cola was not asking network members to do Coke's bidding; rather, CAN was a way for people to "protect and enhance their investment" in the brand. Coke, in short, was simply providing a mouthpiece for employees, shareholders, and consumers to broadcast *their* political voice.[6]

This was the key to CAN's effectiveness: making it seem as if citizens were acting on their own rather than at the direction of the corporation. To be sure, this meta-strategy was not new, as businesses had been engaging in what has been dubbed astroturfing—corporately funded grassroots campaigns—since at least the 1920s. By the mid-twentieth century, astroturfing had become quite common, especially in the soft drink industry. In 1953, for example, beverage, canning, and packaging companies created Keep America Beautiful (KAB), an organization that fought restrictive legislation designed to limit or ban the production and distribution of throwaway containers, which were already becoming a major nuisance to many anti-litter proponents by that time. Though big businesses financed and managed this organization, KAB promoted itself as a grassroots group directed by ordinary citizens concerned about the environment, and it enrolled the support of Boy Scout troops and local community leaders to promote the idea that people, not corporations, were to blame for the nation's waste woes.[7]

By the 1970s and 1980s, businesses increasingly turned to outside public affairs consultants and private lobbying firms to co-ordinate and implement astroturf campaigns similar to those carried out by KAB. This trend was in large part a response to new regulatory legislation designed to clean up the environment and promote consumer health and safety. Businesses felt they needed full-time support to defeat mounting legislation targeting industries, so using outside lobbying firms seemed like a smart move. Between 1972 and 1982, former campaign managers, public relations consultants, and legislative staffers founded roughly 104 new grassroots-consulting firms. In the next decade, 194 such organizations followed. By 1994, grassroots consulting had become an $800 million industry according to *Campaigns and Elections* magazine.[8]

But Coke's Civic Action Network was different from these third-party firms; it connected corporate government relations departments within Coke to outside public advocacy groups and broader political movements. CAN was an in-house feeder organization that seeded corporate grassroots campaigns organized and managed by third-party partners. CAN did its work out of sight and out of mind by design. It did not execute logo-laden public demonstrations or mass marches, and it did not take responsibility for full-page ads promoting company talking points in the *New York Times*; rather, CAN channelled employees, shareholders, and company associates to events and campaigns that featured no CAN branding and asked its members to use their personal email accounts, Facebook pages, and Twitter handles to broadcast corporate messages. In this way, CAN sought to create the illusion that these movements were backed by a groundswell of self-mobilized citizens. To be sure, CAN's attempts to remain obfuscated did not always work, but CAN clearly did not want to be in the public spotlight and believed that it could be most effective if it let its members used their own digital profiles to lobby government officials and shape public opinion.

CAN did not always work the way Coke wanted it to. Over the years, some of Coca-Cola's enemies deftly entered digital portals designed for company loyalists, thereby giving them behind-the-scenes access to company lobbying agendas. These network saboteurs were dangerous because they used their own social media networks to expose the corporate puppeteering behind astroturf campaigns. Thus, digital mobilization networks—once heralded as the key to a new era of corporate lobbying when the Internet expanded in the 1990s—also created vulnerabilities for firms seeking to shape public opinion. The power to create viral social media campaigns through CAN came with the attendant risks of exposing the firm to infection by unwanted company adversaries.

CAN was emblematic of a larger corporate movement at the dawn of the twenty-first century that used digital tools to mobilize company associates in political action campaigns. Though its effectiveness is difficult to assess, considering the lack of publicly available information about membership execution of network directives, CAN maintained a presence online as this book went to press, over two decades after the network's creation, suggesting Coca-Cola still saw utility in this form of political mobilization. As new digital communication systems emerge in the decades ahead, these types of networks will likely remain central to corporate lobbying techniques, which is why it is important to understand their genesis.

*   *   *

For most of its history, the Coca-Cola Company spent a small portion of its budget making Coke cans. After all, Coke's independently owned bottlers were largely responsible for packaging Coca-Cola's product for sale to retailers. This relationship began in 1899, when Coca-Cola's first president, Atlanta pharmacist Asa Candler, reluctantly approved Chattanooga attorneys Benjamin F. Thomas and Joseph Brown Whitehead's request for a bottling franchise. Little did Candler know this decision would give rise to the largest bottling network the world had ever seen.[9]

By 1910 there were over four hundred Coca-Cola bottlers operating in the United States, and two decades later that total would roughly triple. Coca-Cola bottling plants colonized main streets across Jazz Age America with many small town businessmen investing less than $4,000 to get a plant up and running. Within a few years, many early bottlers became millionaires.[10]

The story of Columbus Roberts, of Columbus, Georgia, was typical. Roberts grew up on a tenant farm in Reconstruction-era Georgia and began bottling Coke in Columbus around 1901. Three years later, Roberts claimed over $15,000 in profits and quickly expanded his business. By the time of his death in 1950, he had earned millions, much of which he donated to Mercer University, a Baptist school that is still in operation today. In Columbus, Roberts was king. He was president of the local Kiwanis Club and a deacon at his church, and in 1929 became a representative for Muscogee County in the Georgia General Assembly. Like many Coke bottlers, Roberts was more than just a businessman: he was a civil servant, a church member, someone the community respected.[11]

Candler learned early on that Coke bottlers offered more than just their financial capital and bottling assets to the Coke brand: they also offered up their good name. In 1911, Candler expressed his gratitude to the company's bottlers, men he believed were of "high character" and that "without exception . . . rank with the best and most respected business men of their communities." In the years ahead, Candler would come to see the value of tapping the political and social capital of local bottlers to protect and strengthen the Coke brand.[12]

The importance of local bottlers in shaping Coke's success would not be lost on Coca-Cola's top leadership over the next decades. Whenever a problematic political issue confronted the company, Coca-Cola sent one of its bottlers—typically a respected and politically connected member of the local community—to broker deals in its favour. This was especially true in the case of Coca-Cola's battle against state and federal legislation targeting throwaway containers. In the 1960s and 1970s, thousands of soft drink cans and nonreturnable bottles marred the American landscape, and environmental groups began to call on government to do something about the unsightly waste. By the 1970s, multiple states were considering mandatory deposit laws placing five- to ten-cent deposits on throwaway containers, and Congress was even considering a ban on all no-deposit, nonreturnable bottlers sold in the country. In 1972, Vermont and Oregon became the first states to place a price tag on packaging waste, implementing the first statewide deposit systems.[13]

In this time of crisis, Coca-Cola mobilized its bottling network to stave off what it saw as an existential threat to its business. In 1978, for example, Coca-Cola bottler Craig R. Schmidt, president of the Coca-Cola Bottling Company of Kentucky appeared before Congress to oppose a national mandatory deposit bill. In his statement to the Senate committee, Schmidt made clear that he was a "local bottler" operating a family-run business and claimed that there would be dire consequences for his operation if Congress passed the proposed bill. The story was much the same in 1980 when the US Senate debated yet another mandatory deposit proposal. That year, Edward McGlaston, vice president of Pacific Coca-Cola Bottling based in Oregon, came before Congress to testify about the ill effects the proposed bill would have on his community.[14]

In state and local battles against mandatory deposits, bottlers were also the face of Coke's political campaigns. In 1982, the *Coca-Cola Bottler*, a publication produced for and by Coca-Cola's distributors, praised the efforts of Coke bottlers in Arizona, California, Colorado, and Washington for their efforts in defeating mandatory deposit bills in those states. The "grass roots" campaigns were enormous, with employees reportedly going "door-to-door with pamphlets outlining the disadvantages" of the proposed legislation and mailing "personalized postcards to friends and relatives seeking their 'no' votes." In Ohio, Coca-Cola bottlers worked other local channels to quash a deposit bill. Akron Coca-Cola Bottling

Company chief executive officer Bill Williams reported to the *Coca-Cola Bottler* that he had served on an advisory board to Ohio's governor, Jim Rhodes, where he helped defeat proposed mandatory deposit legislation. Coca-Cola bottlers were working both the streets and the corridors of state capitols.[15]

But despite these successes, by the mid-1980s, some within the Coke family began to question whether Coca-Cola's bottling network could sustain such political campaigns in the years ahead. Since the 1950s, Coca-Cola had begun to streamline its bottling network, buying back big bottlers and forcing smaller distributors to merge with larger operations. In 1983, the *Coca-Cola Bottler* raised the alarm, admitting that many in the Coca-Cola family felt the firm's decentralized political network was "threatened by the recent trend toward consolidated ownership."[16]

Then, in 1986, Coca-Cola made a big decision that would further centralize the company's bottling system. That year, company CEO Roberto Goizueta launched Coca-Cola Enterprises (CCE), a company megabottler that would in the years ahead buy out independent franchise operations. This hastened the pace of Coca-Cola bottling network consolidation, and by 1997 there were roughly one hundred bottlers operating in the United States, down from approximately five hundred just two decades earlier.[17]

Coca-Cola now stood drained of valuable political capital that had helped it fight legislative battles throughout the twentieth century. Local bottlers had been the face of the Coca-Cola Company in its many political campaigns against activists and politicians that challenged its way of doing business over the years. As CCE began to gobble up independent bottling operations, the firm had to reimagine its political strategy for combating unwanted legislation. The company knew that it no longer had the same reputation on Main Street that it once had in the early twentieth century.[18]

In an attempt to build political clout in communities now lacking a local bottler, Coca-Cola decided to create the Coca-Cola Civic Action Network (CAN) in February of 1995 in order to "extend [Coca-Cola's] grassroots reach beyond the fence of [its] bottling plants." In a stock correspondence to over two thousand Coca-Cola employees, Jack Stahl, head of Coca-Cola's US operating division, announced the launch of this "nonpartisan, grassroots organization." As Stahl explained, the company created CAN to mobilize "bottling partners, customers, suppliers, and share owners which had a common stake in protecting our system from discriminatory taxation and unnecessary governmental regulation." The firm was widening its political base.[19]

Just two months after launch, the company happily reported that CAN had over 1,650 active members in New Hampshire, New York, New Mexico, North Carolina, South Carolina, Washington, Oregon, and Minnesota, and expected rapid expansion in the months ahead. Moving forward, CAN was focused on "widening our solicitation" beyond company employees to include stakeholders and consumers outside the firm.[20]

By the end of the 1990s, Coca-Cola's CAN network was undermining pesky mandatory deposit bills that had remained a soft drink industry nuisance. In 1997, several state legislatures, including those in conservative states such as Georgia, Iowa, Texas, and Oklahoma, considered placing deposits on beverage containers to help deal with mounting waste management costs. Coca-Cola believed that CAN members could play a pivotal role in preventing such legislation from being passed. In its newsletter, *Network News*, CAN featured testimonials of organization members engaged in effective campaigning strategies against mandatory deposits. For example, the 1997 newsletter featured the story of William McNeill, identified only as a "Coca-Cola CAN member, Atlanta, Georgia," who had written a letter to his state senator explaining how mandatory deposits were "grossly unfair to middle and low income families." The lack of any further description of McNeill was telling. No longer were local bottlers the main face of Coca-Cola political campaigns. Through its new network, Coke now sought to claim any average citizen as its own in its battles against government.[21]

CAN believed that new technologies, especially the Internet, could help it broaden its lobbying efforts and increase the power of its political message. In October of 1997, CAN announced that *Network News* and "legislative alerts" would be distributed over email. The organization also encouraged its members to use the web to spread lobbying messages: "Remember, many state and federal elected officials are also online, opening up new opportunities to make your voice heard with your elected officials!"[22]

In 1998, CAN reported 12,000 new enrollees in its network, bringing its total membership to over 72,000. That year, CAN announced that it had run successful "campaigns to repeal soft drink taxes in the Carolinas and Washington state," and had also blocked "forced deposit legislation in Pennsylvania, Vermont, California, and Oregon." A year later, the organization detailed its attempts to thwart similar bills in Kentucky, Washington, DC, and Massachusetts. The beauty of Coke's new political network was that it was disaggregated, making it appear as if individual citizens were mobilizing independently. Activists in these communities did not march under a CAN banner or send correspondence on network letterhead. They were encouraged to craft their own missives to state representatives about problems wrought by increased taxes.[23]

CAN's lobbying efforts were not confined to mandatory deposit battles. In 2000, for example, CAN mobilized to stymie a proposed bill in the New Hampshire state legislature that would have placed a 2-cent tax on bottled water to generate revenue to "protect water resources" in the state. CAN members were asked to "communicate to their senators and representatives" their concerns about the measure. A decade later, CAN worked hard to fight sugar taxes and soda bans designed to curb a growing obesity epidemic facing the nation. In 2012, when Mayor Bloomberg banned the sale of soft drink containers over sixteen ounces within New York City, CAN sent out an email encouraging members to "please call or write Mayor Bloomberg and the NYC Health Department," conveniently listing the Mayor's email address and Twitter handle.[24]

In all of these campaigns, CAN encouraged its members to make *their* voice heard, preaching a message of citizen empowerment, but CAN's call for democratic participation did not always yield the results the organization intended. For example, in April of 1999, Brent Tozzer, a self-identified "stockholder in the Coca-Cola Company," penned a fiery missive to CAN's administrative email address calling Coke's failure to use "recycled plastic . . . shameful." He advised Coca-Cola "to be more insightful, progressive, and forward thinking, especially with regard for resource and waste issues." It seemed not everyone was satisfied simply receiving corporate commands from on high; some people saw CAN as a mouthpiece to tell the corporation what to do.[25]

Coca-Cola also unwittingly gave its adversaries an opportunity to infiltrate the firm through the CAN network. Opponents and critics of the company could sign up for the Civic Action Network online and get a first glimpse at Coke's political strategies before they became mainstream. They could even copy and paste legislation alerts and action reports meant exclusively for the eyes of Coke's fandom and spread those materials to discussion forums hostile to Coca-Cola's interests. For example, on July 27, 2012, New York University's famed nutrition and health studies professor, Marion Nestle, reported on her blog that she had "received an email from the Coca-Cola Civic Action Network (CAN)" lauding the fact that Coke would be "refreshing and hydrating the 14,000 athletes, 7,000 officials,

20,000 workers and volunteers and more than 6 million spectators that are expected to flock to the Olympic Park." Nestle asked her readers whether "soda and fast-food companies" should be "sponsoring the Olympics? Is this the message we want sent to kids?" Many people liked her remarks on Facebook and others posted comments, the vast majority supporting her stand. Indeed, this was a new form of democratic participation in corporate lobbying, but perhaps not the one Coke had intended.[26]

Some network members simply did not do what CAN wanted them to do. In what might be called another instance of astroturf sabotage, a man identified only as "B. Busby" on a *Wall Street Journal* blog site directly defied CAN's desires in 2010 when he criticized Coke's funding for the American Academy of Family Physicians (AAFP) educational initiatives on childhood obesity. CAN had explicitly asked its members to comment on the blog, offering a hyperlink to the site. After noting that he had received this CAN correspondence, Busby proceeded to lambast the company for its actions. "Consumers are not as stupid as [corporations] assume," Busby wrote, adding, "Money from Coca-Cola completely derides the credibility of the AAFP."[27]

Such were the perils Coke faced in broadening its political network, but despite these problems, the company continued to utilize CAN communiqués to channel Coke loyalists toward astroturf organizations fighting Coke causes. In September of 2010, just a few months after Busby's betrayal, Coca-Cola wrote its network members to let them know about an organization called Americans Against Food Taxes (AAFT), "a group that includes more than 85,000 consumers and hundreds of business and community organizations." The email asked members to "invite [their] friends and family" to watch an AAFT promotional video and sign a petition opposing food taxes. The message concluded with links to the organizations Facebook and Twitter pages, obviously indicating that CAN hoped its members would use their personal social media profiles to "like" content on AAFT's Facebook and tweet support for the organization.[28]

A month after the AAFT announcement, CAN told its members about another group, the Strategies to Overcome and Prevent (STOP) Obesity Alliance, a self-described "coalition of consumer, provider, government, labor, business, health insurer and quality-of-care organizations" focused on combating obesity. Though the alliance could not be considered a purely astroturf group because it enjoyed strong backing from non-corporate public partners and universities, the Alliance nevertheless promoted ideas that Coke liked and wanted amplified. CAN pointed out a post on the Alliance's blog that urged Americans not to play "the 'blame game,' which unrealistically places the responsibility of the obesity epidemic at the feet of the food and beverage industry." CAN asked its members to comment on this post and to "share the article with [their] Facebook and Twitter friends."[29]

While CAN prodded its members to increase their visibility in the public sphere, the managers of the network quietly reduced CAN's presence on the web in the 2010s. CAN correspondence from 2010–15 included a hyperlink at the bottom of the email directing members to www.civicactionnetwork.com. By 2016, this URL was no longer live; instead it redirected visitors to a generic Coca-Cola website. Nor was a 1-800 number listed in CAN correspondence active. The only way to gain access to CAN was through a buried link deep in Coca-Cola's website on a page dedicated to Coca-Cola shareholders. This link featured no information about CAN's campaigns but merely offered a signup portal for those interested in joining the group.[30]

These moves betrayed CAN's conviction that there were certain benefits to maintaining a low organizational profile online. From CAN's perspective, keeping its organizational brand obfuscated in cyberspace directly contributed to its members' ability to appear as self-mobilized political actors. It also reduced the risk of adversary infiltration of the group. As we have seen, CAN did not always achieve the invisibility it sought, but it nevertheless experimented with new strategies to target only the most loyal supporters of the Coke brand. CAN continued to operate its digital portal in 2016, but very little of the group's activities were broadcast online on a CAN website. The Coca-Cola Civic Action Network remained the cyber roots of more visible astroturf campaigns, operating underground, but seeding movements across the nation.

Coke was by no means the only company to initiate political networking strategies using digital platforms. In the 1990s, other firms experimented with similar tactics to increase their political power. Naturally, telecommunications businesses realized that they had in-house technologies and network tools that would enable them to effectively mobilize company stakeholders. In 1987, Bell South, another firm based out of Atlanta, launched a political action network akin to Coke's CAN. A decade later, the *Atlanta Business Chronicle* described how Bell South's program included regular email communication to shareholders and employees about important political issues. The firm also sent hardcopy legislative action letters penned by the CEO to its network. Bill McCloskey, Bell

South's media relations guru, commented on the effectiveness of the CEO correspondence strategy, saying, "When you get a letter from [Bell South's CEO], by God, you read it."[31]

In 2008, Wal-Mart created its own digital grassroots mobilization system. Dubbed the Wal-Mart Community Action Network (also abbreviated CAN), Wal-Mart cast a broad net, opening up enrolment to the program via a new website, walmartcommunity.com. Virtually anyone could join, though CAN sought to enlist the support of Wal-Mart customers in particular locales where the company was facing resistance to the siting of new stores. In this sense, Wal-Mart's CAN differed slightly from Coke's action network in that it aggressively targeted consumers, rather than just shareholders and employees, which had apparently become by the mid-2010s Coke's main CAN constituency. It was also more visible in that it broadcast corporate messages from CAN Twitter and YouTube accounts. In 2009, Wal-Mart claimed over sixty thousand members in its Community Action Network.[32]

Thus, whether a Bell South employee, Wal-Mart consumer, or Coke shareholder, by the 2010s, Americans were receiving digital invitations to add their voices to new corporate political action networks. In most cases, these were behind-the-scenes operations and they remained a complement to much more visible campaigns carried out by PACs and astroturf organizations. After all, traditional soft money channels for influencing political change had never really dried up. Though the Bipartisan Campaign Reform (McCain-Feingold) Act of 2002 limited contributions to specific political parties and candidate ads, PACs still were able to get around restrictions by ostensibly funding commercials and campaigns that focused on specific issues without naming particular candidates. The Supreme Court's decision in *Citizens United v. Federal Election Commission* in 2010 further ensured that PACs would continue to dominate the American political landscape. It seemed that corporations' worst fears about campaign finance reform in the 1990s never came to pass.[33]

Nevertheless, Coke's CAN network was still sending out emails in 2016, signalling that the corporation still believed this intermediary organization served a purpose in connecting company loyalists to astroturf movements. At that time, it was hard to assess how influential the organization had become or how much its membership had grown. The CAN network tasked its members with using their private Facebook and Twitter accounts and email addresses to lobby for change, making it difficult to connect citizens' actions back to the network. But if Wal-Mart's

CAN revealed anything about broader trends in corporate action network engagement, all signs suggested these organizations were not waning but gaining strength. A glimpse at Wal-Mart's Twitter account in the Internet Archive revealed that the company's CAN Twitter page had just 1,221 followers in August of 2012. Two and a half years later, Wal-Mart's CAN account had 17,500 followers, more than a 1,400 percent increase.[34]

It seemed a new era of corporate grassroots campaigns had blossomed from seeds first laid in the 1990s. With campaign finance reform still a topic of lively debate in the 2010s, multinational firms stood ready to mobilize their new digital networks to broadcast political messages in the years ahead.

18

BOOT
THE BELL

Solidarity as Strategy
in the Neoliberal Era

DAWSON BARRETT

N MARCH 2005, after a four-year boycott, the largest restaurant company in the world agreed to grant Florida farm workers a 75 percent raise and assist them in their efforts to combat modern-day slavery in U.S. tomato fields. Throughout the campaign, the Coalition of Immokalee Workers (CIW), a group of mostly migrant workers with few recognized labour rights and without a common language, had challenged claims by American restaurant officials and university administrators that they were in no way accountable for the working conditions and wages that bolstered their bottom lines. When Yum! Brands (the parent company of Taco Bell, Kentucky Fried Chicken, A&W, Pizza Hut, and Long John Silver's) finally capitulated, the company not only acknowledged responsibility for its entire supply chain but also undermined its own narrative of helplessness in the face of the free market. The campaign against Taco Bell proved that giant corporations could use their considerable power to improve the lives of workers and that they would, if sufficiently pressured.

Taco Bell's operations involved a complex network of corporate offices, farms and distributors, and franchisees (including the food courts of many major universities). In order to find the company's vulnerabilities, the CIW and their many allies targeted all of these points, with varying degrees of success.

Targeting Taco Bell

The campaign against Taco Bell originated in the 1990s efforts of farm workers in Southern Florida. Across the U.S., farm labourers worked long hours for extremely low wages. The work itself was physically punishing, and the workers faced dangers that ranged from the violence and neglect of employers to exposure to toxic pesticides. As Lucas Benitez of the CIW explained in 2003,

> Farm workers . . . contribute their sweat and blood so that enormous corporations can profit, all the while living in sub-poverty misery, without benefits, without the right to overtime or protection when we organize. Others are working by force, against their will, terrorized by violent employers, under the watch of armed guards, held in modern-day slavery. The right to a just wage, the right to work free of forced labor, the right to organize—three of the rights in the United Nations' Universal Declaration of Human Rights—are routinely violated when it comes to farm workers in the United States.[1]

Founded in 1993, the CIW spent its first several years organizing locally, talking to fellow workers and pressuring their employer, the Six L's Packing Company, to raise wages, which had stagnated at 1970s levels. The group built camaraderie by confronting violent crew bosses and launching dangerous undercover investigations that eventually led to the prosecution of five agricultural slavery rings. Labour activists also organized a 230-mile protest march from Ft. Meyers to Orlando and a month-long hunger strike by six CIW members. By the end of the decade, however, the workers had reached a dead end with Six L's. Because the company sold its produce primarily to other businesses rather than the general public, it was virtually invulnerable to public protest. Further, officials could claim, with some validity, that the wages they paid were limited by the poor market value of tomatoes. CIW members quickly realized that their livelihoods depended on reshaping that market.[2]

Pressuring capitalist markets from the bottom up has always been a daunting task for activists, and it has become increasingly difficult in the era of neoliberal globalization. Not only has the line between industry and government been blurred but mergers have created powerful, multinational mega-corporations. On the scale of a local business, consumers can often influence selection, pricing, and even working conditions through strategic purchasing decisions and well-organized boycotts. The global scale, however, is much more complex. The expansion of assembly lines to specialized factories in many different countries and the establishment of "free trade zones," in which environmental and labour standards are all but nonexistent, have created a race to the bottom with few options for the most desperate of the world's workers. And in the global economy, no individual in the supply chain has to claim responsibility for working conditions in contracted, or "outsourced," factories. Factory owners can rightfully claim that they would not receive contracts if they raised wages, while parent corporations can argue that they source based on competitive prices, not their repercussions. Individual consumers make purchasing decisions based on the limited choices they are given and on the limits of their own budgets. All the while, corporate elites and government officials, in rich and poor countries alike, praise the triumphs of "free" trade and dismiss any negative effects as temporary growing pains. No one has to take responsibility for unregulated capitalism, even when its effects include the enslavement of the more than one thousand farm workers freed by Florida law enforcement over the last fifteen years.[3]

The farm workers of Immokalee, of course, were not the first to confront this dilemma. From the 1960s through the 1980s, the United Farm Workers (UFW) and the Farm Labor Organizing Committee (FLOC) conducted a variety of successful nationwide boycotts of Safeway Grocery and Campbell's Soup, among other companies. More recently, United Students Against Sweatshops (USAS) and other student activist groups had targeted American universities as bulk apparel purchasers, with limited but promising results (see Meredith Katz's chapter in this book).

With these examples in mind, the CIW launched a boycott campaign against Yum! Brands, a company so large that a shift in its policies could have an industry-wide impact. Specifically, the workers targeted Yum! subsidiary Taco Bell, which used 10.9 million pounds of Florida tomatoes each year—and whose slogans and imagery casually and cynically played on the border that many CIW members had crossed in search of work. By doing so, however, the CIW also accepted the challenge of decoding the company's complicated labyrinth of franchises, subcontractors, and corporate bureaucracy.[4]

To pressure such a powerful and pervasive company, the CIW needed the help of a broad coalition of allies. Borrowing from the democratic organizing models of other global justice activists, the CIW insisted on autonomy, both for themselves and for their allies. They were not a top-down organization, and they allowed other activists to pursue strategies that played to their respective strengths. So while CIW representatives planned marches and rallies at Yum! headquarters and travelled around the country building support, allied groups targeted Taco Bell from a variety of angles. Religious organizations rallied against the immorality of slave labour and spread the boycott from congregation to congregation. Labour unions focused on the exploitation of workers to encourage their members to join the boycott and participate in solidarity actions.

Student activists, meanwhile, building on a decade of successful anti-sweatshop campaigns, launched a "Boot the Bell" campaign to expel Taco Bell chains from U.S. high schools and universities. By 2005, when Yum! Brands finally reached an agreement with the CIW, student campaigns were active at three hundred colleges and fifty high schools. Booting Taco Bell required the CIW's allied student wing, a loose network of affiliated groups known as the Student/Farmworker Alliance (SFA), to dissect complex university bureaucracies and find ways to pressure key decision-makers. Paralleling the CIW's seasonal membership changes, graduation challenged the stability of SFA campaigns as they stretched from year to year. Ultimately, students at twenty-two schools, including UCLA, Portland State University, and the University of Chicago, succeeded in having their schools cancel or reject contracts with Taco Bell. Although most of the student campaigns failed to expel campus franchises, the mounting pressure of so many simultaneous actions was a key factor in compelling Taco Bell to agree to the CIW's demands. For the company, the risk of spoiling its brand name with its most important target audience became too much to ignore.[5]

Booting the Bell

Each school presented challenges for activists. Just as Taco Bell's elaborate makeup complicated the task of identifying and pressuring power brokers, so too did the complex structures of modern universities. During "Boot the Bell" campaigns at the University of Texas and the University of Notre Dame, student activists engaged with a wide range of opponents, including administrators, Taco Bell officials, and student government representatives. Both campaigns put Taco Bell on the defensive, but students at Notre Dame were ultimately more successful at identifying the vulnerabilities in their school's power structure.

The University of Texas (UT) campaign against Taco Bell started in December 2001, in conjunction with actions in thirty other states, when members of the student Green Party protested and distributed literature about the CIW in front of the campus restaurant. The following October, Green Party members held another demonstration, complete with tomato costumes, which also coincided with similar activities elsewhere. Over the course of the next year, students began meeting with representatives of Aramark, the company contracted by UT to oversee all campus food outlets. By November 2003, the student coalition had broadened to include not only the campus Green Party but also global justice groups like Accion Zapatista and Resist FTAA! In conjunction with a campus visit by CIW members, students held yet another rally and introduced a resolution to the student government that, if passed, would have encouraged the administration to cut ties with Taco Bell. The resolution failed without debate, however, and uninterested student government representatives were seen "working on papers [and] picking their finger nails" during its presentation.[6] Although activists at UT were able to attract publicity, they reached dead ends with both their representatives and the company that held the campus Taco Bell contract.[7]

The following school year, the UT campaign reached its peak. Under the leadership of a group called the Student Labor Action Project (SLAP), the campaign grew to include the support of thirty-five other student organizations. Inspired by a recent victory at UCLA, student activists presented the University of Texas Union Board of Directors (the administrative body responsible for contracting with Aramark) with a petition with over one thousand signatories. Unmoved, board chair Nada Antoun responded that removing Taco Bell would be a "disservice to the students" who were "strapped due to tuition increases" and needed access to cheap food.[8] CIW members again visited the campus, and activists began flooding the school newspaper with letters of support for the campaign. In addition to opinion pieces by students, Austin-area ministers also submitted a letter that pledged support for the boycott by religious groups and quoting former UN High Commissioner for Human Rights Mary Robinson's condemnation of Taco Bell's role in "profiting by exploitation."[9]

In response, Dirk Dozier and Don Barton, respectively CEO and Vice President of Human Resources for Austaco, the company that directly owned the UT Student Union Taco Bell and several others in Central

Texas, began their own media campaign. In February, as the Union Board was gearing up to vote on the issue, Dozier published an opinion piece in the school newspaper defending Six L's as "a very good organization," condemning student and community activists, and asking, "Where is the concern for the tax-paying, wage-earning U.S. citizens—employees of our company—who potentially will lose their jobs for the sake of Florida Immokalee farm workers?" But while Dozier, like Antoun, saw the benefits in exploiting farm workers, he did not explain why a one cent per pound raise for tomato pickers would cause other workers to lose their jobs. Don Barton, meanwhile, maintained that by representing only sixty-eight of the six thousand Taco Bell restaurants in the United States, Austaco was in no position to influence the company. More importantly, Barton also argued that the UT Taco Bell franchise did not buy tomatoes from Six L's and thus was "far removed from what [the CIW was] trying to do." Barton did, however, admit that representing and benefiting from the parent company was "why you become a franchise," and he acknowledged that he had no information on the conditions of the workers who picked his franchises' tomatoes. Despite these contradictions, the Union Board moved to vote on Taco Bell's future at the end of February.[10]

Before the vote, SLAP published additional opinion pieces in the newspaper, and a local church held a public forum on the topic. During the Union Board meeting, SLAP activists held up thirty-six signs, each with the name of a supporting student organization. The board nonetheless voted unanimously to keep Taco Bell, while stipulating that Six L's would be banned from operating at UT—a non-issue, given that Six L's already did not. Although the board's decision ended the students' campaign anticlimactically, Yum! Brands reached an agreement with the CIW the next week.[11]

SLAP and its allies ultimately could not sway either their administration or their student government representatives, but their actions exposed some of the bigger issues confronted by the campaign. Despite Taco Bell's name recognition and seemingly singular identity, the structure of the company was quite complicated. Its distribution and licensing network included other powerful corporations such as Aramark and Austaco. Similarly, the hierarchy of the university also included a variety of powerful decision-making bodies. The problems that the University of Texas students faced were not all structural, however; their campaign also revealed the nature of their opponents' positions. When put on the defensive, the Union Board chair effectively admitted that the exploitation of farm workers benefited students, who themselves were being squeezed by the rising costs of college tuition. Austaco representatives provided a similar response, arguing that the conditions of workers who were not "tax-paying, wage-earning U.S. citizens" were of no concern to their company. Taco Bell apologists initially claimed either ignorance of farm workers' struggles or impotence to affect the situation. When pushed, however, they acknowledged that their financial gain simply trumped the human costs. The campaign at Notre Dame forced a similarly raw response from Taco Bell headquarters.

The Notre Dame "Boot the Bell" campaign, like its Texas counterpart, started in 2001. It reached its peak during the 2003–4 school year. In September, members of the school's SFA affiliate, the Progressive Student Alliance (PSA), met with Notre Dame General Counsel Carol Kaesebier to discuss Taco Bell's official sponsorship of the school's football post-game show. A few months later, after travelling to Kentucky for a protest at Yum! Brand's headquarters and visiting Immokalee over spring break, two PSA members, Melody Gonzales and Tony Rivas, participated in a Cesar Chavez Day forum at which they discussed their involvement in the campaign and their own fathers' experiences as migrant farm labourers. Rivas also began a week-long hunger strike as a lead-up to a protest against Taco Bell.[12]

Importantly, PSA members also identified an additional leverage point with the university: Board of Trustees member Matt Gallo was the director of Gallo of Sonoma Winery, a company accused of unfair labour practices by the United Farm Workers. The Notre Dame students' relied on articulating the contradictions between the school's mission and its relationship to Taco Bell. By targeting Gallo as well, student activists presented a pattern of worker exploitation at the university, which allowed them to embarrass school officials at very high levels and counter attempts to dismiss the Taco Bell issue.[13]

The publicity of Rivas' hunger strike and the subsequent protest, which were part of a national week of student actions, prompted responses from Notre Dame officials and Taco Bell. University spokesperson Matthew Storin told the school newspaper that the fact that Rivas learned about migrant labour issues from a university seminar "should count as University awareness on some level."[14] Speaking on behalf of Taco Bell, Laurie Schalow claimed that the free market was to blame for produce prices, not the restaurant company. She also noted that Taco Bell's Supplier Code of Conduct specified a nine dollar per hour minimum wage, though student activists quickly pointed out that tomato pickers were paid by the bucket, not the hour. Undeterred by Schalow's explanation, PSA members began a letter-writing campaign to University President Father Edward Malloy and launched a forty-person hunger strike. After two weeks of sending letters, dozens of PSA members went to Malloy's office to demand a public statement on the university's relationship with Taco Bell. Though the president's assistant told them that it was "not [Malloy's] style" to meet with students, Counselor to the President Father Peter Jarret agreed to discuss the PSA's conditions for ending their hunger strike.[15]

The administration offered to investigate the students' concerns, but only after receiving an official response from Taco Bell. PSA members, rejecting the university's delaying tactics, instead expanded their hunger strike to include 126 students. They also published editorials that cited the school's previous positions on fair labour practices and accused the university of involvement in "a financial chain that exploits workers."[16] As the hunger strike escalated, university officials demanded an immediate response from Taco Bell representatives, who had been using delaying tactics of their own. A week later, Notre Dame announced that it would postpone renewal of its Taco Bell contract until the company provided an official explanation. President Malloy publicly thanked the students for bringing the issue to his attention but stipulated, "It remains to be seen whether all their concerns were justified."[17] Anxious to maintain a business-friendly appearance, he said the university would not rush to judge Taco Bell before hearing their side of the argument.[18]

In August 2004, the deadline for renewing the annual sponsorship contract passed without the university receiving a sufficient response from Taco Bell. As PSA declared victory, university spokesperson Matt Storin, cautious not to reveal that students had pressured the administration into making a decision, thanked students for bringing up the issue "in a very responsible and studied way."[19]

The Notre Dame campaign against Taco Bell succeeded for several reasons. Chief among them were the students' abilities to establish the moral high ground, articulate the contradiction between the school's mission and its association with the company, and, perhaps most importantly, threaten the image of the school's famed football program. The Texas campaign, by contrast, failed because students were unable to identify or apply pressure on the necessary decision-making bodies, though they remained public and active for the full four-year campaign.

At Notre Dame, the university president, as both an administrative and religious figure, could be compelled by students' morally rooted pressure campaigns. At Texas, however, the bureaucracies of the university and its restaurant operations made decision-makers much less vulnerable. When pressured, officials responded that their obligations were not to any sense of morality but instead to cash-strapped students or to (presumably low-wage earning) "U.S. citizens." Nonetheless, the "pressure from all sides" strategy of the CIW's conflict with Yum! allowed the larger campaign to benefit even from the unsuccessful local campaigns of their allies. The UT Taco Bell remained open, but franchisees and their parent company felt the intended pressure of the students' actions, as demonstrated both by their public reactions and by the eventual agreement between Yum! and the CIW.

On both a broad, national scale and a local university level, the campaign against Taco Bell illustrates some of the difficulties activists face when confronting elaborate bureaucracies. Just as students confronted the complex power structures of American universities, the CIW was forced to navigate a production chain that included an extensive web of farms, distributors, and subcontractors. In order to identify and exploit the right pressure points, the CIW and its allies looked to historical examples and built on the models of more recently successful campaigns. The combination of their efforts eventually forced Yum! to grant the desired concessions, and the CIW has since reached similar agreements with several other companies, including McDonald's, Burger King, Whole Foods, Subway, Trader Joe's, and Chipotle.

Consumer-side activism can only be successful if it pressures a business by threatening to damage its brand image or otherwise impact its profit margin. The Coalition of Immokalee Workers recognized that appeals to individual consumers could not by themselves create enough pressure to influence massive corporations. Instead, the group re-imagined the boycott tactic to include divestment by large institutions. A company like Yum! Brands could afford to lose a few sales of 99¢ burritos. However, the threat of being cut off from thirty thousand student customers at a time—amid accusations of slavery and worker exploitation—forced the company to the bargaining table.

As the structures of modern capitalism become ever more convoluted and decentralized, successful activism will increasingly require larger coalitions that can apply pressure from many angles. Activists will have to think globally and act *everywhere*.

19

WHERE'S THE BEEF . . . FROM?

Boycotting Burger King to Protect Central American Rainforests

KATRINA LACHER

HOLDING A SIGN that read "Boycott Burger King," second-grader Oriana De Forst yelled at passing motorists, "Burger King gets their meat from the jungle!" On April 28, 1984, Oriana and her classmates from Crestmont School assembled in front of the Burger King in Richmond, California, to raise awareness of fast-food companies' use of Central American beef. The students, ranging from first to sixth-graders, designed leaflets, assembled a "press pack," and "even worked out a great dance routine with lots of Michael-Jackson-type moves." One student, dressed as a "Whopper," chased classmates costumed as trees. Other students wrote poems and sent them to Burger King's Miami headquarters. Jamillah Gallman, age ten, penned:

Roses are red,
Violets are blue,
You know you're starving people,
And I'm ashamed of you!

What would motivate children to boycott an all-American institution such as Burger King?[1]

Crestmont School's "Public Awareness Event" was part of a larger campaign in the 1980s to educate consumers about the fast-food industry's use of Central American beef. By the end of the twentieth century, fast food had become part of American culture. Access to cheap beef was a cornerstone not only of the American diet but also of the American lifestyle. In the search for inexpensive meat sources, many fast-food companies increasingly turned to Central and South America, where large landowners in countries such as Costa Rica cleared thousands of acres of old-growth forests and converted them to cattle pasture. Beginning in 1984, conservationists who were concerned about the quickening depletion of rainforests organized a consumer campaign against Burger King, a known and leading importer of Central American meat. Focusing directly on hamburger-loving American consumers and combining direct-action tactics, such as boycotts, with educational campaigns, activists from organizations such as Earth First!, Friends of the Earth, and the newly formed Rainforest Action Network hoped to generate grassroots pressure on corporations and stop deforestation. The movement's organizational structure, focus on consumer education, and implementation of direct action tactics not only forced changes to Burger King's practices but also served as a template for future consumer action and broader environmental activism.

"Americans Must Be Made Aware"

The Burger King boycott had its origins in a study conducted by two researchers at the Center for Applied Human Ecology. In 1981, James D. Nations, a researcher at the Center, wrote to Burger King asking for clarification on the provenance of their beef. The response from "The Home of Whopper" was surprisingly revealing. Jim Lawlor, the media relations manager for the corporation, replied:

> I looked into the subject of imported beef. The details are sparse. However, I am able to pass along some general information . . . suppliers purchase a significant amount of imported beef. This beef comes from several countries including a substantial amount from Central America, particularly Costa Rica. . . . All indications are that demand from imported beef will remain at current levels for the next few years.[2]

Using the above information as a starting point and combing U.S. Department of Agriculture statistics on the origins of imported beef, Nations and fellow researcher Daniel I. Komer set out to uncover more about the extent and potential consequences of U.S. beef imports from Central America.

Their study, published as "Rainforests and the Hamburger Society" in April 1983 in the journal *Environment*, emphasized American consumers' culpability in the destruction of tropical rainforests. Nations and Komer argued that consumers, corporations, and global finance networks—not governments—were essential in addressing the rapid loss of hardwood acreage and the accompanying decline in species diversity. Though acknowledging that "legislation phasing out beef imports from the rainforest regions of Central America" would be helpful, the authors implored that "an even more effective solution to the problem would be to redirect the international finances used to expand extensive beef cattle production in rainforest regions." The researchers' final sentence summarized the unequivocal need for consumer activism: "Americans must be made aware that when they bite into a fast-food hamburger or feed their dogs, they may also be consuming toucans, tapirs, and tropical rainforests."[3]

While researchers like Nations and Komer were exposing the origins of cheap beef, others were already beginning to educate and organize consumers to take action against the damaging effects of America's fast-food industry on the rainforest. Pressuring industry giants such as Burger King soon emerged as a central tactic. Dedicated to building an international movement to preserve rainforests worldwide, John Seed of Australia's Rainforest Information Centre (RIC) toured the United States with Mike Roselle of Earth First!, a relatively new environmental organization that committed itself to using direct action strategies "in defense of Mother Earth." Their 1983–84 "road show" established thirty local action groups who were committed to saving rainforests. But how could two dozen disparate grassroots groups challenge the multibillion dollar fast-food industry? Throughout the mid-1980s and beyond, Seed, Roselle, and environmentalist-filmmaker Randy Hayes developed a multipronged campaign to educate consumers and promote corporate accountability. Crafting a movement that was both grassroots and global, educational and activist, these consumer boycott leaders not only successfully challenged one of the leading corporations in the fast-food industry but also established a model for late twentieth- and early twenty-first-century environmental activism.

Organization

Lead organizers such as Seed, Roselle, and Hayes organized the first action for the last week of April 1984. Deliberately timed to coincide with

Earth Week, "Whopper Stopper" protests built on an existing effective event. A rite of spring on college campuses and in elementary schools across the U.S. since 1970, Earth Day and Earth Week provided a ready-made audience and framework for the nascent rainforest movement.

Frustrated that other environmental groups had not yet devoted significant time and energy to the rainforest issue, Hayes and Roselle pushed for the creation of a new group whose focus would be rainforest preservation. Through 1984 and 1985, Hayes patterned the Rainforest Action Network (RAN) on Seed's Australian RIC model. In short, activists borrowed ideas and tactics from pre-existing organizations (both RIC and Earth Day) to create something novel (RAN). Hoping to forge a network of dozens of international conservation groups, RAN aimed to be an umbrella organization for rainforest activism.

The dual local and global nature of RAN highlighted another aspect of the unique organizational structure of the mid-1980s rainforest campaign. Roselle and his fellow organizers crafted press releases and compiled information kits for nationwide distribution, but they encouraged individual action and grassroots autonomy. The campaign benefited from the large and growing international network, but also from the use of small, non-hierarchical groups of passionate activists and concerned consumers. Blending a global exchange of ideas with a commitment to cultivating grassroots organizing and local control, Seed, Roselle, and Hayes hoped to enact systemic changes.[4]

Tactics and Targets

From the very beginning of the campaign in 1984, the loose coalition of rainforest advocates focused on consumer education and action against Burger King. But why a boycott? Why put the responsibility on consumers and not pressure politicians in Washington, DC, to issue a ban on imported beef? And, why Burger King? Although environmental activists of the previous two decades had relied on lobbying governments and had enjoyed significant legislative success, they found it increasingly difficult to advance conservation measures in the hostile political climate of the 1980s. Following his election in 1980, President Ronald Reagan pursued a rigorous agenda of deregulation, advocated limited government involvement in private enterprise and aggressive resource development "for the betterment of man," and filled key administrative positions with anti-environmental figures, such as James Watt as Secretary of the Interior. Reagan threatened to stall and potentially reverse environmental gains of the previous decades. Realizing that they were unlikely to win legislative battles in the Reagan era, environmental activists employed other tactics, turning away from legislative campaigns and toward campaigns targeting corporations. They hoped that spurring hamburger-loving American consumers to take collective action would elicit lasting corporate change.[5]

Although activists acknowledged that many fast-food establishments used Central American beef, Burger King's open acknowledgement of its use of it made it the clearest target. In numerous press releases, Roselle and other boycott leaders stated that "the use of rainforest beef is an industry-wide problem—not limited to Burger King." Some pamphlets and flyers encouraged protests at other franchises such as McDonald's, Wendy's, Jack-in-the-Box, Bob's Big Boy, and Roy Rogers; however, Burger King was the only company that admitted to using imported meat. In a letter to Earth Firstlers, Roselle explained the campaign's strategy: "There has been enough research done at this point to point a finger at the guilty parties and begin to apply pressure. Burger King seems to be our best target . . . [they] are definitely known to use rainforest beef." Building on evidence uncovered for Nations and Komer's article, organizers chose to focus officially on Burger King but also pulled other industry leaders into the conversation when possible.[6]

Educating consumers was a critical—and challenging—first step. Activists faced a large, internationally known industry with a multimillion-dollar advertising budget and thus used a multiplicity of media to communicate facts about Central American beef exports. Importantly, organizers wanted to make sure consumers knew what the campaign's goals were and why Burger King was the primary target. In one of the first newsletters discussing upcoming actions against Burger King, Roselle offered potential protestors a concise list of goals:

> #1 Obviously, our most important goal is to stop the destruction of rainforests worldwide, with particular attention given to Central America. #2 To raise the issue of global rainforest destruction in the national and international media. . . . #3 Establish a network of rainforest activists. #4 It is important to raise the issue of accountability here. . . . A fact sheet on Burger King is now being compiled and your comments will be appreciated.[7]

Eschewing jargon and broader philosophical musings on concepts such as biocentrism, Roselle and Hayes repeatedly communicated basic "goals of the action."

Organizers realized that it was not just important for their followers to know about and understand the goals of the boycott, but they also needed to get the message out to mainstream media outlets. Roselle and his staff assembled press kits such as, "Where's the Beef . . . From? Don't Eat the Beef. Save the Rainforest," in which they again clearly stated the campaign's goals. In addition to listing details of upcoming demonstrations, the press kit also delineated the objectives of the actions:

> Purpose: To urge Burger King and other fast-food chains to cease importing Central American beef for use in American hamburgers and other fast foods. To draw public attention to the rapid destruction of Central American rain forests, prompted by the American fast-food clamor for Central American beef.

As part of their overall goal to raise awareness and inspire consumer response, rainforest activists used the media to help educate the public. In a memo to fellow organizers, Roselle offered specific instructions on how to maximize media coverage: "Local newspapers and radio stations and the student newspapers are good places to get coverage. Also local conservation publications. Try and keep a file on total news coverage and we will keep a record of it here [Earth First! office in Chico, CA]."[8]

To further broaden the educational campaign, Roselle instructed activists to use a one-page fact sheet titled, "Where's the Beef From?— Do You Know That You Are Eating Rainforest with Every Hamburger?" Providing statistics for protestors to distribute at Burger King stores, the sheet encouraged consumers to "Consider the Facts," such as:

> The U.S. buys 90% of all Central American beef exports. . . . In southeastern Mexico, ten pounds of beef are produced on an acre of land on which Mayan farmers used to grow 6000 pounds of shelled corn and 4000 pounds of root crops before the rainforests were cleared. . . . In the last twenty years over 40% of the Central American rainforest has been converted to cow pasture to provide cheap, low quality beef for America's fast food industry. If it continues, by the year 1990 the most diverse ecosystem on this continent will be lost forever!

The "Where's The Beef From?" pamphlet clearly implicated the fast-food industry in the pace of deforestation, "There is no shortage of domestic beef on the market. The only reason companies purchase Central American beef is that it is cheaper." The sheet, which communicated a sense of urgency, encouraged consumers to boycott Burger King and warned, "time is swiftly running out." Moreover, by using a permutation of the phrase, "Where's the Beef?," a popular Wendy's advertising slogan, activists subtly broadened the campaign beyond Burger King.[9]

Hayes' new group, RAN, adopted a similar media stance. Though focused primarily on Burger King, their print campaign implicated the broader fast-food industry. RAN published full-page advertisements in magazines and newspapers such as the *New York Times*. The ads not only contained statistics on rainforest depletion rates but also used eye-catching visual images and bold "headlines." One RAN ad showed a large snake with the caption, "There's a hidden ingredient in your fast-food hamburger." Under the heading, "Why we're losing 50,000 acres of rainforest a day. . . . Is five cents off a hamburger worth destroying the last rainforests left in Central America?," another advertisement depicted a gluttonous person biting into a massive hamburger. Hand-drawn flyers also used striking visual images. An Earth First! pamphlet announcing a rally and workshop presented a cute frog being enveloped by a large, nefarious-looking burger. The caption read, "You are eating the rainforest, my home."[10]

In these educational fact sheets and advertisements, Roselle and other organizers aimed to broaden the appeal of the campaign against the fast-food industry. Rather than just making a case that rainforests should be preserved for their inherent worth, boycotters also argued that human health was at stake. Stressing that old-growth forests and their rich biodiversity were sources of vital prescription drugs, activists made the issue about more than biocentrism and beauty. One promotional flyer stated, "Rainforests have been described as the 'Lungs of the World' because of their crucial and delicate relationship with the earth's atmosphere—a relationship that is only vaguely understood today, but which is known to be critical to our well-being." In addition to encouraging Americans to think about their own health and survival, rainforest activists also expanded the campaign to include human rights. Highlighting indigenous peoples' displacement, impoverishment, and exposure to toxic pesticides, boycott organizers emphasized the human dimension of rainforest depletion.

In addition to discussing the effect of deforestation on the people of Central America, rainforest activists also accentuated the local and national implications of using imported beef. The Austin, Texas, chapter of Earth First! rallied support for their rainforest campaign by stressing how the practice of importing beef hurt domestic cattle raisers. In their April 9, 1986, boycott letter, Austin Earth First! organizers proclaimed, "The American cattle industry is in a slump today in part because the influx of cow carcasses from Central America, competing with beef grown in the U.S.A. Save the Cowboy! Boycott rainforest beef!"[11] Student leaders at the University of Kansas used similar arguments as they sought to keep Burger King out of their student union food court. Student body president Carla Vogel wrote to the student senate, imploring, "Instead of helping to support the destruction of Central American rain forests by supporting companies that buy beef imported from Central American countries, we can strengthen our local farm economy and increase the University's contribution and commitment to this community by buying from local producers." In short, Vogel, like other rainforest advocates, aimed to make the issue of deforestation about more than saving big trees and cute frogs.[12]

Action

Seed, Roselle, and Hayes also used public demonstrations and other forms of direct action to educate consumers about the problematic source of Whopper meat. Demonstrations, an extension of their education and communication strategy, sought to encourage consumers to pressure the industry to change its practices. Like the print culture of the boycott, activists designed protests to be eye-catching and often humorous. For example, Roselle and the Chico, California, chapter of Earth First! scheduled sidewalk press conferences followed by "informational pickets and educational street theater" in front of a San Francisco Burger King. Costumed as cows, activists "pooped" crumpled up Whopper wrappers as they paraded in front of the Burger King store. Another protestor dressed up as a "little old lady in a parody on the Wendy's ad."[13]

Roselle and other leaders encouraged local groups to "decide on what types of actions they want[ed] to organize." He also reminded grassroots organizers that they did not need many people to make an event effective. In a letter to would-be activists, Roselle wrote, "It should be emphasized that half a dozen people or so will be enough to have a successful demonstration." Across the United States, local activists planned nearly two dozen rallies during the last week of April 1984. As with the main event in San Francisco, many protestors organized lively, attention-grabbing street theatre. In front of dozens of fast-food restaurants, skits and picket signs informed consumers that "Happy Meals" led to unhappy (and non-existent) rainforests.

Some protests offered live music as well. As he continued his international road show, John Seed often performed "The Whopper Song" as another playful way of communicating the importance of the boycott:

> Well, they come into the forest with machines with giant teeth
> Knock a nickel off every Whopper they make with cheap imported
>   beef
> So, won't you lay down your Whopper baby
> Lay down your Whopper and your fries
> Save the rainforest, baby, before the rainforest dies
> . . .
> Well, we've come to make a ruckus, raise our voices and to sing
> Protest the policies of the World Bank and Burger King
> So, won't you lay down your Whopper baby[14]

Helpful not only in gaining media coverage, but also in attracting passers-by, the demonstrations aimed to educate consumers and make them think about the high cost of cheap burgers.[15]

How did Burger King react to these demonstrations and the growing boycott? Local store personnel responded in a variety of ways. Some managers and franchise owners ignored the protests. Others seemed to enjoy the entertainment value of the demonstrations. Still others, concerned about the financial implications of the picket signs and life-size, "defecating" papier mâché cows, were more proactive in responding to the allegations. Employees of the Burger King in Eureka, California, handed out a flyer that "certified" that their store procured all of their meat domestically from Von's Grocery Company of El Monte, California.[16]

As the demonstrations continued sporadically over the next few months, Burger King's headquarters remained silent. Finally, in February 1985, Lisa Zeigler, a representative from Burger King's corporate relations office, replied to Randy Hayes. Citing research conducted by Burger King's public relations department, Ziegler stated that, "It would be our preference that our packers use all domestic beef. And for the most of 1982–83 they did. However, when insufficient lean beef, at affordable prices, becomes a problem, the packers must turn to other approved

USDA sources such as Costa Rica."[17] Though the lines of communication between Burger King and rainforest activists appeared to be opening, as of the fall of 1985, Burger King remained committed to using imported beef for at least a portion of its meat. After several failed attempts to encourage Burger King to finance preservation areas in Central America to offset the continued use of rainforest beef, activists at Earth First! and the Rainforest Action Network acknowledged a more formal boycott would be necessary.

Building on the previous two years of education and grassroots action, in the spring of 1986, the burgeoning coalition of rainforest activists, led by RAN, kicked off a renewed media campaign to encourage a consumer boycott of Burger King. Earth First! circulated a sample letter for frustrated consumers to send to the corporation's headquarters:

> Until I can be assured that you no longer use beef from Central America, my family and I will no longer patronize Burger King. I will also encourage my friends, neighbors, and relatives to do the same. If I become aware of evidence of other fast-food restaurants using rainforest beef, I will boycott them also. Rainforests are worth more than any amount of burgers, or even corporations! Please stop using beef raised in Central American rainforests so that we may once again enjoy your _____. (Try not to puke on the paper while you are writing this last line.)[18]

Though infusing a bit of humour at the end, the rainforest activists were becoming much more serious in their consumer action against Burger King.

Over the course of the next eighteen months, RAN published full-page advertisements in national periodicals such as the *New York Times* and coordinated more lunchtime demonstrations in front of Burger King franchises across the United States. In addition, Hayes' group professionalized its fundraising campaigns and initiated new alliances with groups such as the Farm Animal Reform Movement (FARM) to broaden the boycott's base. Activist publications such as the *National Boycott Newsletter* published articles featuring photographs of the stark results of "slash-and-burn agriculture" in Brazil's Amazon Basin.[19] Throughout 1986 and into 1987, though other national fast-food chains such as McDonald's showed continued growth, Burger King's sales dropped 12 percent. Finally, in July 1987, Burger King cancelled $35 million worth of beef contracts in Central America and announced that they would stop importing rainforest-sourced beef. The boycott was a success.[20]

Conclusions

The Burger King boycott was successful in part because of the movement's unique organizational structure. First, the campaign both worked with existing structures and created new organizational forms. This blend fused familiarity and experience with bold freshness and precision of focus. Second, organizers encouraged a campaign that allowed local autonomy within a larger international crusade. Again, this strategy allowed activists to benefit from a global network of ideas while crafting their own movement. Blending pre-existing structures with new organizations, the multi-pronged, eclectic rainforest campaign forced Burger King to change their practices. In an era arguably hostile to conservation legislation, activists went directly to consumers and corporations. Deploying the knowledge and resources of international activist networks while embracing grassroots autonomy, boycott organizers crafted a powerful template for challenging corporate power.

With the successful boycott of Burger King as a model, other environmental groups adopted similar strategies in the following months, years, and decades. For example, on October 16, 1987, London's Greenpeace chapter organized a "Worldwide Day of Action Against McDonald's." Going forward, RAN used its success with the Burger King boycott to challenge other large international corporations. In 1993, they led a consumer action against Texaco to address its drilling practices in ecologically fragile areas. In 1999, using tactics pioneered in the Burger King action of the mid-1980s, RAN conducted a boycott of Home Depot resulting in the mega-home improvement corporation's cessation of selling old-growth wood in all of its stores. As with the Burger King campaign, RAN's projects in the 1990s and 2000s did not just focus on biocentric concepts of animal rights and species diversity. Arguing that environmental issues were innately human issues, rainforest activists aimed to inspire consumers to "shift the marketplace toward ecological sustainability and human rights."[21]

Though the boycott of Burger King did not inspire a complete overhaul of the fast-food industry, it did highlight the effectiveness of consumer action in eliciting lasting change. As a new generation of activists takes aim at the fast-food industry's low wages, poor working conditions, and growing carbon footprint, they would be well served to reanimate elements of the RAN/Earth First! boycott. In particular, movement coordinators could offer educational materials and support networks but should then encourage local activists to design their own consumer action as part of a broader nationwide boycott. Rather than forcing a strict national agenda and timeline, such flexibility and customization can foster greater authenticity and buy-in among participants.

20

THE
SWEATSHOP EFFECT

Consumer Activism and the
Anti-Sweatshop Movement
on College Campuses

MEREDITH KATZ

O N APRIL 24, 2013, the Rana Plaza factory in Dhaka, Bangladesh, collapsed killing 1,134 workers, making it the deadliest disaster in the history of the garment industry. This tragedy was no accident. The eight-story Rana Plaza building violated multiple building codes, including the illegal construction of the top four floors housing the garment factory. Only one day prior to the collapse, substantial cracks were found in the building structure, and businesses in the lower floors closed immediately. Factory owners demanded garment employees continue to work despite unsafe working conditions.

The collapse of Rana Plaza marked one of three tragedies in the garment industry between 2012 and 2013. Just six months earlier, the electrical fire at the Tarzeen factory in Dhaka, Bangladesh, killed 117 workers and the Ali Enterprises factory fire in Karachi, Pakistan killed 262 workers. With three of the four worst tragedies in the global apparel industry occurring within one year, consumer consciousness of factory working conditions rose.

While the truth about garment factory conditions was a new revelation for some, many individuals and organizations have long resisted and fought against garment worker exploitation. The iconic National Consumers League (NCL) ran the White Label campaign between 1898 and 1919 and compiled a "white list" of approved stores for consumers to patronize based on the company's fair labour practices, "no sweat" apparel, and unionization of workers. The work of the NCL laid the groundwork for many modern consumer movements, including the student anti-sweatshop movement whose origins begin in 1996.[1] At that time, students began focusing attention on sweatshop labour when major athletic brands signed exclusive licensing contracts with university athletic departments. The following summer, students from five universities created the Sweat Free Campus Campaign to pressure their universities to adopt licensing codes of conduct for their athletic apparel contracts. In 1997, the Sweat Free Campus Campaign grew, and students formed United Students Against Sweatshops (USAS). From the outset, USAS chapters demanded universities establish licensing codes of conduct providing schools and licensees with minimum labour standards, including public disclosure of the factories producing their collegiate apparel, inclusion of a living wage clause, and protection for women's rights. Shortly thereafter, in 1999, Nike, faced with the prospect of losing collegiate contracts if they did not adhere to these conditions, agreed to disclose their factory reports. This victory marked the first time any company in the garment industry agreed to make their factory information publicly available. From this point forward, USAS quickly became the largest youth-led organization in North America organizing international solidarity campaigns to fight worker exploitation in all forms.

USAS is a grassroots student-labour solidarity organization, with chapters on over 150 college and university campuses across the United States and Canada, whose members work to expose and change exploitative conditions within the global economy. USAS partners in solidarity campaigns with working people's struggles, of which anti-sweatshop organizing is their flagship. USAS identifies their anti-sweatshop activism as a part of a broader international solidarity campaign that relies on the power of students to petition their schools to join the Worker Rights Consortium (WRC), an independent factory monitoring organization which protects the rights of workers in the global garment industry.

Their organizing philosophy is comprised of five key principles: solidarity, collective liberation, grassroots democracy, diversity of tactics, and pluralism. These standards underlie the organizational structure of USAS and all of their campaign strategies. USAS runs both national level campaigns, including WRC affiliation campaigns, and local-level campaigns specifically focused on fair working conditions for university employees. USAS's global solidarity campaigns have resulted in a series of successes for the labour movement.

For example, after the Rana Plaza collapse, USAS initiated a campaign for universities to cut university licensing contracts with Vanity Fair (VF) Corporation brands, including university licensees Jansport and North Face, for VF corporation's failure to sign the Accord on Fire and Building Safety in Bangladesh.[2] Previous campaigns include the 2013 "Badidas" campaign, where USAS successfully pressured Adidas to compensate 2,700 former Indonesian garment workers who were owed $1.8 million in unpaid severance pay when the PT Kizone factory closed. In 2010, USAS ran a successful "Just Pay It" campaign against Nike, forcing the company to pay 1,800 Honduran workers their $2.5 million severance package when the Hugger de Honduras and Vision Tex factories closed.

USAS Organizing

As can be seen in the previous examples, USAS is extremely successful running campaigns—due in large part to the size and networks of USAS chapters. With over 150 affiliates at colleges and universities across the United States and Canada, USAS's national-level organizing takes multiple forms. Weekly Sunday night solidarity campaign calls are open to all USAS chapters and members. During these discussions, successful strategies and tactics are discussed regarding WRC or other worker justice campaigns. Universities in the midst of WRC campaigns receive organizing packets, complete with sample letters to university administrators, press releases, and organizing points, including rebuttals to common administration responses. If a specific university needs outside support during a campaign, USAS national staff will send out emails to all chapters urging others to call the president's office or sign a petition, complete with all information attached. The institutional support of the USAS network and the main administrative offices of the organization facilitates action at individual colleges and universities across the United States and Canada.[3]

Given the successful track record of USAS, it is important that, as academics and/or activists, we understand USAS's effective organizing strategies. In this chapter, I highlight the successful strategies of USAS to make changes within the global apparel industry. Relying on my own experience co-founding and leading a USAS chapter at Virginia Tech, I detail my experience within the broader context of USAS strategies, as well as the effective tactics we employed to run a successful Worker Rights Consortium affiliation campaign. Specifically, I address the strategic use of media and information gathering from peer institutions to exert pressure on university administrations; the use of existing college and university licensing codes of conduct to hold universities accountable to their already established labour standards; and the advantages of affiliation with the Worker Rights Consortium. These lessons, while specific to the student anti-sweatshop movement, may also help inform other activists about similar tactics and strategies to achieve their movement goals.

Publicity and Opportunistic Timing

It was the fall semester of 2008, and at Virginia Tech, fall means football. I was a first-year graduate student enrolled in a Global Division of Labor course when I first heard about United Students Against Sweatshops. Later that semester, I co-founded the Virginia Tech chapter of USAS, Global Justice Alliance (GJA), with the explicit purpose of Virginia Tech becoming a signatory to the Worker Rights Consortium factory monitoring organization.

At the time, the university athletic department had recently designated two football games every season as "Orange Effect" and "Maroon Effect" games, highlighting the school colours. The university's rationale for these thematic games was to further increase school spirit and solidarity, as if there was not already enough with sixty thousand fans piling into the stadium every Saturday of the season. Furthermore, selling annual t-shirts with the logos "Orange Effect" and "Maroon Effect" was another opportunity to encourage consumption. Virginia Tech licensed-apparel profits consistently topped one million dollars annually, ranking Virginia Tech fortieth in the nation in collegiate apparel revenue sales.[4] For the fall 2008 football season, the university's Orange and Maroon Effect t-shirts for 2008–9 were Gildan branded t-shirts produced in Salvadoran and Honduran factories and sold at a discounted rate for a combined $12. El Salvador and Honduras are the two leading Central American exporters of clothing to the United States.[5] In 2008, workers earned, on average, $1.25 per day working in a garment factory.[6]

The "Effect" t-shirts also provided the key to garnering the attention we knew our WRC campaign needed to be effective. Capitalizing on football season and the popularity of the Effect t-shirts, we named our WRC campaign "The Sweatshop Effect." On maroon American Apparel t-shirts ordered wholesale through a local fair trade and sweatshop free retail store and sold for $12 each, we screen-printed a logo that mimicked the university's "Orange Effect '08" or "Maroon Effect '08" t-shirt designs. Instead, ours read, "Sweatshop Effect '08" in the same font and style as the university's t-shirts. In so doing, we used the provocative tactic of culture jamming or refashioning of a popular image to express a critical message. A common tactic among anti-corporate and anti-sweatshop activists alike, culture jamming is effective because of its ability to elicit a response from viewers.[7] Our Sweatshop Effect t-shirts did just that.

For our newly formed USAS chapter, one advantage of million-dollar revenue sales was that if the university joined the WRC, our association would have that much greater an impact. WRC affiliation ensured the large quantity of collegiate apparel bearing the Virginia Tech logo would be produced in factories with the most stringent monitoring standards available; worker rights would be protected; and factories would be monitored consistently. In addition to the factory monitoring reports publicly available on the WRC website, affiliated universities also receive an email when any of the factories producing its collegiate apparel are monitored. Publicly available reports, coupled with direct emails to universities, means administrators cannot state they are unaware of the labour conditions where their collegiate merchandise is produced.

Education

One of our primary educational strategies was a clothesline of licensed Virginia Tech apparel. For three days during September 2008, students, faculty, and staff walked past a clothesline hung in the centre of campus. Once we had their attention, GJA members and volunteers asked individuals how much they would pay, or did pay, for one of these Virginia Tech t-shirts. After they had responded, with common responses ranging between $15 and $30, we asked then how much they thought the worker who made their t-shirt was paid. While few respondents guessed the worker was paid less than a dollar, the majority mistakenly believed a garment worker earned a few dollars per t-shirt. Respondents were dumbfounded when we told them the truth—for an average $14 t-shirt, factory workers are paid $0.12 per garment, the total cost to the retailer, including shipping costs and labour totals $5.60, with a 60 percent markup to the consumer, and companies profit the remaining $8.33 per t-shirt (O'Rourke Group, 2011).

We continued educating those who stopped by the clothesline, handing out quarter-size sheets of paper illustrating the cost breakdown of a t-shirt, highlighting worker wages. Many people were shocked at how little workers were paid. We asked students, along with faculty and staff, if they wanted these conditions to change. The answer was a resounding yes. We then asked everyone to sign a petition letter to the Virginia Tech President and the Director of University Relations demanding the companies who produce our collegiate apparel are held to higher standards. Specifically, we demanded that the university administration, in accordance with its licensing code of conduct, affiliate with the WRC to ensure the highest protection of garment workers. At the time of the campaign, Virginia Tech was affiliated with the Fair Labor Association (FLA), a corporate-sponsored monitoring organization with a poor track record for protecting worker rights.[8]

Educating an individual, even on the spot, and providing an opportunity for immediate action is a fundamental USAS strategy. If individuals are presented with a problem, and then an immediate way to address the problem, such as signing a petition, they are more likely to feel empowered, connected, and committed to the success of the campaign. In our case, the sweatshop clothesline was part of an effective strategy to heighten the visibility of the campaign, and petition signatures provided an opportunity for immediate connection and action.

Media

The success of the Sweatshop Effect campaign, similar to many other WRC campaigns across college and university campuses, would not have been possible without the strategic use of media. The diversity of media outlets, including television interviews, newspaper stories, and social media publicity, brought attention and awareness to the Sweatshop Effect campaign.

The college town location and overall fandom for Virginia Tech football in southwest Virginia facilitated communication of our story to traditional media outlets. During college football season, it is not uncommon for many local news outlets to highlight Virginia Tech football during a broadcast, making our story more appealing. We called the local CBS station, pitched our story, and they agreed to come to campus to profile our WRC affiliation campaign. The news station came to campus and interviewed me and the other co-founder for a one-time story. We would use this connection later in our campaign to bring the news cameras back to campus.

We also contacted the regional newspaper to write a story. The *Roanoke Times* published an article on September 18, 2008, entitled "Students Rally Behind Sweatshop-Free Clothing." Virginia Tech's student newspaper, the *Collegiate Times*, published "'Sweatshop Effect' Seizes Drillfield" three days later, on September 21, 2008. In the campus news story, I am quoted as stating, "the monitoring is not occurring; the worker's complaints are not being investigated," referencing our dissatisfaction with the FLA monitoring. This same article also quoted the Director of University Relations stating, "I am not aware any of our products are made in sweatshops. We agreed to continue a dialogue and find out what their concerns are." These news stories, at both the campus and regional level, increased the profile and awareness of our campaign to everyone—including the administration.

The media were crucial in not only garnering the attention of university administrators, but their presence and stories also pressured the university to respond. The most strategic use of media occurred on the last day of our three-day clothesline event, when we marched thirty people strong into the president's office with a petition demanding Virginia Tech affiliate with the WRC. The petition included over one hundred signatures we obtained during our clothesline event, as well as the names of other student organizations supporting WRC affiliation. We contacted the local CBS news affiliate who had previously covered our campaign, and the reporter agreed to accompany us into the president's office with television cameras. To say the administration was less than thrilled to see the media was an understatement. However, the administration did agree on camera to discuss our demands at a later date. The presence of the television crew demonstrated the seriousness of our campaign and simultaneously pressured the administration to respond. We met with the Director of University Relations later the same afternoon.

In activist organizing, the strategic use of media is unparalleled in its capacity to bring about an intended outcome. First, media of any form simply helps to increase campaign visibility. Second, the media can be used to apply pressure, positive or negative, to university administrations, forcing them to respond. Given the increasing branding of colleges and universities in the United States, no school wants its name tarnished with negative publicity. USAS chapters and students are keenly aware of this fact, and commonly, as in the case of Virginia Tech, use the university administration's desire to maintain a positive image to their advantage. After all, why would a university want to support sweatshop labour and ignore the demands of students advocating for an alternative?

If you are involved with USAS, or with a similar consumer activist movement, media coverage is essential to the success of your campaign. Pitch your story to local newspapers and television stations. To make an effective pitch, think about your campaign or story from the university's perspective—find something the news station can cover that will elicit, even demand, a response from the university. For USAS chapters, make sure to tell the news media that your group is a part of a broader anti-sweatshop movement, citing the over 180 universities affiliated with the WRC. Establishing the connection between a local campaign and a larger national movement demonstrates to the media the magnitude and impact of the campaign.

The reality is, the Virginia Tech USAS chapter was not very large, a core group of approximately ten students and faculty members. We had support from additional campus organizations, individual students, and faculty, but the core group was small. If you are a small USAS chapter, you can also circulate a statement of support to other campus organizations and student governing bodies. The broader your support, the more difficult it is for the administration to ignore your demands.

Given the Virginia Tech-WRC affiliation campaign was in 2008, our primary use of social media was Facebook. We created an open group with our USAS chapter name, Global Justice Alliance at Virginia Tech, which had approximately fifty members. We used this page to keep interested campus and community members updated on the progress of the WRC campaign, linked media stories to the webpage, and also advertised the clothesline events and football game days we would wear our Sweatshop Effect t-shirts. We did not have a formalized group listserv and instead used Facebook as the primary medium for communication to the public. If starting a similar campaign today, the inclusion of social media outlets Twitter and Instagram as well as a unique hashtag would increase the visibility of your campaign to everyone on campus, including the university administration. The reality is the media pressures stakeholders to respond, at a university or in other organizations.

Strategies of Action

Following the initial delivery of our letter to the university president, we secured meetings with senior level administrators. Over the course of the next four months, a small group of students and faculty, five in total, met with Associate Vice President of University Relations, Assistant Vice President for Marketing and Communications, and Director of Licensing and Trademarks to present our case. In large part, our role was to educate the administration why the university's current affiliation with the FLA, a factory monitoring organization whose very name falsely connotes protection of workers' rights, was insufficient, and why the adoption of the Worker Rights Consortium was imperative. Universities pay $1000 annually or 1 percent of their total licensing revenue, whichever is greater, to the WRC to support their monitoring practice. Hence, the decision to sign on to the WRC was also a financial one. The FLA affiliation cost $5000 annually, but no legal hurdle existed if Virginia Tech chose to maintain their affiliation with the FLA and sign on to the WRC as an additional monitoring organization.

Our initial meetings with the administration were primarily informational in nature. The presence of a sociology faculty member and a business faculty member, both of whom had vast knowledge and experience with labour conditions in garment factories, gave us credibility with the administration. We presented a side-by-side comparison of the FLA and the WRC demonstrating the differences between the two monitoring organizations. We highlighted the insufficient monitoring of the FLA who did not conduct regular factory investigations and whose board was composed of corporate representatives, including two brands from Virginia Tech licensed apparel, Russell and Adidas. We specifically compared and contrasted the FLA with the WRC in terms of transparency, enforcement, corporate board involvement, factory inspection methodology, worker complaints, requirements for a living wage, women's rights, freedom of association, and remediation. The Director of University Relations, who has worked at the university for several decades, recalled a previous USAS group in 1999 petitioning the university to sign on to the FLA, the exact group from which we were asking the university to disaffiliate. Fortunately, our current faculty advisor also advised this previous group and could answer the tough questions regarding why the demand in changing monitoring organizations.[9] Our task was to show clearly that the current monitoring system of the FLA was inadequate and did not ensure the highest protection of workers, despite the name of the organization.

In addition, our organization adopted the long-standing USAS model of using the university's licensing code of conduct to force the administration to adhere to previously established guidelines. Highlighting various elements of the code of conduct, we presented a strong case for the necessity of WRC affiliation. The university's licensee code of conduct applies to all licensees of the university, providing a standard to which USAS chapters can hold a university if licensees do not adhere to the code. Section II of the code specifically states that all licensees must adhere to all principles set forth in the code. During our meetings with the administration, we highlighted the violations of Section IV, employment standards. Specifically, we focused on WRC reports highlighting factory violations with Virginia Tech licensed factories including Jerzees Choloma and Jerzees de Honduras, Thai Garment Export, and TOS Dominicana. In its effort to provide transparent factory monitoring to universities and consumers, the WRC makes all reports publicly available on its website.[10] We provided the administration with licensee reports for those who were in violation of the university's code of conduct. Specifically, we emphasized the violation of Section IV (IX), freedom of association and Section IV (X), violation of women's rights and noted that the FLA does not engage in remediation, leaving these violations unresolved.

Among the strongest arguments we presented for WRC affiliation was the frequency and manner of factory monitoring the WRC employs. WRC regularly conducts independent (not corporate- or union-affiliated) investigations of the health and safety conditions of factories. WRC monitors, unlike the FLA, speak directly with workers in a safe environment away from their bosses.

The transparency and public availability of WRC factory reports hold university administrations to a higher standard. In addition to the publication of factory reports online, universities receive email notifications about new reports of factories in which their licensed apparel is produced. In short, we demonstrated to the administration that the WRC's monitoring practices were more closely aligned with the university's principles and licensing code of conduct than were the FLA's. Since we used the university's existing code of conduct, which falls under contract law, to make our case, the administration could do little to rebut our arguments.

In addition to our dialogue about WRC affiliation on the basis of our licensing code of conduct, we also pressured the university to join the WRC similar to other schools in Virginia Tech's athletic conference. At the time of our campaign, Virginia Tech had recently joined the Atlantic Coast Conference (ACC), and the administration was excited to be a part of an elite division of schools. Five of twelve ACC schools were already affiliated with the WRC (Duke University, University of North Carolina-Chapel Hill, University of South Carolina, University of Virginia, and University of Miami). We used other ACC affiliations with the WRC as a means to apply pressure to the university to also join the WRC. Our rhetoric was that if Virginia Tech wanted to compete in all arenas with conference schools, then joining the WRC was one way to accomplish that goal. This strategy worked remarkably well. Falling behind peer institutions, even within the context of apparel monitoring, is something Virginia Tech was not willing to do. I am convinced this argument tipped our WRC campaign to victory.

Success

Four months after the outset of the Sweatshop Effect Campaign, the Virginia Tech administration agreed to affiliate with the WRC.[11] The affiliation was more than just a change on paper; it meant increased safety and protection for workers producing over one million dollars' worth of Virginia Tech collegiate apparel annually. On January 17, 2009, Virginia Tech joined the ranks of over 180 colleges and universities throughout the United States and Canada affiliated with the WRC.[12]

While we ultimately ran a successful WRC affiliation campaign, we experienced some setbacks. The first challenge we had, similar to many USAS campaigns, was the runaround we received from the university administration. While they were willing to meet with us, administrators constantly gave us more items to research and seemed, for a few months, no closer to making a decision. Frequently we would email University Relations reiterating our points and pressuring for subsequent meetings. Our second challenge was the small number of the core group of involved students. This meant relatively few people were intensely involved and committed a substantial amount of time and energy to this campaign. A stronger and broader base of support would have eased the burden on some of the group's core members. While we did reach out to other campus organizations for their support, our reach could have been broader. Recruiting more allies from less likely sources, such as fraternities and sororities, could have increased the breadth of our support and possibly made our campaign more convincing to the administration. Finally, student turnover in the anti-sweatshop movement, similar to any other movement, is always an issue. Since the VT-SAS chapter in 1999, there had been no anti-sweatshop organizing on campus until our group reinstated a USAS chapter in 2008. Currently, a senior is leading the USAS chapter, but the organization's future leadership is uncertain after she graduates.

Despite the challenges, our successful campaign was no accident. We strategically employed the proven tactics of USAS to convince university administrators to sign on to the WRC. In sum, our campaign was successful for the following reasons: 1) we created visibility and awareness of the WRC campaign within the broader university community; 2) we strategically used media coverage to pressure the university administration into meeting with us; 3) we researched the university's licensing code of conduct, highlighting where the current FLA system failed to uphold the standards of the university's code of conduct; and 5) we strategically used Virginia Tech's admittance into the ACC to pressure the university to join its conference peers and affiliate with the WRC. Many of the strategies we employed were long-standing and widely used tactics of USAS, and without them, our campaign may not have had the same result.

For those of you interested in starting a similar campaign, think about a primary symbol of identity or pride for your school or target organization. Once you have identified this, use it to your advantage. Employ tactics of culture jamming to draw attention to the incongruities, and often the hypocrisy, of what a college or company purports to stand for contrasted with their actual practices. Currently, many universities are concerned about sustainability. Try to expand that conversation to include apparel production and demand your university uphold sustainable practices by affiliating with the WRC. The university's commitment to these practices is likely available on your school's homepage. Identify what your university prides itself on and use that to your advantage.

Since 1997, USAS has become a force to be reckoned with both on college campuses and more broadly within the apparel industry. With over 150 affiliated chapters at colleges and universities across the United States and Canada and a successful campaign track record, there is no reason your university cannot be next.

21

HATING WAL-MART, LOVING TARGET, AND THE CONTRADICTIONS OF SUPPLY CHAIN CAPITALISM

JESSICA STEWART

"We feel they [Target] are worse than Wal-Mart because they are masquerading as this benign employer. [Target] has gotten this pass because they have set up this foundation and have this chic look, and that's more cruel than Wal-Mart. Wal-Mart doesn't pretend."

— Bernie Hesse, director of special projects, Local 789, United Food and Commercial Workers Union, St. Paul, Minnesota[1]

WHAT CAN WE LEARN from understanding the smug shopper, often a liberal, who loves Target but hates Wal-Mart? A great deal, as it turns out. Although Wal-Mart signifies, to many critics, the turn to neoliberalism and has reaped the largest gains from the accompanying shifts in power relations, it is the business model of a new kind of capitalism focused on supply chain management, not one particular company, which proved most consequential for workers.

When the first Targets and Wal-Marts opened in 1962, almost a third of private sector workers belonged to labour unions and working people were experiencing an unprecedented period of prosperity.[2] Fortunes, however, spiralled downward for the working class just as fortunes exploded for the founders of big box retailers, which sold goods made cheaply overseas and crushed small retailers. Now, less than 7 percent of American workers in the private sector belong to a labour union and the wages and living standards of working Americans have stagnated.[3] In 2014, wages for cashiers and other entry level retail store employees were the same at Target and Wal-Mart—around $8 per hour.[4] This is a far cry from the robust wages earned by unionized workers in 1962. Yet these wages are typical for today's working class. Despite decades of efforts, no union has been able to organize big box stores, even as they are at the centre of our consuming and working lives. When the first Wal-Mart and Target opened, no one imagined that fifty years later, in the second millennium, cashiers and stockers would be the face of the working class and the workers along the retail supply chain the key actors in labour's struggle.

Retailers' emphasis on supply chain management lay at the heart of both retailers' success and the transformations in the working class. Both companies seized on the chance to make distribution cheaper and more efficient. "Economically . . . distribution is the process in which physical properties of matter are converted into economic value," noted management theorist Peter Drucker, "it brings the customer to the product."[5] Target and Wal-Mart sought to capitalize on new ways to do just that. In the 1960s, as Wal-Mart and Target grew, newly built interstate roads and rapidly improving communications systems allowed goods to reach stores more quickly and cheaply. Popular stories and business school literature often portray Sam Walton, the founder of Wal-Mart, as a wildly innovative genius who emerged inexplicably from the backwoods of Arkansas to remake the global economy. This story of Walton as hero (or antihero), while dramatic and appealing, fails to account for how Walton, rather than creating innovations out of thin air, was merely the first to act on emerging opportunities. However, he was hardly alone in seizing the moment to gain profits by cutting out inefficiencies in the distribution system. Target, founded the same year, built very similar methods of supply chain management, even as many people imagined the two discounters to be markedly different. Through advertising, community engagement, charitable giving, and shopping experience, Target built an image of being both more upscale and more socially responsible than Wal-Mart. That difference, born of an intentional branding strategy by Target, has led us to focus on Wal-Mart as a "bad apple" rather than recognizing the similarities between the two companies. These shared practices, made possible by new techniques of supply chain management, are the real challenge to the working class—not Wal-Mart alone. Even if Wal-Mart were to fall, workers would still face the constraints and opportunities wrought by supply chain capitalism.

Logistics

Taking control of the supply chains allowed retailers to gain unprecedented power and increase profits. Big retailers' most resounding innovations were not technological but grew from their ability to use technology to shift responsibility for the many links of the supply chain to suppliers and manufacturers, while gaining ever increasing leverage over the entire supply chain. "No matter how good the merchant, distribution is a critical element in the profitability of business," Stephen Pistner, president of Dayton Hudson, told *Women's Wear Daily*.[6] Over time, discount retailers were able to develop this to a very high level and thus became capable, to their great benefit, of "leveraging favorable 'economies' wherever they [were] found on the globe."[7] Strikingly, however, many of the innovations, such as shipping containers and bar codes that proved most pivotal to retailers' success, were created by others. Retailers like Wal-Mart and Target merely had good timing and the wherewithal to act quickly on emerging opportunities.

As is often the case, the world was remade, and supply chain capitalism made possible, chiefly through a collection of seemingly boring innovations and the shifts in power relations flowing from those innovations. Both Target and Wal-Mart made their first big step into what would become the supply chain revolution in the late 1960s when they each took the decidedly undramatic step of opening a distribution centre to supply the growing number of stores in their core regions, Minnesota and Arkansas, respectively. They did not talk about supply chain innovations. During the 1960s, no one talked about supply chains. The term did not exist. Yet, retailers were engaging in building the supply chain systems that would propel their ascendancy. The concept of what is now referred to as the supply chain became a key topic during the 1970s as large firms broke apart and production scattered across the globe. As production dispersed, distribution stepped in to take advantage of the new possibilities. Wal-Mart began its hub and spoke pattern, in which it would open a distribution centre and then open stores around the distribution centre. Target pursued a similar strategy. Although simple, the distribution centre strategy allowed both companies to save vast amounts of money and, as

Drucker said, "convert matter into economic value" with much greater speed and precision. This was the beginning of supply chain triumph.

Improvements in distribution arose to remedy one of capitalism's fundamental contradictions: the lag between supply and demand. In an escalating spiral of improvements, corporate heads and newly discovered "logistics experts" analyzed the supply chain from raw materials to the store. They viewed the supply chain as a continuous system through which goods flowed and sought to eliminate any obstacles to the speedy and precisely directed flow of goods. As the system became more efficient through logistics innovation, goods whizzed through the system and to the consumer at ever faster speeds and with ever greater precision. Retailers wanted to sell what they produced as quickly and efficiently as possible. They did not want piles of unsold sweaters or Christmas mugs cluttering the back rooms of stores. Nor did they want to run out of a favourite item while consumer demand was high. Inventory soaked up working capital—and by extension, profits.

Intermodal shipping containers, which allowed goods to move efficiently across land and sea, made use of the new highways and linked them to ports, which could easily load and unload boxes from ships. Invented during the 1950s by a trucking company owner, Malcolm McLean, shipping containers first gained widespread use by the military for transport of goods to Vietnam. By the 1970s, shipping was transformed.[8] McLean's innovation further reduced costs for big retailers, who could pack the goods into a container in a distant country and not unload the goods until they reached the distribution centre. As with so many fortuitous developments that met Wal-Mart and Target during the 1970s, this was not an innovation of Sam Walton's or any other retailer, and yet they all shared in the possibility. Often, as in the case of ports or highways, these innovations were made possible by state infrastructure, not private genius.

Although Walton is given great credit, similarly, for "making the lowly barcode sing," in fact, both Target and Wal-Mart began testing the bar code during the same year, 1980.[9] With astonishing speed, the bar code became indispensable. Originally conceived by an IBM employee and first used in the 1970s by grocery stores for identifying items, big retailers deployed the bar code to great advantage.[10] Retailers began, on a large scale, to use computers to keep track of who was buying what and where. Earlier innovators had thought about ways to do this during prior decades, but computers were simply too large and expensive to make it profitable.[11] This new knowledge about product sales gave them great power over suppliers. Retailers abandoned cash registers for computerized systems that transmitted point of sale data back to the corporate headquarters, who then transmitted it along the supply chain to producers. Using the point of sale data allowed production and distribution to be closely hitched to sales. Inventory was drastically reduced, and both manufacturers and retailers saved money and moved goods much more quickly, although manufacturers paid dearly for these cost savings in relinquished control.

As supply chains became more integrated, moreover, the relationship became less about trade or even selling than synchronization. Functional barriers between retailers, suppliers, and manufacturers fell. Once guarded with one another, firms moved toward integrated systems that would minimize total cost and maximize speed and turnover of goods. From this position of power, large retailers, such as Wal-Mart and Target, could pressure suppliers to deliver at lower costs and to meet highly specific requirements. No longer did manufacturers make products and then push them onto retailers, instead retailers, with their vast knowledge of consumer behaviour and troves of sales data, told manufacturers what to make and when to make it.

Labour

Target and Wal-Mart's supply chain model allowed them to abdicate responsibility for the conditions under which their stream of stuff was made. "Our primary growth objective has been to compete head-on with other large discounters," Target CEO Robert Ulrich assured shareholders in 1991.[12] Competing head on with Wal-Mart and other large retailers demanded that Target engage in the same business practices as other retailers and ceaselessly seek ways to increase efficiency. The leanness and "power of one" championed by Ulrich, perhaps Target's most successful CEO, meant more work for less pay for workers at all points along the supply chain. As Nelson Lichtenstein has observed, "although these supply chains are highly integrated in a functional sense, legal responsibility is radically attenuated."[13] Even as retailers maintained greater and greater levels of surveillance over the shipping and distribution process, they distanced themselves from the conditions of production.

In the stores, their business models are the same. When the first Target opened in 1962, the company's leaders looked to low-wage housewives and high school students to staff the stores and to a well-paid manager, typically a man, to run the store. An early annual report captured this model by showing an authoritative white man with the accompanying caption, "The store manager—usually a family man himself—holds the key to the drawing power" of Target. Although Wal-Mart has attracted much attention for its low wages and poor labour policies, Target employed nearly identical, and in some cases worse policies for workers. As Target expanded into a national chain, they kept this model and continued to pay low wages. In California, in the early 1980s, Target paid cashiers around $4 per hour. This number became public because clerks protested in 1983 when Target leased thirty-three stores that had been previously run by FedMart, a discount club chain started by Solomon Price, who later founded Price Club.[14] Target refused to hire many of the clerks, who were members of a union and made $6–$7 an hour. Instead, Target hired non-union clerks for $4 per hour. Moreover, the clerks claimed, Target offered fewer and less reliable hours. Almost half of the FedMart employees had been full time, while only 10 percent of the Target positions were.[15]

Target's low wages were once again in the public eye when in 1987, the *Minneapolis Star Tribune* reported that "Dayton's lobbied mightily against [raising the minimum wage] and did not always look like the nice guy, trying to prevent sales clerks from getting a few extra bucks a week. The firm employs a lot of people, yes, but many of them at the minimum wage."[16] According to research by the United Food and Commercial workers, in the early 2000s Target paid between $6.25 an hour and $8 an hour for entry-level, hourly positions in its Twin Cities stores. The union found that Wal-Mart workers earned slightly more with some entry-level positions, getting as much as $8 to $10 an hour in the same region.[17] In 2015 dollars, that is $7.90 to $10 per hour for Target workers and $10 to $12.75 for Wal-Mart workers. Wages are also similar for distribution workers at the two companies. During the 1990s, workers in Target's distribution centres made around $8–9 per hour, or in 2015 dollars, $13–14.[18] Wages were similar for Wal-Mart distribution workers. Like Wal-Mart, the Target business model and rapid growth depended on keeping the minimum wage as low as possible.

Nor was, or is, Target, despite its mantra of "fast, fun, and friendly," a uniquely pleasant place to work.[19] The *Minneapolis Star Tribune* spoke with former Target cashier Mary Murphy of Chanhassen, Minnesota in 2005 and her story illustrates how, for most retail store employees, working conditions at Target are very similar to Wal-Mart. Murphy "said she was proud when Target hired her as a cashier," and that she would never have considered working for Wal-Mart.[20] She was drawn to working for a company that donated 5 percent of its federally taxable income to the communities in which it did business. Hired as a cashier at $7.50 an hour, Murphy was told that she could receive a 50-cent raise, but she was expected to meet Target's quota of selling at least nine credit cards a week to shoppers. "Managers would hover near the checkout lanes to make sure cashiers were pitching the cards with the proper enthusiasm," Murphy said.[21] In order not to "annoy repeat customers," cashiers, while quickly scanning items and making change, were required to vary their sales pitch. Murphy, like others, found the quota impossible to attain. Murphy resigned after nine months without ever receiving the raise and said that, after nine months, all of her colleagues had quit. "If there was a union and a sense that things were going to improve, people might have stayed longer," Murphy said. "Right now, there is absolutely no incentive to stay there for any length of time."[22] Having worked at Target, she now viewed the company in the same light as she once saw Wal-Mart.

Target is Inexpensive, Wal-Mart is Cheap

Yet, despite its contribution to the end of the middle class and harsh new political economy, everyone loved Target, even those on the left. "We've complained to national folks, 'Why is Wal-Mart the bad guy?'" said Bernie Hesse, a UFCW official in Minneapolis who tried to organize Target workers. "But in places like Chicago, the union has zeroed in on Wal-Mart, because it's the retailer people love to hate," he said.[23] People could not hate Target because it allowed them to indulge their fantasies of a classless society. Everyone could have luxury. They sold "attractive, inexpensive interpretations of specialty store merchandise, just a few aisles away from the less sexy but all-important items like milk, white T-shirts and potting soil." Together with inventive advertising, this allowed Target shoppers to feel they were "part of a big, hip national secret."[24]

Consumers' differences in perception of the two stores, although based largely on aesthetics, had significant consequences. A business school study found that "the effect of the rate of anti-Wal-Mart protest is significant and positive: so Target seeks to enter markets when people protest against Wal-Mart." This result prompted the authors to ponder, "Why does Target discount protests against Wal-Mart? Is it because protests are noisy signals? Is it because Target thinks such protests are irrelevant?"[25] According to the study, between 1998 and 2008, Wal-Mart's proposals to open new stores in American communities faced a protest rate of nearly

40 percent while Target's were less than 7 percent. The newspaper articles, public hearing comments, and protest materials accompanying such protests suggested that consumers and citizens, especially those in affluent and liberal locations, saw Wal-Mart as the "poster child of extreme capitalism" and Target as the socially responsible discount store due to its progressive image, highly publicized community engagement and substantial contributions to civic and cultural causes.[26] Surveys of consumer online activity found similar results. Crimson Hexagon, a polling firm, found that "Overall, Target enjoys mostly positive chatter. . . . About 75 percent of conversations were positive." Wal-Mart was "much more polarizing," whereas "people found Target a place for a nice shopping experience."[27] To many consumers, Target represented good taste and a pleasant sensibility.

Although the two companies grew using the same business practices, Target engineered a markedly different consumer experience than at Wal-Mart, which has largely sheltered it from criticism. These distinctions resulted from choices made when each company began. As *Fortune* writer Julie Schlosser recently noted, Target "may have only a fifth of the sales and profits of Wal-Mart, but it reels them in with ten times the panache."[28] The Wal-Mart shopping experience expressed the authenticity of the rural American working class, while Target aspired to, and often created, a shopping experience that hid inequality behind a classless fantasy of democratized consumption. Throughout each company's evolution, the substantial distinctions in image production, sales strategy, and shopping experience remained. Their stores appeared very different even as their supply chain strategies and labour practices converged.

Shopping at Target allowed middle-class consumers to enact a fantasy of being hip, glamorous, and free from fears of downward mobility. When consumers entered Target, they could briefly escape the increasingly precarious world that, ironically, Target and other giant retailers were helping to create. The design of the stores, in particular, was calculated to allow working- and middle-class people to have the sense of escaping the economic worries that dragged them down. Shopping was a vivid, unmediated experience that occurred repeatedly, while advertising and philanthropy were more distant. As marketing professors Patrick Barwise and Sean Meehan noted, "Great advertising might get shoppers into the store once—but only once if the experience and value for money do not meet expectations."[29] Not unlike the department store of the 1920s, they allowed shoppers to enter a fantasy world of luxury. "Target's clothing departments, many set on angles, flow into each other. Back-lit displays, track lighting and wall graphics highlight everything from beauty supplies to sporting goods," noted a writer for *Women's Wear Daily*.[30] Target allowed consumers, through its façade of "democratized design," to relish the illusion of a classless society.[31]

In a skilful exploitation of paradox, Target allowed consumers at once to be reasonable budget seekers and indulge their fantasies of luxury. As an internal Wal-Mart memo leaked to the media in 2006 lamented, "Target has been incredibly successful at resetting the bar of what people expect from a discount store. Their fundamental premise is democratizing great design. . . . They feel like the 'new and improved' while Wal-Mart often feels like the 'old and outdated.'"[32] If Wal-Mart invoked mountain of poverty to some consumers, Target invoked big-city glamour. "Going to Target" became "a cool" experience, observed *Fortune* writer Shelley Branch. At Target, saving money was cool, not cheap. In the performance of class and coolness, the repeated shopping experience mattered most because, as Nietzsche noted long ago, "the doing itself is everything."[33] Middle-class shoppers loved Target as much as they hated Wal-Mart. Articles about Target celebrated it as the "center of urban cool."[34] Customers were led to feel that they were achieving a shopping coup—getting a department store experience and designer fashions at discount store prices.

To middle-class consumers, Target was "fancy at a reasonable price," while Wal-Mart was just cheap.[35] The clean, uncluttered aisles, tasteful lighting, and crisply contrasting red and white suggested disciplined, sensible, and orderly consumption. "I see Target as cleaner, better organized and less trashy" than Wal-Mart, remarked engineer Steve Hansberry as he shopped at Target on a Saturday morning.[36] Unlike Wal-Mart, which stoked middle-class anxiety about poor people, Target stores soothed middle-class shoppers' fears of becoming like poor shoppers recklessly spending their meagre dollars on cheap junk. Social anxieties about undisciplined poor people ruining society remained at bay within the Target shopping experience. If anybody could afford Target, why would anyone shop at Wal-Mart? Something must be wrong with Wal-Mart customers, the thinking went, something that made them poor. If they shopped at Wal-Mart when they could shop at Target, then obviously they made bad choices in life.

Wal-Mart had the country, but Target had the cities—or at least the urbane. Robert Ulrich, a key executive during the 1980s and 1990s widely credited with building the chic image of Target, created a trend department during the image-conscious 1980s, which built on and expanded Target's fashionable leanings. First, he brought over fashion scouts from Dayton Hudson, who started with the modest goal of expanding the colour palette for T-shirts. "I can remember all the skepticism," noted George Jones, a Target executive during the 1980s, and later CEO of Borders Books. "No one in mass had anything like this."[37] Ulrich persisted, and his efforts paid off. Target became known as sophisticated and hip. Even New York City socialite Blaine Trump described herself as a "huge fan of Tarjay" and noted that she would not go "anywhere else for her running gear and thongs."[38]

In 1987, Ulrich became CEO of Target Stores, and the company's efforts at being cool grew bolder, led by John Pellegrene, a theatre major who began working at Target in 1988 and later ran the marketing department. Ulrich and Pellegrene created a marketing message that "dared to suggest that shoppers could get joy from buying a broom or a toothbrush."[39] Even everyday goods could be differentiated. Pellegrene's marketing strategy allowed, in the words of an enthusiastic reporter, "Target [to] spearhead a giant self-esteem program for the middle class."[40] Target's design aplomb offered middle-class shoppers the possibility to both be thrifty budget shoppers and indulge in a small piece of the luxury that was so prominently displayed by an increasingly prominent wealthy elite during the 1980s and 1990s.

At a time when middle-class consumers felt their futures to be increasingly precarious, Target helped them to feel they were still on top of the game. They could buy the same running gear as Blaine Trump and have fancy tea kettles, so all was not lost. "1998 was exceptional," crowed the cover of Dayton Hudson's annual report from that year. Part of that success derived from the rollout of their designer collaborations. "At last we can afford to buy some of the things we design," the annual reported quoted Michael Graves, an architect and designer who created a budget line for Target, as saying.[41] Consumers flocked to stores to buy whimsical kettles and Mossimo shirts, more than willing to pay for a sense of class security.

Shopping at Wal-Mart, to many middle-class consumers, would have been embarrassing and cheapened their identity, but even celebrities and the rich shopped at Target. They saw shopping at Target almost as a form of resistance against the classifications imposed by consumer society—much like how hip Brooklynites viewed flea market shopping. It was this remarkable feat that caused women to form blogs like *Slave to Target* in which the writer gushed,

> I am madly and deeply in love. I can't help myself. I go to see him every day and push around his big, red, hot, rock hard cart. We stroll, we ooh and ahh and we always end up in trouble. Everyone looks at us like we are crazy but they too know how amazing our love affair is. They feel the same passion and know that I will be coming back for more. . . . It is simple diary, I am smitten and I can't get enough. I am in love with Target.[42]

By shopping at Target, upper-class people saw themselves as engaging in a safe "form of market sanctioned cultural experimentation" or even rebellion.[43] Celebrities, New Yorkers, and other style guides gleefully engaged in the carefully controlled rebellion associated with Target shopping and in so doing invited middle-class consumers to safely embrace Target. Target became a free choice that they made as independent, savvy consumers, while Wal-Mart would have been a prison sentence imposed by poverty or lack of taste.

Although people loved to hate Wal-Mart, Target longed to be Wal-Mart. As a retrospective article in *Home Textiles Today* noted, "Despite the differences in marketing attitude between the two chains—Wal-Mart's just-folks conceit vs. Target's sleek modernism—Wal-Mart is clearly Target's benchmark."[44] In the same article, then-CEO Douglas Scovanner admitted, "We pay far, far, far more attention to what Wal-Mart is up to than what Kohl's is up to."[45] Scovanner's admission illustrates the key point that class appeal mattered far less than business model in the construction of a system of retail capitalism that defines how goods are produced, shipped, and purchased and indeed shapes the class structures that make up society. Target and Wal-Mart differed in the consumer experience but in everything else—labour policies, inventory management, supply chain management, procurement—they were the same. As contemporary inequality hit levels that make the luxury fetish of the 1980s and 1980s look quaint, Target faces an uncertain future. The world that relentless and brutal supply chains produced, by increasing precarity and killing well-paid manufacturing jobs, was the reason that Target shoppers flocked there. But now, even those shoppers have lost their jobs. Target can no longer feed off the anxieties of a declining middle class and an economy in transition. The transition to extreme inequality is already over.

The Triumph of Supply Chains, the End of Big Boxes

Maybe it is neither Kohl's nor Wal-Mart that should worry Target. Instead, it is the lowly dollar store that now threatens the mighty discount titans. The beginning of the end of the reign of big discounters is in progress. Small box stores may mean the end of big box stores. Target is closing its stores in Canada and is rumoured to be losing its edge. Wal-Mart is not faring much better.[46] Only Costco, of the big box stores, with its much different business model, seems to be faring well. Although store formats are changing, the supply chain structure remains at the centre of retail's hegemony and labour's challenges.

Dollar stores sell even cheaper goods than Target and Wal-Mart and have many more stores. Their niche in the "extreme value sector" enables them to do well even in dire economic times. Some dollar stores, like Dollar Tree, sell all goods for one dollar, but most sell items that range between one and ten dollars. Many dollar stores sell food staples such as milk, bread, chips, and eggs in addition to cheap household items and plastic trinkets.[47] If Target thrived on the anxieties wrought by an economy in transition, dollar stores thrive on inequality.

Discount retailers now face one of the classic contradictions of capitalism. The world they hastened into existence through supply chain capitalism is one in which there is a declining market for their goods due to wealth inequality. The masses of working- and middle-class people who once flocked to discount retailers now find themselves increasingly financially constrained and unable to consume at the levels that propelled discount retailers to supremacy. In this new landscape, consumers' perceptions of Wal-Mart have dramatically changed. No longer is Wal-Mart seen as the least expensive place to shop.[48] Target, widely, albeit inaccurately, perceived to be more expensive than Wal-Mart, has been even more impacted by consumers' price scrutiny. If consumers feel Wal-Mart is too pricey, they certainly are not going to Target with its fancy ambience. "The recession accelerated shoppers' respect for dollar stores," observed retail analyst Wendy Liebmann. "Wal-Mart shoppers, particularly, its most frequent shoppers, agree that dollar stores have lower prices and more national brands than Wal-Mart, and dollar stores are becoming more accepted by shoppers as being mainstream."[49] Faced with this conundrum, discount retailers grasped at odd solutions, such as rapid expansion into the grocery market. They hoped, through expansion into grocery, long a low-margin wasteland, to find a way to draw consumers in and capture their entire wallet, yet such an approach is fraught with logistical perils.

As inequality has become more extreme, shopping patterns have diverged. Amazon, small businesses, and the maker movement are drawing away more affluent big box consumers. Essentials such as diapers, toilet paper, and even breakfast cereal can now be gotten overnight on Amazon.com. For middle- and upper-class consumers, who buy their bread from artisans, their vegetables at farmers' markets, and their shirts at boutiques, this time-saving convenience is a boon and may trump the thrifty cool of Target.

Chains like Dollar Tree specialize in an even cheaper version of chic than Target, carrying items like plastic champagne glasses, cocktail umbrellas, and wrapping paper. Upper-class suburbanites derive a thrill from scoring party items for a buck.[50] These are higher profit margin dollar stores and are more commonly located in suburban areas. Indeed, in 2014 and 2015, Dollar Tree had much higher gross margins than Wal-Mart. Other dollar stores, like Family Dollar, reap much lower margins and serve the poorest customers in urban and rural areas isolated from larger grocery and retail stores.

Especially in the case of high margin stores like Dollar Tree, dollar stores are exploiting the supply chain networks built by Wal-Mart and Target and seeking to gain profits by operating more efficiently and flexibly than the large and relatively more unwieldy large discount retailers in much the same way that steel mini-mills displaced the once unshakable US Steel.[51] Wal-Mart is finding that, as David Harvey argued, "competitive advantages (higher profits) from superior organisational forms, machines or, for example, tighter inventory control [are] usually short-lived."[52] As well, because dollar stores are smaller and less scrutinized, they can pay even lower wages than Target and Wal-Mart. In some cases, dollar stores break wage and hour laws with an impunity no longer available to the giant retailers.[53] In much the same manner that discount stores disrupted the department store business during the 1950s and 1960s, dollar stores now disrupt the hegemony of Wal-Mart and Target. By observing the changing of store formats and the triumph of the supply chain, labour activists stand to gain crucial strategic insights.

Conclusion

Wal-Mart is an enormous company and clearly the company shapes political economy in important ways, but it is easy for workers and their allies to become awed by the company's size and forget the rapidity with which the retail landscape can change. For the working class to prosper in the long term, labour must gain leverage over the retail supply chain, which is the true enemy of working-class prosperity, not bring virtue to Wal-Mart.

The labour movement's choice to focus on Wal-Mart grew from practical concerns. Their leaders had to make the most of limited resources and were operating in an unfavourable political and legal climate. Labour leaders hoped that by targeting the largest company, they would set a process in motion that would transform the industry through pattern bargaining, or some extension of that concept, as had been done so successfully in other sectors.[54] However, to focus on one company implied to the public and even to those within the movement that the problem inhered within the particular moral or political outlook of one company and thus led the movement down numerous strategic dead ends.

One of these dead ends was to focus on consumers and moral outrage. Consumers have been, and will continue to be, part of the struggle to remake the supply chains in ways that give labour power, but moral persuasion alone was, and is, no match for the exploitation that occurred along the supply chains of giant retailers. Moreover, such an approach imagined capitalism as a moral force and failed to reckon with the self-justifying power of hegemony. As the class politics of Wal-Mart and Target make clear, capitalism has tremendous power to subvert moral messages and justify conditions, relationships, and processes that, in the absence of hegemony, many people would reject. Blogger Carrie Kirby illustrated this point when she wrote on her blog, *Wisebread*, about why she boycotts Wal-Mart but loves Target: "People have to buy things someplace, and for many, especially those outside urban areas, that someplace is going to be a big box store. A boycott is an easier sell if it isn't an undue burden on those who are asked to participate."[55] Ultimately, for many middle-class consumers like Kirby, it was about feeling ethical, not changing power structures. Labour's historic victories arose not from appeals to the morality of either capitalists or consumers, but through actions focused on capital's vulnerabilities.

Another dead end came from focusing on Wal-Mart stores and not the retail supply chain. To achieve victory, activists and unionists must recognize that it is a new structure of capitalist relationships, not Wal-Mart, that is the enemy. As retailers like Wal-Mart and Target "create a seamless supply chain, slashing inventories and delivering goods "just in time" to the customer," their supply chains become intertwined along the way.[56] "Ships, intermodal yards, and trucks have been transformed into mobile warehouses."[57] Some of these systems of mobile warehouses are distinct to each company, but in many cases are intertwined. Each company is distinct in image, but their supply chains cannot be teased apart in a way that makes it advantageous confront only one company.

One of labour's most profound and celebrated achievements has been to inspire brave and bold action among its ranks. To do so effectively today it must appropriate the courage and commitment of past labour campaigns, but must apply that energy to today's circumstances with a keen awareness of how contemporary capitalism operates. Although the transformations in employment wrought by supply chain capitalism have weakened worker power in well documented ways, the exigencies of the supply chain also confer tremendous power to small groups of strategically placed workers. Just in time supply chain practices leave companies vulnerable to disruption at chokepoints. Conceptualizing new forms of resistance must not confuse the retailer for the supply chain. Successful activism must consider the entirety of the supply chain for meaningful shifts in power relations to occur. Focused actions at key points along the supply chain could allow labour to regain some of the power it has lost over during recent decades and set the stage for a new era of labour militancy and victory.

22

PORTS ARE THE
NEW FACTORIES

Supply Chains and Labour Power in the Twenty-First Century

LOUIS HYMAN

"A merchant, it has been said very properly, is not necessarily the citizen of any particular country. It is in a great measure indifferent to him from what place he carries on his trade; and a very trifling disgust will make him remove his capital, and together with it all the industry which it supports, from one country to another."

— Adam Smith, *The Wealth of Nations*

N NOVEMBER 2012, union activists across the country celebrated what they saw as the latest opportunity to kick-start the moribund labour movement: a strike at Wal-Mart on Black Friday. Retail workers, or as Wal-Mart calls them, "associates," across the United States were to walk out on the busiest shopping day of the year. The walkout was to signal the national unity of retail workers and strike a blow that would stagger the giant from Bentonville. At the same time, it would galvanize liberal consumers who would support the walkout by their refusal to shop at Wal-Mart. Bringing together consumers and workers, union activists believed, would force America's largest retailer, and staunchest foe of unionization, to the negotiating table.

Despite the hype, the Black Friday strike failed. It turned out, as one might expect, that co-ordinating a walkout at thousands of locations across the country was hard—even in this age of social media. Walkouts were erratic. Most Wal-Mart workers, already pressed, did not want to risk their jobs. Shoppers, most of whom were hard-pressed themselves, thought more about the presents than the picket lines—if there were any. Attempts to remount the Black Friday Wal-Mart strike in the subsequent two years also failed.

At the same time, in 2012, as the well-publicized Wal-Mart strike was fizzling out, another strike was taking place that also threatened Wal-Mart's ability to deliver all those cheap Chinese-manufactured goods throughout the country. However, because this strike—in the container port at Long Beach, California—provided neither the visceral satisfaction nor spectacle of underpaid workers or politically conscious consumers picketing the world's most powerful retailer, it attracted hardly any media attention. The organization took much less work since it was in only one place. But the Long Beach strike was much more important than the Black Friday strike—not only because it was successful, but because it pointed to the real opportunity to re-establish worker power in consumer capitalism. Understandably, the press saw greater news value in discussing evil Wal-Marts than it did boring ports. But the port strike, unlike the retail boycott, actually shut down the movement of all those goods to all those Wal-Mart stores, freezing a billion dollars of goods every day. Without those goods, Wal-Mart, and every other retailer, cannot make money. This strike, over six hundred workers, was more important, I think, because it suggests a way to organize all those Wal-Mart stores and rejuvenate the American labour movement.

Misremembering History

The hope that the planners and earnest activists of the Wal-Mart strike placed on it was based on commonly-held—but quite mistaken—assumptions about consumer capitalism. Retail stores, we are told, are the new factories. We live in a service economy, after all, and customer service representatives are the new proletariat. Since solidarity among factory workers is what made unions strong in the decades following the Second World War, we need now to organize retail workers. This will bring back the union strength that made possible America's postwar prosperity. We need to organize the stores.

This argument, which feels so right, is fatally flawed. Today's Wal-Mart stores are not postwar General Motors' factories.

Retail chains sprawl across the country. When a union tries to organize a store, that particular location can simply close up shop, move somewhere else, and hire new staff. Inventories can be easily moved. New buildings can be easily leased. Workers can be trained in a week. Retail is essentially flexible. Everything and everybody can be replaced. To retailers like Wal-Mart, the cost of unionization would be higher than the cost of reopening a store (which are opening every day somewhere else anyhow).

The success of the factory labour movement in the twentieth century depended on conditions that were the opposite of what we have in retail: workers, inventory, location, and plant were inflexible.

It also must be remembered that the powerful postwar labour movement—which brought us things like pensions and weekends—came about not in the midst of prosperity but in the middle of the Great Depression, exactly when we would think it would be most difficult to organize. Consider what many labour historians regard as the kickoff for the last great labour movement in the twentieth century: the Flint Sitdown Strike of 1936. In the midst of the Depression, workers fought and won against what was then the most powerful, and anti-union, corporation in America, General Motors, after which their union, the United Auto Workers, determined the pattern of union contracts for the entire country.

The Flint Sitdown Strike is remembered for its militant control of a factory and giving birth to the UAW. Nostalgic labour advocates celebrate the solidarity of the workers who occupied an unheated auto body plant in December of a Michigan winter, facing down water hoses, rifles, and tear gas. Yet these labour proponents have remembered the wrong lesson of that strike. The solidarity, while necessary, was not sufficient to win it. Militancy, in and of itself, was not enough. What mattered was *where* the strike occurred.

What is forgotten is that the workers *chose* that particular factory—Fisher Body Plant No. 1—among GM's hundreds of locations, because it made auto bodies that could be made in only one other factory in the whole country, in Cleveland. The dies that stamped metal into car bodies were there in Flint and could not be replaced. Workers realized that in order to cripple production, to bring it to a halt, they did not need to control every GM factory in the U.S., much less all the car dealerships.

Such an organizing feat would have been impossible. When the UAW shut down that one factory—with only a few hundred workers—all of GM stopped. Production collapsed from fifty thousand cars a month to nearly zero. All of its suppliers stopped as well. The largest corporation in America was brought to its knees. Police could not forcibly storm the plant because they could not risk the irreplaceable machines being damaged. GM could not wait six months for the workers to give up, nor could they wait six months to make new dies. Forty-four days later, General Motors recognized the UAW as the sole bargaining agent for its workers, and all autoworkers in America subsequently got raises.

Today labour remembers the solidarity but not the strategy. It pins its hopes on organizing Wal-Mart through a strike because Wal-Mart is powerful like GM was, but it draws the wrong lessons from history. Activists hope that they can organize every Wal-Mart in America. Such a strike would link their consumerist disdain with their romantic half-understood memories of factory strikes. But to organize those tens of thousands of stores one by one, or even all at once, is not possible. We have tried for a generation and failed.

These factories in China, or even the remaining factories in the U.S., are not chokepoints. Equally impossible, for cultural and political reasons, would be organizing the thousands of Chinese factories that supply those stores, but the real reason is today's manufacturing technology. Production technology is programmed, not built. Dies can be replaced with some programming. Fordist manufacturing relied on economies of scale, where huge volumes of the same product produced low unit costs. We live in a post-Fordist era, where profits come from machines that can flexibly produce different products—what economists call economies of scope. The great variety in the factory and the store does not impede profit as it would have during the early twentieth century. All manufacturing and retail capital is replaceable. But the situation is not hopeless. Flint workers in the 1930s also understood these strategic realities. Instead of just solidarity, they looked to weaknesses in the inflexibility of capital.

What would a success on the scale of the Flint Sitdown Strike look like in today's economy with Chinese factories, container ports, and Wal-Mart stores? A successful strategy, just like in 1936, has to focus on the place where capital cannot move, where it is vulnerable to militant occupation, and where that control would disrupt not only that one site but the entire movement of commodities.

Between the factories and the stores—the ports— is the new opportunity for a rejuvenated labour movement.

The Distribution Economy

We are blind to the reality of our economy. Most people today would say that we live in a service economy and that Wal-Mart workers are a part of it, as are doctors and lawyers. But what does it mean to be part of a service economy? To be a "service worker"? I think this term "service" obscures the realities of contemporary capitalism. The "service" economy is a leftover category from an earlier period when the economy was defined as agriculture, manufacturing and everything else. This "everything else" was classified as service. "Service" is just a residual that does not explain anything. Doctors and lawyers have nothing in common (in terms of economic function) with checkout clerks and truck drivers, yet all are "service" workers.

What I think we do live under is a "distribution" economy. Mechanization of field and factory has eliminated the majority of production jobs. Most of our workforce is in moving those commodities around. Service jobs, like lawyers and doctors, are in the service sector, but working people are in distribution. They unload at warehouses. They check you out at the register. Wal-Mart, Target, and all the other big box retailers that take advantage of cheap Chinese manufacturing compete in how they can most cheaply move goods from Asia to North America. The movement of goods information is where innovation is happening today—and it is in distribution networks that capital has become the least flexible. Corporations can easily source products in a new Guangzhou factory or open a new big box store on the other side of town, but between the factory and the store, capital is vulnerable. In a distribution economy, workers need to control the chokepoints in the supply chain that have become the auto body plants of today.

Even in the depths of the Great Recession in 2009, the U.S. imported $523 billion in goods, accounting for 12 percent of global trade. Even at the worst of times, then, the United States imports about a billion-and-a-half dollars' worth of goods every day. If those imports stop, not just American capitalism, but global capitalism grinds to a halt.

The centrality of ports to capitalism today could easily be seen during the heyday of the Occupy movement. During 2011, cities around the country and the world faced sudden tent cities in parks full of protesters. The movement was extraordinarily effective at highlighting the new inequality in American capitalism. For most people, it was from coverage surrounding Zuccotti Park that they first learned the term "1 percent." Yet for all its successes, Occupy, in New York and elsewhere, failed to disrupt the operation of capitalism in any meaningful sense. Financial transactions do not occur in parks. Urban police were perhaps not happy about the tent cities, but actual violence against protesters was less severe than at the IMF protests of the late 1990s or even the annual G-7 conferences— except when the protesters targeted the container ports.

When the occupiers headed for the Port of Oakland, the police brought out the billy clubs. Police defended the port, and the occupiers were pushed back. Actual disruption of the global flow of commodities could not be allowed. Unlike in the Flint strike of 1936, Oakland occupiers were not well-organized. They were not connected with the longshoremen's union. Police were able to attack them because they did not physically occupy the port machinery. Without control of the physical plant, occupation is theatre, not militancy.

Container ports cannot be readily moved or replaced. New ones can't be built. Harbours with the depth to handle container ships generally already have ports. Even if new harbours could be found, the machinery would take billions of dollars of investment capital and years of construction. The skilled workers, moreover, who operate the specialized computers cannot be replaced easily. Without the container ports, the entire supply chain, not only for Wal-Mart but for the economy, grinds to a halt. What is less obvious, perhaps, is that if these ships are stranded without a dock, billions of dollars in cargo will be undeliverable. Undeliverable cargo represents the crucial opportunity for American labour in the twenty-first century. Financial capital can't be stopped, but invested capital—in the form of inventory—can. A small group of committed people can have a disproportionate effect. Workers can have power.

In the next few years, labour will have a rare opportunity to organize against global capital. The Panama Canal, which connects the Atlantic markets with Chinese factories, is currently undergoing an upgrade. For only $5 billion, the canal is being widened so that bigger "Panamax" ships can traverse the isthmus. As wide as a ten-lane highway and as long as the Empire State building, these Panamax ships will be able to hold thirteen thousand standard twenty-foot containers. The largest ships today can only handle five thousand. The economies of scale for larger ships are obvious. Once shipping prices fall, it will be impossible for retailers and manufacturers to go back to the smaller ships.

While the Panama Canal is widened, few east coast U.S. ports have been dredged to handle these much larger ships. Currently, only the ports of Baltimore and Norfolk can handle ships of this size. New York's port is blocked by the Bayonne Bridge. Occupying two ports and shutting down the flows of goods from China to the U.S. would be a disruption of the global supply chain that would make the Flint strike of 1936 pale in comparison. This opportunity will only last for a few years, as east coast ports will eventually dredge their harbours and instal the new unloading machines for these Panamax ships. As it was in 1936, the opportunity to disrupt a supply chain is not on-going, but temporary. However, even in the long run, the centrality of the container port—like the factory before—to this current era of capitalism will be the deciding factor in the strategic success of American labour.

Supply Chain Unionism

The question for the labour movement is how to leverage this port power into benefits, not only for longshoremen but for workers across America. If port unions are already successful in organizing the ports, then why would they want to reach out to the rest of American labour? This same question confronted craft unions when American business began to be dominated by the heavy investments of industrial capitalism. Steel and autos may have used carpenters and bricklayers, but most of the workers were unskilled. Traditional craft unions would not organize them and refused to support industrial unions. As a consequence, industrial capital became ever-stronger and, by the 1910s, began to crush craft unions as well. The AFL limped through the 1920s since they could not control the growing sectors of the economy. Only when labour leaders began to imagine new kinds of industrial unions through the Congress of Industrial Organizations were they able to organize more broadly in the 1930s. The CIO's strength brought post-war prosperity to industrial workers—and strength to the American labour movement, including the AFL. Eventually the AFL and CIO reunited in 1955, bringing unprecedented influence, and money, to American workers.

Today's port unions are in the same position as the craft unions of the 1920s. They could do all right for a while by keeping to themselves, but eventually they will be made illegal or broken in some other way. The only alternative is to embrace a new vision of the labour movement whose organization reflects that of capital—supply chain unionism. The industrial union no longer has strength because industries are not fixed, they are along the supply chain. The out-sourced corporation requires a union that can face it down where it is. Port unions have an opportunity to reach out along that supply chain to build a new kind of labour movement—and save themselves in the process.

Supply chain unionism, to be clear, is illegal. American unions during the postwar era began to think their political power was the source of their power and became ever-more dependent on labour law to enforce their demands. After the Second World War, American unions swapped militancy for legitimacy. In the Taft-Hartley Act of 1947, unions—in addition to agreeing to expel all communists—agreed to give up the secondary strike, in which workers in an unrelated industry strike to support another industry. Longshoremen can't legally strike in support of Wal-Mart workers. In return for these concessions, the Taft-Hartley Act boosted the enforcement powers of the National Labor Relations Board (NLRB) to enforce labour law on corporations.

Today, forty years of Reagan neoliberalism have made the NLRB toothless. More importantly, the sources of potential working-class strength have shifted from manufacturing to distribution, following the shift in the economy. Distribution workers are not inherently less able to organize than manufacturing workers, but the law, as written, makes them weaker. While bottom-up organizing is necessary to control the ports, top-down legal activism is necessary to restore the freedom to strike. In an era when more private sector workers are temps than unionists, the Taft-Hartley compact that swapped union militancy for union security is no more and needs to be struck down.

Even without the legal backing, even if sitdown strikes remain illegal, controlling the ports can still be a source of power for unions. Seizing private property in Flint in 1936 was also illegal, and yet the UAW was successful. Labour law didn't make Flint possible, union power did. Union power made labour law possible, and to think otherwise neglects the reality of power under capitalism.

When the labour movement acknowledges the lessons of the past and the realities of the present, unions will once again be able to empower American workers, even in the midst of an economic downturn like the Great Recession. Effective strategy, in addition to solidarity, is necessary to fight back against capital. When the next wave of occupation comes, I hope that it will be occupation like in 1936, controlling the machines that cannot be replaced and replacing the laws that keep working people down. We can shop for change, but we should not forget, at the same time, that every consumer has a job, and to make sure all those retail jobs are good jobs, we will need to organize.

23

TO SPEAK
IN ONE VOICE

Dynamics of a Cross-Movement
Coalition for Financial Reform

ROBERT N. MAYER
and LARRY KIRSCH

THE HOLY GRAIL for progressives in the United States and elsewhere is building a social movement that overcomes differences in social class, race, ethnicity, and gender to secure broad advances in economic and social justice. During the last few years in the U.S., glimmerings of such a movement have appeared in pursuit of two fundamental progressive goals: health insurance reform and financial reform. In both cases, a broad and pragmatic coalition spanning multiple social movements successfully pressed for landmark legislation. In the case of health care, the cross-movement coalition Health Care for America Now helped enact the Affordable Care Act.[1] With respect to financial reform, Americans for Financial Reform (AFR) brought together consumer, labour, civil rights, and other progressive groups to propel passage of the Dodd-Frank Wall Street Reform and Consumer Protection Act.[2]

From the perspective of consumer protection, the most important element of the Dodd-Frank Act was the creation of a new agency—the Consumer Financial Protection Bureau (CFPB) to set standards and enforce reasonable lending practices for all consumer financial products and all types of consumer financial institutions. This chapter discusses the role of a cross-movement coalition—Americans for Financial Reform (AFR)—in passing the Dodd-Frank Act. The success of the coalition was hardly pre-ordained. Indeed, on learning of AFR's launch in June 2009, left-wing blogger Jane Hamsher penned a blog post titled "Americans for Financial Reform: Waste. Of. Time." Hamsher predicted that AFR would be just "another group that will redouble every mistake made by every such liberal group since the 1970s. They'll put together a bunch of experts [and] issue some 'white papers,' nobody will care."[3]

The mechanisms by which AFR overcame the challenges of mobilizing, managing, and maintaining a diverse coalition and built an alliance with substantial expertise and clout are of particular interest to those seeking to make change. Creating an effective cross-movement coalition began with the recruitment of an experienced, professional leadership team. This team, in turn, established strong internal norms of dedication and subordination to common goals, raised sufficient financial resources for a field operation to support ongoing media and messaging and direct Congressional lobbying, and adopted an ambitious yet pragmatic political approach.

Research on Social Movement Coalitions

Social movement organizations join coalitions when they believe they can more effectively pursue their political and policy objectives by working in concert with other organizations.[4] Most models of social movement coalitions posit that a minimum condition for deciding to join a coalition is the belief that the likely benefits of participation exceed the likely costs.[5] The potential benefits of coalitions within and across social movements are indeed substantial. They include enhanced public legitimacy and visibility, greater political clout, and better access to financial and human resources.[6]

Balanced against the high potential benefits of coalitions are corresponding potential costs. Coalitions require the contribution of human and/or financial resources—resources that a coalition member may find in short supply and needed somewhere else. Membership in a coalition may also entail loss of freedom of action, as when a coalition member finds itself on the losing side of a group decision. Perhaps most important, participation in a coalition may threaten an organization's identity. Social movement organizations typically compete for members, financial support, and policy influence. Therefore, they expend a great deal of effort branding themselves in terms of goals, ideologies, and tactics. Joining a coalition can compromise an organization's unique identity by associating it with an organization it regards as tainted or a policy stand it has rejected in the past.

When multiple organizations agree to enter into a coalition, the management tasks are formidable.[7] Mechanisms of self-governance must reconcile competing values and visions of the coalition's goals and strategies; harmonize alternative orientations and different ways of working on problems and resolving disputes; smooth out any tensions resulting from past interactions among organizations; overcome the "free rider problem" to obtain necessary resources by creating incentives for each coalition member to contribute its fair share for the common good; and find ways of capturing synergies between groups with different skill sets and other characteristics.[8] Disagreements between more radical and reformist partners in a coalition can be particularly difficult to manage.[9]

The challenges of managing a coalition differ between single movement and cross-movement coalitions. Coalitions within a single social movement bring together organizations that have similar goals and constituencies but for that very reason may compete for funding, recognition, and other resources. The members of a cross-movement coalition are less likely to compete directly with one another, and they are less likely to harbour resentments from past interactions, but this type of coalition must often reconcile different views regarding the nature, causes, and remedies for the problems they are jointly seeking to address.[10] The management challenges of cross-movement coalitions are exacerbated when these coalitions knit together groups whose memberships vary widely in terms of social class, race, ethnicity, age, gender, and/or political philosophy.[11]

Some cross-movement coalitions take on a bigger bridging challenge than others. For example, passing food safety legislation in the first part of the twentieth century, promoting a woman's right to choose to end a pregnancy in the 1960s to 1980s, or opposing the U.S. invasion of Iraq in 2003 were all campaigns involving different but cognate social movements.[12] On the other hand, so-called "blue-green" alliances between labour unions and environmental or energy conservation groups involve blending movements with potentially deep divides of goals, ideology, and membership characteristics.[13] The same holds true for "environmental justice" campaigns that typically bring together civil rights activists and environmentalists.[14]

External conditions such as an economic crisis, war, or massive building project typically propel the formation of cross-movement coalitions.[15] Once formed, the major internal challenges for maintaining the coalition include setting a common agenda, securing leadership, building a durable organizational structure, acquiring adequate financial and human resources, developing a "master frame" that motivates and integrates participants, and developing effective patterns of self-governance built on trust and durable participation.[16]

This chapter focuses on the means by which Americans for Financial Reform addressed these organizational tasks in pressuring for passage of the Dodd-Frank Act, with special attention to AFR's efforts to create a new consumer agency to protect borrowers. This chapter incorporates information from more than thirty in-depth interviews conducted with the leaders of the consumer, civil rights, community development, and labour organizations that came together in AFR.[17]

Magic Moment and Coalition Formation

The economic crisis that gripped the United States beginning in the fall of 2008 made it virtually certain that *something* would be done by the Obama administration and the Congress to address the causes of the crisis and reduce the likelihood of a recurrence. But the exact nature of that policy response was very much up for grabs because so many different actors had their individual explanations of who was to blame. The various culprits included mortgage brokers, lenders, and securitizers; credit rating agencies; housing speculators; the Federal Reserve; government-sponsored enterprises Fannie Mae and Freddie Mac; and even consumers themselves. Financial institutions preferred a narrative that attributed the crisis to federal policies that forced them to make unwise loans and to naïve or greedy consumers who took out risky mortgages.[18]

Consumer, civil rights, and fair lending organizations had their own story: the crisis was due to corporate greed and stupidity, the dismemberment of the watchdog agencies that had been tasked to control financial institutions, and an absence of robust consumer protection.[19] A public suffering from agonizing levels of unemployment and home foreclosures was predisposed to concur with the explanation for events offered by progressive organizations, but members of these organizations needed to act fast if they hoped to translate public support into meaningful policy reforms.

With respect to enhanced consumer protection, Harvard law professor Elizabeth Warren had offered a bold proposal in 2007 to create a new federal agency to protect the interests of consumers in financial markets. Warren proposed a Financial Product Safety Commission that would protect consumers from dangerous financial products just as the Consumer Product Safety Commission protects people from hazardous household products such as microwaves and toasters. In addition to being the proposed agency's intellectual architect, Warren would prove to be a savvy political entrepreneur. At the time, though, most people, even consumer activists, considered her proposal to be a long shot. Warren later recalled that "not many organizations were willing to listen. Shoot, there weren't even many academics, the people who are in the business of producing pipedreams, who wanted to listen. It was too ambitious, too far reaching, too impossible."[20]

After the Democratic Party's sweep in the November 2008 election, what had been a long shot was now upgraded to a remotely winnable political dogfight. Leaders of labour and consumer organizations, building on a recent history of working together toward eventual passage of the Credit Card Accountability Responsibility and Disclosure Act of 2009, held informal but pivotal meetings in late 2008 and early 2009 to discuss financial reform. Ahead of the first meeting, Ed Mierzwinski, head of consumer policy for U.S. Public Interest Research Group (the federation of state-level public interest research groups), sent an email to a variety of advocacy groups. Without any real follow-up, representatives of about fifty organizations showed up.

A second, standing-room-only meeting took place shortly thereafter. Elizabeth Warren and John Sweeney, then president of the AFL-CIO, addressed the attendees. It was at this point that the participants realized that a broad coalition was not only possible but indispensable. People sensed that it was time to get out of their respective silos and get to work on building an unprecedented partnership. According to Maureen Thompson, who had prior connections to several organizations in attendance, people recognized that only a broad-based effort would have a chance of besting the powerful financial services industry.[21] A few months later, the result of this recognition would be the formation of Americans for Financial Reform.

It was one thing for advocates to have energy, talent, goodwill among themselves, and the political winds at their back. It was another to mobilize quickly. Within a few months, AFR managed to put in place an official agenda, experienced leadership, a clear decision-making structure, and adequate financial resources.

A special challenge was agreeing on a set of explicit goals, the lack of which often dooms broad coalitions. In this instance, not everyone was immediately convinced that the people in the potential coalition shared the same goals. For instance, the AFL-CIO focused on issues of corporate governance, derivatives, and shareholder rights. The American Federation of State, County and Municipal Employees (AFSCME) was especially interested in fiduciary duties in conjunction with its pension funds. And many of the consumer and civil rights groups had a history of specializing in credit markets and consumer regulation.

Fortunately, several leaders of the early coalition meetings recognized that a common agenda might already exist in the form of the general principles for financial reform articulated in the Special Report on Regulatory Reform of the Congressional Oversight Panel (COP) of January 29, 2009. The COP was five-person panel charged with monitoring implementation of the $700 billion Troubled Asset Relief Program (TARP), which involved the U.S. government attempting to steady a reeling national economy by investing in the stock of financial institutions and purchasing some of their illiquid mortgage-backed securities. Elizabeth Warren served a chair of COP, and Damon Silvers, the AFL-CIO's Policy Director, held the position of deputy chairperson.

In early April, Steve Abrecht of the Service Employees International Union told U.S. PIRG's Ed Mierzwinski and Gary Kalman to "forget about drawing up a mission statement and just take Elizabeth Warren's road map and say this is what we agree on."[22] Abrecht was referring to the eight general recommendations contained in the COP Special Report, recommendations that provided a little something for all of the major constituencies in the budding coalition. The tangible result of adopting the COP's recommendations as a basis for moving forward was a "Call to Action" issued on April 8 and signed by more than a hundred consumer, labour, civil rights, community, and responsible-investing organizations from across the United States. The document called for "bold action" to deal with "a full-blown global economic crisis."[23] Although many challenges of organizational cohesion lay ahead, a potentially divisive fight over the official goals of the new coalition was avoided.

Coalition Leadership and Organizational Structure

Throughout the campaign to pass Dodd-Frank, Elizabeth Warren was inseparable in the public mind from the idea of a new agency. As chair of the COP, Warren also came to embody the broader national impulse to hold financial firms accountable for their role in the economic crisis. Her dexterous use of the media to tell the story of broken financial institutions and their threat to the middle class was crucial to mobilizing and motivating a broad-based constituency.

As important as Warren's leadership was throughout the campaign to pass the Dodd-Frank Act, Heather Booth and Lisa Donner—the executive director and deputy director of AFR, respectively—also mustered crucial support for the passage of the Act, including the new consumer agency. The AFR leaders had a record of social activism stretching back to the 1960s and spanning the civil rights, antiwar, women's, and labour movements. In the early 1970s, Booth founded the Midwest Academy, a training institute for progressive community organizers. In leading the Academy for decades, Booth was known to many of the leaders of the organizations that would comprise AFR and in some cases had trained these leaders personally.

Donner, though somewhat younger than Booth, also had credibility based on years of organizing experience. After graduating from Harvard, she cut her political teeth as an organizer for the Service Employees International Union in its Justice for Janitors campaign. Donner also spent eleven years heading ACORN's Financial Justice Center, tackling issues such as payday lending, tax refund anticipation loans, and subprime mortgage loans. Donner's knowledge of consumer issues complemented Booth's wider experience in social justice movements. In retrospect, few people could have gained trust so readily within AFR and guided its diverse members as skilfully as Booth and Donner. They oversaw AFR's outward strategy, day-to-day tactics and operations, mechanisms of self-governance, and organizational culture.

Even before recruiting Booth and Donner, the founders of AFR arrived at an organizational structure in which decision-making would be made by a small Executive Committee and a slightly larger Steering Committee. Booth held membership on both. The Steering Committee, as AFR's primary decision-making body, had the role of approving the organization's policy positions and letters to the U.S. Congress. If time proved short, the Executive Committee would serve as the rapid response team. The original members of the Executive and Steering Committees were selected to represent the key constituencies within the coalition.

Although AFR's resources paled in comparison to those of its industry foes, the coalition generated a respectable financial base. In addition to a prompt infusion of foundation funding ($200,000 from Arca, $550,000 from Atlantic Philanthropies, and $150,000 from Panta Rhea), member organizations provided in-kind support and in some cases obtained permission from funding sources to repurpose other grants. Organizations represented on the Steering Committee also contributed funds and staff support to the coalition.[24]

The major activities of AFR—legislative policy, field mobilization, and communication—were organized by task forces, the most important of which was the Policy Task Force. This task force was in turn divided into eight mini-task forces. The one most relevant to the proposal to create a Consumer Financial Protection Agency was the Consumer Protection Task Force, with Ed Mierzwinski of the U.S. Public Interest Research Group (U.S. PIRG) as its co-ordinator.

Whereas the task forces were comprised primarily of representatives of Washington, DC-based organizations, AFR also had a plan for communicating with state and local organizations. This effort was headed by Eileen Toback, who joined AFR after stints with the United Steelworkers and the AFL-CIO. Toback held conference calls every Friday to ensure that the troops in states like Massachusetts, Illinois, and Iowa were marching to the beat set by AFR's leaders in Washington, DC. These calls were used to organize lobbying efforts to reach local opinion leaders, such as the members of newspaper editorial boards or clergymen. In a few instances, AFR was able to provide small amounts of money in support of these efforts, but in retrospect, AFR's leaders opined to us that the field component of their campaign might have been far more effective had it been more robustly funded.

Self-Governance

In addition to using task forces to advance the work of AFR, its leaders had to develop effective methods of governance for the coalition. In particular, they faced the challenge of promoting productive social norms among AFR's member organizations.[25] Among these social norms, the most important were trust among coalition partners, support of the common agenda, accountability and reward for work contributed, and disavowal of free-riding. AFR's leaders faced two other related tasks: co-ordinating the needs of the coalition while providing sufficient autonomy for its members; and managing ideological differences, especially those between more radical and more reformist parties in the coalition.

The diversity of the coalition complicated the task of building trust, and there were multiple lines of cleavage that could have fractured AFR. There were differences in broad political objectives as well as familiarity with the intricacies of the U.S. financial system. Some coalition members, such as the Roosevelt Institute and a group of progressive economists organized as SAFER (Stable, Accountable, Fair and Efficient Financial Reform) sought deep, structural change in U.S. financial institutions and had no trouble conversing in the language of derivatives, leverage, proprietary trading, and executive compensation. Others, such as the Consumer Federation of America and the National Consumer Law Center, focused on reforms with more everyday consumer relevance (e.g., transacting a mortgage, borrowing for a car, getting a credit card). Willingness to work with the Obama administration and leading Democrats was another tricky divide to span. Some AFR members viewed cultivating these insider relations as essential to achieving reform, but others preferred the outsider's role and the freedom to be publicly critical of the government.

Many members of AFR had only a limited history of working together, and in some cases, there was palpable distrust. Recalling her first meeting with AFR's organizers, Heather Booth explained, "When I came into this, there was electricity in the room [but also] very thick tension. Many of the people did not know each other, did not trust each other." She heard comments like, "Why do we need these think-tank people in the room? What do they contribute? Won't they just slow us down?" Other people asked why the AFR needed "some specific grassroots organizations in there."[26]

One means of building trust was operating transparently on matters such as budgets and contacts with legislators and staff. Each meeting was preceded with a detailed agenda and followed by a set of minutes that did much to pre-empt misunderstandings and suspicions. With transparency and broad representation on AFR's executive bodies, members could not plausibly claim that they were surprised by or left out of AFR's decisions.

There were clear differences of priorities across movements (and sometimes within movements). To take the CFPB as an example, creating a new agency ranked at the top of the financial reform agenda for groups like Consumers Union, U.S. PIRG, the Consumer Federation of America, and AARP. It was placed further down the agenda by most labour unions and civil rights organizations. Given these varying priorities, the AFR coalition had to explicitly address the concern that the priorities and work contributed by any single group might be sacrificed in the final legislative bargaining process. The solution AFR employed was to assure its members that the coalition would not trade off one organization's major priority in favour of another's.

The assurance to honour the goals of each major faction within AFR was tested early in the campaign. President Obama's White Paper on Financial Reform had proposed strengthening enforcement of the Community

Reinvestment Act (the 1977 law that creates strong incentives for banks to meet the consumer credit needs of low- and moderate-income communities in which they operate) by moving it into the new consumer agency. This proposal was of paramount importance to civil rights and community development groups. Not surprisingly, banks and other financial institutions reacted negatively to this idea. Aware of their resistance, House Financial Services Committee Chairman Barney Frank viewed retaining the CRA portion of the President's plan as seriously endangering the prospects for a new consumer agency, and he decided to drop the idea from the bill he introduced in July 2009. At this point, the civil rights and community development groups could have abandoned the coalition. They certainly thought about it.

Nancy Zirkin, executive vice president for policy for the Leadership Conference on Civil and Human Rights, told us she was extremely frustrated by the exclusion of the CRA from Frank's bill because attacks on the CRA as the cause of the mortgage crisis were "the dumbest thing [she] had ever heard." As she explained, the exclusion of the CRA "was a big loss for our organization, but we still needed the housing piece, and we still needed the whole consumer bureau."[27] After some hesitation, the civil rights and fair lending organizations not only stuck with their fellow coalition members but devoted considerable resources to creating the CFPB and enacting financial reform legislation.

In building a work ethic for the coalition, Booth and Donner led by example, but they weren't bashful about asking others to pitch in. David Arkush of Public Citizen remembers Heather Booth lining him up for a job the very first time they met. Arkush was in the lobby of the AFL-CIO headquarters in Washington, DC when Booth walked up to him and said, "Oh, I'm Heather Booth" and told him that she might be playing a role in a coalition. She said to Arkush, "I heard you get work done. Could I get you to chair a task force, possibly on policy?"[28] Booth placed Arkush at the head of the influential Policy Task Force, and Arkush lived up to the responsibility. His position of leadership had an additional benefit. Among consumer groups, Public Citizen had a reputation for not being willing to compromise or give up any of its independence of action. By having Arkush serve as the task force's chair, Booth virtually assured that Public Citizen would be an integrator rather than an insurgent.

The work expectations for AFR members went beyond leveraging their established relationships with congressional members and staffers. AFR adopted a lobbying process in which a lead organization, say, one interested in executive compensation, always made lobbying calls accompanied by members of other partner organizations. This made it possible for the lead organization to project more interest and support for its agenda items to the congressional target. At the same time, this method educated the other groups who could then disperse to raise the same issue with other congressional contacts.

Beyond building a results-oriented culture within the coalition, AFR leaders had to balance two potentially competing processes: achieving a high level of co-ordination among organizations while also permitting sufficient autonomy for each one. Having a certain degree of autonomy was especially important for AFR's larger member organizations, several of which were worried that they might be expected to agree with every position taken by AFR and have to pre-clear every action with AFR's governing bodies.

Donner and Booth enforced no such requirement. Member organizations were free to act on their own, although there was an implicit understanding that they would not act against the common interest. This arrangement, according to Janis Bowdler of the National Council of La Raza, worked well:

> We considered everything that we were doing to be aligned with AFR and we would try to time things as best that we could. . . . So for example, if there was a big call-in day in a certain state, we would be sure to let our members know. . . . But in another way, we branded our own campaign out to the field, and often would link back to AFR materials either directly or through cross posting. And so we did our own national calls, really making the case of why, from a civil rights and within our community's perspective, we had to be pushing for XYZ, this particular limit and provision, or these market provisions. And we saw that as feeding into the broader AFR efforts.[29]

The freedom of AFR's member organizations to pursue independent actions functioned largely as a means of reassurance for its members because, in practice, these actions reinforced rather than undermined AFR's priorities.

Framing

With experienced leadership, reasonable funding, and emergent norms of co-operation in place, AFR confronted the additional task of "framing" the public debate—the process by which social movements promote their definition of the problem they are addressing to the general public, policy makers, and the mass media as well their own members.[30] Elizabeth War-ren developed a frame for the debate over the Dodd-Frank Act and the CFPB, and the AFR coalition found her framing to be useful for their purposes.

Warren's earlier research on the causes of consumer bankruptcy had portrayed middle-class households living on the financial precipice. A dis-location caused by a job loss, illness, or divorce could easily tip them into financial insolvency.[31] Contrasting the interests of "Main Street" (code for the middle class) with those of Wall Street, Warren hammered on the theme of middle-class suffering before and throughout the campaign to pass Dodd-Frank.

And why were middle-class consumers suffering? Borrowers were vic-timized by countless "tricks and traps." Warren repeatedly compared the extensive safety regulation that pertained to the lowly household toaster to the lack of social control of mortgage products. Her influential 2007 article in *Democracy* argued: "It is impossible to buy a toaster that has a one-in-five chance of bursting into flames and burning down your house. But it is possible to refinance an existing home with a mortgage that has the same one-in-five chance of putting the family out on the street."[32] Throughout the Dodd-Frank campaign, Warren repeated the toaster analogy, and members of AFR and President Obama employed it as well.[33]

The final element in Warren's framing of the crisis facing Main Street was that existing regulators with the responsibility to protect consumers from abuse had been asleep at the switch, or worse, they were knowingly collusive with the financial services industry. The only viable remedy, in Warren's view, would be the creation of a new agency with a tough-minded devotion to consumers and strong weapons at its disposal. Again, Warren used a simple image to frame her message; the new agency would be the consumer's "cop on the beat."

Polling conducted for AFR confirmed that the framing constructed by Elizabeth Warren would be a sturdy basis for their efforts. They found her imagery to be useful for both communicating internally to mem-bers and externally to the press and policy makers. Advocates of financial reform wanted to be perceived as representing middle-class Americans— not the bankers receiving bailouts and bonuses. Because this "defending the little guy" framing was so potentially powerful, opponents of financial reform tried to use it as well. Political consultant Frank Luntz advised his business clients to describe financial reform efforts as creating a "permanent bailout fund" for big private companies.[34] Similarly, in an advertising campaign, other lobbying material, and congressional testimony, the U.S. Chamber of Commerce attacked the idea of a new consumer agency on the grounds that it would be a nightmare for small businesses.[35]

While framing a new agency in terms of its benefits to the middle class had the great advantage of acting as a "big tent" for a cross-section of Americans, it did carry some potential liabilities for AFR. The civil rights groups, in particular, needed some convincing that all this talk about middle-class suffering would not obscure the fact that there was still a two-tiered market for financial services, with poorer people and people of colour facing higher prices and more predatory practices. Lisa Rice of the National Fair Housing Alliance confided to us that the civil rights groups felt they already had a coalition and might not need AFR. Janis Bowdler of the National Council of La Raza had similar concerns. Elizabeth Warren and the leaders of AFR assured her and others, however, that the middle-class frame was simply a point of entrée to discuss the consumer problems facing all consumers, both middle-class *and* lower-income. Warren's track record on issues of racial discrimination also helped win support from La Raza and other groups.[36]

Ambitious Pragmatism

A further crucial task for AFR was managing ideological differences within the coalition. More radical members of the alliance wanted nothing less than the nationalization of the nation's largest banks and the imprisonment of their CEOs. (To this day, Elizabeth Warren still expresses outrage that not a single Wall Street banker has been put behind bars for their role in the financial debacle.[37]) Others, probably the majority of AFR's members, were more reformist. Reconciled to the incremental nature of political change in the U.S., they were going to be satisfied with more modest gains. The fear within AFR's leadership was that at some crucial moment, the radicals might decide that a compromised bill was not worth having, thereby threatening the coalition's clout and credibility.

AFR's overall strategy for reconciling differing political philosophies was adopting a form of ambitious pragmatism. The coalition was ambitious inasmuch as it communicated externally and internally that it sought the strongest possible reforms. Deputy Director Lisa Donner described her underlying "theory" of the campaign this way: "Our view of how to pass this bill was always that having the strongest possible bill was the best way to get votes for it. . . . You do better for yourself in the end by, rather than compromising a lot, making the bill good so that people will fight for it."[38]

Still, AFR was steadfastly pragmatic, especially with respect to creating the CFPB. This pragmatic approach put AFR in tune with Barney Frank who, during a commencement address at American University a month before AFR came into existence, told those assembled: "Idealism without pragmatism is just a way to flatter your ego."[39]

The pragmatists who led AFR did not—and could not, even if they had wanted to—work to prevent incautious statements by some of their colleagues. At no time was this better illustrated than in March 2010, when Senator Chris Dodd was trying to move forward a financial reform bill with bipartisan support out of the Senate Banking Committee. Negotiations with Republican Senator Richard Shelby went nowhere, and a potentially more promising excursion with Senator Bob Corker ended at the same destination. Dodd chose to incorporate some Republican ideas into his legislative proposal, including placing the CFPB within the Federal Reserve instead of making it fully independent. John Taylor, president of the National Community Reinvestment Center, was not impressed by where things were heading. He said:

> If the intention was a compromise on the independence of the agency, then why do it twice over? Putting the agency at the Federal Reserve and giving the Systemic Risk Council veto power ensures that this agency will be totally hamstrung by the very agencies that failed to prevent this crisis in the first place.[40]

Barney Frank greeted the idea of putting the new consumer agency within the Federal Reserve by calling it "a bad joke."[41] Previously, Elizabeth Warren had also warned against a weak bill, asserting that if the Senate committee could not produce a strong consumer agency, her second choice was "no agency at all and plenty of blood and teeth left on the floor."[42]

AFR's leaders realized that having some strident voices within the pro-reform movement could be quite functional so long as they did not alienate legislators. In fact, the expression of extreme views by some members of the pro-reform coalition made it easier for moderate Democrats to vote for Dodd's bill. An interviewee close to the action observed:

> There wasn't a moderate Democrat on the Committee who wanted to have a vote on it. They don't like tough votes there. . . . [But

because of the stinging criticism of Dodd's compromises] centrist Democratic senators from Republican-leaning states . . . could report to their constituents that they had reached across the aisle and supported a more modest version of the new consumer protection agency. In a sense, the louder advocates complained about Dodd's compromises, the safer they made it for any wavering Democrats to vote for the bill.[43]

Meanwhile, within AFR, its more pragmatic leaders urged colleagues to focus on the specifics of Dodd's proposal rather than the symbolism. One of these leaders, Mike Calhoun of the Center for Responsible Lending, told us that he and Travis Plunkett took the lead in trying to convince other organizations that putting the CFPB in the Fed would be okay. Officially, AFR would continue to call for a stand-alone agency for purposes of rallying support at the grassroots level, where anything less than a fully independent agency would be a hard sell. Calhoun said:

> Much more so than within the Beltway, it's a more complicated field organizing cry to say, "Let's fight for an agency embedded within the Federal Reserve." I think it actually helped at the end of the day to have this workable compromise because conversely the rallying cry for the Chamber of Commerce and other industry groups had been no independent agency. And so having it embedded in the Fed complicated messaging for both sides. It was much harder for [the CFPB's opponents] to say the bureau embedded in the Fed is going to be this rogue agency.[44]

Publicly criticizing the idea of locating the CFPB within the Fed while privately building support for the idea turned out to be a brilliant political strategy by AFR.

Conclusion

AFR effectively navigated the shoals that so often strand collective action. In the abstract, multi-movement coalitions are an appealing idea for bringing about important societal reforms. In practice, there are many centrifugal forces that work to pull apart such coalitions. These obstacles include (but are by no means limited to): differing goals and political philosophies among coalition partners; a lack of "social capital" among partners, perhaps arising from past competition for resources and influence; and difficulty in extracting contributions of labour and money from coalition members. However, AFR's initial organizers recruited seasoned, professional leaders who brought out the best in the coalition's partners. These leaders helped AFR build a durable organizational structure, develop effective patterns of self-governance, construct a strategy for framing the campaign's issues, and fashion an overall political approach characterized by ambitious pragmatism.

Despite effective coalition management and a political environment marked by a supportive president, a Democrat-controlled Congress, and an angry citizenry, it is worth remembering that the Dodd-Frank Act passed by a single vote in the U.S. Senate. Moreover, the challenges of achieving significant, long-lasting financial reform only begin with the passage of legislation. They continue during the regulatory process, where advances are always threatened by intense business lobbying, the corrupting influences of the "revolving door" by which government personnel are recruited from and/or later hired by the industries whose conduct the agency is supposed to control, and a public that participates in the regulatory process even less avidly than it does in the legislative process. Cross-movement coalitions for progressive change must be durable and effective in all public forums—not only the legislative process—if they are to be fully effective.

24

ON DEMAND

TRACEY DEUTSCH

ɪꜰ ᴄʜᴏɪᴄᴇ is the idea that animates neoliberalism, demand is its silent accomplice. Demand is how individual choice matters to grander calculations and systems. It is the reason, according to many businesses, that firms change what or how they sell. Changes in consumer "demand" can explain everything from McDonald's switch to "humanely raised" chicken to the stores that sell "fast-fashion," produced with little regard to humane standards at all. Demand, in short, is frequently taken as the most important justification for what businesses do.

The rhetoric of demand has particular importance for this volume. Changing consumer demand, e.g., via boycotts and protests, is commonly taken as a potent way of forcing businesses to change. Both lack of demand (e.g., through a boycott) and increased "demand" (e.g., for fair trade goods) are put forth as mechanisms for change. Alternatively, in this way of thinking demand can emerge as a barrier to change—people "want" large big box stores or low prices, and stores must deliver regardless of social cost. This collection of essays on the history and possibilities of consumer activism encourages us to think differently—to question assumptions about consumption itself. One of those assumptions is that consumption is by nature a relatively (perhaps disturbingly) smooth process in which buyers get the products they want. We can ask why we think of consumption as a system in which consumers have power, and what it is they might really be wanting.

This essay questions how contemporary economics theorizes consumption. Rather than seeing protest, disruption, or difficulty as an exception to a world of streamlined shopping, we might see charged, politicized, constrained purchasing as the norm—the position from which all shoppers work but which contemporary economics has obscured.

As many of the contributors to *Shopping for Change* make clear, people have not always gotten what they wanted from stores, not even when they made purchases. Using the ideas of earlier economists, we can extend this point: consumer society cannot be explained by looking at what consumers buy. Consumer society is structured by power, by institutions, and by complex social dynamics—not just by purchases. This essay is part of the broader effort of this volume to ask how consumers have acted politically and how we might rethink consumption as a result.

In particular, it analyzes the language of "demand" historically, tracing how the term achieved new meanings in post–Second World War economic thought and policy, especially in the U.S. and to a slightly lesser extent in Europe. Economic thinking encompassed relatively complicated and politically charged ways of thinking about consumption before the war; these became obscured in the middle decades of the twentieth century by the now orthodox way of thinking about demand. The main actors in the analysis are economists, rather than the activists so well documented by other authors in this volume. And the kind of consumption studied is the everyday work of shopping which economists so powerfully framed in their writing, rather than the moments of protest that are the focus of other essays.[1] Seemingly esoteric changes in the field of economics dramatically narrowed both popular and academic visions of consumption on the right *and* the left. Consumption became both more important in economic theory—and also framed by a single, predictable, controllable factor: consumer demand.

"Demand," with its connotations of focused insistence on a few discernable objects, has become crucial to modern economic thought. Consumers and consumption are legible in economic thought as purchasers with clear needs and with unrelenting desires to meet those needs. In the process of meeting those needs, they force change onto producers and, indeed, power entire economies. When supply meets their demand, we have "equilibrium"—a functioning economy. The idea of consumer "demand" also implies that broader social concerns, issues, and priorities are of secondary concern to businesses, which must "supply" what is being demanded. Firms must respond to demand or go out of business. Consumers are people who, for good or for ill, get what they want.

This is a change, however. Many U.S. economists earlier in the century, while they occasionally used the term "demand," asserted that consumers did *not* always get what they wanted and saw consumption's significance in terms of individual or household well-being rather than aggregate spending power. Consumers were people with broad and complicated concerns, issues, and priorities. Purchases were guided by constraint as much as desire. This was as true of businesses as shoppers, since entrepreneurs were also shaped by "institutional" policies, restrictions, etc. What shoppers bought indicated what they could get, not what they wanted.

Through the mid-twentieth century, economists and many retailers continued to discuss openly the politics of purchase. But gradually these came to seem irrelevant to economists and economies more broadly. By equating what people buy with what they want, the notion of "demand" gave consumers seeming importance in modern society, but little power as citizens or members of groups. (Indeed, in this formulation they have little need for power, since they exert authority via individual purchases.) This has led to misguided views of consumption among both conservative and progressive groups that focus on changing people's "demand" rather than the structures that shape that demand.

Whereas we often consider modern economic thought as abstracting labour and value, consumption, too, has often been abstracted, with systems of coercion that force (or prevent) certain kinds of consumption made less visible. In this way of thinking, boycotts, protests, regulations, and even consumer complaints are disruptions to consumption—not predictable aspects of the work of shopping. In order to really effect change, consumption and retail spaces need to be seen as sites of everyday struggle—places full of politics, resistance, and possibility. "Shopping for change" reveals a grainy, textured, bumpy economy, a vision that is flattened by many contemporary uses of "demand."

This requires some intellectual history. Unlike today's (nearly) uniform adherence to neoclassical economics, the first decades of the twentieth century were a time when respected economists could employ many different models of economic behaviour. It was in particular the highpoint of "institutionalist economics." The name refers to the shared understanding that exchange was embedded in institutions. Members of this very loose school emphasized the wide variety of factors that shaped people's abilities to buy and sell goods. Institutionalists were not the first economists to centre consumption in economic studies, but they were among consumption's most important students. Most institutionalists "emphasized the social nature of the formation of consumption habits and . . . socially defined 'standards of living.'"[2] In doing so, they drew on the work of Thorstein Veblen and C. Wesley Mitchell, early economic thinkers who forwarded influential theories about consumption and consumer spending. Veblen's "theory of the leisure class," for instance, emphasized comparison and social status as spurring purchases and consumption. He wrote, "The motive that lies at the root of ownership is emulation."[3] That is, what people purchased and how they did so depended on socially constructed identities (which social group they aspired to)—not on inherent needs or rational calculations. Mitchell, in his work on spending, emphasized constraints on consumers. As he wrote in "The Backwards Art of Spending Money," "Our faults as spenders are not wholly due to wantonness, but largely to broad conditions over which as individuals we have slight control."[4] Mitchell went on to acknowledge the gender dynamics of household labour, limited income, and false advertising as some of these constraints.

For these authors, consumption was fascinating precisely because it was both different from other kinds of economic activity (like wage labour) and yet clearly so central to them. They saw economies as the conglomeration of the work of families, communities, business firms, and government laws. Mitchell and other institutionalists largely shared the underlying beliefs that how people obtained goods was inherently social and political in nature and that consumption constituted a proper subject of economic inquiry. Unfettered exchange was hardly imaginable in this model. Economies, business firms, shopping—all worked precisely *because* of institutional policies and structures.

Located at schools such as the University of Wisconsin, Columbia, Harvard, and the University of Chicago, institutionalist economists had a presence throughout academia, in professional associations, state and federal government agencies, and as popular commentators on contemporary problems of poverty and business failure. These were public intellectuals in every sense of the term: John Commons, for instance, was intimately involved in drafting workers' compensation legislation and other Progressive Era policy for the state of Wisconsin but was also quoted on the need for dietary reform. Richard Ely, a well-known labour economist and contributor to much progressive policy in Wisconsin, also spoke publicly on everything from real estate assessments to proper regulation of telegraphy.[5]

Many prominent members of this school emphasized regulation and law as crucial factors in economies. Gardiner Means' studies of, and later his oversight over, "administered prices" is one example of this.[6] But others examined firm structure, the internal systems through which wages were determined, trade associations and efforts to coordinate production, the dynamics of business cycles, the cost of living for Americans of different classes, and the dynamics of family spending.[7] The capacious set of interests made, and makes, institutionalists difficult to pigeonhole. However, it also documents the many topics that this group of economists felt properly fell under their purview as they sought to understand economies.

One example conveys institutionalists' expansive vision of what was involved in consumption. Hazel Kyrk's prizewinning dissertation and later book, *A Theory of Consumption*, was particularly concerned with developing fuller and more sophisticated understandings of individual buying. Her analysis included ways in which consumers might be defrauded but went beyond this to acknowledge how firms' profit-motive inevitably made this uneven territory: "The consuming process takes place by means of a productive organization which limits and conditions it in manifold ways." Kyrk felt that addressing the problem of well-being required fuller understandings of consumption itself. Consequently, the book included sections on everything from the intellectual history of the notion of freedom of choice, to discussions of income inequality, industrial processes, legal and financial constraints on consumer goods, efforts to test and grade consumer goods, and social dynamics and cultural identities, concluding with a call for attention to "standards of living" as a force in people's expectations and purchasing. She wrote, "The study of consumption is [a study] of almost all the desire and purposes which move men to action."[8]

As Kyrk's work suggests, questions posed by institutional economists often reflected their intellectual interest in a higher "standard of living." The "standard of living" was a favourite phrase of the time and particularly important to these academics.[9] Historically speaking, it reveals their interests in how and why people bought what they did, and often in establishing what goods and services people needed in order to live. Many, although certainly not all, shared a sense that better living conditions and more economic equality were marks of healthy economies.[10] Paul Douglas, for instance, urged the provision of the "subsistence-plus" standard of living which, he argued, "would permit families to enjoy a few of the decencies of life without making inroads upon their health."[11]

Interest in subsistence could for some also inform political commitments. Paul Douglas later became an important U.S. Senator who fought for civil rights. But we should not romanticize their work. The very notion of a standard of living leaves room for enormous inequality, and the assumption that some groups of people would naturally require a lower standard of living than others. Indeed, John Commons went out of his way to articulate his nativist and racist hierarchy of Americans in his 1907 book, *Race and Immigrants in America*, asserting that African Americans and many immigrants would never be fully integrated into the American society.[12] It would be a mistake to think that all institutionalist economists were immune to the racist thinking of their political moment.

Rather than politics, these economists were united by their interest in the ways that institutions of all kinds—businesses, families, etc.—shape what and how people buy. Institutionalists were particularly likely to see the significance of governments in shaping consumption and well-being more generally. Adolph Berle, working for the government on the eve of the Second World War, took as a matter of course that democratic governments would be expected to provide a minimal standard of living for their citizens and that this would include "social security provision for the nonproductive periods of life, including childhood, maternity, sickness, and old age."[13] Thinking like this had also informed John Maynard Keynes' *General Theory of Employment, Interest, and Money*, one of the most prominent economics texts of the interwar period. Keynes insisted that although the scope of his analysis differed from many institutionalists', he shared the belief that consumption was central to economic health. They also shared the belief that promoting widespread consumer purchases required action (in Keynes' case, deficit spending) by central governments.

Many of these economists were also distinguished by their method. Keynes and interwar institutionalists studied businesses, industries, families, workers, and consumers in concrete, highly specific, terms.[14] It was this openness to the nuance and detail of lived experience more than their political program of improving the standard of living and their focus on consumption, which distinguished them from later neoliberal and neoclassical work. We can apply Malcolm Rutherford's description of New Deal economist Walter Hamilton more broadly, and safely say that the goal for most institutionalists was "to get behind the abstractions of demand and supply, and to come to understand why a price is what it is."[15] Rather than generalities or aggregate effects, institutionalists emphasized variation and specificity.[16] Their studies were not necessarily ethnographic (although sometimes they did involve interviews) but they were often detailed and emphasized the particularities of the local. This method was linked to their shared belief that what people bought did not necessarily reflect their needs nor even desires, but rather could be mediated by a host of factors. It was not consumers' power, but the inherent complexity of exchange, that struck economists.

These economists' analyses of consumption reflected widespread beliefs that everyday shopping was a vexed task. Consumers' struggles to get what was needed, to make a budget stretch, to choose from among many alternatives, were palpable, and visible (no doubt witnessed by many economists themselves) in stores and spaces of consumption. Economists, business owners and observers all acknowledged individual consumers' desire for personal attention and the unruliness—the ungovernability—of spaces of consumption.

Institutionalists took particular note of the gendered division of labour in homes and the social systems that gave so much of the work of provisioning to women. Hazel Kyrk, Wesley Mitchell, and many others made clear that what looked like overspending or unwise purchases by housewives did not reflect inherent stupidity on women's part, but rather their limited knowledge, limited time, and most importantly their desires for social and cultural belonging, alongside material well-being. As C. Wesley Mitchell said, "For her gains are not reducible to dollars, as are the profits of a business enterprise, but consist in the bodily and mental well-being of her family."[17] They understood that women provisioners bore multiple responsibilities and consequently were unpredictable or even difficult shoppers.

This understanding of women as both difficult and demanding shoppers was reinforced in how stores operated and also in much popular discourse around shopping. As numerous scholars have documented, consumer purchases for most of U.S. history required personal negotiation and give-and-take. This made retail a somewhat disorderly space in which the multiple pressures acting on consumers were obvious. Even the most refined of stores—e.g., department stores—expected that customers would require personalized attention.[18] By the 1930s, many consumers, women in particular, joined movements to influence businesses, for example around fair hiring and honest labeling. All of this is to say that institutional economists' views of consumption reflected widely held understandings of women's experiences as consumers.

Institutionalists continued to exert influence over government policy during the Second World War—for instance in government efforts to set prices for retail goods. However, in the postwar years the field of economics, theories of consumption, and both the discourse and nature of shopping that economists would have seen around them, changed dramatically. Quantitative methodology and a neoclassical framework, both of which had existed before the war, assumed new prominence and new resonance. Economists emphasized demand as an abstract, predictable, action of self-interested rational actors. Their work often is categorized as "neoclassical" for their attachment to older notions of self-interest as the key to modern economies.

These economists shared with institutionalists a belief in the significance of consumption; indeed, the centrality of consumer spending to economic health became an article of faith among economists in the years surrounding the war. But the interest in structural constraints and institutional context in which spending occurred quickly became muted. By the 1970s and 1980s, the political impulse toward state or institutional intervention, particularly intervention that aimed to decrease economic or social inequality, virtually disappeared.[19]

The shift happened for a variety of reasons. Like many academics/professionals, economists had long sought political salience and influence. In the years during and after the Second World War, they achieved this. But they did so through an embrace of quantitative methodology hinging on mathematical representation of qualitative action. A new generation of economists, led by Paul Samuelson and Gunnar Myrdahl, encouraged econometric analysis and, more importantly, econometric models that promised policymakers new help in economic planning.[20] Models offered predictions and quantitative certainty and therefore appealed to policymakers facing difficult social problems and enormous pressures to solve them.

Other historians have argued that the impulse toward abstraction happened for more intellectual reasons. Classical economics, Ivan Moscati, has argued, had long been committed to "a systematic theory of consumer demand." Simply put, the focus of neoclassical economists on abstract theory was in place from the beginning of the field; practitioners simply became better at articulating a general theory. Newer economists directed their ire toward institutional economists and the interest in "unobservable" phenomena such as psychology or cultural identity.

This shift toward quantification involved a focus on variables that, for these academics, revealed overarching truths rather than the distractions of real-world detail. Milton Friedman wrote in a review of Thomas Wilson's *Inflation* that "the analysis is verbal, neither mathematics nor graphs playing any appreciable role" and that the book had no clear central thesis and was "reportorial, nonrigorous, largely undocumented."[21] Similarly, Paul Samuelson worked beginning in the 1930s, but with more success over time, to measure "utility," and also to equate utility with the value and meaning of goods in people's lives.[22] Indeed, Samuelson opened the first edition of what would become his famous textbook, *The Foundations of Economic Analysis*, by announcing that he would borrow "the principle of generalization by abstraction" stated by the mathematician E. H. Moore and work out its implications for economics.[23]

This field-wide transition in method transformed the ways in which consumption was understood. Mark Blaug asserts that, beginning in the 1950s, a "formalist revolution" reified economic activity into mathematical equations in which price was the only response firms might make and purchasing the only positive action individuals might take. In other words, the moment of purchase was a lens onto all relevant behaviour of economic actors. Other responses—changes in location or refusals to serve or purchasing less of a good without substituting it with something else —were simply written out of most studies of economics (although they were retained in business studies).[24] Friedman and Samuelson were important leaders of a field-wide shift to quantitative modelling and methodology, but more importantly to an emphasis on utility as the only meaningful and relevant way of understanding consumption. In so doing, economists emphasized price and other "observable" variables over "unobservables" such as beliefs.

These intellectual trends reflected and were sustained by a new politics of economics departments and journals. Anticommunist surveillance of "heterodox" economists, narrower criteria for tenure and for publication in leading journals, and shifting interests of foundations and funders all contributed to the shift to a quantitative methodology and neoclassical model.[25] McCarthyist investigators focused particularly on economists who argued for government intervention or promoted "Marxist" notions (such as the labour theory of value). In other words, there were structural (one might say institutional) as well as intellectual reasons for the narrowing of economics; indeed the two entwined in ways nearly impossible to untangle.[26]

The neoclassical model that remained both celebrated and assumed that people, firms, and institutions would further their own self-interest and that this would ultimately benefit everyone. Consumer purchases would "correct" for over- or under-production of desirable goods by suppliers. In this model, purchase was a crucial node—indeed in many models the only relevant node—between economic actors. And all important actors were economic actors.

Between 1946 and the mid-1960s, a stripped down model of markets powered by consumer "choice" was forwarded as a worthy political goal in and of itself. Friedrich Hayek, Milton Friedman, and others created the famous "Chicago School of Economics" to argue for the benefits of "free markets" as the best response to problems of poverty, inequality, and other concerns. Friedman and others promoted a vision of economies free of institutionalist and Keynesian visions of state and large-scale intervention. Rather than nuanced understanding of local contexts or consumers' (and citizens') constraints and desires, collective identities and collective struggles, Friedman and others increasingly forwarded the notion that individual purchases were the truest measure of what people wanted and best mechanism for achieving what economists came to call equilibrium—a balance of supply and "demand."[27]

Econometric models that emphasized rational action (defined as the pursuit of self-interest) and individual choice (as the mechanism through which self-interest was pursued) were now routinely applied beyond conventional economics. Gary Becker, Friedman's colleague at the University of Chicago, epitomized this trend in his 1976 book, *The Economic Approach to Human Behavior*.[28] In a chapter on fertility, for instance, he posited "Abstracting from the kind of satisfaction provided by children makes it possible to relate the 'demand' for children to a well-developed body of economic theory." Becker went on to create equations that predicted the effects of income on fertility and the "quality" of children produced.[29] In 1992, Becker's reduction of human behaviour to the pursuit of self-interest and "utility" was rewarded with the Nobel Prize in Economics "for having extended the domain of microeconomic analysis to a wide range of human behaviour and interaction, including nonmarket behavior."[30]

Becker's professional success marked the transformation of economics from what had been a pluralist discipline, in which varying theoretical models could be legitimately deployed, into a decidedly more uniform field in which non-neoclassical economists were increasingly dismissed (sometimes literally) from academic institutions and public intellectual life.[31] The sort of careful theorizing of consumption and consumer spending done by economists like Hazel Kyrk decades earlier were, if they were done at all, now under the auspices of "home economics" or "family studies."[32] In labour economics, studies of firm structure largely disappeared from predictions of wages and profits. "Heterodox" scholars who insisted on studying the contexts in which consumers bought goods and theorizing a marketplace that functioned via institutional policies found homes in other disciplines or left academia entirely. The broad sweep of issues previously understood as "economic" now seemed beside the point. There was an important gender component here: economics remained a bastion of men's work even as women won new ground in social science and other disciplines.[33]

For most working economists, these scholars' concerns with cultural beliefs, or family dynamics, or household need or institutional structure could be encompassed by simple reference to notions of utility, and by assurances that any action could be usefully understood as maximizing utility (and that problems in families, or in businesses, or in society, would disappear if individuals were allowed to pursue their self-interest in maximizing utility). Questions of structural constraint and the social meanings of goods, and of the significance of the context in which goods were purchased or distributed within homes, were secondary to questions of purchase, and therefore outside of mainstream economics.

Importantly, economists continued to emphasize the importance of consumer goods and consumer purchasing. Indeed, in some ways, interest in consumption intensified. Household spending was an important theme in the work of Friedman, Becker, and others. Federal and state governments dramatically expanded the scale and scope of consumption-related data they collected, shifting at the same time from a focus on the cost of living for working-class and immigrant families to large-scale snapshots of how much all Americans were spending, on all kinds of goods, as an indicator of national well-being.[34]

In emphasizing "rational" self-maximizing behaviour, the complexities of consumption and the factors that intervened between individuals and individuals getting what they needed or wanted—in other words the limitations of a market—were lost. Because of the political reach of this postwar orthodoxy, this limited understanding of contextualized economic life had real social costs. These included devastating effects on social safety nets, collective action, and public services, as many scholars have demonstrated.[35]

But it also had some intellectual costs. Importantly, perniciously, and largely unnoticed by most social scientists, what people bought came to be, by definition, equated with what they wanted.[36] Business responses to changes in buying patterns, then, were equated with meeting people's actual needs and desires, rather than simply responding to purchases. Alternative analyses of consumption as reflecting structural inequalities were silenced by McCarthyist attacks on activists, particularly those articulating holistic or feminist analyses.[37] Importantly, the resulting limited discourse of consumption was repeated as much by critics of consumption as its supporters. [38] For better or worse, received wisdom was that consumers were guileless, materialistic, satisfied shoppers.

And here we can return to the language of "demand." The term was barely used by the first generation of institutional economists (it appears six times in Veblen's 1899 *Theory of the Leisure Class*) but grew more common over time. (Milton Friedman's *A Monetary History of the United States*, published in 1971, featured it 138 times). The significance of demand as an abstract and immutable force is even more striking than these numbers suggest. Demand became significant to economists as a variable that might be predicted in equations. Indeed, demand received its most celebrated attention from theorists interested in models; Ivan Moscati has shown that when economists performed real-world experiments on "demand theory," the results had almost no impact on other economists, even (perhaps especially) when these experiments showed that models did not accurately predict outcomes.[39] Variances were explained away as the effects of local, and therefore, limited, contexts. For economists, demand had come to seem everywhere and, in terms of its real world embeddedness, nowhere.

Simultaneously, demand took on particular powers in popular rhetoric. That is, satisfying "demand" was used to justify a range of actions— from decisions about where stores should locate to whom they should exclude, from justifications for selling "quality" goods to selling clearly shoddy products. This was as true for business and policy elites as for people in more mundane positions. In March 2012, Ben Bernanke, then head of the U.S. Federal Reserve, justified the reserve's continued efforts to hold down interest rates because, he said, low consumer demand weighed against more encouraging signs, such as job growth.[40] And to take one of many possible illustrative contemporary examples of how "demand" is used to transcend conventional notions of ethics and common sense, in explaining how an investment firm could successfully sell subprime auto loans in spite of their incredible risk (defaults were increasing, the firm that originated the loans had received a subpoena regarding lending practices) analyst Christopher Donat said simply, "You do deals when there is demand."[41] In these and other moments, demand emerged as a kind of deus-ex-machina, an unnamed but enormously powerful force that had to be obeyed.

Visions of what customers (or citizens) wanted narrowed in the mid-twentieth century, even as the term "demand" was invoked more frequently and was, among economists, elevated to a mathematical variable. Rather than difficult, individualist, and diffuse prewar shopping, postwar shopping was increasingly presented as co-ordinated, streamlined, and pleasurable. Moreover, this sort of "mass" consumption was taken as crucial to business prosperity, the economy, and a distinctively American way of life. Malls, supermarkets, and even standardized homes were sites of a new wildly successful model of retail.

As had been the case earlier, this shift in thinking about consumption reflected new ways of seeing (or not seeing) women. Nothing exemplifies this better than *Life* magazine's 1955 special issue, "Food, Farm, Government." Featuring a disembodied woman's gloved hand delicately pushing a full shopping cart, the issue celebrated a remarkable system of distribution and consumers' eager embrace of it. With titles like "How Beef Gets to a Beef Eating Nation" page after page lovingly described the nation's "modern" food systems, focusing on how they met postwar desire for new foods. Women's food buying, previously understood as difficult and requiring personalized attention, now powered streamlined, large-scale, economies.[42]

The emphasis on standardization and the success of consumption— both in popular thought and in economists' writings—is striking because so much in later years suggested the limits of mass consumption, and of demand itself, as a factor in retail operations. The most striking examples of the explanatory limits of demand come from attacks on stores themselves. The 1960s and 1970s saw extraordinary numbers of urban racial insurrections that targeted neighbourhood businesses. Simultaneously, academics, local residents, and journalists routinely demonstrated that many stores charged more in poor neighborhoods than in wealthier ones, or simply avoided poor areas entirely. Economists and many others continued to trumpet the notion that markets could offer what people most wanted and that the lure of profits would end discrimination, at the same time that many Americans made clear that neither stores nor "markets," nor the economy had given them anything like what they wanted.[43]

We can, however, recapture earlier ways of understanding consumer frustration. In moments where the dynamics of consumption were studied carefully, such as earlier in the twentieth century, economic analyses reflected an embedded notion of consumption that took the shortcomings of the market into account. The resulting economic thought reflected understandings that women acted politically, by themselves but also collectively, in the realm of consumption. But in moments when the dynamics of consumption were less visible in scholarship, when women shoppers were cast as apolitical and gullible (or unfeminine or non-normative if they were assertive), versions of unimpeded consumer choice resonated more strongly. The recent crackdowns on mall protests, the removal of patrons suspected of stealing, the time, effort, and social costs required to confront a clerk or manager—all of these reflect the requirements of smooth-running consumption.

Why does this history matter to the present moment? Because the notion that individualized demand is the most important factor in economic change and business activity makes it difficult to organize successful social movements. If demand is really what drives things like sales of soft drinks or gas-guzzling cars, then people's basic tastes would have to shift for change to happen—any regulation would be anti-democratic. But if consumer spaces are and have always been political, then changing how business is done does not require changing people's basic desires but rather acknowledging the fullness of those desires—for fairness, for religious and racial identity, for health, for affordable and convenient goods and services, for sociality. The pressures faced by a woman in a grocery store might be discussed, rather than eliminated as "exogenous." If consumption has always been political, then political solutions might be applied to remedy its inequalities and problems it creates.

This brief history of economists' efforts to know and control demand reveals a fuller notion of consumption that was eclipsed over time. It speaks to the limits of understanding demand as a disembedded variable that powers economies. It also speaks to the rewards of seeing consumers as complicated, constrained, and hopeful social actors. As the economist Hazel Kyrk wrote nearly one hundred years ago, our goal remains to understand, and to act on, "the world behind the demand curve."[44]

CONTRIBUTORS

Kyle Asquith is assistant professor in the Department of Communication, Media & Film at the University of Windsor. His research has been published in venues such as *Critical Studies in Media Communication*, *Popular Communication*, the *Advertising & Society Review*, and the *Canadian Journal of Communication*.

Dawson Barrett is assistant professor of history at Del Mar College in Corpus Christi, Texas. He is the author of *Teenage Rebels: Successful High School Activists from the Little Rock Nine to the Class of Tomorrow* (Microcosm Publishing, 2015).

Lawrence Black, a former Fulbright Scholar, is professor of modern history at the University of York, UK. He is author and editor of six books, most recently *Redefining British Politics: Consumerism, Culture and Participation* (Palgrave-Macmillan, 2010) and *Reassessing 1970s Britain* (Manchester University Press, 2013, paperback 2015).

Madeline Brambilla works in marketing at a leading organic ingredient supplier. She develops educational online and print materials on the importance of sustainability and organic agriculture in the food industry.

Joshua L. Carreiro is assistant professor of sociology at Springfield Technical Community College, Springfield, MA. His current research explores the history of consumers' co-operatives in the United States with a particular emphasis on their role in black American economic development and ideologies of black self-segregation. He has previously published research on the intersection of workers, consumers, and unionization campaigns in the contemporary United States.

H. Louise Davis is associate professor of American studies and chair of the Interdisciplinary and Communication Studies Department at Miami University. She is co-editor with Karyn J. Pilgrim and Madhudaya Sinha of *The Ecopolitics of Consumption: The Food Trade* (Rowman & Littlefield, 2016). Her scholarship and teaching focus on poverty and power, transnational media based activism, social and environmental justice movements, and ethical commodity fetishism.

Jeffrey Demsky is assistant professor of history at San Bernardino Valley College, CA. His research focuses on American Holocaust memory. He is the author of various articles, book chapters, and encyclopedia entries. In addition to his teaching duties, Professor Demsky is a historical consultant who helps secondary schools to design and implement their Holocaust and Genocide Studies curriculum.

Tracey Deutsch is associate professor of history at the University of Minnesota-Twin Cities. She is the author of *Building a Housewife's Paradise: Gender, Politics and American Grocery Stores in the Twentieth Century* (University of North Carolina Press, 2010) and several articles on food politics and consumer society.

Mara Einstein is professor of media studies at Queens College, City University of New York. She is a former senior marketing executive with stints at advertising agencies, as well as NBC and MTV Networks. She is the author of numerous books on advertising and marketing including *Compassion, Inc.: How Corporate America Blurs the Line between What We Buy, Who We Are and Those We Help* (University of California Press, 2012).

Bart Elmore is assistant professor of environmental history at The Ohio State University and author of *Citizen Coke: The Making of Coca-Cola Capitalism* (W. W. Norton, 2015).

Sarah Elvins is associate professor of history at the University of Manitoba. She is the author of *Sales and Celebrations: Retailing and Regional Iden-*

tity in Western New York State, 1920–1940 (Ohio University Press, 2004), and articles on scrip, consumption, and cross-border shopping.

Daniel Faber is professor of sociology at Northeastern University and director of the Northeastern Environmental Justice Research Collaborative. He is a board member of Coming Clean, the Alliance for a Healthy Tomorrow (AHT), and the Massachusetts Environmental Justice Alliance (MEJA). His most recent book is *Capitalizing on Environmental Injustice: The Polluter-Industrial Complex in the Age of Globalization* (Rowman & Littlefield, 2009).

Julie Guard is associate professor in history and labour studies at the University of Manitoba and coordinator of the Labour Studies Program. Her book, *Radical Housewives: Price Wars and Food Politics in Mid-Twentieth Century Canada*, is forthcoming from the University of Toronto Press. She is co-editor with Wayne Antony of *Bankruptcies and Bailouts* (2009). Her work on women, gender and ethnicity in left, labour, working-class and social justice movements has been published in *Labour/Le Travail, Journal of Women's History, Labor: Studies in Working-Class History of the Americas*, and *International Labor and Working-Class History*.

Louis Hyman, a former Fulbright Scholar and McKinsey consultant, is associate professor of history and director of the Institute for Workplace Studies at the ILR School of Cornell University. He is the author of *Debtor Nation: The History of America in Red Ink* (Princeton, 2011) and *Borrow: The American Way of Debt* (Knopf, 2012).

Meredith Katz is instructor of sociology at Virginia Commonwealth University and the co-founder and former president of United Students Against Sweatshops (USAS) at Virginia Tech, where she earned her PhD in sociology. She currently serves as faculty advisor for USAS at Virginia Commonwealth University. Her research focuses on ethical consumption, collegiate anti-sweatshop organizing, and garment workers' rights.

Randall Kaufman is chair of the Department of Humanities and Social Sciences at Miami Dade College-Homestead Campus. He is a PhD student at Florida International University completing his dissertation: "For Humanity's Sake: The American Anti-Nazi Boycotts (1933–1938)."

Larry Kirsch is an economist and managing partner of IMR Health Economics, a consulting firm in Portland, OR. He is co-author, with Robert N. Mayer, of *Financial Justice: The People's Campaign to Stop Lender Abuse* (Praeger, 2013).

Katrina Lacher is assistant professor of history at the University of Central Oklahoma. Her work focuses on direct-action environmental organizations and the rise of anti-environmentalism.

Bettina Liverant is an adjunct assistant professor in history at the University of Calgary. She is the author of *Buying Happiness: The Development of Consumer Consciousness in Canada, 1890–1963* (University of British Columbia Press, forthcoming). Her research focuses on consumer society and corporate philanthropy.

Amy Lubitow is assistant professor of sociology at Portland State University. She teaches and conducts research on environmental sociology, social movements, and sustainability.

Robert N. Mayer is professor of family and consumer studies at the University of Utah. He is co-author, with Larry Kirsch, of *Financial Justice: The People's Campaign to Stop Lender Abuse* (Praeger, 2013) and co-editor, with Stephen Brobeck, of *Watchdogs and Whistleblowers: A Reference Guide to Consumer Activism* (Greenwood, 2015).

Michelle McDonald, a former Fulbright Scholar and NEH Fellow, is associate professor of history at Stockton University. She is the co-editor of *Public Drinking in the Early Modern World: Voices from the Tavern* (Pickering and Chatto, 2011) and *Caffeine Dependence: Coffee and the Economy of Early America* (University of Pennsylvania Press, forthcoming).

Wendy Wiedenhoft Murphy is associate professor of sociology at John Carroll University. She is the author of *Consumer Culture and Society* (SAGE, 2016) and has published research on consumer activism in *Social Movement Studies*, *Journal of Consumer Culture*, and *Peace and Change*.

Mark W. Robbins is associate professor of history at Del Mar College and holds a PhD in history from Brown University. His work on labour history, memory, and consumer politics has appeared in journals including

Labor History, The Public Historian, Oral History Review, and the *Historical Journal of Massachusetts.* He is the author of the forthcoming book, *Middle Class Union: Organizing the 'Consuming Public' in Post-World War I America* (University of Michigan Press).

Jessica Stewart is a graduate of Cornell University where she was Rawlings Scholar and Merrill Presidential Scholar. Before studying at Cornell, she was an activist focused on issues of economic justice.

Joseph Tohill, a former Fulbright Scholar and labour activist, teaches American and Canadian history at York University and Ryerson University. His research and writing focuses on comparing the politics of consumption and public policy in the United States and Canada.

Allison Ward has a PhD in Canadian History from Queen's University, Kingston. She has taught at both Queen's University and McMaster University.

Philip Wight is a Rose and Irving Crown Fellow and PhD candidate in history at Brandeis University.

NOTES

INTRODUCTION

1 Before Piketty and Saez used "1 percent" as the metric of inequality, the most common measure used by economists was the unintuitive "Gini coefficient." We think that this shift in economic language helped make inequality much more visible. See Thomas Piketty and Emmanuel Saez, "Income Inequality in the United States, 1913–1998," NBER Working Paper 8467 (Cambridge, MA: National Bureau of Economic Research, 2001), piketty.pse.ens.fr/fichiers/public/PikettySaez2001.pdf.

2 On conceptualizing consumer activism, see Dietlind Stolle and Michele Micheletti, *Political Consumerism: Global Responsibility in Action* (New York: Cambridge University Press, 2013), Michelle Micheletti, *Political Virtue and Shopping: Individuals, Consumerism, and Collective Action*, 2nd ed. (New York: Palgrave Macmillan, 2010); Lawrence B. Glickman, *Buying Power: A History of Consumer Activism in America* (Chicago: University of Chicago Press, 2009); Matthew Hilton, *Prosperity for All: Consumer Activism in an Era of Globalization* (Ithaca: Cornell University Press, 2009); Matthew Hilton, *Consumerism in Twentieth-Century Britain: The Search for a Historical Movement* (New York: Cambridge University Press, 2003).

3 See, for example, Dan Zuberi, *Differences that Matter: Social Policy and the Working Poor in the United States and Canada* (Ithaca: Cornell University Press, 2006).

4 Glickman, *Buying Power*, 2–3.

5 Hilton, *Prosperity for All*; Glickman, *Buying Power*; Donatella Della Porta and Mario Diani, *Social Movements: An Introduction*, 2nd ed. (Malden, MA: Blackwell, 2009), esp. 49–53.

6 Glickman, *Buying Power*, 2. See also T. H. Breen, *The Marketplace of Revolution: How Consumer Politics Shaped American Independence* (New York: Oxford University Press, 2004); Lawrence B. Glickman, "'Buy for the Sake of the Slave': Abolitionism and the Origins of American Consumer Activism," *American Quarterly* 56, no. 4 (December 2004): 889–912; Margaret Finnegan, *Selling Suffrage: Consumer Culture and Votes for Women* (New York: Columbia University Press, 1999); Robert Weems, *Desegregating the Dollar: African American Consumerism in the Twentieth Century*

(New York: New York University Press, 1998).

7   Robert V. Kozinets and Jay M. Handelman, "Adversaries of Consumption: Consumer Movements, Activism, and Ideology," *Journal of Consumer Research* 31 (December 2004): 694–95.

8   Micheletti, *Political Virtue and Shopping*.

9   Micheletti and Stolle offer a succinct discussion of such criticisms in *Political Consumerism*, chapters 7–8.

10 Roopali Mukherjee and Sarah Banet-Weiser, eds., *Commodity Activism: Cultural Resistance in Neo-Liberal Times* (New York: New York University Press, 2012), ix–xi, 1–17.

11 Gillian Creese, "Exclusion or Solidarity? Vancouver Workers Confront the 'Oriental Problem,'" in *Canadian Working-Class History: Selected Readings*, 3rd ed., ed. Laurel Sefton MacDowell and Ian Radforth (Toronto: Canadian Scholars Press, 2006), 202; Gerald Tulchinsky, *Canada's Jews: A People's Journey* (Toronto: University of Toronto Press, 2008), 301–3; United States Holocaust Memorial Museum, "Father Charles Coughlin," *Holocaust Encyclopedia*, www.ushmm.org. See also Donica Belisle, "Conservative Consumerism: Consumer Advocacy in *Woman's Century* Magazine during and after World War I." *Social History/Histoire Sociale* 47, no. 93 (May 2014): 111–38.

12 Stolle and Micheletti, *Political Consumerism, 48*.

13 Stolle and Micheletti, *Political Consumerism*. See also Erma Angevine, ed., *Consumer Activists, They Made a Difference: A History of Consumer Action Related by Leaders in the Consumer Movement* (New York: National Consumers Committee for Research and Education and Consumers Union Foundation, 1982).

14 The best overviews of historical and contemporary consumer activism, respectively, are Hilton, *Prosperity for All*, and Stolle and Micheletti, *Political Consumerism*. Among the most important works in American history are Meg Jacobs, *Pocketbook Politics: Economic Citizenship in Twentieth-Century America* (Princeton: Princeton University Press, 2005); Lizabeth Cohen, *A Consumers' Republic: The Politics of Mass Consumption in Postwar America* (New York: Knopf, 2003); Dana Frank, *Purchasing Power: Consumer Organizing, Gender, and the Seattle Labor Movement, 1919–1929* (New York: Cambridge University Press, 1993); Susan Levine, "Workers' Wives: Gender, Class, and Consumerism in the 1920s United States," *Gender & History* 3, no. 1 (Spring 1991): 45–64. Significant Canadian works include Julie Guard, "A Mighty Power against the Cost of Living: Canadian Housewives Organize in the 1930s," *International Labor & Working-Class History* 77 (Spring 2010): 27–47; Magda Fahrni, "Counting the Costs of Living: Gender, Citizenship, and a Politics of Prices in 1940s Montreal," *Canadian Historical Review* 83, no. 4 (2002): 483–504; Joy Parr, *Domestic Goods: The Material, the Moral, and the Economic in the Postwar Years* (Toronto: University of Toronto Press, 1999); Joan Sangster, "Consuming Issues: Women on the Left, Political Protest, and the Organization of Homemakers, 1920–1960," in *Framing Our Past: Canadian Women's History in the Twentieth Century*, ed. Sharon A. Cook, Lorna R. McLean, and Kate O'Rourke (Montreal and Kingston: McGill-Queen's University Press, 2001), 240–47.

15 Glickman, *Buying Power,* 302.

16 Breen, *Marketplace of Revolution;* Francis Back, "L'étoffe de la liberté: politique tex-
    tile et comportements vestimentaires du mouvement patriote," *Bulletin d'Histoire
    Politique* 10, no. 2 (2001): 58–71.

17 Glickman, *Buying Power,* 87, 155–62. See also Hilton, *Prosperity for All.*

18 Glickman, *Buying Power,* 255–74, 280–84; Hilton, *Prosperity for All,* 21–50.

19 As is so often the case, the Canadian side is much less well covered by historians,
    but for a brief overview see Joseph Tohill, "'A Consumers' War': Price Control and
    Political Consumerism in the United States and Canada during World War II"
    (PhD diss., York University, 2012), 447–58; Donald A. N. Wallace, "The Confi-
    dent, the Ascetic, and the Vigilant Consumer: Discourses of Mass Consumption
    and Subjectivity in Post-War Canada and the United States" (PhD diss., Carleton
    University, 2003), 203–15; Glickman, *Buying Power,* 275–302; Hilton, *Prosperity for
    All,* 161–75.

20 This decline is detailed in Hilton's *Prosperity for All,* 153–254.

1: CONSUMING WITH A CONSCIENCE

 1 Special thanks to Kevin Konrad, a recent graduate of Stockton University's Ameri-
    can Studies program, and my graduate assistant during the 2012–13 academic year.
    It was his careful culling of newspaper advertisements that gave names and com-
    modities to Philadelphia's free produce market. C. Gilpin, *Conscience versus Cotton;
    or, the Preference of Free Labour Produce,* 2nd ed. (London: C. Gilpin), 1–3.

 2 T. H. Breen, *The Marketplace of Revolution: How Consumer Politics Shaped American
    Independence* (Oxford: Oxford University Press, 2004).

 3 Gilpin, *Conscience versus Cotton,* 4.

 4 Lawrence B. Glickman, "'Buy for the Sake of the Slave': Abolitionism and the Ori-
    gins of American Consumer Activism," *American Quarterly* 56, no. 4 (December
    2004): 889–912. Glickman draws on the earlier work of Ruth Nuermberger, *The Free
    Produce Movement: A Quaker Protest Against Slavery* (Durham: Duke University Press,
    1942) and Julie Joy Jeffrey, *The Great Silent Army of Abolition: Ordinary Women in the
    Anti-Slavery Movement* (Chapel Hill: University of North Carolina Press, 1998).

 5 Gilpin, *Conscious versus Cotton,* 2; Michael Lamb and Benjamin Lundy first adver-
    tised their free produce store in the *Genius of Universal Emancipation,* August 5,
    1826.

 6 See Marc Egnal, "The Changing Structure of Philadelphia's Trade with the British
    West Indies, 1750–1775," *Pennsylvania Magazine of History and Biography* 99, no. 2
    (April 1975): 156–79; Frederick Tolles, *From Meeting House to Counting House: The
    Quaker Merchants of Colonial Philadelphia, 1682–1763* (New York: W. W. Norton,
    1963).

 7 Sara Fanning, *Caribbean Crossing: African Americans and the Haitian Emigration
    Movement* (New York: New York University Press, 2015), 61–70.

 8 For the free produce wedding of Angelia Grimke, see "Angelina Grimke to Weld,"
    May 6, 1838, in *Letters of Theodore Dwight Weld, Angelina Grimke Weld, and Sarah*

Grimke, 1822–1844, ed. Gilbert H. Barnes and Dwight L. Dumond, 2 vols. (New York: D. Appleton-Century, 1934), 2: 665. For Garrison's early support for free produce, see Nuermberger, *The Free Produce Movement*, 101–2 and Glickman, "'Buy for the Sake of the Slave,'" 890–92. David Lee Child advertised his free produce business in the *National Enquirer*, April 29, 1838. For more on Richard Allen, see *Fanning, Caribbean Crossings*, 90, and Richard Newman, *Freedom's Prophet: Richard Allen, the AME Church, and the Black Founding Fathers* (New York: New York University Press, 2008), 264–68.

9   *Minutes of Proceedings of the Requited Labor Convention held in Philadelphia* (Philadelphia: Merrihew and Gun, 1838), 12; Alain Chatriot, Marie-Emmanuelle Chessel, and Matthew Hilton eds., *The Expert Consumer: Associations and Professionals in Consumer Society* (Burlington: Ashgate, 2006), 29.

10 *Minutes of Proceedings of the Requited Labor Convention*, 13.

11 Robert Lindley Murray advertisement, *National Era*, October 5, 1848.

12 For more on J. Miller McKim, see Ira Brown, "Miller McKim and Pennsylvania Abolitionism," *Pennsylvania History* 30, no. 1 (January 1963): 55–72; David Brion Davis, "Abolitionists and their Freedmen: A Review Essay," *Journal of Southern History* 31, no. 2 (May 1965): 164–70; and John L. Myers, "The Early Anti-Slavery System in Pennsylvania, 1833–1838," *Pennsylvania History* 31, no. 1 (January 1964): 62–86.

13 George W. Taylor advertisements, *National Era*, March 4, 1847, and July 18, 1850. See also W. P. Garrison, "Free Produce among the Quakers," *Atlantic Monthly* 22 (October 1868): 485–94.

14 Ezra Town advertisement, *National Era*, October 13 and November 30, 1854; J. Miller McKim advertisement, *Frederick Douglass' Paper*, August 20, 1852.

15 George W. Taylor advertisements, *National Era*, August 23, 1855, and February 5, 1857.

16 *Minutes of Proceedings of the Requited Labor Convention*, 11.

17 Robert Lindley Murray advertisement, *National Era*, October 5, 1848.

18 Eli Adams advertisement, *Pennsylvania Freeman*, July 11, 1839.

19 G. B. Stebbins advertisement, *North Star*, December 1, 1848; Robert McClure advertisement, *Pennsylvania Freeman*, July 15, 1837, and June 21, 1838; C. & E. Adams advertisement, *Pennsylvania Freeman*, May 3, 1838.

20 Mark Brook advertisement, *Pennsylvania Freeman*, August 17, 1848; C. & E. Adams advertisement, *Pennsylvania Freeman*, June 21, 1838.

21 James Willis advertisement, *Pennsylvania Freeman*, November 20, 1845; similar ads appear on April 29, 1847, and December 22, 1853.

22 Lydia White advertisement, *Pennsylvania Freeman*, May 3, 1838. By the following year, White had expanded to include four different kinds of sugar, East India and American rice, coffee, teas, and a variety of cotton cloths. *Pennsylvania Freeman*, May 9, 1839.

23 Laetitia Bullock advertisement, *Pennsylvania Freeman*, December 22, 1853.

24 *Minutes of the Adjourned Session of the Twentieth Biennial American Convention for Promoting the Abolition of Slavery and Improving the Condition of the African Race* (Baltimore: published by the convention, November 1828), 5. It is interesting to note

that this first report also included "or by Slaves, whose condition has been so meliorated as to approach the condition of freemen, shewing what are the relative advantages between free and slave labor." This distinction, however, was not repeated in subsequent committee reports.

25 William Lloyd Garrison is cited in "The Free Produce Question," *Liberator*, March 1, 1850, 1, while Wendell Phillips appeared in "Sketches of the Sayings and Doings at the New England Anti-Slavery Convention," *Liberator*, June 4, 1847, 91. See also James B. Stewart, "Heroes, Villains, Liberty, and License: the Abolitionist Vision of Wendell Phillips" in *Antislavery Reconsidered: New Perspectives on the Abolitionists* (Baton Rouge: Louisiana State University Press, 1979), 168–91.

26 T. Stephen Whitman, "Free Produce," in *World of a Slave: Encyclopedia of the Material Lives of Slaves in the United States*, ed. Martha B. Katz-Hyman and Kym S. Rice (Santa Barbara: Greenwood, 2011), 236–37.

27 Cecelia Gowdy-Wygant, *Cultivating Victory: The Women's Land Army and the Victory Garden Movement* (Pittsburgh: University of Pittsburgh Press, 2013), 63; Adam Shprintzen, *The Vegetarian Crusade: The Rise of an American Reform Movement, 1817–1921* (Chapel Hill: University of North Carolina Press, 2013), 2.

2: BOYCOTTS, BUYCOTTS, AND LEGISLATION

1 There is a growing historiography of consumer activism during the Progressive Era, including Tracey Deutsch, *Building a Housewife's Paradise: Gender, Politics, and American Grocery Stores in the Twentieth Century* (Chapel Hill: University of North Carolina Press, 2010); Dana Frank, *Buy American: The Untold Story of Economic Nationalism* (Boston: Beacon Press, 1999); Frank, *Purchasing Power: Consumer Organizing, Gender, and the Seattle Labor Movement* (Cambridge: Cambridge University Press, 1994); Lawrence B. Glickman, *Buying Power: A History of Consumer Protest in America* (Chicago: University of Chicago Press, 2009); Lawrence B. Glickman, *A Living Wage: American Workers and the Making of Consumer Society* (Ithaca: Cornell University Press, 1997); Meg Jacobs, *Pocketbook Politics: Economic Citizenship in Twentieth-Century America* (Princeton: Princeton University Press, 2005); Kathryn Kish Sklar, "The Consumers' White Label Campaign of the National Consumers' League, 1898–1918," in *Getting and Spending: European and American Consumer Societies in the Twentieth Century*, ed. Susan Strasser, Charles McGovern, and Matthias Judt (Cambridge: Cambridge University Press, 1998), 17–35; Theda Skocpol, *Protecting Soldiers and Mothers: The Political Origins of Social Policy in the United States* (Cambridge: Cambridge University Press, 1992).

2 Leo Wolman, *The Boycott in American Trade Unions* (Baltimore: John Hopkins Press, 1916), 25–26.

3 National Consumers League (NCL), *Fourth Annual Report* (March 1903), 46; NCL, *Fifth Annual Report* (March 1904), 18; Florence Kelley, "Aims and Principles of the Consumers' League," *American Journal of Sociology* (1899), 290.

4 Monroe Friedman, *Consumer Boycotts* (New York: Routledge, 1999).

5 Walter Macarthur, "Union Label First Prize Essay," *American Federationist* (July 1904), 573–75; M. E. J. Kelley, "The Union Label," *North American Review* (1897), 27;

Ernest Spedden, *The Trade Union Label* (Baltimore: John Hopkins Press, 1910), 22.

6 Maud Nathan, *The Story of an Epoch-Making Movement* (Garden City: Doubleday, 1926).

7 NCL, *Fourth Annual Report* (March 1903); *NCL Report for the Years 1914–1916* (February 1917).

8 *American Federationist* (May 1901), 166; Samuel Gompers, *Labor and the Employer* (New York: E. P. Dutton, 1920); *American Federationist* (February 1904), 161; *American Federationist* (May 1907), 352; Wolman, *The Boycott in American Trade Unions*, 34.

9 Nathan, *The Story of an Epoch-Making Movement*.

10 NCL, *Eighth Annual Report* (March 1907); *NCL Report for the Years 1914–1916* (February 1917).

11 John Graham Brooks, "The Label of the Consumers League," *Proceedings of the American Economic Association* (February 1900), 252.

12 Samuel Gompers, "Report to the 23rd Annual Convention," *American Federationist* (1903), 1284; NCL, *Memorandum on the Label* (February 1918).

13 This brief is popularly referred to as the Brandeis Brief, which became renowned for establishing the acceptance of social science research in legal proceedings.

14 NCL, *Tenth Report for Two Years* (March 1909). The AFL did not pursue labour legislation for its own members during the Progressive Era, but it did support it for female and children workers.

15 Clive Barnett, Paul Cloke, Nick Clarke, and Alice Malpass argue in *Globalizing Responsibility: The Political Rationalities of Ethical Consumption* (Chichester, UK: Wiley-Blackwell, 2011) that the current success of the fair trade movement is not simply a case of consumer activism but also organizations helping to co-ordinate individual consumer practices.

3: MAKING A MARKET FOR CONSUMERS

1 "Only Three Bylaws Out of the Ten Were Carried Yesterday," *Morning Albertan* (Calgary), May 1, 1914, 1, 7. Support for the public market led the polls, followed by support for sewer and waterworks extensions. Requests for additional funds for the fire brigade and other public services were rejected.

2 Reports in the *Globe and Mail* (Toronto), one of Canada's major daily papers, included "Bread Riots Break Out in Lisbon," August 5, 1911, 1; "The French Food Riots Break Out a Fresh," September 14, 1911, 1; "Fierce Food Rioting," September 18, 1911, 2; "Berlin Dear Food Riots," October 25, 1912, 4. On protests in America, see Meg Jacobs, *Pocketbook Politics: Economic Citizenship in Twentieth-Century America* (Princeton: Princeton University Press, 2007), 42–44.

3 Georgina Newhall, "An Adventure in Economics," *Saturday Night* (Toronto), February 14, 1914, 41.

4 "Consumers' League Mass Meeting," *Calgary Daily Herald*, May 22, 1913, 16.

5 Newhall, "An Adventure in Economics," 41; "Consumers' League Now an Organized Reality Here," *Morning Albertan*, May 29, 1913, 1.

6   "Consumers' League Now an Organized Reality Here." The constitution was drawn up on May 21 and approved on May 28.

7   "Consumers' League Adopts Constitution; Makes Ready to War on the High Cost of Living," *Morning Albertan*, May 22, 1913, 4.

8   "Consumers League Drew Big Crowd to Its Annual Meeting, Women Have Put the Public Market on a Paying Basis," *Calgary Daily Herald*, September 18, 1913, 14, 19; "The Consumers' League," *Calgary Daily Herald*, September 19, 1913, 6; Max Foran, "Idealism and Pragmatism in Local Government: The Calgary Experience 1911–1930," *Journal of Canadian Studies* 18, no. 2 (Summer 1983), 96.

9   "Consumers' League to Continue System," *Calgary Daily Herald*, September 25, 1914, 12. Of the key players, the most is known about Newhall and Gale. Georgina Newhall, an Ontario native, was the first woman to edit the women's section in a major Canadian daily newspaper, one of the first woman stenographers in Canada, and an executive secretary in a prominent Toronto law firm. After marriage, Newhall left paid employment and became active in the women's club movement. A native of England, Annie Gale had been one of the first women to take the Oxford Entrance Examinations in the early 1890s. As it was not possible for women to attend Oxford at that time, she worked in the family grocery business before marrying and immigrating to Calgary in 1912. Frustrated by high living costs, Gale joined the Consumers League early on, filling an instrumental role as the corresponding secretary. Leveraging her experience and good reputation, Gale entered municipal politics and was elected as an alderman in 1917, the first woman elected to public office in Canada. On this generation of woman activists, see Veronica Strong-Boag, *The Parliament of Women: The National Council of Women of Canada* (Ottawa: National Museum of Canada, 1976), 187. On Newhall, see Donica Belisle, "Conservative Consumerism: Consumer Advocacy in *Woman's Century* Magazine during and after World War I," *Histoire sociale/Social History* (May 2014): 111–38; "A Student of Food Economics," *Canadian Magazine* 52, no. 1 (November 1918), 605–6; "Tribute to Late Mrs. G. Newhall," *Calgary Herald*, November 19, 1932, 17; "Woman Writer Dead," *Montreal Gazette*, November 12, 1932, 14. On Gale, see "A Charming Progressive," *Canadian Magazine*, 52, no. 1 (November 1918), 604; Heather Foran, "Annie Gale: Reformer, Feminist and First Woman Alderman in Calgary," in *The Citymakers: Calgarians after the Frontier*, ed. Max Foran and Sheilagh Jameson (Calgary: Historical Society of Alberta, Chinook Country Chapter, 1987), 196–207.

10 On resistance from the Board of Trade, see "Consumer League Discusses Cost of Living in Calgary," *Calgary Daily Herald*, November 28, 1913, 21; "Consumers' League Favours Wholesale Market for City," *Morning Albertan*, April 29, 1914, 1. For an industry response, see "Get Rid of Consumers' Leagues," *Canadian Grocer* (Toronto), July 4, 1913, 31.

11 "Consumers League Opening of the Public Market Notable Success," *Morning Albertan*, June 23, 1913, 1.

12 "Purchasing Public, Whose Money It Saves, Should See That the Public Market Bylaw Is Passed," *Morning Albertan*, April 29, 1914, 1.

13 "Petition of Consumers' League is Only Partially Acceded to by the Aldermen," *Morning Albertan*, June 24, 1913, 8.

14 Mrs. Arthur Lewis, "A Woman Suffragist in Canada," *The Vote* (London), June 23, 1916, 4.

15 "Butchers' Licenses Reduced to $1 A Year; Vote Taken Under the Eyes of Women Advocates," *Morning Albertan*, November 25, 1913, 8.

16 *Calgary Daily Herald*, November 28, 1913, 21; *Labour Gazette* (Ottawa: Canada Department of Labour), August 1914, 181; "How Calgary Women Broke the Food Combine," *Quebec Telegraph*, November 4, 1916, 5.

17 "Retail Grocer Explains Reliable Business Methods," *Morning Albertan*, November 28, 1913, 11.

18 Newhall, "An Adventure in Economics," 49.

19 "Tells Edmontonians How Cost of Living May Be Reduced," *Edmonton Bulletin*, March 19, 1914, 1.

20 "Consumers' League Drew Big Crowd to Its Annual Meeting," *Calgary Daily Herald*, September 18, 1913, 19.

21 "Consumers' League Drew Big Crowd," 14.

22 "Consumers' League Drew Big Crowd," 14. On differences between the Calgary Consumers League and the National Consumers League, see Newhall, "An Adventure in Economics," 41; "Consumers' League to Continue System" and "Citizens Should Buy Calgary-Made Goods," *Calgary Daily Herald*, September 25, 1914, 12.

23 "The Consumers' League and Its Great Problems," *Calgary Daily Herald*, August 4, 1914, 12, 15; "Members of Consumers' League Overworked at the Market," *Calgary Daily Herald*, August 7, 1914, 11.

24 Newhall wrote that "the great diversity of interests occupying the attention of women [along with] the overlapping of objectives and methods of attack which the possession of the franchise has brought upon the women of Canada" and the hope that "the Government would at last do something worthwhile in reference to Household Economics" undercut commitment to the league. *The Year Book of the National Council of Women of Canada* (Toronto: 1919), 106–7. See also Strong-Boag, *Parliament of Women*, 413–15.

25 She is most remembered as the author of a cookbook emphasizing thrift for the war effort. Elizabeth Grant Deachman, *Home Canning by Mrs. R. J. Deachman, President of the Calgary Consumers' League* (Calgary, 1916). See also "Consumers' League Would Encourage Greater Use of Dairy Products in City," *Calgary Daily Herald*, June 22, 1917, 11; "Consumers' League Starts Canning Clubs for Red Cross Society," *Calgary Daily Herald*, July 7, 1917, 11; "How Calgary Women Broke the Food Combine," 5.

26 See "Women Heckle Men Who Would Serve Calgary in the High Places," *Morning Albertan*, December 6, 1913, 1.

27 Philip Ethington, "Recasting Urban Political History: Gender, the Public, the Household, and Political Participation in Boston and San Francisco during the Progressive Era," *Social Science History* 16, no. 2 (Summer 1992), 304.

28 "Appeals to Women to Stand Behind the Public Market," *Morning Albertan*, December 20, 1920, 7.

4: MAKING A MIDDLE CLASS "PUBLIC"

1 Thomas R. Marshall, "The Awakening Middle Class," *New York Times Magazine*, October 5, 1919.

2 Marina Moskowitz, *Standard of Living: The Measure of the Middle Class in Modern America* (Baltimore: Johns Hopkins University Press, 2004); Jennifer Scanlon, *Inarticulate Longings: The "Ladies' Home Journal," Gender, and the Promises of Consumer Culture* (New York: Routledge, 1995).

3 Many activists and commentators characterized their actions as a revolt against high prices, profiteers, and organized labour. For a few examples, see Frederic Haskin, "Rogers Park Rent Revolt," *Chicago Daily Tribune*, June 6, 1920; "Middle Class Union Formed to Fight Costs," *Nashville Tennessean*, February 9, 1920; Edward Slosson, "Denim and Gingham," *The Independent*, May 1, 1920. This chapter suggests that by the post–First World War period, many people defined a "middle class" identity differently than Robert Johnston's characterization of the middle class. In contrast to Johnston's "radical" pro-labour middle class, the activist movements discussed in this chapter largely criticized both wealthy people and striking workers, advocated within the framework of capitalism, and appealed to cultural traditionalism. Robert D. Johnston, *The Radical Middle Class: Populist Democracy and the Question of Capitalism in Progressive Era Portland, Oregon* (Princeton: Princeton University Press, 2003).

4 For similar and expanded treatment of many themes in this essay, see Mark W. Robbins, *Middle Class Union: Organizing the "Consuming Public" in Post-World War I America* (Ann Arbor: University of Michigan Press, 2017).

5 "Two of Our Needs," *San Francisco Bulletin*, March 25, 1879.

6 Calculated from "professional service" and "clerical occupations" categories in Bureau of Labor Statistics (BLS), *Handbook of Labor Statistics, 1924–1926* (Washington: GPO, 1927), 420. C. Wright Mills, *White Collar: The American Middle Classes* (New York: Oxford University Press, 1956).

7 See Moskowitz, *Standard of Living*, Scanlon, *Inarticulate Longings*, and Janice Williams Rutherford, *Selling Mrs. Consumer: Christine Frederick and the Rise of Household Efficiency* (Athens: University of Georgia Press, 2003).

8 See Lawrence B. Glickman, *Buying Power: A History of Consumer Activism in America* (Chicago: University of Chicago Press, 2009).

9 See, for instance, Dana Frank, "Where are the Workers in Consumer-Worker Alliances? Class Dynamics and the History of Consumer-Labor Campaigns," *Politics & Society* 31, no. 3 (September 2003): 363–79.

10 BLS, *CPI Detailed Report: Data for November 2014* (Washington: Dept. of Labor, 2014), 70.

11 BLS, *Handbook of Labor Statistics*, 705.

12 *Tampa Tribune*, March 31, 1920; April 1, 1920; April 3, 1920; and April 5, 1920.

13 United States Senate, Select Committee on Reconstruction and Production, *Reconstruction and Production* (Washington: GPO, 1921), 941–44.

14 David Montgomery, *Workers' Control in America* (New York: Cambridge University Press, 1979), 97; *Montgomery Advertiser*, July 24, 1919.

15 John Corbin, *The Return of the Middle Class* (New York: Scribner's, 1923), 12, 13, 15.

16 *Oregonian*, April 11, 1920; "The People and Their Daily Troubles," *Los Angeles Times*, June 17, 1920; "Organizing the Salaried Man," *Montgomery Advertiser*, August 12, 1919.

17 *Rocky Mountain News*, October 16, 1922; *New Orleans Times-Picayune*, October 12, 1919; Speech, June 1, 1921, folder 7, box 8, Series 5, Lowden Papers, University of Chicago Special Collections.

18 Corbin, *Return of the Middle Class*, 11.

19 "Cheese Club to Wage Warfare on Profiteers," *Ogden Standard-Examiner*, April 23, 1920; "Overall Club Idea Growing," *Charlotte News*, April 14, 1920; "Member Appears…," *St. Louis Post-Dispatch*, April 18, 1920.

20 "White Collar Man is for Overall Remedy," *Sault Ste. Marie Evening News*, April 29, 1920.

21 "In Overalls," *Bristol Daily Courier*, April 23, 1920.

22 *Chicago Daily Tribune*, February 9, 1921; *San Antonio Evening News*, June 9, 1920.

23 "War on City's Rent Gougers," *Denver Post*, February 16, 1920.

24 *Portsmouth Daily Times* (Ohio), June 20, 1920; *Chicago Daily Tribune*, February 8, 1920, and May 15, 1920; "People's League," *New York Tribune*, January 11, 1920; "Public's Union," *Boston Post*, April 23, 1920.

25 Meg Jacobs describes how in the early twentieth century, white-collar workers paid increasing attention to the high cost of living and "felt particularly victimized by price increases" but largely emphasizes how rising prices gave workers and the middle class common ground in opposing profiteers and trusts. Lawrence Glickman notes how progressive and similarly minded consumer activists of the first few decades of the twentieth century linked the categories of consumer and citizen. Many of them focused on protecting the interests of workers, while other consumer activists, during the 1920s, for instance, aimed to protect themselves from price increases or dishonest practices. The white-collar activists discussed in this chapter similarly cast consumers as the citizenry but also attempted to link these categories to the "middle class" and frequently characterized the labour movement as hostile to their values and priorities. Meg Jacobs, *Pocketbook Politics: Economic Citizenship in Twentieth-Century America* (Princeton: Princeton University Press, 2005), 40–41; Glickman, *Buying Power*, 156–218.

26 "A Middle Class Union," *New York Tribune*, September 10, 1922; *Denver Post*, February 2, 1920.

27 "People's League to Aid U.S. Unorganized Masses," *New York Tribune*, January 11, 1920.

28 "The New Middle Class Union," *Sandusky Register*, May 2, 1920.

29 Robert Murray, *Red Scare: A Study in National Hysteria* (Minneapolis: University of Minnesota Press, 1955).

30 See, for instance, "News, Notes, and Comments," *Steam, Shovel and Dredge*, June 1920.

31 "White Flays Both Labor and Capital," *Omaha World Herald*, September 21, 1938.

32 It is worth noting that a tension emerged within the consumer movement of the 1930s over whether to prioritize the interests of the purchaser or workers/social

justice for the working class. This tension was especially on display during and after the 1935 Consumers' Research strike. See Lawrence B. Glickman, "The Strike in the Temple of Consumption: Consumer Activism and Twentieth-Century American Political Culture," *Journal of American History* 88, no. 1 (June 2001): 99–128. Jacobs, *Pocketbook Politics*, 133–35.

33 See Lizabeth Cohen, *A Consumers' Republic: The Politics of Mass Consumption in Postwar America* (New York: Random House, 2003).

34 See Jacobs, *Pocketbook Politics*, 250–52.

35 Shane Hamilton, *Trucking Country: The Road to America's Wal-Mart Economy* (Princeton: Princeton University Press, 2008), 153; "Meatless Meals: A Middle Class Revolt," *Boston Globe*, April 4, 1973.

36 Frank, "Where are the Workers"; Lou Dobbs, *War on the Middle Class* (New York: Viking, 2006), ix, 10.

5: YOU ARE PURCHASING PROSPERITY!

1   *Hamilton Spectator*, "Ambitious City Gives Movement Fine Support," June 1, 1929.

2   Dominion Bureau of Statistics, *Census of Canada, 1931: Cross-Classification*, vol. 3 (Ottawa: Dominion Bureau of Statistics, 1934), 900–912.

3   C. W. Kirkpatrick, "Hamilton, Canada: A City of Opportunity," 1928, Industrial Commissioner Papers, RG 17, Historical Records of the City of Hamilton, Local History and Archives Division, Hamilton Public Library, Hamilton, Ontario (hereafter Hamilton Records).

4   John Maynard Keynes, *The Means to Prosperity* (London: MacMillan, 1933), 5–12.

5   Tom Traves, *Canadian Manufacturers and the Federal Government, 1917–1931* (Toronto: University of Toronto Press, 1979), 160–67.

6   Lawrence B. Glickman, *Buying Power: A History of Consumer Activism in America* (Chicago: University of Chicago Press, 2009), x.

7   *Hamilton Spectator*, "'Work'," November 9, 1932; Minutes of Hamilton Board of Control, May 8, 1932, Board of Control Papers, RG5, Hamilton Records.

8   Minutes of the Meeting of the Executive Committee, June 29, 1926, vol. 5, Canadian Manufacturers' Association fonds (CMA fonds), MG 28 I 230, Library and Archives Canada, Ottawa (LAC).

9   Ernest R. Forbes, *The Maritimes Rights Movement, 1919–1927: A Study in Canadian Regionalism* (Montreal and Kingston: McGill-Queen's University Press, 1979); Michael Lansing, *Insurgent Democracy: The Nonpartisan League in North American Politics* (Chicago: University of Chicago Press, 2015), 50–53; Donald V. Smiley, "Canada and the Quest for a National Policy," *Canadian Journal of Political Science* 8, no. 1 (March 1975): 40–62.

10 *Hamilton Spectator*, "Ambitious City Gives Movement Fine Support."

11 Minutes of the Meeting of the Hamilton and Brantford Branch Executive Committee, August 29, 1930, vol. 18, CMA fonds, MG 28 I 230, LAC.

12 Report of the Executive Committee to the Hamilton and Brantford Branch, May 3, 1935, vol. 19, CMA fonds, MG 28 I 230, LAC.

13 *Hamilton Spectator*, "Choose Gifts that Give Canadians Jobs!," December 1, 1930.

14 *Hamilton Spectator*, "Canadian Gifts," December 1, 1930; *Hamilton Spectator*, "Buy Now," November 11, 1930.

15 Joseph Pigott, president, et al., *Annual Report of the Hamilton Chamber of Commerce, April 1st 1932 to March 31st 1933* (Hamilton, Ontario: Hamilton Chamber of Commerce, 1933), 1–2, Hamilton Chamber of Commerce Papers, Local History and Archives Division, Hamilton Public Library, Hamilton.

16 Sarah Elvins, *Sales and Celebrations: Retailing and Regional Identity in Western New York, 1920–1940* (Athens, Ohio: Ohio University Press, 2004), 106–38.

17 Robert Douglas, president, et al., *Annual Report of the Hamilton Chamber of Commerce, April 1st 1931 to March 31st 1932* (Hamilton, Ontario: Hamilton Chamber of Commerce, 1932), 16–17, Hamilton Chamber of Commerce Papers.

18 *Hamilton Herald*, "Hamilton Day," October 27, 1931.

19 *Hamilton Herald*, "Wednesday to See 100,000 Shoppers in Search of Bargains," October 24, 1931.

20 *Labor News*, "The Anti-Chain Store News, Published for the Best Interest of Our People," September 28, 1931.

21 *Labor News*, "Store vs. Independent Merchant," September 28, 1931. The fight for independent stores has broader roots in the fight against chain department and grocery stores in both Canada and the United States. Mark Levine, *The Great A&P and the Struggle for Small Business in America* (New York City: Macmillan, 2011); Donica Belisle, *Retail Nation: Department Stores and the Making of Modern Canada* (Vancouver: UBC Press, 2011). However, the connection between supporting local producers and independent stores is not made in these cases.

22 Douglas, *Annual Report of the Hamilton Chamber of Commerce, April 1st 1931 to March 31st 1932*, 16–17.

23 Charles Peebles, president, et al., *Annual Report of the Hamilton Chamber of Commerce, April 1st 1934 to March 31st 1935* (Hamilton, Ontario: Hamilton Chamber of Commerce, 1935), 5, Hamilton Chamber of Commerce Papers.

24 Joan Sangster, *Earning Respect: the Lives of Working Women in "Small-Town" Ontario, 1920–1960* (Toronto: University of Toronto Press, 1995).

25 Carolyn M. Goldstein, *Creating Consumers: Home Economists in Twentieth-Century America* (Chapel Hill: University of North Carolina Press, 2012), 1–20; David Monod, *Store Wars: Shopkeepers and the Culture of Mass Marketing, 1890–1939* (Toronto: University of Toronto Press, 1996), 196–200.

26 Janet Inman, letter to the editor, *Hamilton Spectator*, December 1, 1937; Isabel Malloy, letter to the editor, *Hamilton Spectator*, May 5, 1938.

27 *Hamilton Spectator*, "She Shops at Home before She Buys," December 14, 1930.

28 *Hamilton Herald*, "ACT!," November 19, 1930; *Hamilton Spectator*, "ACT!," November 20, 1930. A similar ad ran on December 3, which read "We'll work for prosperity!" and featured a stereotypical workman with a wrench in his hands and his sleeves rolled up. These two ads clearly delineated the expected gendered roles Hamiltonians should live by in the Depression. *Hamilton Herald*, "We'll Work for Prosperity!," December 3, 1930.

29 Quebec's government and business owners launched similar protectionist campaigns. Their "achat chez nous" campaigns were based on protecting a shared language and culture against Anglo-Canadian or immigrant businesses, especially the growing number of Jewish-owned businesses, rather than a localized protection of production. James W. St. G. Walker, *"Race," Rights, and the Law in the Supreme Court of Canada: Historical Case Studies* (Waterloo, Ontario: Wilfrid Laurier University Press, 2006), 188.

30 Nora-Frances Henderson, "Women Understand the Spirit," *Hamilton Herald*, July 23, 1930.

31 Motion Regarding Women and Relief, January 18, 1933, file 1, vol. 60, National Council of Women fonds, MG 28 I 25, LAC.

32 Kirkpatrick, "Hamilton, Canada: A City of Opportunity."

33 John Peebles, Mayor, speaking to the City of Hamilton, City Council, *Minutes of Hamilton City Council, 1933* (Hamilton, Ontario: Hamilton City Council, 1934), April 25, 1933.

34 Herbert Wilton, Mayor, speaking to the City of Hamilton, City Council, *Minutes of Hamilton City Council, 1934* (Hamilton, Ontario: Hamilton City Council, 1935), May 29, 1934.

35 *Hamilton Spectator*, "Empire Preferences Keeping Thousands at Work Here," October 8, 1933.

36 *Hamilton Spectator*, "Buy Home Products," October 17, 1933.

6: MAKING MONEY IN HARD TIMES

1 Karl H. Starkweather to Professor Irving Fisher, February 13, 1933, Plymouth, Michigan, Irving Fisher Collection, New York Public Library. Aided by his assistant Hans Cohrssen, Fisher maintained correspondence about scrip with representatives from five hundred communities across the country. Cohrssen sent Starkweather materials about how to start a scrip plan.

2 For more on the role of individual consumers in combatting the economy, see Sarah Elvins, *Sales and Celebrations: Retailing and Regional Identity in Western New York State, 1920–1940* (Athens, Ohio: Ohio University Press, 2004), 110–12.

3 "Stamp-Scrip Remedy," *Syracuse Herald*, February 19, 1932.

4 Donna Fisher, "Family Life in Nyack Is Suspended as 'Trade-itis' Epidemic Sweeps Town," *New York World Telegram*, December 22, 1932.

5 "Barter Movement Spreads in South," *Washington Evening Star*, January 23, 1933, A-6; "Southwest is Also Trying Barter Plan," *The Bee* (Danville, VA), January 24, 1933, 3.

6 Joel W. C. Harper, "Scrip and Other Forms of Local Money" (PhD diss., University of Chicago, 1948); Wayne Weishaar and Wayne W. Parrish, *Men Without Money* (New York: G.P. Putnam's Sons, 1933), Loren Gatch, "Local Money in the United States during the Great Depression," *Essays in Economic & Business History*, 26 (2008): 47–61.

7 "Barter Plan Being Put on Solid Basis," *Christian Science Monitor*, January 14, 1933, 1.

8 Malcolm Ross, "Ohio Barter Plan Began in College, *New York Times*, January 22, 1933, E6.

9 "The Growing Barter-and-Exchange Movement," *Literary Digest*, February 11, 1933, 19.

10 "New Bartering Plan to Extend Over Wide Area," *Christian Science Monitor*, January 17, 1933, 1.

11 George Tselos, "Self-Help and Sauerkraut: The Organized Unemployed, Inc., of Minneapolis," *Minnesota History* 45 (1977): 306–20.

12 "Organized Unemployed, Inc. Minneapolis, Minnesota," typescript manuscript produced by the Organized Unemployed, n.d., 3, George Tselos Collection, Minnesota Historical Society, St. Paul, Minnesota.

13 Darragh Aldrich, "Putting the Town on the Potato Standard," *Household Magazine*, April 1933, 14.

14 J. B. Farber and Clyde W. Buell, "Cooperative Self-Help in Minnesota and the United States," a research project sponsored by the Minnesota Department of Dairy and Food, June 1935, Minnesota Historical Society.

15 Hector Lazo, "Scrip and Barter: Their Use and Service," bulletin prepared by the Assistant Chief, Marketing Service Division, Bureau of Foreign and Domestic Commerce, Department of Commerce, 1933, typescript manuscript, Rare Books, Library of Congress, 1.

16 Silvio Gesell, *The Natural Economic Order* (Berlin, 1916).

17 Sarah Elvins, "Scrip Money and Slump Cures: Iowa's Experiments with Alternative Currency during the Great Depression," *Annals of Iowa* 64, no. 3 (Summer 2005): 221–45; Elvins, "Stamp Scrip in the Great Depression: Lessons for Community Currency for Today?" *International Journal of Community Currency Research* 14 (2010): A29–45; Hugo Godschalk, "Does Demurrage Matter for Complementary Currencies?" *International Journal of Community Currency Research* 16 (2012): D58–69.

18 *The Hawarden Centennial, 1887–1987: One Hundred Years on the Right Track* (Hawarden, Iowa: Le Mars Daily Sentinel, 1987), 905.

19 Loren Gatch, "The Professor and a Paper Panacea: Irving Fisher and the Stamp Scrip Movement of 1932–1934," *Paper Money* 260 (March–April 2009): 125–42.

20 Charles Zylstra to Irving Fisher, Hawarden Iowa, December 31, 1932, Irving Fisher Collection, New York Public Library.

21 Irving Fisher, *Stamp Scrip* (New York: Adelphi, 1933).

22 Fisher, *Stamp Scrip*, chapter 1.

23 "States & Cities: For Money," *Time*, January 9, 1933. Charles Zylstra told a version of this story in a piece in the *Hawarden Independent*, August 4, 1932, 2. Irving Fisher repeats the story again in *Stamp Scrip*, chapter 3.

24 "The Little Pink Trade Check," *Enid Events*, March 9, 1933. Cited in Loren Gatch, "Money Matters: The Stamp Scrip Movement in Depression-Era Oklahoma," *Chronicles of Oklahoma* 84, no. 3 (Fall 2006), 276.

25 Stuart Chase, "500,000 Turn to Use of 'Wooden Money,'" *New York Times*, January 15, 1933, E8.

26 Gatch, "The Professor and a Paper Panacea," 132.

27 "Scrip Dollars Circulated in Evanston, Ill.; Merchants Back Issue and New Aid to City," *New York Times*, December 29, 1932, 20.

28 "Tax-Anticipation Scrip Shows Up Best," *American City*, June 1932, 93.

29 "Back Barter in Harlem," *New York Times*, January 10, 1933, 40.

30 "Council Votes Issuance of Scrip to Meet City Pay Roll," *Atlanta Constitution*, December 13, 1932, 1.

31 Gatch, "Money Matters," 263.

32 Charles Zylstra to Irving Fisher, October 28, 1932, Irving Fisher Papers, New York Public Library.

33 Weishaar and Parrish, *Men Without Money*, 49.

34 Weishaar and Parrish, *Men Without Money*, 5.

35 Elvins, *Sales and Celebrations*, 106–38.

36 "Look! You Keep a String on Every Dollar You Spend at Home" (advertisement by the Red Card Merchants), *Key West Citizen*, April 10, 1932, 6.

37 Bankhead-Pettengill Bill, February 7, 1933. It was presented but not passed by Congress.

38 "Scrip Problems," *Business Week*, July 22, 1933, 13.

39 Gatch, "The Professor and a Paper Panacea," 138.

40 Farber and Buell, "Cooperative Self-Help in Minnesota and the United States," 35–36.

41 "Exchange Born in Hard Times Will Liquidate," *Washington Post*, August 16, 1933, 12.

42 The classic study of the persistence of consumer culture's messages even during the Depression is Roland Marchand, *Advertising the American Dream: Making Way for Modernity, 1920–1940* (Berkeley: University of California Press, 1985).

43 Gerald Goss, "'No Handouts for Us,' Say Hundreds to Whom Self-Help Exchange Means New Hope," *Washington Post*, December 31, 1939, E3.

44 Weishaar and Parrish, *Men Without Money*, 111.

45 Jerome Blanc, "Classifying 'CCs': Community, Complementary, and Local Currencies," *International Journal of Community Currency Research* 15 (2011): 4–10.

46 Thomas Greco, *Money: Understanding and Creating Alternatives to Legal Tender* (White River Junction, VT: Chelsea Green Publishing, 2001); Gwendolyn Hallsmith and Bernard Lietaer, *Creating Wealth: Growing Local Economies with Local Currencies* (Gabriola Island, BC: New Society Publishers, 2011).

47 Prominent local scrip programs in the United States include the BerkShares of Massachusetts, the Ithaca, NY, Hours program, and the Bay Bucks of Traverse City, Michigan. For a sense of some current experiments in local currency, see the *International Journal of Community Currency*, available online at ijccr.net. Another resource for information about scrip and barter exchanges is the Schumacher Center for a New Economics, centerforneweconomics.org.

7: PROTECTING THE "GUINEA PIG CHILDREN"

1 Histories of American interwar advertising, including anti-advertising activism, include: Lawrence B. Glickman, *Buying Power: A History of Consumer Activism in America* (Chicago: University of Chicago Press, 2009); Pamela Walker Laird, *Advertising Progress: American Business and the Rise of Consumer Marketing* (Baltimore: Johns Hopkins University Press, 1998); Roland Marchand, *Advertising the American Dream: Making Way for Modernity 1920–1940* (Berkeley: University of California Press, 1985); Kathy Newman, *Radio Active: Advertising and Consumer Activism, 1935–1947* (Berkeley: University of California Press, 2004); Susan Smulyan, *Selling Radio: The Commercialization of American Broadcasting, 1920–1934* (Washington: Smithsonian Institution Press, 1994); Inger L. Stole, *Advertising on Trial: Consumer Activism and Corporate Public Relations in the 1930s* (Chicago: University of Illinois Press, 2006); and Susan Strasser, *Satisfaction Guaranteed: The Making of the American Mass Market* (New York: Pantheon Books, 1989).

2 This paradigm shift can be witnessed in the sheer quantity of marketing to children by the 1930s. See Lisa Jacobson, *Raising Consumers: Children and the American Mass Market in the Early Twentieth Century* (New York: Columbia University Press, 2004) and Kyle Asquith, "Join the Club: Food Advertising, 1930s Children's Popular Culture, and Brand Socialization," *Popular Communication* 12 (2014): 17–31.

3 E. Evalyn Grumbine, *Reaching Juvenile Markets: How to Advertise, Sell, and Merchandise Through Boys and Girls* (New York: McGraw-Hill, 1938), 197.

4 Minutes of Representatives Meeting, April 16, 1930, box 2, J. Walter Thompson Staff Meeting Minutes, Rare Book, Manuscript, and Special Collections Library, Duke University.

5 Glickman, *Buying Power*, 192.

6 Stole, *Advertising on Trial*, 174.

7 Peter Morrell, *Poisons, Potions and Profits: The Antidote to Radio Advertising* (New York: Knight, 1937), 9.

8 Rachel Lyn Palmer and Isidore M. Alpher, *40,000,000 Guinea Pig Children* (New York: Vanguard Press, 1937), 3.

9 Warren B. Dygert, *Radio as an Advertising Medium* (New York: McGraw-Hill, 1939), 80.

10 The original book was also published by Vanguard Press. Ruth Brindze's story is republished in Julie L. Mickenberg and Philip Nel, ed. *Tales For Little Rebels* (New York: New York University Press, 2008), 64–68.

11 "Broadcasters Act to Curb 'Bogeyman,'" *New York Times*, February 28, 1933, 21.

12 "The Children's Hour," *The Nation*, April 5, 1933, 362.

13 Clara Savage Littledale, "Better Programs for Children," *Parents' Magazine*, May 1933, 13.

14 A. Mann, "Children's Crime Programs," *Scribner's*, October 1934, 244–46.

15 Larry Wolters, "Juvenile Show Sponsors Meet a Threat in East," *Chicago Tribune*, February 17, 1935, N6.

16 "Adopt Radio Formula For the Children," *New York Times*, December 19, 1939, 21.

17 Joel Spring, *Educating the Consumer-Citizen: A History of the Marriage of Schools, Advertising, and Media* (Mahwah, NJ: Lawrence Erlbaum, 2003), 121.

18 Scott Bruce and Bill Crawford, *Cerealizing America: The Unsweetened Story of American Breakfast Cereal* (Boston: Faber and Faber, 1995), 84.

19 See Stole, *Advertising on Trial*, 138–58 for an account of this legislation.

20 "New Rules for Food and Drugs," *Consumers Guide*, July 11, 1938, 3–7.

21 "Candy," *Consumers' Research Bulletin*, December 1936, 17–19.

22 "So You Have a Sweet Tooth?," *Consumers Guide*, January 30, 1939, 19.

23 In 2006, North American children's food advertisers created the "Children's Food and Beverage Advertising Initiative." This self-regulatory effort is overseen by the Council of Better Business Bureaus (in the United States) and Advertising Standards Canada (in Canada).

24 Bill Jeffery, "The Supreme Court of Canada's Appraisal of the 1980 Ban on Advertising to Children in Quebec: Implications for 'Misleading' Advertising Elsewhere," *Loyola of Los Angeles Law Review* 39 (2006), 246.

25 Glickman, *Buying Power*, 12.

26 Robert W. McChesney, *Telecommunications, Mass Media, and Democracy: The Battle for the Control over U.S. Broadcasting, 1928–1935* (New York: Oxford University Press, 1993), 115.

8: OUR ECONOMIC WAY OUT

1 Anne Meis Knupfer, *Food Co-ops in America* (Ithaca: Cornell University Press, 2013).

2 Jessica Gordon Nembhard's *Collective Courage: A History of African American Cooperative Economic Thought and Practice* (University Park: Penn State Press, 2014) provides a rare and detailed analysis of black consumers' co-operation. Lizabeth Cohen's *A Consumers' Republic: The Politics of Mass Consumption in Postwar America* (New York: Alfred A. Knopf, 2003) and Barbara Ransby's *Ella Baker and the Black Freedom Movement: A Radical Democratic Vision* (Chapel Hill: University of North Carolina Press, 2003) consider the place of black consumers' co-operation within the context of early twentieth-century American consumer activism and the life of civil rights activist Ella Baker, respectively.

3 Cheryl Lynn Greenberg, *Or Does It Explode? Black Harlem in the Great Depression* (New York: Oxford University Press, 1991).

4 Robert E. Weems, *Desegregating the Dollar: African American Consumerism in the Twentieth Century* (New York: New York University Press, 1998).

5 Wayne L. Villamez and John T. Beggs, "Black Capitalism and Black Inequality: Some Sociological Considerations," *Social Forces* 63, no. 1 (1984): 117–44.

6 T. Clair Drake, "Why Not Cooperate?" *Opportunity* 14 (August 1936), 233.

7 For a summary of Du Bois's position: W. E. B. Du Bois, "The Economic Future of the Negro," *Publication of the American Economic Association* (New York: Macmillan, 1906); "The Class Struggle," *The Crisis* 22, no. 4 (1921), 151–52; "Marxism and the

Negro Problem," *The Crisis* 40, no. 5 (1933), 103–4; "A Negro Nation within the Nation," *Current History* 42 (1935): 265–70. For a review of race and the American labour movement, see Philip S. Foner, *Organized Labor and the Black Worker* (New York: Praeger, 1974).

8 W. E. B. Du Bois, "The Immediate Program of the American Negro," *The Crisis* 9, no. 6 (1915), 310–12.

9 W. E. B. Du Bois, "Cooperation," *The Crisis* 15, no. 1 (1917), 10.

10 W. E. B. Du Bois, "A Negro Nation within the Nation."

11 W. E. B. Du Bois, "The Economic Future of the Negro."

12 W. E. B. Du Bois, "Segregation," *The Crisis* 41, no. 1 (1934), 20.

13 W. E. B. Du Bois, "Cooperation," *The Crisis* 16, no. 6 (1918), 268.

14 W. E. B. Du Bois to the Twentieth Century Club, February 13, 1941, MS312, W. E. B. Du Bois Papers, Special Collections and University Archives, University of Massachusetts, Amherst.

15 George Schuyler, "An Appeal to Young Negroes," n.d., box 2, folder 3, Ella Baker Papers, Schomburg Center for Research in Black Culture, New York Public Library, New York.

16 "Schuyler Heard at Brookwood College," *New York Amsterdam News*, August 5, 1931.

17 "Schuyler Heads Up League," *Pittsburgh Courier*, October 24, 1931.

18 "Cooperative Movements Point Way, Says Schuyler," *New York Amsterdam News*, December 23, 1931.

19 H. M. Johnson, "Defends Schuyler on Liberia, 'Coop' Issues," *Pittsburgh Courier*, March 10, 1934; George S. Schuyler, "Views and Reviews," *Pittsburgh Courier*, August 18, 1934.

20 Bertram B. Fowler, "Miracle in Gary: The Negro Gropes toward Economic Equality," *Forum and Century*, September 1936, 135–38.

21 J. L. Reddix, "The Negro Finds a Way to Economic Equality," *Consumers' Cooperation* 11, no. 10 (1935): 173–75.

22 Fowler, "Miracle in Gary."

23 W. C. Matney to W. E. B. Du Bois, April 22, 1936, MS312, W. E. B. Du Bois Papers.

24 "Bluefield Students Conduct Practical Business Course," *Afro-American* (Baltimore, MD), April 23, 1927.

25 Chappy Gardner, "350 Harlem Families Operate Grocery Stores: Educational System Reaching Masses," *Pittsburgh Courier*, July 6, 1935; "Many Groups Merge to Consider Coops," *New York Amsterdam News*, November 5, 1938; Ellen Tarry, "Sugar Hill Purchases 'Sugar' at Consumers' Coop," *New York Amsterdam News*, September 12, 1942.

26 Tarry, "Sugar Hill Purchases 'Sugar' at Consumers' Coop."

27 Earl Ofari, *The Myth of Black Capitalism* (New York: Monthly Review Press, 1970).

28 W. E. B. Du Bois, "Reconstruction," *The Crisis* 18, no. 3 (1919), 130–31.

29 Margedant Peters, "Little Ohio Town Sees Coop Work Miracles," *Chicago Defender*, March 27, 1943.

30 "Harlem's Oldest Cooperative to Expand," *New York Amsterdam News*, October 15, 1949.

31 Venice Spraggs, "Big D.C. Coop Food Store Open after Long Fight," *Chicago Defender*, August 5, 1944.

32 John Hope, "Rochdale Cooperation among Negroes," *Phylon* 1, no. 1 (1940): 39–52.

33 Robert Smith, "Labor's Front," *New York Amsterdam News*, September 19, 1942.

34 Samuel Lloyd Myers, "Consumers' Cooperation: A Plan for the Negro" (master's thesis, Boston University, 1942).

35 Lawrence Mishel et al., *The State of Working America*, 12th ed. (Ithaca: Cornell University Press, 2012).

36 Kelly M. Bower et al., "The Intersection of Neighbourhood Racial Segregation, Poverty, and Urbanicity and its Impact on Food Store Availability in the United States," *Preventative Medicine* 58 (2014): 33–39.

9: NOT BUYING IT

1 Rafael Medoff, *Blowing the Whistle On Genocide: Josiah E. Dubois, Jr., and the Struggle for a US Response to the Holocaust* (West Lafayette: Purdue University, 2009), 6.

2 While scholars emphasize the absence of dedicated coverage, writers published thousands of reports about the destruction of European Jewry. See Laurel Leff, *Buried by the Times: The Holocaust and America's Most Important Newspaper* (New York: Cambridge University Press, 2005), 2–3.

3 Michael Birdwell, *Celluloid Soldiers: The Warner Bros. Campaign against Nazism* (New York: New York University Press, 1999), 25–30.

4 Richard A. Hawkins, "'Hitler's Bitterest Foe': Samuel Untermyer and the Boycott of Nazi Germany, 1933–1938," *American Jewish History* 93, no. 1 (2007): 21–50.

5 Theodore Hamerow, *Why We Watched: Europe, America, and the Holocaust* (New York: W. W. Norton, 2008), 389.

6 Lynne Olson, *Those Angry Days: Roosevelt, Lindbergh, and America's Fight Over World War II, 1939–1941* (New York: Random House, 2013), 129.

7 Victoria Saker Woeste, "Insecure Equality: Louis Marshall, Henry Ford, and the Problem of Defamatory Anti-Semitism, 1920–29," *Journal of American History* 91, no. 3 (2004): 877–905.

8 Carole Fink, *Defending the Rights of Others: The Great Powers, the Jews, and International Minority Protection, 1878–1938* (New York: Cambridge University Press, 2004), 54.

9 Pauline Maier, *From Resistance to Revolution: Colonial Radicals and the Development of American Opposition to Britain, 1765–1776* (New York: W. W. Norton), 73.

10 William Lockwood, "Economics of a Silk Boycott," *Far Eastern Survey* 6, no. 22 (1937): 249–51.

11 Lawrence B. Glickman, *Buying Power: A History of Consumer Activism in America* (Chicago: University of Chicago Press, 2009), 226, 241.

12 As quoted in Glickman, *Buying Power*, 225.

13 For discussion of this question see Nathan Becker, "The Anti-Japanese Boycott in the United States," *Far Eastern Survey* 8, no. 5 (1939), 51.

14 Michael Denning, *The Cultural Front: The Laboring of American Culture in the Twentieth Century* (London: Verso, 1998), 129.

15 Michael Zalampas, *Adolf Hitler and the Third Reich in American Magazines, 1923–1939* (Bowling Green: Bowling Green State University Popular Press, 1989), 168.

16 "Who Stands Behind Hitler?" *Nation Magazine*, February 22, 1933, 197.

17 "Leave the Jewish Problem Alone," *Christian Century*, April 25, 1934, 556.

18 David Kennedy, *Over Here: The First World War and American Society* (New York: Oxford University Press, 1980), 54–55.

19 "Our Protest Parade," *The Jewish Veteran*, April 1933, 8–9.

20 "Protest on Hitler Growing in Nation," *New York Times*, March 23, 1933.

21 Louis Anthes, "Publicly Deliberative Drama: The 1934 Mock Trial of Adolf Hitler for "Crimes against Civilization," *American Journal of Legal History* 42, no. 4 (1998), 400–401.

22 "Takes Effect Saturday," *New York Times*, March 29, 1933.

23 "Ban on Jews Spreads," *New York Times*, March 28, 1933.

24 Edwin Black, *The Transfer Agreement: The Untold Story of the Secret Agreement Between the Third Reich and Jewish Palestine* (New York: MacMillan, 1984), 36.

25 Hannah Ahlheim, *"Deutsche, kauft nicht bei Juden!" Antisemitismus und politischer Boykott in Deutschland 1924 bis 1935* (Göttingen: Wallstein Verlag, 2011), esp. chapter 3.

26 Melvin Urofsky, *A Voice That Spoke For Justice: The Life and Times of Stephen S. Wise* (Albany: State University of New York Press, 1982), 266.

27 William Orbach, "Shattering the Shackles of Powerlessness: The Debate Surrounding the Anti-Nazi Boycott of 1933–1941," *Modern Judaism* 2, no. 2 (1982), 155.

28 Urofsky, *Voice*, 268.

29 "Nazi Attacks Stir British Catholics," *New York Times*, March 24, 1933.

30 "Ban on Jews Spreads."

31 Three years later, the so-called Battle of Cable Street occurred in this district, pitting pro- and anti-fascist forces against each other. See Iain Channing, "Freedom of Expression from the 'Age of Extremes' to the 'Age of Terror': Reflections on Public Order Law and the Legal Responses to Political and Religious Extremism in 1930s Britain and the Post 9/11 Era," *Law, Crime and History* 1, no. 2 (2011), 35.

32 As quoted in Sharon Gewitz, "Anglo-Jewish Responses to Nazi Germany 1933–39: The Anti-Nazi Boycott and the Board of Deputies of British Jews," *Journal of Contemporary History* 26, no. 2 (1991), 260.

33 "Nazi Attacks Stir British Catholics."

34 Ben Urwand, *The Collaboration: Hollywood's Pact With Hitler* (Cambridge: Belknap Press of Harvard University Press, 2013), 19.

35 Arnd Krüger, "United States of America: The Crucial Battle," in *The Nazi Olympics: Sport, Politics, and Appeasement in the 1930s*, ed. Arnd Krüger and W. J. Murray (Urbana: University of Illinois Press, 2003), 53.

36 As quoted in Gewitz, "Anglo-Jewish Responses," 262.

37 Karl Schleunes, *The Twisted Road to Auschwitz* (Urbana: University of Illinois Press, 1970), 140.

38 "Jewish Reaction on Reich," *New York Times*, May 15, 1933.

39 Schacht's support for Nazism and allegiance to Nazi leaders steadily deteriorated. See Harold James, "Schacht's Attempted Defection from Hitler's Germany," *Historical Journal* 30, no. 3 (1987), 730.

40 Moshe Gottlieb, "The First of April Boycott and the Reaction of the American Jewish Community," *American Jewish Historical Quarterly* 57, no. 4 (1968), 516.

41 Joseph Broadman to R. H. Macy and Co., November 21, 1933, box 20, "Miscellaneous," Joint Boycott Council of the American Jewish Congress and Jewish Labor Committee, Manuscripts and Archives Division, New York Public Library, New York (hereafter Joint Boycott Papers).

42 Edwin Marks to Joseph Broadman, November 23, 1933, box 20, "Miscellaneous," Joint Boycott Papers.

43 Broadman to R. H. Macy and Co., November 21, 1933, box 20, "Miscellaneous," Joint Boycott Papers.

44 Melissa Klapper, "'Those by Whose Side We Have Labored': American Jewish Women and the Peace Movement between the Wars," *Journal of American History* 97, no. 3 (2010), 653.

45 Moshe Gottlieb, "In the Shadow of War: The American Anti-Nazi Movement in 1939–1941," *American Jewish History Quarterly* 62, no. 2 (1972): 146–61.

46 "Woolworth Stores Handle Nazi Goods," "Woolworth," box 12, "Miscellaneous," Joint Boycott Papers.

47 Dan J. Puckett, "Reporting on the Holocaust: The View from Jim Crow Alabama," *Holocaust and Genocide Studies* 25, no. 2 (2011): 219–51.

48 "Radio Address," June 14, 1934, box 20, "Miscellaneous," Joint Boycott Papers.

49 Benjamin Alpers, *Dictators, Democracy and American Public Culture: Envisioning the Totalitarian Enemy, 1920s–1950s* (Chapel Hill: University of North Carolina Press, 2003), 17, 38.

50 Loring Black, *Congressional Record*, H 73, 1st sess. (May 12, 1933), 3373.

51 Emanuel Celler, *Congressional Record*, H 73, 1st sess. (April 20, 1933), 2019.

52 Samuel Untermyer to Samuel Dickstein, January 12, 1934, box 4/2. Samuel Dickstein Papers, 1923–44, American Jewish Archives, Cincinnati (hereafter Dickstein Papers).

53 Mrs. Mark Harris to Richard Rollins, October 18, 1937, box 4/2, Dickstein Papers.

54 "For Immediate Release," April 13, 1938, box 4/2, Dickstein Papers.

55 "Declaration of Adherence," box 20, "Miscellaneous," Joint Boycott Papers.

56 For discussion of Polish boycott activity see "Polish Jews Condemn Germany," *New York Times*, March 21, 1933. For South Africa see "African Jewish Board of Deputies to Joint Boycott Council," August 16, 1938, box 5, "S," Joint Boycott Papers. For Latin America see "II Minutes: January 1936–1940," March 3, 1939, box 20 "Mixed Materials," Joint Boycott Papers.

57 "Peace and Democracy Rally," March 15, 1937, box 4, "P," Joint Boycott Papers.

58 Robert Marcus to Marion Newman, March 6, 1939, Woolworth," box 12, "Miscellaneous," Joint Boycott Papers.

59 Joseph Tenenbaum to Nathan Braun, January 30, 1936, box 5, "W," Joint Boycott Papers.

60 Max Goldberg to Joseph Tenenbaum, April 17, 1936, box 11, "Excerpts," Joint Boycott Papers.

61 Henry Ashby Turner, *General Motors and the Nazis: The Struggle for Control of Opel, Europe's Biggest Carmaker* (New Haven: Yale University Press, 2005), 152.

62 As late as 1939, James Mooney, president of the company's overseas operations, defended Hitler's "right to regain for his people the things they lost" following the First World War. Turner, *General Motors and the Nazis*, 107.

63 See, for example, Douglas Miller, *You Can't Do Business With Hitler* (Boston: Little, Brown, 1941).

64 Joseph Tenenbaum to Alfred Sloane [sic], March 11, 1936, box 11, "Excerpts," Joint Boycott Papers.

65 Alfred Sloan to Joseph Tenenbaum, March 23, 1936, box 11, "Excerpts," Joint Boycott Papers.

66 E. C. Riley to Joseph Tenenbaum, May 12, 1936, box 11, "Excerpts," Joint Boycott Papers.

67 E. C. Riley to Joseph Tenenbaum, May 12, 1936, box 11, "Excerpts," Joint Boycott Papers.

68 As quoted in Orbach, "Shattering," 162.

69 Richard Breitman and Alan Lichtman, *FDR and the Jews* (Cambridge: Belknap Press of Harvard University Press, 2013), 59, 116.

10: CANADA'S CITIZEN HOUSEWIVES

1 Temma Kaplan, *Taking Back the Streets: Women, Youth, and Direct Democracy* (Berkeley: University of California Press, 2004), 46.

2 See, for instance, Tarah Brookfield, *Cold War Comforts: Canadian Women, Child Safety, and Global Insecurity, 1945–1975* (Waterloo, Ontario: Wilfred Laurier University Press, 2012) and Brian T. Thorn, *From Right to Left: Women's Political Activism in Postwar Canada* (Vancouver: UBC Press, 2016).

3 "Housewives Association Starts War on Prices," *Evening Telegram*, November 9, 1937, 21; "Housewives Plan 'High Prices' Boycott: Plan City-Wide Union To Fight Food Costs Control Board Told," *Toronto Daily Star*, November 3, 1937, 1.

4 Alice Cooke, "Weekly Letter," *Daily Clarion*, November 16, 1938.

5 Pat Chytyk, interview by author, February 27, 1997, Sudbury, Ontario.

6 Alice Cooke, "Housewives' Association," *Daily Clarion*, May 7, 1938.

7 "Keep Controls or Prices May Rise 50 P.C.—Gordon," *Toronto Daily Star*, November 5, 1946, 7.

8 Peter S. McInnis, "Planning Prosperity: Canadians Debate Postwar Reconstruction," in *Uncertain Horizons: Canadians and Their World in 1945*, ed. Greg Donaghy (Ottawa: Canadian Committee for the History of the Second World War, 1997), 231–60.

9 "Curb Corporation Profits, Housewives' Brief Demands," *Toronto Daily Star*, May 31, 1947, 15.

10 "Panic-Buying of Meat Starts; Back Market Terms Out of Control," *Globe and Mail*, April 19, 1946, 1–2.

11 *Canada Year Book 1947–1948*.

12 Anne Ross to James Gardiner, Minister of Agriculture, December 23, 1946, file 1, Anne Ross papers, 5941, Provincial Archives of Manitoba (PAM), Winnipeg.

13 Mrs. E. Molinski, President, the Mothers' Club of All People's Church to the Housewives' Association, September 28, 1946, Ross papers, file 5, PAM.

14 "Price Control Debate Billed for First Week of 6 Months' Session," *Globe and Mail*, January 24, 1948, 3.

15 "Prices Push Incomes below Family Health 'Danger Line,'" *Globe and Mail*, January 8, 1948, 1–2.

16 "The Congress Memorandum," *Canadian Unionist*, April 5, 1946, 79–82; Brief to the City of Regina Council, "Reduce the Cost of Living," vol. 3466, Housewives and Consumers Association of Regina, 1946–52, RG 146, Library and Archives Canada (LAC), Ottawa.

17 "Believe They Got 'Brush-Off' Housewives Angry, Return Home," *Ottawa Citizen*, June 26, 1947 (clipping), 3353 supp. 1 vol. 1, Housewives and Consumers Federation of Canada (HCFC), RG 146 vol., LAC.

18 "Price War," *Time*, January 26, 1948; "Price War," *Time*, February 9, 1948.

19 "Price Control Possible, Up to House: Abbott," *Globe and Mail*, January 10, 1948, 1.

20 "Pork Prices Skid Some With Butchers Finding Stiff Buyer Resistance," *Globe and Mail*, January 10, 1948, 1–2; "Hit 'im again, Missus, 'We' are Winning!" editorial cartoon, *Toronto Star*, January 13, 1948, 6.

21 Press release, Housewives Consumer Association, February 20, 1948, HCFC, LAC.

22 "Women Back Milk Price Freeze, Propose CCW Leader for Board," *Canadian Tribune*, March 26, 1951 (clipping), HCFC, LAC.

23 Donez Xiques, "Early Influences," in *Challenging Territory: The Writing of Margaret Laurence*, ed. Christian Erich Reigel (Edmonton: University of Alberta Press, 1997), 187–210.

24 Mrs. Mary Aveline, letter to the editor, *Globe and Mail*, December 14, 1942, 6.

25 *Act Now! Tell Ottawa Prices Must be Held!* (Ottawa: CCF National Office, 1948).

26 "'Million Names' Drive Backed by Coldwell, Issue Convention Called," *Canadian Tribune*, February 28, 1948 (clipping), HCFC, LAC.

27 Robert Bothwell and William Kilbourn, *C.D. Howe: A Biography* (Toronto: McClelland and Stewart, 1979), 200.

28 "Biggest Petition in History Demands King Act on Prices," *Canadian Tribune*, April 17, 1948 (clipping), vol. 3440, part 2a, Housewives Consumers Association, Toronto, RG 146, LAC.

29 Joy Parr, *Domestic Goods: The Material, the Moral, and the Economic in the Postwar Years* (Toronto: University of Toronto Press, 1999), 64–83.

30 "Housewives Consumers Association," *House of Commons Debates*, April 14, 1948, 2952.

31 "Wives' League Rebuffed as Dupe of Communists; Butter Speculation Bared," *Montreal Gazette*, April 14, 1948 (clipping), HCFC, LAC.

32 Dominique Clément, *Canada's Rights Revolution: Social Movements and Social Change, 1937–82* (Vancouver: UBC Press, 2008), 40.

33 "Canadians Duped to Aid Red 5th Column," *Windsor Daily Star*, March 10, 1948, reprinted in *Halifax Herald*, March 13, 1948 (clipping), HCFC, LAC.

34 Ronald Williams, "Are Reds Behind Housewives?" *Financial Post*, April 24, 1948, 1, 3.

35 "Mr. Abbott Makes a Discovery," *Ottawa Journal*, April 16, 1948 (editorial).

36 Landon R. Y. Storrs, *The Second Red Scare and the Unmaking of the New Deal Left* (Princeton: Princeton University Press, 2013).

37 Veronica A. Wilson, "'Now You Are Alone': Anticommunism, Gender, and the Cold War Myths of Hede Massing and Whittaker Chambers," *Diplomatic History* 36, no. 4 (2012): 699–722; and "Elizabeth Bentley and Cold War Representation: Some Masks Not Dropped," *Intelligence and National Security* 14, no. 2 (1999): 49–69.

38 Deborah A. Gerson, "'Is Family Devotion Now Subversive?': Familialism against McCarthyism," in *Not June Cleaver: Women and Gender in Postwar America, 1945–1960*, ed. Joanne Meyerowitz (Philadelphia: Temple University Press, 1994), 151–76.

39 "Abbott Charges Housewives Inspired by Communists," *Ottawa Journal*, April 15, 1948 (clipping), HCFC, LAC.

40 Williams, "Are Reds Behind Housewives?"

41 Ronald Williams, "Are You a Stooge for a Communist?" *Chatelaine*, April 1949, 90–94.

42 Dan Azoulay, "'Ruthless in a Ladylike Way': CCF Women Confront the Postwar 'Communist Menace,'" *Ontario History* 89, no. 1 (1997): 23–52.

11: "THE CONSUMER GOES TO WAR"

1 Galbraith is quoted in Studs Terkel, *"The Good War": An Oral History of World War Two* (New York: Pantheon, 1984), 323. The emphasis on selfish consumption has been particularly prominent in Canada. See, for example, Graham Broad, *A Small Price to Pay: Consumer Culture on the Canadian Home Front, 1939–45* (Vancouver: UBC Press, 2013); Jeff Keshen, *Saints, Sinners, and Soldiers: Canada's Second World War* (Vancouver: UBC Press, 2004).

2 Lawrence B. Glickman's *Buying Power: A History of Consumer Activism in America* (Chicago: University of Chicago Press, 2009) passes lightly over the wartime period, but it is given a more central place in Meg Jacobs, *Pocketbook Politics: Eco-*

nomic Citizenship in Twentieth-Century America (Princeton: Princeton University Press, 2005) and Lizabeth Cohen, *A Consumers' Republic: The Politics of Mass Consumption in Postwar America* (New York: Knopf, 2003).

3 OPA Washington District Office, "How You Can Tell Top Legal Prices: The Wartime Consumer's Bill of Rights," Pamphlet, September 1943, Women's Adviser's File 1944–1946, box 41, file Labor Conferences, Office of Price Administration, Executive Offices, Labor Office, UD 98, RG 188, National Archives at College Park (NACP), Maryland.

4 On the twentieth-century consumer movement as a transnational phenomenon, see Matthew Hilton, *Prosperity for All: Consumer Activism in an Era of Globalization* (Ithaca: Cornell University Press, 2009).

5 The final chapter of Ware's 1942 book, *The Consumer Goes to War: A Guide to Victory on the Home Front* (New York: Funk & Wagnalls, 1942), was titled, "Shall We Win the Peace?"

6 The arguments in this chapter draw on Joseph Tohill's "'A Consumers' War': Price Control and Political Consumerism in the United States and Canada during World War II" (PhD diss., York University, 2012).

7 Ware, *The Consumer Goes to War*, 1–3.

8 Ware, *The Consumer Goes to War*, 224–41. On Caroline Ware's thought and activism, see Eleanor Capper, "Caroline Ware, Consumer Activism and American Democracy during the New Deal, 1933–45," *Cultural and Social History* 9, no. 1 (2012): 85–101.

9 Historians Meg Jacobs and Lizabeth Cohen largely ignore this internal conflict in their examination of the OPA's consumer protection efforts. See, for example, Jacobs, *Pocketbook Politics*; Cohen, *A Consumers' Republic*. Landon R. Y. Storrs, however, correctly suggests that the "state building from the bottom up" with which Jacobs credits OPA leaders actually "had to be forced on them by the women of the Consumer Division." Storrs, "Left-Feminism, the Consumer Movement, and Red Scare Politics in the United States, 1935–1960," *Journal of Women's History* 18, no. 3 (Fall 2006), 52–53.

10 "What Is Wrong with the OPA," *Newsweek*, and James A. Wechsler, "Citizen Hurst Fights for High Prices," *PM*, June 10, 1943, both in box 27, File O.P.A.–About Recent Price Control, Henderson Papers, Franklin Roosevelt Presidential Library.

11 Chester Bowles, *Promises to Keep: My Years in Public Life, 1941–1969* (New York: Harper & Row, 1971), 43–45.

12 Natalie Davis Spingarn, "Chester Bowles: A Crusader out of the Ranks of Business," *PM*, January 5, 1946, Portraits of OPA Officials, box 1, File Bowles–Biography etc., OPA, RG 188, Still Pictures Branch, NACP; Howard B. Schaffer, *Chester Bowles: New Dealer in the Cold War* (Cambridge, MA: Harvard University Press, 1993), 2–16.

13 Imogene H. Putnam, *Volunteers in OPA* (Washington: Office of Price Administration, 1947), 29, 32–33. See also "Policing of Prices Slated as Task for Local Boards," *New York Times*, April 28, 1942; "Trained Shoppers to Check for OPA," *New York Times*, May 1, 1942.

14 Putnam, *Volunteers in OPA*, 90.

15 W. B. Harvey (OWI Domestic Branch) to J. Latham (Program Manager, OWI Domestic Branch), "Government-Consumer Relations Regarding Rationing in Canada," Report, April 12, 1945, Records of the Deputy Director Maurice Hanson, PI 56 Entry 66 (Hanson Records), box 14, file Reports, Office of War Information (OWI), RG 208, NACP.

16 "Report of National Conference, 17–21 January 1944," Report, n.d., Consumer Branch Conferences, ser. 1240 Consumer Branch Records 1941–1947, vol. 1447, file A-10-29-11 v. 2, WPTB, RG 64, Library and Archives Canada, Ottawa.

17 Julie Guard has written extensively on the role of anticommunism in stifling the postwar consumer movement, including in her contribution to this volume. See especially her "Women Worth Watching: Radical Housewives in Cold War Canada," in *Whose National Security? Canadian State Surveillance and the Creation of Enemies*, ed. Gary William Kinsman, Dieter K. Buse, and Mercedes Steedman (Toronto: Between the Lines, 2000). On the American side, see Landon Storrs, *The Second Red Scare and the Unmaking of the New Deal Left* (Princeton: Princeton University Press, 2013).

12: FROM THE GREAT SOCIETY TO GIANT

1 Lawrence B. Glickman, *Buying Power: A History of Consumer Activism in America* (Chicago: University of Chicago Press, 2009), 27; Esther Peterson, "Consumer Representation in the White House," in *Consumer Activists: They Made a Difference, A History of Consumer Action Related by Leaders in the Consumer Movement*, ed. Erma Angevine (New York: Consumers Union, 1982); *Advertising Age*, April 17, 1972.

2 Esther Peterson and Winifred Conkling, *Restless: The Memoirs of Labor and Consumer Activist Esther Peterson* (Washington, DC: Caring Publications, 1995), 34–45, 75, 81, 94–114; Landon Storrs, *The Second Red Scare and the Unmaking of the New Deal Left* (Princeton: Princeton University Press, 2013).

3 See Daniel Horowitz, *The Anxieties of Affluence: Critiques of American Consumer Culture, 1939–79* (Boston: University of Massachusetts Press, 2004).

4 *Supermarket News*, April 24, 1972; Presidential Committee on Consumer Interests (PCCI), *Summary of Activities, 1964–67* (1967), 32, box 65, file 1246 (65/1246), Esther Peterson Papers, Radcliffe Institute (hereafter EP); "Consumer Affairs Departments in the Retail Food Industry: Voice for the Consumer Interest?" (1976), 12, EP74/1470.

5 Peterson, Democratic Party Platform Committee (August 15, 1964), EP65/1249.

6 Consumer Message to Congress (February 5, 1964), www.presidency.ucsb.edu/ws/?pid=26058.

7 Letter of transmittal, Peterson to Johnson, n.d., c. March 1967, EP65/1243.

8 Peterson, *Restless*, 119–22; Peterson to Johnson, January 15, 1965, EP65/1260; Peterson, "Consumer Representation," 204–6.

9 *Supermarket News*, October 24, 1966; Lizabeth Cohen, *A Consumers' Republic: The Politics of Mass Consumption in Postwar America* (New York: Vintage, 2004), 367–70.

10 *Grocer's Spotlight*, October 11, 1966; *New York Post*, October 28, 1966; C. Mauritz Erkkila to Peterson, November 22, 1966, EP66/1274.

11 Giant Supermarkets, *50 Years of Caring* (Washington DC: Giant, 1986), 59; Peterson, *Restless*, 130–32; Peterson to President, December 9, 1964, EP65/1260.

12 *Advertising Age*, January 16, 1967; "Draft Review," 7, EP65/1246; David Swankin and John Walsh, "Government Consumer Programs in Europe . . . Their Significance for the US," 1966, 23, EP65/1255.

13 Memos, March 20, 1967, April 5, 1967, EP65/1246; PCCI, *Summary of Activities*, 26–28, 38–40.

14 Storrs, *The Second Red Scare*; Meg Jacobs, *Pocketbook Politics: Economic Citizenship in Twentieth-Century America* (Princeton: Princeton University Press, 2007), 267.

15 Peterson, "Consumer Representation," 210.

16 Giant, *50 Years*, 20, 46–48; Forbes to Peterson, January 22, 1965, EP74/1471.

17 "Peterson, Inside, Looks Out," *Supermarket News*, September 21, 1970; Danzansky, September 20, 1974, EP75/1477; Note, September 3, 1976, EP75/1476; Peterson, *Restless*, 140–41.

18 *NCL Newsletter*, September 15, 1974; Domestic Affairs Task Force, January 1976, EP80/1581.

19 Peterson, John Hechinger paper, EP80/1582; Eizenstat to Pertschuk, July 29, 1976, EP80/1588.

20 Consumer Advisory Committee (CAC), November 15, 1975, EP75/1479; CAC, January 21, March 4, April 15, 1971, EP75/1480.

21 Giant, *Annual Report* 1971, 4; Giant, "Computer-Assisted Check-Out" (1975), EP74/1467; Peterson, "Consumer Participation in Business" in Angevine, *Consumer Activists*, 251; Severna Park, MD survey, February 1975, EP77/1532.

22 Giant, *Annual Report* 1974, 13; Consumer Action Taskforce, January 31, 1971, EP75/1473; Nutrition Group, n.d., EP76/1514; James Turner, *The Chemical Feast* (New York: Grossman, 1970); *Canning Trade*, March 8, 1971.

23 "What's This, Giant, a Follower?," November 11, 1974, EP77/1525.

24 Brenda Kelly, February 17, 1976, EP150/3520.

25 Forbes to Danzansky, October 7, 1970; Barnett to Peterson, September 18, 1970; Consumer Action Taskforce, October 6, 1970, EP75/1472; CAC, July 9, 1976, EP150/3522; Giant press release, December 19, 1972, EP74/1468.

26 CAC, January 9, 1976, EP150/3520; CAC, April 15, 1971, EP75/1480.

27 Peterson, report, November 22, 1975, EP150/3520; Severna Park Survey, February 1975.

28 CAC, July 9, 1976, EP150/3522; Peterson, "Unit Pricing—Giant Step for Consumers," n.d., EP77/1528.

29 "Speaking Out for Consumers," *Chain Store Age Supermarkets*, December 1981.

30 Giant, Feedback Report, February 2, 1975, EP76/1511.

31 Peterson, *Restless*, 147, 148, 150.

32 King Soopers visit, October 23, 1970, EP75/1472. Peterson, *Restless*, 143; Jennifer Cross, *The Supermarket Trap* (Indianapolis: University of Indiana Press, 1970).

33 Esther Peterson, "Consumerism as a Retailer's Asset," *Harvard Business Review* (May-June 1974), 99–100; Ad Woman of the Year, EP78/1555.

34 Peterson, "Consumer Participation," 251, 254; Peterson to Bernie Murphy, SMI, June 10, 1975, EP75/1488.

35 "Shoppers Give Giant the Edge in Washington, DC," *Chain Store Age Supermarkets*, December 1981.

36 Consumer Action Taskforce, January 31, 1971; Peterson to Chairman, June 21, 1971, EP75/1473.

37 Giant press release, January 5, 1972, EP74/1478; Peterson to Lynn Lyons, April 5, 1972, EP75/1510.

38 Peterson, "Retailer's Asset," 91; *Advertising Age*, April 24, 1972; Peterson, *Restless*, 142.

39 Giant, *50 Years*, 59; Giant *Consumer Guide* pamphlets, EP74/1467.

40 "Consumer Affairs . . ."; *NCL Bulletin*, December 1973.

41 Peterson notebook, October 25, 1970, EP75/1472; Giant, Press release, June 9, 1971, EP76/1515.

42 Peterson, *Restless*, 156, 158; Glickman, *Buying Power*, 275–79; Matthew Hilton, *Prosperity for All: Consumer Activism in an Era of Globalization* (Ithaca: Cornell University Press, 2009), 171–75; Peterson, "Consumer Representation," 210.

43 Hilton, *Prosperity*, 121–24, 179–82; Peterson, *Restless*, 142; Giant, *50 Years*, 60; Glickman, *Buying Power*, 292–94.

44 Odonna Matthews, *New York Times*, January 22, 1997; David Frost, *The Americans* (New York: Stein & Day, 1970), 115.

13: THE COUNTERCULTURAL ROOTS OF GREEN CONSUMERISM

1 Tracey Deutsch, "On Demand," this volume.

2 Sam Binkley, "The Seers of Menlo Park: The Discourse on the Heroic Consumption in 'The Whole Earth Catalog,'" *Journal of Consumer Culture* 3, no. 2 (November 2003), 292.

3 Andrew Kirk, *Counterculture Green: The Whole Earth Catalog and American Environmentalism* (Lawrence: University Press of Kansas, 2007), 39.

4 Fred Turner, *From Counterculture to Cyberculture: Stewart Brand, the Whole Earth Network, and the Rise of Digital Utopianism* (Chicago: University of Chicago Press, 2008), 59–60.

5 Stewart Brand to Mr. Edward Cornish, 1968, box 6, folder 5, Stewart Brand Papers, M1237, Special Collections and University Archives, Stanford University Libraries (hereafter SBP); J. Baldwin and Stewart Brand, eds., *Whole Earth Ecolog: The Best of Environmental Tools and Ideas* (New York: Harmony, 1990), 128.

6 "Windmill Power," *Time*, December 2, 1974, 12.

7 Stewart Brand to Joe Bonner, August 12, 1969, box 6, folder 6, SBP.

8 Thomas Albright, "The Environmentalists," *Rolling Stone* 48 (December 13, 1969), box 30, folder 1, SBP.

9   Turner, *From Counterculture to Cyberculture*, 32.

10 Turner, *From Counterculture to Cyberculture*, 77.

11 Stewart Brand, "Game Design," in *The Last Whole Earth Catalog* (New York: Random House, 1972), 35.

12 Interview with Stewart Brand, *Focus: Introductory Frame*, box 7, folder 1, SBP; Binkley, "The Seers of Menlo Park," 307–8.

13 Baldwin and Brand, *Whole Earth Ecolog*, 3.

14 Turner, *From Counterculture to Cyberculture*, 36.

15 Stewart Brand, ed. *The Updated Last Whole Earth Catalog: Access to Tools* (Menlo Park, CA: Nowles, 1971), 43.

16 Albright, "The Environmentalists."

17 Stewart Brand, "Money," in *The Last Whole Earth Catalog*, 438.

18 Albright, "The Environmentalists"; Stewart Brand to Ken Kesey, January 19, 1973, box 7, folder 2, SBP.

19 Stewart Brand to Lois Brand, box 7, folder 1, SBP.

20 Stewart Brand, journal entry, July 11, 1971, box 18, folder 1, SBP.

21 Turner, *From Counterculture to Cyberculture*, 121

22 "Fight to Save the Earth From Man," *Time*, February 2, 1970.

23 Commoner interview with Jim Clarke, box 46, folder: WMAL TV Mr. Jim Clarke, May 2, 1972, and Commoner on "Firing Line," box 46, folder: May 1, 1973, "Firing Line" with William Buckley, Barry Commoner Papers, Library of Congress, Washington, DC (hereafter BCP).

24 Commoner speech, box 39, folder: "Pollution and the Profit Motive," 1971, BCP.

25 Commoner speech, box 38, folder: November 21, 1971, "Quality of Life" Seminar, BCP.

26 Commoner interview with WBBM Radio, Chicago, January 25, 1974, box 48, folder: WBBM Radio, BCP.

27 Commoner speech, box 44, folder: November 28, 1972, SF "Jobs and the Environment" Conference, BCP.

28 Commoner speech, International Youth Conference on the Human Environment, Toronto CA, August 24, 1971, box 41, folder: Youth Conference on the Human Environment, BCP.

29 Commoner interview with WBBM Radio, Chicago, January 25, 1974, box 48, folder: WBBM Radio, Chicago, BCP; Commoner interview with KETC-TV, Forest Park, Illinois, box 47, folder: May 16, 1973, KETC-TV, BCP.

30 Commoner interview with WBBM Radio, Chicago, January 25, 1974; Commoner interview with KETC-TV, May 16, 1973.

31 Commoner interview with KETC-TV, May 16, 1973.

32 Commoner speech, Onway, Michigan SIPI-UAW Sponsored National Action Conference, May 3, 1976, box 52, folder: National Action Conference, BCP.

33 Meg Jacobs, *Panic at the Pump: The Energy Crisis and the Transformation of American Politics in the 1970s* (New York: Hill and Wang, 2016), 9.

34 *Time*, April 23, 1990.

35 Bill McKibben, "Global Warming's Terrifying New Math," *Rolling Stone*, July 19, 2012.

36 Gutowski et al., "Environmental Life Style Analysis," Massachusetts Institute of Technology, 2008.

37 Nicholas Stern, *The Economics of Climate Change: The Stern Review* (Cambridge, UK: Cambridge University Press, 2007), viii.

38 Marcello Graziano and Kenneth Gillingham, "Spatial Patterns of Solar Photovoltaic System Adoption: The Influence of Neighbors and the Built Environment," *Journal of Economic Geography* 15 (2014): 815–39.

39 Peter Rugh, "'We Have to Be the Carbon Tax': An Interview with Tim DeChristopher," *Waging Nonviolence*, November 7, 2013.

14: PURCHASING CHANGE

1 Stephen Mayfield, "The Green Revolution 2.0: The Potential of Algae for the Production of Biofuels and Bioproducts," *Genome* 56, no. 10 (December 2013), 552.

2 R. Quentin Grafton, Tom Kompas, Ngo Van Long, and Hang To, "US Biofuels Subsidies and CO2 Emissions: An Empirical Test for a Weak and a Strong Green Paradox," *Energy Policy* 68 (2014), 554.

3 Brian Wright, "Global Biofuels: Key to the Puzzle of Grain Market Behavior," *Journal of Economic Perspectives* 28, no. 1 (2014), 73.

4 Mayfield, "The Green Revolution 2.0," 552.

5 Wright, "Global Biofuels," 75.

6 Alison Mohr and Sujatha Raman, "Lessons from First Generation Biofuels and Implications for the Sustainability Appraisal of Second Generation Biofuels," *Energy Policy* 63 (2013), 116; José Goldemberg, Francisco F.C. Mello, Carlos E. P. Cerri, Christian A. Davies, and Carlos C. Cerri, "Meeting the Global Demand for Biofuels in 2021 through Sustainable Land Use Change Policy," *Energy Policy* 69 (2014), 16.

7 Wright, "Global Biofuels," 86.

8 Mayfield, "The Green Revolution 2.0," 552.

9 Wright, "Global Biofuels," 86.

10 Zainul Abideen, Abdul Hameeda, Hans-Werner Koyro, Bilquees Gul, Raziuddin Ansari, and M. Ajmal Khan, "Sustainable Biofuel Production from Non-Food Sources—An Overview," *Emirates Journal of Food & Agriculture* 26, no. 12 (2014), 1057.

11 "How Much Gasoline Does the United States Consume?—FAQ—U.S. Energy Information Administration (EIA)." Accessed May 24, 2015. www.eia.gov.

12 Grafton et al., "US Biofuels Subsidies and CO2 Emissions," 551.

13 US EPA, OAR, "Renewable Fuel Standard (RFS)," *Overviews & Factsheets*, November 15, 2011, www.epa.gov.

14 Jadwiga Ziolkowska, William H. Meyers, Seth Meyer, and Julian Binfield, "Targets and Mandates: Lessons Learned from EU and US Biofuels Policy Mechanisms," February 7, 2011, www.agbioforum.org.

15 US EPA, "Renewable Fuel Standard (RFS)."

16 Cormac Sheridan, "Big Oil Turns on Biofuels," *Nature Biotechnology* 31, no. 10 (October 1, 2013), 870–71.

17 S. Venghaus and K. Selbmann, "Biofuel as Social Fuel: Introducing Socio-Environmental Services as a Means to Reduce Global Inequity?" *Ecological Economics* 97 (2014), 86.

18 Abideen et al., "Sustainable Biofuel Production from Non-Food Sources," 1058.

19 The EPA considers sugar to be G2, even though sugar is a food source.

20 Rostek Ewa and Krzysztof Biernat, "Liquid Biofuels of the First and Second Generation: The Method of Preparation and Application," *Journal of Polish CIMAC* 7, no. 1 (2012), 193–94.

21 Abideen et al., "Sustainable Biofuel Production from Non-Food Sources," 1058–60.

22 Mayfield, "The Green Revolution 2.0," 552–54.

23 Abideen et al., "Sustainable Biofuel Production from Non-Food Sources," 1062.

24 Mohr and Raman, "Lessons from First Generation Biofuels," 118.

25 Gohin, "Assessing the Land Use Changes and Greenhouse Gas Emissions of Biofuels," 575.

26 Mohr and Raman, "Lessons from First Generation Biofuels," 118.

27 Abideen et al., "Sustainable Biofuel Production from Non-Food Sources," 1057.

28 Sheridan, "Big Oil Turns on Biofuels," 870.

29 Grafton et al., "US Biofuels Subsidies and CO2 Emissions," 551.

30 Sheridan, "Big Oil Turns on Biofuels," 870.

31 Mohr and Raman, "Lessons from First Generation Biofuels," 116.

32 Alexandre Gohin, "Assessing the Land Use Changes and Greenhouse Gas Emissions of Biofuels: Elucidating the Crop Yield Effects," *Land Economics* 90, no. 4 (November 2014), 575.

33 Mohr and Raman, "Lessons from First Generation Biofuels," 116.

34 Natural Resources Defense Council, "Biofuel Sustainability Performance Guidelines" (July 2014), 5.

35 Mohr and Raman, "Lessons from First Generation Biofuels," 116.

36 Mayfield, "The Green Revolution 2.0," 115.

37 For specific data on US biofuel imports see "U.S. Total Crude Oil and Products Imports," www.eia.gov.

38 Ruth Kelly, with contributions from Monique Mikhail and Marc-Olivier Herman, "The Hunger Grains," Oxfam Briefing Paper 161, Oxfam GB for Oxfam International, September 17, 2012, 2, www.oxfamnovib.nl.

39 Mohr and Raman, "Lessons from First Generation Biofuels," 118.

40 Mohr and Raman, "Lessons from First Generation Biofuels," 116.

41 Kelly, Mikhail, and Herman, "The Hunger Grains," 23.

15: BUYING A BETTER WORLD

1 "New Study Reveals: Men Really Do Have a Heart," *Barkley*, www.prnewswire. com.

2 "Sponsorship Spending Receded for the First Time in 2009," *IEG*, accessed August 19, 2010, www.sponsorship.com.

3 Mara Einstein, *Compassion, Inc.: How Corporate America Blurs the Line between What We Buy, Who We Are and Those We Help* (Berkeley: University of California Press, 2012).

4 "Carol Cone: Cause Marketing is Dead. (It's All about 'Purpose')," *On Philanthropy*, onphilanthropy.com; Rance Crain, "Marketers Shouldn't Dominate Charities: Brands Needn't Convey Their Social Values in Every Ad," *Advertising Age*, June 4, 2013, 100.

5 "Cause Marketing—US—August 2011," Mintel, oxygen.mintel.com.

6 Sophia A. Muirhead, *Corporate Contributions: The View from 50 Years* (New York: The Conference Board, 1999).

7 Craig Smith, "The New Corporate Philanthropy," *Harvard Business Review* (May-June 1994): 105–16.

8 Jonas Collander and Michael Dalhen, "Following the Fashionable Friend: The Power of Social Media," *Journal of Advertising Research* 51, no. 1 (2011): 313–20.

9 "Global Advertising Consumers Trust Real Friends and Virtual Strangers," *Nielsen*, www.nielsen.com.

10 Mark Andrejevic, *iSpy: Surveillance and Power in the Interactive Era* (Lawrence: University Press of Kansas, 2007); "Service and Social Media: You're Not Social (Enough)," *DestinationCRM.com*, www.destinationcrm.com.

11 Greg Dickinson, "Selling Democracy: Consumer Culture and Citizenship in the Wake of September 11" *Southern Communication Journal* 70, no. 4 (2005): 271–84.

12 Einstein, *Compassion, Inc.*

13 Hamish Pringle and Marjorie Thompson, *Brand Spirit: How Cause Marketing Builds Brands* (New York: John Wiley, 1999); Jeffrey Hollender and Stephen Fenichell, *What Matters Most: How a Small Group of Pioneers is Teaching Social Responsibility to Big Business, and Why Business is Listening* (New York: Basic Books, 2004); Daniel C. Esty, *Green to Gold: How Smart Companies Use Environmental Strategy to Innovate, Create Value, and Build Competitive Advantage* (New Haven: Yale University Press, 2006).

14 Philip Kotler et al., *Good Works! Marketing and Corporate Initiatives that Build a Better World . . . and the Bottom Line* (New York: John Wiley & Sons, 2012); P. S. Bronn and A. B. Vrioni, "Corporate Social Responsibility and Cause-Related Marketing: An Overview," *International Journal of Advertising* 20, no. 1 (2001): 207–22; Cone Inc. *Cone 2010 Brand Evolution Study, Cone Communications*, www.coneinc. com; Brian D. Till and Linda I. Nowak, "Toward Effective Use of Cause-Related Marketing Alliances," *Journal of Brand Management* 9, no. 7 (2000): 427–84; Corrinne Upton, "What 'Gives' With Cause Marketing? Strengthen Your Business, Enhance Your Image, and Give Back," *Public Relations Quarterly* 51, no. 4 (2006), 40–41; Srdan Zdravkovic, Peter Magnusson, and Sarah M. Stanley, "Dimensions

of Fit between a Brand and a Social Cause and Their Influence on Attitudes," *International Journal of Research in Marketing* 27, no. 2 (2010): 151–60.

15 Einstein, *Compassion, Inc.*; Angela M. Eikenberry, "The Hidden Costs of Cause Marketing," *Stanford Social Innovation Review* 7, no. 3 (Summer 2009): 51–55; Josee Johnston, "The Citizen-Consumer Hybrid: Ideological Tensions in the Case of Whole Foods Market," *Theory and Society* 37, no. 3 (2008): 229–70; Inger Stole, "Philanthropy as Public Relations: A Critical Perspective on Cause Marketing," *International Journal Of Communication* 2 (2008): 20–40; Sarah Banet-Weiser and Charlotte Lapsansky, "Red is the New Black: Brand Culture, Consumer Citizenship and Political Possibility," *International Journal of Communication* 2 (2008): 1248–68; Samantha King, *Pink Ribbons, Inc.* (Minneapolis: University of Minnesota Press, 2006); M. Bergland and C. Nakata, "Cause-Related Marketing: More Buck Than Bang?," *Business Horizons* 48 (2005): 443–53; Donald R. Lichtenstein, Minette E. Drumwright, and Bridgette M. Braig, "The Effect of Corporate Social Responsibility on Costumer Donations to Corporate-Supported Nonprofits," *Journal of Marketing* 68, no. 4 (2004): 16–32; Michael Jay Polonsky and Greg Wood, "Can the Overcommercialization of Cause-Related Marketing Harm Society?," *Journal of Macromarketing* 21, no. 1 (2001): 8–22.

16 Einstein, *Compassion, Inc.*

17 "The Broken Buy One Give One Model. Three Ways to Save TOMS Shoes," *Fast Coexist*, www.fastcoexist.com.

18 www.toms.com/coffee.

19 "Is Warby Parker Too Good to Last?," *Wired*, www.wired.com.

20 "H&M Releases 2012 Sustainability Report," *Triple Pundit*, www.triplepundit.com.

21 Jennifer Aaker et al., *The Dragonfly Effect: Quick, Effective, and Powerful Ways to Use Social Media to Drive Social Change* (New York: John Wiley, 2010), xiv.

22 Jessica Pressler, "20/30 Vision: Warby Parker has Trained its Sights on the Stylish, 'Post-Wealth' Millennial Set—As Customers and Employees," *New York Magazine*, nymag.com.

16: WHAT ABOUT THE CAUSE?

1 Amy Lubitow and Mia Davis, "Pastel Injustice: The Corporate Use of Pinkwashing for Profit," *Environmental Justice* 4, no. 3 (2011): 139–44.

2 Phil Brown, Stephen M. Zavestoski, Sabrina McCormick et al., "Print Media Coverage of Environmental Causation of Breast Cancer," *Sociology of Health and Illness* 23, no. 6 (2001): 747–75.

3 "Industry Statistics: Global," *American Chemistry Council*, www.americanchemistry.com.

4 Government of Canada, "The Canadian Trade Commissioner Service: Chemicals and Plastic," www.international.gc.ca.

5 Michael P. Wilson and Megan R. Schwarzman, "Toward a New U.S. Chemicals Policy: Rebuilding the Foundation to Advance New Science, Green Chemistry,

and Environmental Health," *Environmental Health Perspectives* 117, no. 8 (2009), 1202.

6   Robin E. Dodson, Marcia Nishloka, Laurel J. Standley et al., "Endocrine Disruptors and Asthma-Associated Chemicals in Consumer Products," *Environmental Health Perspectives* 120 (2012): 935–43.

7   Jane Houlihan, "Testimony before the United States House of Representatives, on the Discussion Draft of the 'Food and Drug Administration Globalization Act' Legislation: Device and Cosmetic Safety," May 14, 2008. Available at www.ewg.org.

8   Centers for Disease Control and Prevention. *Fourth National Report on Human Exposure to Environmental Chemicals* (Atlanta: CDC, 2009), 1–529.

9   Environmental Defence Canada, *Pre-Polluted: A Report on the Toxic Substances in the Umbilical Cord Blood of Canadian Newborns* (Toronto: EDC, 2013).

10 Janet Gray, *State of the Evidence: The Connection between Breast Cancer and the Environment*, 6th ed. (San Francisco: Breast Cancer Fund, 2010).

11 Philippe Grandjean, David Bellinger, Ake Bergman et al., "The Faroes Statement: Human Health Effects of Developmental Exposure to Chemicals in Our Environment," *Basic Clinical Pharmacology and Toxicology* 102, no. 2 (2008): 73–75.

12 Carl F. Cranor, *Legally Poisoned: How the Law Puts Us at Risk from Toxicants* (Cambridge, MA: Harvard University Press, 2011).

13 Gray, *State of the Evidence*, 1–33.

14 Wilson and Schwarzman, "Toward a New U.S. Chemicals Policy," 1202–9.

15 Canada's Economic Action Plan, *Taking Action on Toxic Chemicals* (2013), actionplan.gc.ca.

16 Michael E. Belliveau, "The Drive for a Safer Chemicals Policy in the United States," *New Solutions* 21, no. 3 (2011): 359–86.

17 Heather Sarantis, Lisa Archer, Stacy Malkan et al., "Market Shift: The Story of the Compact for Safe Cosmetics and the Growing Demand for Safer Products," *Campaign for Safe Cosmetics* (2011), 1–24.

18 Campaign for Safe Cosmetics, "FDA, Cosmetics Industry Lock Out Consumer, Public Health Groups from Meeting" [Press Release 2007], www.safecosmetics.org.

19 "Exposures Add Up—Survey Results. A Survey on Personal Care Produce Use in the U.S.," Environmental Working Group, 2004, www.ewg.org.

20 Environmental Defence, *The Manscape: The Dirt on Toxic Ingredients in Men's Body Care Products* (Environmental Defence, 2012), 4–6.

21 Daniel Faber, *Capitalizing on Environmental Injustice: The Polluter-Industrial Complex in the Age of Globalization* (Lanham, MD: Rowman & Littlefield, 2008).

22 Stacy Malkan, *Baby's Tub Still Toxic* (San Francisco: Campaign for Safe Cosmetics, 2011).

23 Saranti et al., "Market Shift," 1–24.

24 Interagency Breast Cancer and Environmental Research Coordinating Committee, *Breast Cancer and the Environment: Prioritizing Prevention* (Washington, DC: National Institute of Environmental Health Sciences, 2013).

25 Silent Spring Institute, *Breast Cancer and the Environment* (Newton, MA: Silent Spring Institute, 2015).

26 National Cancer Institute, "Cancer Costs Projected to Reach at Least $158 billion in 2020," National Institutes of Health, January 12, 2011, www.cancer.gov.

27 IBCERCC, *Breast Cancer and the Environment, 1,1–1,6* (Washington, DC: National Institute of Environmental Health Sciences, 2013).

28 Lubitow and Davis, "Pastel Injustice," 139–44.

29 Margaret Cuomo, *A World Without Cancer: The Making of a New Cure and the Real Promise of Prevention* (New York: Rodale, 2012).

30 Karen M. Kedrowski and Marilyn Stine Sarow, *Cancer Activism: Gender, Media, and Public Policy* (Chicago: University of Illinois Press, 2007).

31 Kedrowski and Sarow, *Cancer Activism*, 198.

17: THE MAKING OF A COKE CAN

1 Grace Hale, "When Jim Crow Drank Coke," *New York Times*, January 29, 2013, A23.

2 That dissertation is now *Citizen Coke: The Making of Coca-Cola Capitalism* (New York: W. W. Norton, 2015).

3 Email, Civic Action Network (civicactionnetwork@na.ko.com) to Bartow Elmore, "Setting the Record Straight—Coca-Cola Responds to NY Times Op-Ed," January 29, 2013.

4 Memorandum, Nehl Horton to the National Soft Drink Association (NSDA), April 19, 1995, American Beverage Association (ABA) Information Center, Washington, DC (hereafter ABA Information Center). ABA employees granted the author access to the Information Center for a limited period from 2009 to 2010.

5 "Businesses Mobilize Employees for More Clout," *Atlanta Business Chronicle*, August 11, 1997.

6 "Businesses Mobilize Employees for More Clout."

7 US Treasury Secretary Lloyd Bentsen allegedly coined the phrase "astroturfing" to refer to corporate grassroots campaigns in 1985. On the early emergence of corporately financed interest groups during the Progressive Era, see Christopher M. Loomis, "The Politics of Uncertainty: Lobbyists and Propaganda in Early Twentieth-Century America," *Journal of Policy History* 21, no. 2 (2009): 187–213; Caroline Lee, "The Roots of Astroturfing," *Contexts* 9, no. 1 (Winter 2010): 73–75. Political sociologist Edward T. Walker highlights the tobacco industries' 1920s corporate grassroots campaigns in *Grassroots for Hire: Public Affairs Consultants in American Democracy* (New York: Cambridge University Press, 2014), 53. See also Bart Elmore, *Citizen Coke*, 234–35.

8 Walker, *Grassroots for Hire*, 24, 58, 61–76; Benjamin C. Waterhouse, *Lobbying America: The Politics of Business from Nixon to NAFTA* (Princeton: Princeton University Press, 2014), 247–52. On the rise of professional advocacy groups in the second half of the twentieth century, see also Theda Skocpol, "Government Activism and the Reorganization of American Civic Democracy," in *The Transformation of American Politics: Activist Government and the Rise of Conservatism*, ed.

Paul Pierson and Theda Skocpol (Princeton: Princeton University Press, 2007), 39–67.

9   For the early history of Coca-Cola bottling, see Mark Pendergrast, *For God, Country, and Coca-Cola: The Definitive History of the Great American Soft Drink and the Company That Makes It* (New York, Basic Books: 2013), 66–78.

10 Constance L. Hays, *The Real Thing: Truth and Power at the Coca-Cola Company* (New York: Random House, 2004), 11; Frederick Allen, *Secret Formula: How Brilliant Marketing and Relentless Salesmanship Made Coca-Cola the Best-Known Product in the World* (New York: HarperBusiness, 1994 (hardback); 1995 (paperback)), 108. Page references are to the paperback version.

11 Mike Cheatham, *"Your Friendly Neighbor": The Story of Georgia's Coca-Cola Bottling Families* (Macon, Georgia: Mercer University Press, 1999), 61, 65, 67, 71.

12 Quoted in Charles Howard Candler, "Coca-Cola Company Bottling Company 50th Anniversary Address," November 21, 1950, box 15, folder 4, Charles Howard Candler Papers, Manuscript Archive and Rare Book Library (MARBL), Emory University, Atlanta, Georgia (hereafter MARBL); Charles Howard Candler, *Asa Griggs Candler* (Atlanta: Emory University, 1950), 143.

13 For more on the battle over mandatory deposits, see Bartow J. Elmore, *Citizen Coke*, 232–48, 253–61.

14 Senate Subcommittee for Consumers of the Committee on Commerce, Science, and Transportation, *Beverage Container and Reuse*, 95th Cong., 2nd Sess., January 25, 26, and 27, 1978, 156–58; Senate Committee on Commerce, Science, and Transportation, *Reuse and Recycling Act of 1979*, 96th Cong., 2nd Sess., March 3, 1980, 66–68.

15 "Western Bottlers Helped Lead Drive for 'No' Votes on Mandatory Deposits," *Coca-Cola Bottler* 73, no. 17 (December 1982), 1, box 50, folder 1108, Central Coca-Cola Bottling Company, Inc., 1906-2003, Manuscript Collection (hereafter Central Coca-Cola Manuscript Collection), Mss3 C3332 a FA2, Virginia Historical Society, Richmond, Virginia (hereafter Virginia Historical Society); "Bottlers Intensifying Efforts to Battle Forced Deposits," *Coca-Cola Bottler* 73, no. 15 (October 1982), 4, box 50, folder 1108, Central Coca-Cola Manuscript Collection, Virginia Historical Society.

16 "Involvement in Grassroots Politics Vital to Keeping Industry Healthy," *Coca-Cola Bottler* 74, no. 1 (January 1983), 10, box 50, folder 1109, Central Coca-Cola Manuscript Collection, Virginia Historical Society.

17 Constance L. Hays, *The Real Thing*, 11, 182.

18 Coca-Cola explicitly stated that bottling consolidation led to the creation of CAN in a video entitled *The Coca-Cola Company Civic Action Network Video*, created by the Coca-Cola Company Government Relations Department in the 1990s, ABA Information Center.

19 Memorandum from Nehl Horton to the National Soft Drink Association (NSDA), April 19, 1995; Memorandum from Jack Stahl to Coca-Cola Employees, February 1995, ABA Information Center.

20 Memorandum from Nehl Horton to the National Soft Drink Association (NSDA), April 19, 1995, ABA Information Center.

21 "Several States Recycle Forced Deposit Legislation: Coca-Cola CAN Members Voice Opposition to Outdated Idea," *Network News*, a publication of the Coca-Cola Company Government Relations Department, vol. 3, no. 1 (April 1997), ABA Information Center.

22 "Communicating with Coke CAN," *Network News* 3, no. 2 (October 1997), box 32, folder 801, Central Coca-Cola Manuscript Collection, Virginia Historical Society.

23 Douglas Ivester to Betty Sams Christian, Central Coca-Cola Bottling Company, Inc., January 2, 1998; "Victory 1998: Coca-Cola CAN Delivers!" *Network News* 4, no. 2 (December 1998), box 32, folder 801, Central Coca-Cola Manuscript Collection, Virginia Historical Society.

24 Robert Foster, *Coca-Globalization: Following Soft Drinks from New York to New Guinea* (New York: Palgrave Macmillan, 2008), 163; Email, Civic Action Network (civicactionnetwork@na.ko.com) to Author, "Coca-Cola Responds to New York City Health Department's Health Proposal to Ban 'Large' Portion-Sized Beverages," May 31, 2012.

25 A 1998 letter from Douglas Ivester to Betty Sams Christian encapsulated Coke's message of citizen empowerment. In that missive, Ivester urged, "Please remember that your voice and your vote carry an enormous weight in the democratic process." Douglas Ivester to Betty Sams Christian, January 2, 1998, Central Coca-Cola Manuscript Collection, box 32, folder 801, Virginia Historical Society; Email, Brent Tozzer to Coca-Cola Civic Action Network, April 15, 1999, leaked to the Grassroots Recycling Network, greenyes.grrn.org.

26 Marion Nestle, "Should Soda and Fast-Food Companies Sponsor the Olympics?" *Food Politics* (blog), July 27, 2012, www.foodpolitics.com.

27 Email, Civic Action Network to Author, "AAFP—Let us know your thoughts!," July 20, 2010; Comments by B. Busby to "Coca-Cola Funds Family Doc Group: What Do You Think?" *WSJ Blogs*, July 29, 2010, blogs.wsj.com.

28 Email, Coca-Cola Civic Action Network to Author, "New TV Ad from Americans against Food Taxes," September 22, 2010.

29 Email, Coca-Cola Civic Action Network to Author, "New Editorial by Dr. Richard Carmona," October 21, 2010. Information about the STOP Alliance can be found at www.stopobesityalliance.org.

30 In 2016, the CAN page could be found at www.coca-colacompany.com/investors/coca-cola-civic-action-network-can.

31 "Businesses Mobilize Employees for More Clout," *Atlanta Business Chronicle*, August 11, 1997.

32 Walker, *Grassroots for Hire*, 114–15; Wal-Mart's CAN website: walmartcommunity.com; Wal-Mart CAN Twitter account, February 3, 2015: twitter.com/walmartaction; Wal-Mart CAN YouTube page: www.youtube.com/user/WalmartCommunity/about.

33 Citizens United v. Federal Election Commission, 558 U.S. 310 (2010); Waterhouse, *Lobbying America*, 255.

34 Wal-Mart CAN Twitter page, August 25, 2012, Internet Archive, web.archive.org/web/20120825062726/twitter.com/walmartaction; Wal-Mart CAN Twitter account, February 3, 2015: twitter.com/walmartaction.

18: BOOT THE BELL

1 Statements made at the Robert F. Kennedy Human Rights Awards Ceremony, November 20, 2003, blogs.nysut.org.

2 Elly Leary, "Immokalee Workers Take Down Taco Bell," *Monthly Review*, October 2005; Kari Lydersen, "Farm Workers Walk for Freedom," *Alternet*, November 17, 2003; Rob Augman, "The Coalition of Immokalee Workers and the IWW," Industrial Workers of the World, May 12, 2001, www.iww.org; David Solnit, "Taco Bell Boycott Victory—A Model of Strategic Organizing: An Interview with the Coalition of Immokalee Workers," *Left Turn*, August 1, 2005; Rob Gurwitt, "Power to the Pickers," *Mother Jones*, July 1, 2004; Coalition of Immokalee Workers, "About CIW," www.ciw-online.org.

3 On globalization, see *The Global Assembly Line*, directed by Lorraine W. Gray, New Day Films, 1986; *Life and Debt*, directed by Stephanie Black, New Yorker Films, 2003; Saskia Sassen, "Global Cities and Survival Circuits," in *Global Woman: Nannies, Maids, and Sex Workers in the New Economy*, ed. Barbara Ehrenreich and Arlie Russell Hochschild (New York: Henry Holt, 2002); Lori Wallach and Michelle Sforza, *Whose Trade Organization? Corporate Globalization and the Erosion of Democracy* (Washington, DC: Public Citizen, 1999). Wayne A. Cornelius, "Death at the Border: Efficacy and Unintended Consequences of US Immigration Control Policy," *Population and Development Review* 27, no. 4 (December 2001), 661, 669–70; Barry Estabrook, *Tomatoland: How Modern Industrial Agriculture Destroyed Our Most Alluring Fruit* (Riverside, NJ: Andrews McMeel Publishing, 2012), xv, 75–100.

4 Oxfam America, *Like Machines in the Field: Workers Without Rights in American Agriculture*, Research Report (Boston: Oxfam America, 2004); Estabrook, *Tomatoland*; Coalition of Immokalee Workers, "Consciousness + Commitment = Change," in *Globalize Liberation: How to Uproot the System and Build a Better World*, ed. David Solnit (San Francisco: City Lights Books, 2004), 347–60; Leigh Muzslay, "Cal State Dropping Taco Bell," *San Bernardino Sun*, December 26, 2004.

5 Student/Farmworker Alliance, "March 12, 2005 Press Release: Taco Bell Concedes to Boycott Pressure, Commits to End Sweatshop Conditions in the Fields of Florida," *Student/Farmworker Alliance*, www.sfalliance.org.

6 Lauren Sage Reinlie, "Students Join Farmworkers to Boot the Bell at UT," *UT Watch*, November 2003.

7 Courtney Morris, "Students Join 3-day Protest of Taco Bell," *Daily Texan*, December 1, 2001; Elizabeth Esfahani, "Students Protest Practices of Fast Food Chain," *Daily Texan*, November 1, 2002; "Viewpoint: Yo No Quiero Taco Bell," *Daily Texan*, October 7, 2003; Reinlie, "Students Join Farmworkers to Boot the Bell at UT."

8 Sarah Michel, "Student Group Encourages Taco Bell Boycott," *Daily Texan*, October 29, 2004.

9 Michel, "Student Group Encourages Taco Bell Boycott"; "Viewpoint: Stop—What's in Your Taco?" *Daily Texan*, November 10, 2004; Rev. Lou Snead and Rev. Tom Heger, "Churches Join Bell Boycott," *Daily Texan*, January 19, 2005.

10 Dirk Dozier, "Taco Bell's Response to Boycott," *Daily Texan*, February 1, 2005; Melissa Mixon, "Union Board to Consider Taco Bell's Fate," *Daily Texan*, January

31, 2005; Lauren Sage Reinlie, "Taco Bell Boycott Continues . . . But is Student Demand Subsiding?" *UT Watch*, February 2005.

11 Mixon, "Union Board to Consider Taco Bell's Fate"; Patrick George, "Forum Addresses Taco Bell," *Daily Texan*, February 8, 2005; Reinlie, "Taco Bell Boycott Continues"; Adrienne Lee, "Taco Bell Faces Final Union Vote," *Daily Texan*, February 25, 2005; "Viewpoint: Rotten Tomatoes," *Daily Texan*, February 24, 2005; Laura Heinauer, "Taco Bell Isn't Facing Expulsion from UT," *Austin-American Statesman*, February 25, 2005; Melissa Mixon, "Unanimous Board Vote Keeps Taco Bell in Union," *Daily Texan*, February 28, 2005; "Put Bell on the Ballot," *Daily Texan*, March 2, 2005; Adrienne Lee, "Taco Bell Boycott Finally Over," *Daily Texan*, March 9, 2005.

12 Silvia Giagnoni, *Fields of Resistance: The Struggle of Florida's Farmworkers for Justice* (Chicago: Haymarket Books, 2011), 103–7.

13 The Notre Dame Student/Farmworker Alliance, "Take Charge of Your Taco," *Notre Dame Observer*, April 4, 2001; Kamaria Porter, "Boycotts Benefit Farmworkers," *Notre Dame Observer*, September 29, 2003; Maria Smith, "Partners in the Fight for Justice," *Notre Dame Observer*, March 30, 2004.

14 Smith, "Partners in the Fight for Justice."

15 Claire Heininger, "Protests Prompt Taco Bell Response," *Notre Dame Observer*, April 5, 2004; Observer Viewpoint, "Voicing Dissent," *Notre Dame Observer*, April 6, 2004; Claire Heininger, "PSA Descends on Office of the President," *Notre Dame Observer*, April 15, 2004; Kamaria Porter, "Staying on the Path," *Notre Dame Observer*, April 20, 2004.

16 Porter, "Staying on the Path."

17 Claire Heininger, "Notre Dame Issues Statement on Taco Bell," *Notre Dame Observer*, April 28, 2004.

18 Claire Heininger, "Taco Bell to Respond to ND Letter," *Notre Dame Observer*, April 19, 2004; Heininger, "Notre Dame Issues Statement on Taco Bell"; Porter, "Staying on the Path."

19 Claire Heininger, "ND Cancels Contract with Taco Bell," *Notre Dame Observer*, August 26, 2004.

19: WHERE'S THE BEEF . . . FROM?

1 Numerous newspapers reported on the April 1984 event including the *Richmond Independent*, *West County Times*, and the *Oakland Tribune*.

2 John M. Lawlor to James D. Nations, July 20, 1981, Dave Foreman Papers, 1982–1998, box 2, Western History Collection, CONS 223, Denver Public Library (hereafter DFP).

3 James D. Nations and Daniel I. Komer, "Rainforests and the Hamburger Society," *Environment* 25, no. 3 (April 1983): 12–20.

4 "Burger King Protest: Background Information," April 1984, DFP.

5 "Remarks at Dedication Ceremonies for the New Building of the National Geographic Society," June 19, 1984, *The Public Papers of Ronald W. Reagan*, Ronald Reagan Presidential Library, Simi Valley, California.

6   Mike Roselle to Earth First!ers, March 4, 1984, DFP.

7   Mike Roselle to Earth First!ers, March 4, 1984, DFP.

8   Press Kit, "Where's the Beef . . . From? Don't Eat the Beef. Save the Rainforest," April 24, 1984, DFP.

9   Fact sheet, "Where's the Beef From?—Do You Know That You Are Eating Rainforest with Every Hamburger?," 1984, DFP.

10 Rainforest Action Network advertisements, DFP.

11 Boycott letter from Earth First! Austin, April 9, 1986, DFP.

12 "Vogel Vetoes Move to Include Fast-Food for Diners at Union," *University Daily Kansan*, April 27, 1984.

13 Santa Fe, New Mexico, Earth First! organizer to Dave Foreman and Mike Roselle, April 23, 1984, DFP.

14 "The Whopper Song," Bill Oliver, 1986.

15 Mike Roselle to Earth First!ers, March 4, 1984, DFP.

16 Western Union telegram to J. Rane from Herman Stein, April 27, 1984, DFP.

17 Lisa Zeigler to Randy Hayes, February 15, 1985, DFP.

18 "Whopper Stopper Demonstration," Earth First! newsletter, Chico, California, 1987, DFP.

19 "Here's the Beef . . . Now Where's the Rainforest?" *National Boycott Newsletter*, Seattle, Washington, Late Winter-Early Spring 1986.

20 "Annual Review of Top 100 Chains," *Nation's Restaurant News*, 1989; United States House of Representatives (101st Congress), Committee on Small Business, *Franchising in the Economy: Prospects and Problems* (Washington, DC: US Government Printing Office, 1990); Rainforest Action Network, "Challenging Corporate Power," *2010 Annual Report*.

21 Rainforest Action Network, "Making the Radical Appear Reasonable," *2010 Annual Report*.

20: THE SWEATSHOP EFFECT

1   On the history of anti-sweatshop campaigns, see Lawrence B. Glickman's *Buying Power: A History of Consumer Activism in America* (Chicago: University of Chicago Press, 2009).

2   The Accord on Fire and Building Safety in Bangladesh is an independent, legally binding agreement between brands and trade unions in Bangladesh. Signatories to the Accord agree to independent factory inspection, public disclosure of all factory inspection reports, democratically elected health and safety committees at each factory, a commitment to support worker remediation if necessary, and worker empowerment training. To date, over 190 apparel brands in over 20 countries have signed onto the Accord. For more, visit www.bangladeshaccord.org.

3   For more specifics regarding the strategic advantages of collegiate anti-sweatshop activism, see Dale Wimberley, Meredith Katz, and John Paul Mason, "Mobilization, Strategy, and Global Apparel Production Networks: Systemic Advantages for

Student Antisweatshop Activism," *Societies Without Borders* 10, no. 1 (2015): 1–32.

4 Information on collegiate revenues can be found at "NCAA Finances," *USA Today*, accessed August 29, 2016, sports.usatoday.com/ncaa/finances.

5 The vast majority of brands do not own the factories where their apparel is produced and must subcontract production to multiple factories, often to the lowest bidder. Hence, it is common industry practice for one brand of t-shirts in one season to be produced in multiple factories and countries.

6 Worker Rights Consortium, "Global Wage Trends for Apparel Workers, 2001-2011," *Center for American Progress*, cdn.americanprogress.org.

7 Culture jamming is a tactic used by anticonsumerist activists to subvert media culture and turn corporate power against itself through the co-option or recontextualization of meaning. For more information, check out the Canadian magazine *Adbusters*, the premier culture jamming magazine, or Jonah Peretti, "The Nike Sweatshop Email: Political Consumerism, the Internet, and Culture Jamming," in *Politics, Products, and Markets: Exploring Political Consumerism Past and Present*, ed. Michele Micheletti et al. (New Brunswick: Transaction Publishers, 2004).

8 The Fair Labor Association was created in 1998 out of the Clinton administration and the sweatshop revelations surrounding Kathie Lee apparel production in Honduras. The FLA's strategy is to have corporations join the association and then require them to monitor their own factories around the world for adherence to a code of conduct determined collectively by the members of the Association. However, a strong conflict of interest exists, as the FLA members are corporations charged with enforcing codes of conduct in the factories in which their companies produce apparel. Moreover, six of the twelve FLA Board of Directors are from corporations including Hanes, Patagonia, Adidas, and New Balance.

9 In 1999, the VT-SAS (Students Against Sweatshops) group successfully pressured the university to sign a licensing code of conduct establishing standards for university licensed apparel. At that time, VT-SAS also campaigned for the university to join the FLA, the only monitoring organization in existence at the time. Shortly thereafter the WRC was established, but the university maintained its FLA affiliation until our 2008 campaign.

10 Even though Virginia Tech had yet to affiliate with the WRC at this point, we were able to access these factory reports via the public database on the WRC website.

11 Initially, the university administration decided to keep its affiliation with the FLA, even after signing onto the WRC. Since then, Virginia Tech has dropped its FLA affiliation and maintains only its affiliation with the WRC, citing better and more detailed factory reports from the WRC.

12 In almost all instances, WRC affiliation came as a result of USAS campaigns. In a handful of cases, a broader living wage campaign or worker justice group unaffiliated with USAS prompted the affiliation. It is also important to note that some USAS chapters have started and then ended due to student turnover and may have re-emerged at a later date. For more information on affiliated schools, please visit www.workerrights.org.

2 1: HATING WAL-MART, LOVING TARGET, AND
THE CONTRADICTIONS OF SUPPLY CHAIN CAPITALISM

1 Miguel Bustelo and Anne Zimmerman, "In Cities That Battle Wal-Mart, Target Gets a Welcome," *Wall Street Journal*, October 14, 2010, www.wsj.com.

2 Leo Troy, *Trade Union Membership, 1897–1962*, National Bureau of Economic Research, www.nber.org/chapters/c1707.pdf, 2.

3 "Union Members—2014," *Bureau of Labor Statistics*, January 23, 2015, www.bls.gov.

4 Kari Lyderson, "Target: Wal-Mart Lite," CorpWatch, April 20, 2006, www.corp-watch.org.

5 Peter Drucker, "The Economy's Dark Continent," *Fortune*, April 1, 1962, 104.

6 Sharon Stangenes, "Dayton Hudson: Cost Saving a Chain Reaction," *Women's Wear Daily*, April 5, 1978, 28.

7 Peter Klaus, "Logistics Research: A 50 Years' March of Ideas," *Logistics Research* 1, no. 1 (March 2009), 53.

8 See Marc Levinson, *The Box: How the Shipping Container Made the World Smaller and the World Economy Bigger* (Princeton: Princeton University Press, 2006).

9 Nelson Lichtenstein, *The Retail Revolution: How Wal-Mart Created a Brave New World of Business* (New York: Picador, 2010), 42; *Dayton Hudson Annual Report 1982*.

10 Stephen A. Brown, *Revolution at the Checkout Counter* (Cambridge, MA: Harvard University Press, 1997).

11 Brown, *Revolution at the Checkout Counter.*

12 *Dayton Hudson Annual Report 1991.*

13 Nelson Lichtenstein, "The Return of Merchant Capitalism," *International Labor and Working-Class History* 8 (April 2012), i.

14 Arthur Markowitz, "Discounting Hall of Fame: Sol Price: His Deeds Speak Louder Than Words—Founder of Price Club," *Discount Store News*, August 22, 1988.

15 Anthony Ramirez, "Union Calls for a Boycott of all New Target Stores," *Los Angeles Times*, March 5, 1983, A5; "Target Stores Boycotted by Local in San Diego," *Women's Wear Daily*, March 8, 1983, 8.

16 Robert Whereatt, "Legislators Labored to Project Right Image for Dayton's Session," *Minneapolis Star Tribune*, June 25, 1987, 16A.

17 Chris Serres, "Teflon Target: While Wal-Mart is Seen as the Evil Empire, Target Has Sterling Image," *Minneapolis Star Tribune*, May 25, 2005, reclaimdemocracy.org.

18 Marilyn Krause, "Waukesha County Residents Dominate Target Center Hiring," *Milwaukee Journal*, June 22, 1994.

19 *Target Annual Report*, 1998.

20 Serres, "Teflon Target."

21 Serres, "Teflon Target."

22 Serres, "Teflon Target."

23 Miguel Bustelo and Anne Zimmerman, "In Cities That Battle Wal-Mart, Target Gets a Welcome," *Wall Street Journal*, October 14, 2010, www.wsj.com.

24 Jennifer Steinhauer, "Stores that Cross Class Lines, *New York Times*, March 15, 1998, www.nytimes.com.

25 Lori Qingyuan, Yue Hayagreeva Rao, and Paul Ingram, "Information Spillovers from Protests against Corporations: A Tale of Walmart and Target," *Administrative Science Quarterly* 58, no. 4 (December 2013): 669–701.

26 Qingyuan, Rao, and Ingram, "Information Spillovers."

27 Brian Morrissey, "In Online Chatter, Target Bests Walmart," *Adweek Online*, September 4, 2009.

28 Julie Schlosser, "How Target Does It," *Fortune*, October 18, 2004, archive.fortune.com.

29 Patrick Barwise and Sean Meehan, "Bullseye: Target's Cheap Chic Strategy," *Harvard Business School Working Knowledge*, August 16, 2004, hbswk.hbs.edu.

30 Joel Hoekstra, "Red Hot," *Minnesota Monthly*, September 2007, www.minnesotamonthly.com.

31 Jackie Fox, "Target's Design Democracy," *Blink: Perspectives on Design*, September 16, 2011, blink.hdrinc.com.

32 Hoekstra, "Red Hot."

33 Friedrich Nietzsche, *On the Genealogy of Morals*, quoted in Judith Butler, *Gender Trouble: Feminism and the Subversion of Identity*, 2nd ed. (New York: Routledge, 2006), 25.

34 Julie Schollser, "How Does Target Do It?," *Fortune*, October 18, 2004, money.cnn.com.

35 Jim Cramer, "Why WMT Should Worry about TGT," *CNBC.com*, February 25, 2015, video.cnbc.com.

36 Chris Serres, "Target Wants to Score Bullseye with 'Hip' Image," *Minneapolis-St. Paul Star Tribune*, September 26, 2005.

37 Jennifer Reingold, "Target's Inner Circle," *Fortune* 157, no. 6, March 31, 2008, 74–86.

38 Zoe Heller, "Fashion: Power Comeback: Movin' on Up," *Vogue* 193, no. 3, March 1, 2003, 554–59.

39 Reingold, "Target's Inner Circle."

40 Reingold, "Target's Inner Circle."

41 *Dayton Hudson Annual Report 1998.*

42 "Dear Diary," *Slave to Target* (blog), July 31, 2005, slavetotarget.blogspot.com.

43 Douglas Holt, "Why Do Brands Cause Trouble? A Dialectical Theory of Consumer Culture and Branding," *Journal of Consumer Research* 29, no. 1 (June 2002), 89.

44 "Target 40 Years of Retailing: The Importance of being Target," *Home Textiles Today* 23, no. 38, May 27, 2002, 16–17.

45 "Target 40 Years of Retailing."

46 Jillian Berman, "Wall Street Analysts Predict the Slow Demise of Walmart and Target," *Huffington Post*, July 30, 2014, www.huffingtonpost.com.

47 Phil Wabha, "Why Wal-Mart Should Worry about Family Dollar's Fate," *Fortune*, August 18, 2014, fortune.com.

48 Sharon Edelson, "Study: Wal-Mart Losing Price Edge," *Women's Wear Daily*, August 4, 2011, 6.

49 Edelson, "Study: Wal-Mart Losing Price Edge."

50 Louis Hyman, "A Tale of Two Dollar Stores," *New York Times*, August 3, 2014, www.nytimes.com.

51 Hyman, "A Tale of Two Dollar Stores."

52 David Harvey, *Seventeen Contradictions and the End of Capitalism* (New York: Oxford University Press, 2015), 93.

53 Andrew Elrod, "Dollar Store Syndrome: Low Prices, Lower Pay," *Al Jazeera*, September 12, 2104.

54 See, for example, David Moberg, "The Union behind the Biggest Campaign against Walmart in History May Be Throwing in the Towel. Why?," *In These Times*, August 11, 2015, inthesetimes.com; Dave Jamieson, "Labor Groups Are Taking On Walmart and McDonald's. But Who Will Fund Their Fight?," *Huffington Post*, June 2, 2016, www.huffingtonpost.com. As well, May 2015 conversations at Cornell University between the author and OUR Walmart organizers confirm this point.

55 Carrie Kirby, "Is Target Really Just as Bad as Wal-Mart?," *Wisebread*, March 2008, www.wisebread.com.

56 Mark Brenner, "As Cargo Chains Grow, So Does Workers' Leverage," *Labor Notes* 347 (February 2008), 8–9.

57 Brenner, "As Cargo Chains Grow, So Does Workers' Leverage."

23: TO SPEAK IN ONE VOICE

1 Peter Dreier, "Lessons from the Health-Care Wars," *American Prospect* (May, 2010), 29–34; Richard Kirsch, *Fighting for Our Health* (New York: Rockefeller Institute Press, 2012).

2 Robert G. Kaiser, *Act of Congress* (New York: Alfred A. Knopf, 2013); Larry Kirsch and Robert N. Mayer, *Financial Justice: The People's Campaign to Stop Lender Abuse* (Santa Barbara: Praeger, 2013).

3 Jane Hamsher, "Americans for Financial Reform: Waste. Of. Time.," *FireDogLake.com* (blog), June 29, 2009, fdlaction.firedoglake.com.

4 Paul A. Sabatier, "Toward Better Theories of the Policy Process," *PS: Political Science and Politics* 24, no. 2 (June 1991): 147–56; Edella Schlager, "Policy Making and Collective Action: Defining Coalitions within the Advocacy Coalition," *Policy Sciences* 28, no. 3 (August 1995): 243–70.

5 Michael T. Heaney and Fabio Rojas, "Coalition Dissolution, Mobilization, and Network Dynamics in the U.S. Antiwar Movement," in *Research in Social Movements, Conflict and Change*, vol. 28, ed. Patrick G. Coy (Bingley, UK: Emerald Group, 2008), 39–82; David S. Meyer and Catherine Corrigall-Brown, "Coalitions and Political Context: U.S. Movements Against Wars in Iraq," *Mobilization* 10, no. 3 (October 2005): 327–44; Christopher M. Weible, Paul A. Sabatier, and Kelly McQueen, "Themes and Variations: Taking Stock of the Advocacy Coalition Framework," *Policy Studies Journal* 37 (2009): 121–40.

6 Michael T. Heaney and Fabio Rojas, "Hybrid Activism: Social Movement Mobilization in a Multimovement Environment." *American Journal of Sociology* 119, no. 4 (2014): 1047–103.

7   Stijn Brouwer and Frank Biermann, "Towards Adaptive Management: Examining the Strategies of Policy Entrepreneurs in Dutch Water Management," *Ecology and Society* 16, no. 4 (2011): 5–18.

8   Renee Beard and John Williamson, "Social Policy and the Internal Dynamics of The Senior Rights Movement," *Journal of Aging Studies* 25, no. 1 (January 2011): 22–33; Sonia M. Ospina and Angel-Saz Carranza, "Paradox and Collaboration in Network Management," *Administration & Society* 42, no. 4 (2010): 404–40.

9   Christopher K. Ansell, *Schism and Solidarity in Social Movements* (Cambridge: Cambridge University Press, 2001); Herbert H. Haines, *Black Radicals and the Civil Rights Mainstream* (Knoxville: University of Tennessee Press, 1988).

10 Thomas D. Beamish and Amy J. Luebbers, "Alliance Building Across Social Movements: Bridging Difference in a Peace and Justice Coalition," *Social Problems* 56, no. 4 (August 2009): 647–76.

11 Brian Mayer, "Cross-Movement Coalition Formation: Bridging the Labour-Environment Divide," *Sociological Inquiry* 79, no. 2 (May 2009): 219–39.

12 Jeffrey Haydu, "Frame Brokerage in the Pure Food Movement, 1879–1906, *Social Movement Studies* 11, no. 1 (2012): 97–112; Meyer and Corrigall-Brown, "Coalitions and Political Context"; Suzanne Staggenborg, "Coalition Work in the Pro Choice Movement: Organizational and Environmental Opportunities and Obstacles," *Social Problems* 33, no. 5 (June 1986): 374–90.

13 Andrew Battista, *The Revival of Labor Liberalism* (Urbana: University of Illinois Press, 2008); Mayer, "Cross-Movement Coalition Formation"; Brian Mayer, Phil Brown, and Rachel Morello-Frosch, "Labor-Environmental Coalition Formation: Framing and the Right-to-Know," *Sociological Forum* 25, no. 4 (December 2010): 746–68; Brian K. Obach, *Labor and the Environmental Movement: The Quest for Common Ground* (Cambridge, MA: MIT Press, 2004); Fred Rose, *Coalitions across the Class Divide: Lessons from the Labor, Peace, and Environmental Movements* (Ithaca: Cornell University Press, 2000).

14 Susan Cutter, "Race, Class, and Environmental Justice," *Progress in Human Geography* 19, no. 1 (1995): 111–22; David Faber, "A More 'Productive' Environmental Justice Politics: Movement Alliances in Massachusetts for Clean Production and Regional Equity," in *Environmental Justice and Environmentalism: The Social Justice Challenge to the Environmental Movement*, ed. Ronald Sandler and Phaedra C. Pezzullo (Cambridge, MA: MIT Press, 2007), 135–64; Eileen M. McGurty, "Warren County, NC, and the Emergence of the Environmental Justice Movement," *Society & Natural Resources* 13 (2000): 373–87.

15 Kirsch and Mayer, *Financial Justice*; Meyer and Corrigall-Brown, "Coalitions and Political Context"; Nella Van Dyke, "Crossing Movement Boundaries: Factors that Facilitate Coalition Protest by American College Students, 1930–1990," *Social Problems* 50, no. 2 (2003): 226–50.

16 Marshall Ganz, "Leading Change: Leadership, Organization and Social Movements," in *Handbook of Leadership Theory and Practice*, ed. Nitin Nohria and Rakhesh Nhurana (Boston: Harvard Business School Publishing, 2009), 527–68; Jurgen Gerhards and Dieter Rucht, "Mesomobilization: Organizing and Framing in Two Protest Campaigns in West Germany," *American Journal of Sociology* 98, no. 3 (November, 1992): 555–96; Aldon Morris and Suzanne Staggenborg, "Lead-

ership in Social Movements," in *The Blackwell Companion to Social Movements*, ed. David Snow, Sarah Soule, and Hanspeter Kriesi (Malden, MA: Blackwell Press, 2004); Gordon Müller-Seitz, "Leadership in Interorganizational Networks: A Literature Review and Suggestions for Future Research," *International Journal of Management Reviews* 14, no. 4 (December 2012): 428–43; Lynn Rivas, *Built to Last: Preventing Coalition Breakdowns* (PhD diss., University of California, Berkeley, 2007); Nella Van Dyke and Holly J. McCammon, eds. *Strategic Alliances: Coalition Building and Social Movements* (Minneapolis: University of Minnesota Press, 2010).

17 Kirsch and Mayer, *Financial Justice*.

18 *The Role of Government Affordable Housing Policy in Creating the Global Financial Crisis of 2008*, Staff Report, U.S. House of Representatives, 111th Congress, Committee on Oversight and Government Reform, Originally released July 1, 2009, updated May 12, 2010, oversight.house.gov.

19 *Community and Consumer Advocates' Perspectives on the Obama Administration's Financial Regulatory Reform Proposals*, Hearing before the Committee on Financial Services, U.S. House of Representatives, 111th Congress, July 16, 2009. Washington, DC: U.S. Government Printing Office, 2009, www.gpo.gov.

20 Elizabeth Warren, "Remarks at the Consumer Federation of America Financial Services Conference," press release of the U.S. Department of the Treasury, Washington, DC, December 2, 2010, www.treasury.gov.

21 Kirsch and Mayer, *Financial Justice*, 36.

22 Kirsch and Mayer, *Financial Justice*, 38.

23 AFL-CIO and 200 Other Groups, "A Call to Action for Real Financial Services Reform," April 9, 2009, ourfinancialsecurity.org.

24 Kirsch and Mayer, *Financial Justice*, 48.

25 Elinor Ostrom, *Governing the Commons: The Evolution of Institutions for Collective Action* (Cambridge: Cambridge University Press, 1990); Ostrom, *Understanding Institutional Diversity* (Princeton: Princeton University Press, 2005).

26 Kirsch and Mayer, *Financial Justice*, 63.

27 Kirsch and Mayer, *Financial Justice*, 83.

28 Kirsch and Mayer, *Financial Justice*, 65.

29 Kirsch and Mayer, *Financial Justice*, 61.

30 Robert D. Benford and David A. Snow, "Framing Processes and Social Movements: An Overview and Assessment," *Annual Review of Sociology* 26 (2000): 611–39; David A. Snow, E. Burke Rochford, Jr., Steve K. Worden, and Robert D. Benford, "Frame Alignment Processes, Micromobilization, and Movement Participation," *American Sociological Review* 51, no. 4 (1986): 464–81.

31 Teresa A. Sullivan, Elizabeth Warren, and Jay Westbrook, *The Fragile Middle Class* (New Haven: Yale University Press, 2001); Elizabeth Warren and Amelia Warren Tyagi, *The Two-Income Trap: Why Middle Class Parents are Going Broke* (New York: Basic Books, 2004).

32 Elizabeth Warren, "Unsafe at Any Rate," *Democracy* 5 (Summer, 2007): 8–19.

33 Brady Dennis, "Consumer Groups Praise Idea of Financial Protection Agency," *Washington Post*, July 17, 2009, www.washingtonpost.com; Transcript of Obama's Interview on "The Tonight Show," *Wall Street Journal*, March 20, 2009, online.wsj.com.

34 Frank Luntz, *The Language of Financial Reform* (Alexandria: WordDoctors, January 2010).

35 The Chamber's "toolkit" for stopping what was then called the CFPA can be found at www.uschamber.com/consumer-financial-protection-agency-toolkit.

36 Elizabeth Warren, "The Economics of Race: When Making It to the Middle Is Not Enough," *Washington & Lee Law Review* 61, no 4 (2004): 1777–79, scholarly-commons.law.wlu.edu.

37 S. A. Miller, "Elizabeth Warren Demands Jail Time for Wall Street Bankers," *Washington Times*, September 9, 2014, www.washingtontimes.com.

38 Kirsch and Mayer, *Financial Justice*, 93.

39 Barney Frank, Commencement address at American University, Washington, DC, May 9, 2009, www.american.edu.

40 National Community Reinvestment Center, "Dodd Bill Offers Compromised Consumer Financial Protection Agency," press release, March 15, 2010, www.ncrc.org.

41 Eamon Javers and Victoria McGrane, "Barney Frank: Chris Dodd Deal like 'A Bad Joke,'" *Politico*, March 2, 2010, www.politico.com.

42 Shahien Nasiripour, "Fight for the CFPA Is 'A Dispute between Families and Banks,' Says Elizabeth Warren," *HuffPost Business*, March 3, 2010, www.huffingtonpost.com.

43 Kirsch and Mayer, *Financial Justice*, 93.

44 Kirsch and Mayer, *Financial Justice*, 95.

24: ON DEMAND

1 In the course of this essay, I distinguish among several schools of economic thought. However, I am not trying to map economists onto a modern political spectrum of "good" or "bad," "progressive" or "liberal." As I discuss later, some people I identify as institutionalists, a group often concerned with class inequality, went out of their way to articulate racist and nativist positions. Some later economists often took it upon themselves to study ways that (however incorrectly, in my opinion) neoclassical economic policy could help to end racial discrimination. Many of the people I discuss shared connections to each other; Wesley C. Mitchell, for instance, was an important mentor to Milton Friedman. Rather than elide complicated differences and overlaps, I want to highlight intellectual trends and the meaning of these trends for contemporary politics of consumption.

2 Malcolm Rutherford, *The Institutionalist Movement in American Economics, 1918–1947* (New York: Cambridge University Press, 2011), 44–45, 47.

3 Thorstein Veblen, *The Theory of the Leisure Class: An Economic Study in the Evolution of Institutions* (New York: Macmillan, 1899), 25.

4 Wesley C. Mitchell, "The Backwards Art of Spending Money," *American Economic Review* 2 (June 1912), 269.

5 "Better Diet Needed: Cooking Schools Absolutely Necessary For All Classes," *Chicago Daily Tribune*, October 15, 1893, 10; Richard T. Ely, "Heavy Tax Burden Depreciates Value," *New York Times*, July 31, 1932, RE 1; Ely, "The Telegraph Monopoly," *North American Review* 149 (July 1889): 44–53.

6 Frederic S. Lee, *A History of Heterodox Economics: Challenging the Mainstream in the Twentieth Century* (New York: Routledge, 2009), 34–35; Lee, "From Multi-Industry Planning to Keynesian Planning: Gardiner Means, the American Keynesians, and National Economic Planning at the National Resources Committee," *Journal Of Policy History* 2, no. 2 (April 1990): 186–212.

7 Gardiner Means with Adolf Berle, *The Modern Corporation and Private Property* (New York: Columbia University, Council for Research in Social Sciences/Commerce Clearing House, 1932); Wesley C. Mitchell, *Business Cycles: The Problem and Its Setting* (New York: National Bureau of Economic Research, 1927); Edwin Nourse, *The Chicago Produce Market* (New York: Houghton Mifflin, 1918); Nourse, *Price Making in a Democracy* (New York: Brookings Institution, 1944); Paul H. Douglas, *Wages and the Family* (Chicago: University of Chicago Press, 1925); Hazel Kyrk, *Economic Problems of the Family* (New York: Harper, 1933).

8 Hazel Kyrk, *A Theory of Consumption* (New York: Houghton Mifflin, 1923), quotes from 21–22, 6.

9 For a fuller discussion of the term's significance, see Marina Moskowitz, *Standard of Living: The Measure of the Middle Class in Modern America* (Baltimore: Johns Hopkins University Press, 2004).

10 Rutherford, *The Institutionalist Movement in American Economics*, 78–79, 82–83, 296–97; Geoffrey Hodgson, *How Economics Forgot History: The Problem of Historical Specificity in Social Science* (New York: Routledge, 2001), 217.

11 Paul H. Douglas, "The Problem of the Basic Wage," *University Journal of Business* 3 (December 1924): 1–17.

12 John R. Commons, *Race and Immigrants in America* (New York: Macmillan, 1907).

13 Adolf A. Berle, Jr., "Government Function in a Stabilized National Economy," *American Economic Review* 33, no. 1: Part 2, Supplement, Part 2 (March 1943): 27–38.

14 Keynes, of course, emphasized the importance of aggregate spending and large-scale policy interventions. But he was not at all supportive of theoretical modelling for its own sake. For an introduction to Keynes's complicated relationship to math and modelling, see Robert Skidelsky, *Keynes: A Very Short Introduction* (London: Oxford University Press, 2010), esp. 149–51.

15 Rutherford, *The Institutionalist Movement in American Economics*, 83.

16 For summaries of this critique, see Rutherford, *The Institutionalist Movement in American Economics*, and Lee, *A History of Heterodox Economics*.

17 Mitchell, *Business Cycles*, 276.

18 Although the narrative is rarely stitched together, numerous works support this view of retail spaces as disorderly and powered by a gender ideology in which women required individual attention. See, for instance, Derek Valliant, "Peddling Noise: Contesting the Civic Soundscape in Chicago, 1890–1913," *Journal of the Illinois State Historical Society* 96 (Autumn 2003): 257–87; Adam Mack, *Sensing Chicago: Noisemakers, Strikebreakers, and Muckrakers* (Urbana: University of Illinois Press, 2015); Susan Porter Benson, *Counter Cultures: Saleswomen, Managers and Customers in American Department Stores, 1890–1940* (Urbana: University of Illinois Press, 1986); Tracey Deutsch, *Building a Housewife's Paradise: Gender, Politics, and American Grocery Stores*

in the Twentieth Century (Chapel Hill: University of North Carolina Press, 2010).

19 For an overview of this history, see Lee, *A History of Heterodox Economics.*

20 See, for instance, Michael Bernstein, "American Economics and the National Security State," 1941–1953," *Radical History Review* 68 (1995): 8–26; Esther-Mirjam Sent, Roger E. Backhouse, A. W. Bob Coats, John B. Davis, and Harold Hagemann, "Perspectives on Michael A. Bernstein's *A Perilous Progress: Economists and Public Purpose in Twentieth Century America,*" *European Journal of the History of Economic Thought* 12 (March 2005), 129. On economists' embrace of abstract, "scientific" studies of demand as a way of claiming professional and political status, see Bernstein, *A Perilous Progress*, 119.

21 Milton Friedman, "Review of *Inflation,*" *American Economic Review* 51 (December 1961), 1051. Tellingly, Friedman also felt he had to recuperate the work of his teacher Wesley C. Mitchell as more than "arid description" by arguing that it was a contribution to theories of economic change in spite of its empirical basis. Friedman, "Wesley C. Mitchell as an Economic Theorist," *Journal of Political Economy* 58 (December 1950): 465–93.

22 See, for instance, Paul Samuelson, "A Note on Measurement of Utility," *Review of Economic Studies* 4 (Feb 1937): 155 61. Here Samuelson is clear that overlooking real-world experience was precisely the advantage of his model. "In order to arrive inductively at the measurement of utility, essentially a subjective quantity, it is necessary to place the individual (*homo economicus*) . . . under certain ideal circumstances where his observable behaviour will render open to unambiguous inference the form of the function which he is conceived of as maximizing" (155). Samuelson also argued that purchases best indicated likes or dislikes in his widely influential article, "A Note on the Pure Theory of Consumers' Behavior," *Economica* 5, no. 17 (Feb 1938): 61–71. This was the basis for "revealed preferences theory."

23 Paul Samuelson, *Foundations of Economic Analysis* (Cambridge, MA: Harvard University Press, 1947).

24 Mark Blaug argues that by the 1950s, a hegemonic framework had emerged in which "price adjustments [were] the only way markets ever respond to shocks." Blaug, "The Formalist Revolution of the 1950s," *Journal of the History of Economic Thought* 25, no. 2 (2003): 145–56, quote from 153.

25 See Rutherford, *The Institutionalist Movement in American Economics*, 313–33, esp. 322–23. Bernstein has also suggested this sort of intentional and unintentional dismissal of much of previous economics and its move to mathematical modelling. Michael Bernstein, "American Economics and the National Security State." See also Lee, *A History of Heterodox Economics*, esp. 35–39, 68–71.

26 These attacks were not restricted to institutionalists. Samuelson was himself the target of active campaigns to ban his textbook, on the grounds that it occasionally encouraged government intervention. Lee, 38.

27 This was most famously articulated in his co-authored 1980 book *Free to Choose*, in which he and his wife, Rose, repeatedly asserted that any action, by definition, benefited both parties unless participation was coerced. Freidman was particularly concerned with government control. Seen this way, even public schools were problematic in that children were forced to attend them. Milton and Rose Friedman, *Free to Choose* (New York: Harcourt, 1980).

28 Gary Becker, *The Economic Approach to Human Behavior* (Chicago: University of Chicago Press, 1976).

29 The constraints of his theory meant that Becker had to go to great lengths to explain that while more "expensive" children would be categorized as "higher quality" (in much the same way, he explained, that a Cadillac is understood as higher quality than a Dodge) readers should not believe that children that cost more were "morally better." Instead, it indicated simply that their parents "obtain additional utility from the additional expenditure." Becker, 173.

30 www.nobelprize.org/nobel_prizes/economic-sciences/laureates/1992.

31 Blaug, "The Formalist Revolution of the 1950s," esp. 145 and 154.

32 The place of women and tasks understood as "women's work" had long been tenuous in economics departments. The postwar shift secured longstanding professionalization efforts to distance economists from studies of unpaid labour. The effect limited women's presence in professional economics. See Bernstein, *A Perilous Progress*, 26–27 for a history of these efforts in the 1910s.

33 The proportion of articles authored or co-authored by women in leading journals actually declined between 1963 and 1973; it has since risen, albeit slowly. Daniel Hamermesh, "Six Decades of Top Economics Publishing: Who and How," *Journal of Economic Literature*, 51, no. 1 (2013), 164. On the lag between economics departments and other fields in hiring and promoting women, see Shulamit Kahn, "Women in the Economics Profession," *Journal of Economic Perspectives* 9, no. 4 (1995): 193–205; Stephen J. Cecil, Donna K. Ginther, Shulamit Kahn, and Wendy M. Williams, "Women in Academic Social Science: A Changing Landscape," *Psychological Science in the Public Interest*, 15, no. 3 (2014): 75–141.

34 The first studies of consumer expenditures were conducted by state labour departments as a way of gauging the well-being of urban working-class families. By the early twentieth century, the U.S. Labor Department was collecting data to determine average costs of living. It established the cost of living index in 1936 and then the Consumer Price Index in 1945. The CPI expanded its survey to include rural and single "consumers" in 1960–61 and became a continuous (rather than decennial) survey in 1980. See "How Family Spending has Changed in the U.S.," *Monthly Labor Review* (March 1990): 20–27, esp. 24; *The First Hundred Years of the Bureau of Labor Statistics*, 158, www.bls.gov.

35 See, for instance, Lisa Duggan, *The Twilight of Equality? Neoliberalism, Cultural Politics, and the Attack on Democracy* (Boston: Beacon Press, 2003); Jennifer Silva, *Coming Up Short: Working-Class Adulthood in an Age of Uncertainty* (New York: Oxford University Press, 2013).

36 Economists do not operate wholly without a sense of the complications to demand. There have been assertions at least since the 1970s that demand does not necessarily decrease as prices rise (in the language of economists, that the demand curve does not necessarily slope downwards). See Geoffrey Hodgson, "The Mirage of Microfoundations," *Journal of Management Studies* 49, no. 8 (2012), 1389. Most recently, historians of economics have identified this slippage between purchases and actual desires. See, for instance, Hodgson, *How Economics Forgot History*, 276–77. Nonetheless, as numerous scholars have shown, demand continued to be both crucial and an utterly abstract variable that represented material self-interest.

37 Feminists who had gained positions in the U.S. government after the Second World War on the basis of their consumer activism in the 1920s and 1930s were frequent targets. See Landon Storrs, "Attacking the Washington 'Femocracy': Antifeminism in the Cold War Campaign against 'Communists in Government,'" *Feminist Studies* 33 (Spring 2007): 118–52. Consumer politics and theories about consumers' power narrowed at the same time and for similar reasons to the narrowing of economic thought. Importantly, in both instances, women's leadership and emphasis on the links between housekeeping and structural economic problems were excluded from legitimate thought and action.

38 This discourse was as true for critics of consumption as its proponents. See, for instance, the similarities between the *The Stepford Wives* (1975), which concludes its critique of suburban life with a scene of vacant animatronic women pushing carts, and conservative Cold War iconography of peaceful domestic scenes. On the latter, see Beatriz Colomina, *Domesticity at War* (Cambridge, MA: MIT Press, 2007).

39 Ivan Moscati, "History of Consumer Demand Theory, 1871–1971: A Neo-Kantian Rational Reconstruction," *European Journal of Economic Thought* 14 (March 2007): 119–56; Moscati, "Early Experiments in Consumer Demand Theory, 1930–1970," *History of Political Economy* 39 (2007): 359–401.

40 "Bernanke: Economy Lacks Strength to Sustain Gains," March 22, 2012, www.cbsnews.com.

41 Michael Corkery and Jessica Silver-Greenberg, "Many Buyers for Subprime Auto-Loan Bundle," *New York Times*, March 15, 2015, www.nytimes.com.

42 "Food, Farm, Government," *Life*, January 3, 1955.

43 For discussions of efforts to expand "demand" and ease consumption in the face of market failures see Louis Hyman, "Ending Discrimination, Legitimating Debt: The Political Economy of Race, Gender, and Credit Access in the 1960s and 1970s," *Enterprise & Society* 12 (March 2011): 200–232 and Deutsch, *Building a Housewife's Paradise*, ch. 7, "Babes in Consumerland."

44 Kyrk, *A Theory of Consumption*, 19.

INDEX